SOCIAL AND ECONOMIC HISTORY OF GERMANY
1888-1938

Social and Economic History of Germany from William II to Hitler

1888 - 1938

A Comparative Study

by

W. F. BRUCK
M.A., Ph.D. (Leipzig)

Visiting Professor and Research Scholar in the Department of Industrial Relations in the University College of South Wales and Monmouthshire, Cardiff; formerly Professor Ordinarius of Political Economy in the University of Münster/Westphalia

With a Foreword
by
J. F. REES
M.A. (Oxon.)

Formerly Scholar of Lincoln College, Oxford; Principal of the University College of South Wales and Monmouthshire

NEW YORK
RUSSELL & RUSSELL · INC
1962

" There is no Economic History without the use of theoretical conceptions. How can I describe facts, without putting them into an order, and how can I put them into an order without distinct points of view which alone enable me to create such an order? How much work on Economic History has largely been wasted because it did not rest on the sound foundation of an appropriate system. No wonder, that some work on Economic History turned out to be a mere description of the institutions of individual States and their administration. If authors do not base their descriptions on theoretical conceptions, economic facts cannot be systematised and their development cannot be comprehended."

E. LEDERER
(" Economic Theory "),

FIRST PUBLISHED IN 1938
REISSUED, 1962, BY RUSSELL & RUSSELL, INC.
BY ARRANGEMENT WITH THE UNIVERSITY OF WALES PRESS
L. C. CATALOG CARD NO: 62—13828
PRINTED IN THE UNITED STATES OF AMERICA

To
my wife

CONTENTS

FOREWORD by Principal J. F. Rees, ix
ACKNOWLEDGMENTS xii.
INTRODUCTION, xiii.

CHAPTER I
Elements and Forces of the Period.

(1) The Problem - - - - - - - - 1
   (a) The Right " Pre-conception " of Economic History? 1
   (b) German Social and Economic History and the Theory of History, 4; (c) Economics and Sociology, 12; (d) Individualism and Socialism, in general and in this period, 19.

(2) Forces that Influenced the Trend of Development.
   (a) Ideology and Sociology I, 26.

   General remarks, 26; Prussianism: its ethnological derivation, 27; its mercantilist economic expression in History, its influence on the mind and on the social structure of Germany—Mercantilism (Cameralism) and the " *Beamtenstaat*," 35—Troeltsch on pre-war militarism 39—liberal ideas, 41.

   (b) Ideology and Sociology II.

   German type of State philosophy and of Socialism in the 19th century and later, 48: its origins §1 Prussian mercantilism (State-socialism), 49; §2 the idealistic and later schools, 51; §3 certain socialist schools, 56; §4 differing views on ethics, 60.

   (c) Some aspects of the period before William II in their relation to later development - - 66

   (The main features of the Economic system.)

CHAPTER II
The Era of William II
A. Up to the Great War.

(1) Facts and Forces of a new Capitalist Age - - 73
   (a) Large Scale Enterprise (introduction) - - - 75
   (b) Finance Capitalism.
   §1 Banks and Industralisation, 80; §2 Technicalities, 84; §3 New Forms, 88.

  (c) Large Scale Enterprise (cartelisation, trustification) 92; §1 General outlines of combines in German history, 92 ; §2 Cartels in German theory, 100 ; §3 a short account of how cartels and trusts originate and of their position as monopolies, 104; §4 Market systems outside free competition, 108.

(2) Commercial Policy, World and Colonial Policy, 110.
  (a) Commercial, 112 ; (b) World and Colonial Policy, 120.
  §1 General, 120 ; §2 German Banking Policy in Foreign Countries, 121.

(3) Social Policy, 124.

    B. War-Time Economy - - - 134

CHAPTER III
The Weimar Reich

(1) Development, 1918-1933
  (a) The Chaos - - - - - - - 143
  (b) Recovery, Crisis, Relapse
   §1 Socialism in the Weimar Reich, 149 ; §2 Stabilisation, 162 ; §3 Boom and Crisis, 177.

(2) Some Special Problems - - - - - - 191
  (a) Industry and its Financing, 191.
  (b) Cartel Policy and Legislation, 196.
  (c) Mixed Public and Private Enterprise, 198.

CHAPTER IV
The Third Reich

(1) Ideological Remarks, 204.

(2) Economic Policy (general survey), 210.

(3) Special Problems
  (a) Monopolies and *Marktordnung*
   §1 the motives for planning, 219 ; §2 Cartels since 1933 and the *Marktordnung*, 222 ; §3 Growing demand monopolies, 228 ; §4 New Joint Stock Law, 231 ; §5 A few remarks on trusts, 237.
  (b) Public Control and Public Finance, 241.
  (c) Agricultural Policy, 256.
  (d) Social Policy before and during the Third Reich, 265.

FOREWORD

Dr. Werner Friedrich Bruck has now been in Cardiff for nearly four Sessions, and he has been able to devote some of his time to the elucidation of the leading phases of the economic development of modern Germany. Here he presents his findings. His qualifications for undertaking the enquiry on which they are based may be briefly recorded. With a training in biology, as well as in economics, he wrote as early as September, 1914, an article in which he insisted on the importance of cultivating within Germany itself crops necessary for the textile industry. This pioneer essay on self-sufficiency attracted the attention of Walther Rathenau, who was then in charge of the economic resources of the country. Dr. Bruck was subsequently appointed a Commissioner of the Cotton Control Board which he did much to organise. Contacts with such men as Walther Rathenau and Wichard von Moellendorff naturally turned his mind to the general problem of " economic planning "—*Planwirtschaft*— a term which he believes von Moellendorff to have been the first to invent. In his *Geschichte der Baumwoll Kriegswirtschaft* (Berlin, 1920) Dr. Bruck gave an account of the achievements of the Cotton Control Board. After serving for some time as the head of one of the sections of the Ministry of Economic Affairs, he was in 1922 elected Professor Ordinarius in the University of Münster. There he had the direction of a Research Institute and his work brought him into close touch with the leading politicians and industrialists.

This practical experience of the working of war and post-war control, combined with economic teaching and research, provides a key to the point of view adopted in this work. It explains the twofold approach, sometimes so strictly academic, and sometimes so insistent on practical considerations. Dr. Bruck has had first-hand experience of economic planning as it was developed to meet emergency conditions, and, whatever may be said of our country, it is hardly possible to represent such conditions as temporary in Germany. After the war, the period of high inflation gave place to that of rationalisation, and rationalisation has been followed by the ambitious projects of economic control initiated by the Third Reich. State control in the economic sphere has reached proportions hardly contemplated even under the stress of war. This portentous growth of planning naturally raises the question whether circumstances were favourable to it even in the pre-war years. Does the policy run with the grain of German society? To answer this question Dr. Bruck carefully analyses the progress of industrialisation in Germany. He demonstrates that what we with our prepossessions are apt to regard as aberrations are natural developments in Germany. To the historian the most revealing part of the book perhaps is the affiliation of ideas which the author suggests. The roots of " planned economy " run deep in German soil. Dr. Bruck submits its growth to minute examination and in particular shows that it had produced the cartel and the mixed public and private enterprise as well as the more comprehensive schemes of to-day.

Dr. Bruck's treatment of his subject is at once historical and theoretical. In some ways it will seem strange to English readers. With us there has been a growing separation between economic history and economic theory. The historians have applied themselves to the collection of facts and, although they have not been without some general guiding principles of interpretation, their attention has not been greatly engaged by them. They have been vaguely conscious that the struggles of social classes, the process of state-formation and the predominance of certain ethical-religious conceptions have been factors in economic development. Karl Marx, Gustav Schmoller and Max Weber have each exercised some influence; but our economic historians have hesitated to follow them very far. They have felt some misgivings and like Hamlet have sought to salve their consciences by reflecting that these may be false spirits attempting to lure them to their destruction. The reader will find that Dr. Bruck is not prepared to approach economic history on these terms. For him, as for Emil Lederer, there is no Economic History without the use of theoretical conceptions; he makes this the text of his treatise. In the introduction he endeavours to define his canons of interpretation. Incidentally this discussion serves another purpose. Nothing is more difficult to grasp than the subtle difference between points of view with regard to the same phenomena. To understand the significance of German economic speculation one has to study its background. Here Dr. Bruck is a highly competent guide and the disquisitions on underlying assumptions, which we would not expect in an English work on Economic History, are not only perfectly relevant to his thesis, but are in themselves of the greatest value.

Sir William Ashley once remarked that " the economist tends to be too abstract, insufficiently cognizant of fact, and the historian to be too concrete, too heavily burdened with fact." We have seen that Dr. Bruck agrees with this criticism of the historian; he would also subscribe to the indictment of the economist. For, if in his opinion, our economic historians seem to make shift with a slight modicum of theory, our economists indulge in refinements of theory which have little or no relation to facts. While he deplores the writing of history without conscious guiding principles, he challenges the economists to consider actual conditions and the policies which are adopted to meet them. To the English reader, therefore, this book presents a criticism of much of our historical and economical literature. It is a stimulating criticism and the author would be the last to resent replies to it. But, apart from these fundamental considerations, there is here a wealth of information about the economic evolution of Germany. We are shown that the essential elements in the present situation can be traced back for a century or more. Our own pre-occupation with theories, which as far as we were concerned fitted in with our experience in the nineteenth century, has made us too apt to assume that those theories had a universal application. Departures from them seemed to be a temporary dislocation which would ultimately correct itself. The presumption with us was that change surged up from below; in Germany that it was initiated and should be guided by the State. Writers in the two countries often used a different language in a more profound sense than that of words or idioms. There is now a general departure from the conception of an economy, spontaneous, self-acting and individualist. The tragedy of the War and the ineptitudes of the post-war period have now set us all to seek the principles of a new order. The clue to it is to be found somewhere in the welter of ideas which are at present bewildering us; for the past and future are bound together by an unbroken chain. When so many panaceas are noisily pressed upon our attention, choice may seem easy or difficult according to our temperament and training. But if history has any lesson to teach it is that there is no panacea, and that when men submit to the force of circumstances and cease to grapple with the problems of life stagnation inevitably sets in.

J. F. REES.

16th March, 1938.

ACKNOWLEDGMENTS

My grateful thanks are due to Principal J. F. Rees and Professor H. A. Marquand for all they have done to make possible the continuance of my scientific work. Without their help this book could never have been published. I am also indebted to the Rockefeller Foundation for the Research Scholarship which I held from 1934 to 1936.

Most foreigners write their books in their own language and have the good fortune of having them translated by *one* expert. For my part, I have been dependent on the kind assistance of a number of friends who have helped me to improve my English and at the same time to simplify many of the complications that would have been incomprehensible to English readers. Above all, I am indebted to Mr. A. Sheinfield for his friendly help and searching criticism. Further, I thank my friends and colleagues in Cardiff, Miss Katherine Hughes (Penarth), Mr. Evan John Jones, Mr. D. Gwilym James, Mr. B. J. Morse, Mr. L. N. Hopper, Mr. K. V. Stephens and Mr. John C. Harries.

In spite of all the assistance I have had, I know that, as a foreigner, I still retain many vestiges of my native idiom and many traces of the world of ideas in which I was brought up. It has been found necessary to quote from German literature. I trust that its appearance in English garb will not do injustice to the original.

W. F. BRUCK.

UNIVERSITY COLLEGE,
CARDIFF.
February, 1938.

INTRODUCTION

It is, perhaps, a little venturesome to write an Economic History of recent events. If it is to be more than a mere catalogue of facts, the author will find himself inextricably involved in the controversies of economists on general problems, as well as on every important particular aspect of the subject, such as currency, competition or control, or the causes of unemployment.

Quite apart from the divisions of politicians there are some fundamental differences between the British and the German mind which it is my duty, in writing a German History, to try to make comprehensible; and I may add that these differences do not make my task, as a foreigner coming from Germany and writing for English readers, an easy one.

First of all, Social and Economic History, despite special analysis, depend on the same *Problematik* as General History—that of how to use facts and analogies to form a philosophy. Both are in a stage of transformation. German historians who accept evolutionary development are in one way or another trained in the School of Hegel. They have never reached a functional theory of Society as expounded in England after the War. The main point of divergence is in regard to the ideal of Society and the ideal State.

To imagine Hegel on the stage of political history in England would be as impossible as to imagine Cobden or Gladstone on the German stage. It is true, the Hegelian ideas of State and freedom became "baroque." But we live again at a time when baroque forms are characteristic of political and economic systems, each with its own logic and justification. Architectural styles in most ages begin with simple unornamented functional forms; but they often become complicated by strange exuberances until finally reaction creates simpler forms again. Such baroque eccentricities exist in the excesses of the orthodox economic liberalism of our days as well as in the exaggerations of the socialist and planned systems (and of other grossly misused ideas which are rife in present-day political systems). Apart from the world of the exchange mathematician or the planocrat, we see the human individual for and through whom the economy is created.

Social and Economic History is a "History of Deviations from the Ideal Scheme of Economy" which follows its own laws. Since exchange of goods and services is the expression of the economic relations among men, the theory of economic mechanics which investigates this exchange, must necessarily form one of the historian's foundations. This theory shows how the economic organism can function at its best as long as laisser faire rules. But it is neither the end of theory nor a guide to policy. If this knowledge were enough, the statesman could carry about with him a dictionary of economic solutions, which he could consult for his actions—finding monetary problems under " M "; but in practice he is like the physician for whom the study of the organism functioning at its best is not enough. He has rather to be a pathologist or, if necessary, a surgeon. Perhaps pathology is most analogous to the treatment of these " deviations "; yet we cannot glibly assume that these " abnormal " phenomena are not the normal state. Every such deviation from the principle of competition has a tendency to grow. With the enormous increase of these deviations, derived from non-economic influences, history may become tragedy, but how can it find its way back to the ideal scheme? If we follow Marx and (to a certain extent) Clark, Schumpeter and others, this question is wrong, however, if the large scale organisation is the normal outcome of competition and the ideal scheme is merely a static one. True, on its foundation, modern schools are trying to build the theory of the structure and dynamics of the capitalist market. This is in essence the subject of the new theory. It is the things belonging to social psychology, of which politics is mainly a part, that determine this capitalist change and give first the true picture of history. But this social psychology also depends on laws and develops ideal schemes, which are, however, still far too immature to form the new theory. And will this be the last theory of our economy?

Even those few ideologies which man has tried and found good had, before acceptance, to overcome long years of resistance. We mortals ourselves must be modest, for our knowledge is not enough to scan history from these scientific foundations. We have to take refuge in simpler working hypotheses. So the writer must beware of the cramping influence of any grand fundamental theory. It is, perhaps, unfortunate that this book is the history of a country, in which, throughout the centuries, all the great "real" facts manifest a clear contradiction to *the* economic theory so venerated in Britain. Perhaps the very existence of Germany, like that of other countries, depended on that contradiction. It is pertinent to ask, whether the history of a society neither more nor less prosperous and happy than that of other countries should remain unwritten because of these contradicting " realities." Are not these realities history?

As regards approaching research from different starting points, it is a peculiarity of German economists, for instance, Max Weber, Brentano, Bücher, that, unlike the thinkers of Great Britain and Austria, they do not produce or follow " general laws." They realised that such laws cannot embrace the complex socio-economic phenomenon. Can we blame a practical statesman, if he turns away from his theoretical advisers when he finds that behind the positive results of their individual theories they grope in the dark? On what principle can the man who makes history choose his " Brain Trust "? His task is clear, like that of the physician. He must act at some given moment. Bismarck once said: " Politics is the art of the possible." The statesman has to use a working conception of his own. His decision is always in the nature of an experiment, yet it should show some signs of order and reason. He anticipates the proof of the theorist.

This tends to show that the historian must follow the man who makes history—or who is the agent of whatever dynamic forces it is that make history—and trace out his motives or those of his group. This will lead him to the spirit animating certain epochs or to a general line of development whose guiding principles, unfortunately, cannot be embraced in one dogma after the fashion of various exponents, whether it be Boehm-Bawerk, Schaeffle, Marx or Spann. I shall try to find the philosophical starting point for the investigation of the problem. So I shall first of all deal with the principles underlying our historical problem (see " The Problem," p. 1). In this way I shall discuss how far the historical presentation of economic processes can go in using or criticising social and economic theories. So much I hold to be true, that the historian will not understand this chapter of history without considering social psychology and historical evolution together with the rôle of the exchange economy.

Quite apart from these problems I propose to show that throughout the last 200 years, leaving out of consideration some points of new ideology (race, etc.), there has been a certain logical sequence in Prussian-German History. In a nutshell, it was and is the expression of Cameralism, the peculiar German type of Mercantilism. This phenomenon will also explain much of the attitude of German economists. I have kept in the foreground the idea of Germany's great political and economic organization (the *Wirtschaftsverfassung* of this period) which is so important in a nation which has always shown a mastery of organization.

I think I need not explain that the material compels me to emphasise certain subjects. The reader will, no doubt, understand my deliberate choice. I would refer the English reader to Professor Clapham and Dr. W. H. Dawson for details of other general subjects and to Professors Liefmann and H. Levy for more detailed trade problems. Much good work in English has also been published on Germany's trade cycle and her monetary problems. The chapter dealing with the Third Reich can only be a cursory survey owing to the fluctuating conditions of things.

As I am writing a comparative study for English readers, I have stressed those points which expressly show the main difference between the British outlook and the German. I have been compelled to discuss some difficult theoretical economic and even philosophical questions. The less advanced student or general reader may find it best to skip the chapter on " The Problem " and the sections on " Monopolies " in Chapters II and III.

Chapter I

ELEMENTS AND FORCES OF THE PERIOD

"In peaceful neighbourhood our fancies abide;
Impenetrably facts with facts collide."
(*Schiller, Wallenstein*—translated by
Professor W. J. Roberts)

(1) THE PROBLEM

(a) The Right "Pre-conception" of Economic History?

"He who maintains that our Economy is rational and purposeful, is sadly mistaken. He falls far short of the truth. Economic Society aims at stable equilibrium, but never succeeds in attaining it because it involves the unceasing creation and development of dynamic forces which at times produce revolutions of historic importance . . ."

"The dynamic impulses are stimulated by the material and spiritual upheavals of Society when subjected to immense strain. In the task of using massed forces fully and without apparent loss, for social purposes, only powerful peoples approach success and then only at rare peaks in their history. Such success is achieved after centuries of tentative experiment involving devious struggles and much waste of energy . . ."

I have quoted Wieser's[1] words at the beginning, because they give the general picture of history in a nutshell, and because they hint at the special relations between Economic Society and historical development. In this investigation I shall try to describe the " dynamic impulses " and the " material and spiritual upheavals " to which the German people were subjected during the period under review. What were the " tentative experiments " which resulted? This is a clear objective of research; it deals with ideas and policies which have become history. To this extent I agree with economic theorists that one cannot properly fulfil the task of writing economic history with a mere description of events uninformed by a theoretical conception. One can only describe facts truly if one sets them in order.[2] The theory of cognition involves certain ideas and, for my present purpose, I pick out only some of the most well known. An investigation of reality, including economic reality, is not sufficiently based on the object of experience itself. The things we see are shaped by our point of view. Furthermore, the research of centuries has created certain conceptions of order for every " reality " of a particular subject. With this the object of investigation has become divided into an *object of experience* (the total presented social fact) and an *object of cognition* (the presented situation as interpreted by thought). Even the natural sciences do not work on the naive observation of an object of experience.

How then should the economic historian approach his subject? Which pre-conception should he choose? Here argument begins, because opinions on subject and methods differ. A history book for English students cannot evade this discussion, for the leading economic school in this country which, no doubt, has the most clear cut theory, claims for economics independence of other disciplines. As I have said in my preface, the present state of our knowledge does not permit us to apply an all-embracing theory. The theories in any one of the divisions of our subject—history, sociology or economics—are either not always valid or not yet developed with such clarity as to be decisive for our purpose. Nor can we know whether future events will allow the application of existing methods.

The various schools of economics have taken up different positions with regard to methods of research. Mercantilists recognised no difference between an object of cognition, in this case of economic theory, and the objects of experience gained from practical economy. The mercantilists will occupy us greatly in this investigation; for their influence in Germany, both on practice and on theory, has continued to be strong up to the present day. The physiocrats first proposed some general hypotheses which seemed acceptable to reason, and from these deduced their cognition of economic processes. There was here no methodological difference from Euclidean geometry, which was built up on a groundwork of axioms[3] (once all these had a certain relation to reality!). As is well known, the sciences have always used the expedient of such working hypotheses when fuller knowledge is lacking, and on this basis great laws have been established.

To Adam Smith[4] the reality of economic experience of his own time was one with cognition, that is to say that he did not proceed by the use of only one sweeping generalisation; from his theoretical point of view there consequently arose a maxim of " right " acting, and he recognised the practical influence of the profit motive on theory. But he also believed in the possibility of an economic policy advantageous to all, and in its perceptibility by the light of reason. In contrast to some of his followers, Adam Smith, who built up the law of exchange economy, did not intend to do more than state the laws of " economics "; he left social psychology, ethics and law to other investigations. This is shown in his Theory of Moral Sentiments, and of Natural Law, which latter was never published. He never presumed to recommend the price economy as the panacea for innumerable ills. Ricardo, living at the dawn of the industrial era, when Sismondi already reflected its trend, had no such optimistic outlook, but was not yet an exponent of the modern pure economics which separates theory completely from policy. After Ricardo, economics developed in three directions—the *historical*, the *static-theoretical*, and the *dynamic-theoretical*. The historical direction branches in two ways. On the one hand the Marxian, connected in some ways with the Hegelian idea of history, and on the other hand the historical and institutional school which was mainly developed in Germany and which, as I shall show in another paragraph, had certain affinities to the methods of the mercantilists. This school flourished between the two great German wars and directed itself against any form of deductive theory. Closely connected or even identical with the *Kathedersozialisten* (professorial socialists—this was a nickname), it aimed at digging out the new facts which in its eyes were the outcome of the capitalist development, and to reveal the causes of the change from one epoch to another. It was the fate of this school that it followed the blind alleys of detailed research. But it is recognised, especially in Germany, that this school contributed much to the empirical research which led to the creation of economic sociology.

The second direction produced the system called " pure economy " or " theory." This theory relates all economic problems to the exchange economy, which offers a fundamental conception for the carrying out of all possible economic policies, but from which no individual practical policy can be deduced as necessary or desirable. One of its foremost exponents, Böhm-Bawerk, drew a picture of economic mechanics in which economic processes are deliberately made independent of historical developments. Ricardo, who clearly outlined outstanding changes in economic processes during his days, formulated a theory of capitalist economy which covered all possible patterns. Böhm-Bawerk, however, not only applied all fundamental conceptions to all stages and forms of economy in the same way, but also connected his conceptions and inserted them in the whole scheme in a manner which presupposed unchangeableness : he was not concerned as to how much may be changed in reality ; *a theory of economy holds good for all times and all forms of Society.* This view, widely adopted in England, was rejected by German writers of all non-liberal economic systems, and these were at all times in the majority. Recently it has again been discussed, for example by E. Lederer, or to take an economist of very different views, A. Spiethoff.[5] According to these views, with which I agree, there cannot exist an economic theory valid throughout all times, as with the laws of some exact natural sciences, and an abstract scheme can only be given separately for each of the main economic epochs or forms. As Lederer puts it, here following Marx to a certain extent, "the economy of an epoch is its decisive form, as it were the catchword of the epoch, which often reveals much that its political history disguises."[6]

But I shall dwell more fully in section (*c*) on the differences which showed themselves between the school of economics representing the " static type," and certain sociological schools.

The static type had long ago its opposite in Karl Marx, in his capacity as economic theorist (and here I do not refer to Marx as exponent of a labour theory of value). "His great systematic achievement was the discovery that large-scale organisation and permanent technical progress determined the structure and dynamics of the capitalist market process. On this basis he recast the classical system by supplanting some of its sociological 'middle principles' by others."[7] "... What makes him a pioneer is his idea of constructing another economic theory of circular flow and evolution at the same level of abstraction as the classical writers, but on substantially different assumptions, and the conscious tenacity of his hold on the sociological implications of his economic theory"[8] (Löwe). There are some writers, with different views, among them J. B. Clark, Wicksell, Schumpeter, Oppenheimer, who are at one with Marx, in so far as they see in the capitalist change the dynamic process which is the subject-matter of a new theory.

(b) German Social and Economic History and the Theory of History.

Before going further into these highly controversial matters I turn to another, without which our "pre-conception" would be incomplete. Social and economic history after all remains history, and to understand the process we must subject it to the methods similar to those of general history. It is beyond my task to unravel in this special investigation all the determinant factors of history. I can only touch on such factors when I feel that an important one is wrongly conceived and so must inevitably lead to a misinterpretation of the whole complex problem. This analysis may seem to savour of a certain adherence to a materialist conception which is not necessarily involved, because other influences are not excluded. The sociological interpenetration of history is not doubted and so, too, the economic interpenetration of sociology. History, as a social system involves the whole range of fundamental economic problems; among them the observational approach, whether we see things statically or dynamically. From this point I wish to approach the historical problem; this in its turn is identical with the socio-economic problem. In anticipation—it is *the problem of periodic transformations evolved by economic powers*. How these factors influence the social system and in what ways and to what extent they influence history in its totality has not yet been proved in clear cut theory. So long as our knowledge does not go farther, we must accept the handicap of seeing sociology (outside its positive findings) " in supra-historical generalisations and social interrelations " (Löwe), or even in pure " speculation." In this way many a successful theory has begun. Where empirical research ceases there is much room for the play of imagination. This holds good for Schumpeter's dynamic system as well as for the liberal school. Curiously enough, after having worked out such exact proof of perhaps only one of the several component parts, the followers of this school tend to fall a victim to their imagination and, under its influence, they explain the entire theoretical ground as well as the practical policy. Our object of *cognition* is still in the making. The interdependence of history and sociology compels us first to use working rules.

Wieser's statement (p. 1)—which gave me the cue to this approach—shows that he, in contrast to the classicists, did not assume a harmonious development ever moving upward. His picture hints at the great change which determines our epoch; it also shows that the same features of those historical philosophers whose interpretation I have selected are related, though not very definitely. Most writers coming under Hegelian influence regard the process of history as the "dialectism" of social and economic forces. Every epoch fulfils itself, as its dominant idea reaches maturity, and then, and for that very reason, gives way to another epoch whose main idea had contested the way with its predecessors. So to Hegel development is a progress through the conflict of opposites. The history of biological evolution, quite independent of Hegel's thoughts, showed analogous ways of development.[9] Laws, empirically discovered since Darwin's time, were proved by the exact methods of the students of the mechanics of evolution.

Marx, too, formed his picture of history on Hegelian lines. He gave a theory of evolutionary development which embraced economic development and economic theory. With the flow of development the productive forces advance. But they are never to be seen out of the perspective of their background, the social conditions. Therefore, for Marx the technical development of a certain period corresponds to its social structure, which includes the domination of certain social classes. He pictured feudalism followed by capitalism which in turn was to be followed by other movements— each epoch ending with revolution. Marx saw in these productive forces the dynamic factors which influenced the social structure, as well as the dynamic social forces which influenced the productive forces. Every historical epoch shows in its economic form its political structure; for Society is always regarded as a system of domination. Marx, building on Hegel, saw very distinctly the dialectical process in the change of the opposite guiding ideas and facts of two successive epochs. It was in the nature of *large scale organisation* that Marx found the vision of the theory of capitalist change. Capitalism, to him, is dominated by the tendency towards accumulation and concentration of capital; this, in conjunction with the growth of the forces of production, sows the seed of its own destruction. Marx's theory here grew beyond the boundaries of a theory of pure history. With this we see that it is hardly possible to separate general history from economic history.

The historical process, in its totality, is a dialectical process in which individual epochs are to be distinguished; whether it be according to the stage of development of the productive forces, or according to the preponderance of an individual dominating social class. In every epoch economic life runs according to certain laws which, however, are not included in the cognition of dialectic change, for the theory holds good only for the cognition of the historical process in its totality. Economic theory has to reveal the laws of a particular epoch and those which explain the dynamic transition from one epoch to another. Most clearly Marx and other authors with their theories of dynamics marked the starting point for a new economic theory, independent of the static one, and which had to show its own laws based upon the sociological and economic data. No doubt, a titanic task!

German social and economic history in the last 70 years may illustrate the realisation of these dynamic theories. But as to the individual interpretations by the authors mentioned above, one must reserve judgment. In this recent period the effects of the industrial revolution can be seen more clearly than in Marx's time. The development of monopolistic forms steps beyond the boundary of a market economy, the essence of the " pure " theory. I do not wish to state this essential change as general, *for our period is a stage of marked transition in which self-regulation and planning (i.e., consciously directed economy) uneasily contest the scales*. This point is of outstanding importance especially for economic policy; it is in this way dependent on two different principles which cannot logically be reconciled in theory. In practice, however, pure theory may be a rule of conduct, showing how an economy under certain rules may act at its optimum. The planner whose task is identical with pure economy—to create an optimal economy (the one by planning, the other by self-regulation)—here finds an ideal scheme, valid under fixed points of agreement. The abandonment of this ideal scheme, for admittedly it cannot meet many things because of its " institutional framework," would prevent us from applying it where it is valid. *To the " institutional framework " of a world market operated on the lines of " pure " theory belongs a corresponding international political system of like-minded people. Where this premise is destroyed the " pure " theory is excluded or at least limited* (cf. p. 10). Yet we need the system of self-regulation for our transitional time where conscious direction interacts with the competitive system. And there are many other reasons, such as perhaps human inability to tackle the enormously difficult problems of planning, which might therefore make preferable laisser faire. Without doubt growing experience of planning, where underlying facts are investigated, may make more inroads possible or even imperative. But the problem begins where unexpected events occur, or where non-economic factors make the examination of economic processes impossible.

In this connection I recommend the reading of Sir William Beveridge's Essay on " Planning under Socialism," etc. (1936).

It considers the various factors which hinder or permit the successful development of planned schemes.

On the other hand, to believe that we can use pure theory as a panacea and deny the great change that has occurred and consider large scale organisations (monopolies) as aberrations, involves and leads to wrong reasoning. My extended description of the main institutions which interfere with free competition—cartels—will make it quite clear that the flow of development makes this organisation grow into a class of its own. Recently they have become important organs of the whole political system of individual countries in which they perform the duties of departments of Public Administration. With this and their position in certain economic systems they grew to something totally different from combines of competing producers, from which they once originated, and became subject to other laws. History and the history of science show many such adaptations caused by permanent working on the lines of other systems. This reminds me of an example from biological evolution. Whales, being mammals, once changed their terrestrial life to that of fish. Terrestrial motion and respiration were adapted to swimming under water. So whales became subject to different rules of life. How can one compel these animals to go back to their original terrestrial habits? Can a cartel, which has grown into a place of its own in a political system, be considered only as an "aberration" because it once excluded laisser faire? How can a political system based on such institutions go back to a system which is subject to other and exclusively economic rules?

There is another factor which must be observed. The point where "interference" began was, with "pure" theorists, never a matter determined by fundamental principles. The question of interference was always a question of how much, and not a question whether it existed or not. Even in the great days of laisser faire, it was recognised that authoritative interference was necessary in some things, for we find that the staunchest liberals were at all times ready to regulate the monetary system.

The two realities, relating the ages of small and large scale enterprises, which respectively underlie the static and dynamic theory show a fundamentally different technical state and technical progress. The rôle of labour and capital in the exchange system appears completely changed.

Supply and demand are connected in this new system by planning which has asserted itself gradually: The *joint supply and demand undertaking* appeared as a new economic phenomenon at the end of the nineteenth century. *The modern process of production which makes the producers of the successive stages the consumers of the previous stage, until the last consumer is reached, is mainly planned* (cf. II A (1) (a). Production, as it grew in scale with the consequent immobilising of great capital, became, in the still capitalist economy, a new economic factor on which capital risk and social risk were dependent. The dynamic development as it expressed itself in the trade cycle induced conscious interference in the economic sphere to meet the risks. Large scale conditions need large scale methods embracing successive stages of producer-consumers up to the last consumer. Sometimes monopolistic buying agents of the consumers organised the whole process of production and distribution. The new industries, the electrical industry foremost of all, instance the process which requires new methods of organising and financing production and distribution. For these industries reveal that there is no longer much competition between suppliers in the individual stages; although in many cases, when new discoveries and inventions mark technical progress, competition always appears; it also appears during certain phases of the trade cycle and in other conditions which I cannot describe here. But after a relatively short time the competitors reconcile their interests either in strong combines or in building up a machinery which comprehends both supply and demand. No longer does competition or "imperfect competition" show itself, but a system in which producers and consumers are included in the same apparatus which finances them. In a special chapter I shall deal with this phenomenon. The electrical industry, connected with all its raw material producers and with its consumers at the various stages of production, with the power ultimately transformed into supply and transport organs, illustrates this system clearly, both in the home and in the foreign market. The road transport undertaking—to give an instance of the interlocking of production and consumption—is owned in part by the great electrical manufacturing company which furnishes it with most of its material, in part by the great railway company controlling the transport of the district, and in part also by the big power station, private or public, which provides the ultimate consumer in the community with its goods and services. And there are examples enough where industries interested in the transport of their employees co-operate in the control of such bus-line transport undertakings. Again, raw material furnishers, manufacturing companies and power stations are interlocked by many other technical and financial chains.

Our example—one among many in every province of goods and services and the corresponding credit and monetary processes—has shown a change of general significance in the satisfaction of wants with comparable goods before and during the last eighty years. At the beginning of this period, wants were satisfied by a mainly free competitive system. *Whilst forty years ago a partially excluded competition, in which monopolistic formations played a part, appeared, to-day the supply and demand of various goods and services show extensively a complex whole of which the particular electrical example is only a part. Competitive processes in this whole are intensively restricted.*

During this period of eighty years, we see appear a finance capitalism, an excrescence of private enterprise, and, by degrees, we see groups within the community and even the State itself coming into the fore as planners of production and distribution. With large scale organisation, managed trade, industry and agriculture, managed monetary system and managed labour showed themselves by degrees in the period under review. All these data become symptoms for the historian; he pronounces the 18th and 19th centuries as the time for relatively small scale business activities—the reality to which " pure " theory corresponds. Another period since the last decades of the 19th century develops with large scale organisations, mostly of private character, formed by the people who strictly followed their self-interest. Competition at this stage is largely excluded. Then the historian realises the varying intensity of State control. Even totally planned economic systems, without any kind of self-regulation, appear. The competitive system, the basis of " pure " theory at its proper time, the era of expansion of advanced industrial nations, seduced these theorists to the belief that these temporary circumstances were a general verification of the classical theory, whereas the line of evolution was entirely different from the deduction of the classical school. This era was based on self-interest and utilitarianism, the incentives of the economic man, according to Adam Smith and Bentham. Since the dynamic process brought forth the large scale enterprise, not only the forms of capitalist market organisations but also the incentives changed their significance. Active policy to a great extent is influenced by the new developments. Self-interest has found other competing incentives.

The period under review shows two curious worlds of ideas, the one is that of the nations successful in their conquests and the other of those which, though equally desirous of conquest, had less success. The idea of the Nation which, before our period, showed itself often and in various forms in world history, appears in new clothes in Germany, and for that matter throughout the whole world. From the time of the idealistic period, this has been one of the strongest incentives of German life as a whole, stronger than self-interest, the incentive of the competitive system. The natural instinct of preservation of a destitute country, crippled by its enemies, inspires the incentive of nationalism, and leads easily to exaggerations. Liberal capitalism, based on self-interest, in State-socialist Germany, was only an episode, but for the Anglo-Saxon World, living in an atmosphere opposed to State interference, it is the whole life. Yet Western liberal ideology and social progress found no difficulty in living together with great conquest, expansion and imperialism.

Thus I shall deal with a period of instability, when human Society was struggling desperately to find new forms for itself appropriate to its social progress. But the primitive instincts to conquer and oppress still held sway; and these crude forces, like the blows of a hammer on some delicate mechanism, inflicted grievous harm on the highly complicated economic and technical structure within which the social organism had developed. Characteristic of this period, especially in Germany, was the fact that the State assumed a position of special importance in every aspect of social, economic and political life. Its power was held in check by that of the controllers of various political systems as well as by the idea of the humanitarian State. This however differs greatly from the view of the supporters of the functional theory of Society. The conception of the " Nation " within the framework of the State, at first based on mercantilist and romanticist ideas, developed into a philosophy of the national State which dominated Germany's international relations during the period under review. While Imperialism flourished all round her, the late-comer, armed with this philosophy which became an instrument of power-policy, inevitably came into conflict with other nations. In this struggle of the " haves " to maintain their static position, national egoism advanced—*economic nationalism* became the weapon of the " have nots." And the Treaty of Versailles added to it greatly. The Treaty divided the world into two groups, the super-nationalist countries who enriched their economic power at the expense of the vanquished, and the vanquished countries. A nation composed of 67 million people, which to a large extent lived by export trade, was doomed to be crippled. The Treaty, the occupation of the Ruhr and other incidents increased the tendency to keep away the world market from this vanquished people. An international policy of sufficiently like-minded people is the premise of a world market working on the principle of a " general law " of economics. Politics prevented this and created political counteractions. The rest of my book shows the political and economic defence set up by the vanquished : economic nationalism. Briefly, in consequence of various disturbances, economics is no longer ruled by the English-Austrian subjective law of the market. And deviations from the law of free play of economic forces have a special tendency to grow. So political follies finally produce economic follies.

Our period shows conspicuous developments as well as conspicuous setbacks, from the point of view of exchange economy. At its commencement, the Industrial Revolution had united the nations in a world economy. National markets, both for goods and credit, were merged into the world market. At the end of our period, there is a return to a primitive system of economics. The isolated self-sufficient countries are the signs of this. The result has been the almost total destruction of the world economy and its dismemberment into individual States proportionally weak.

Wieser's words and the symptoms—given so far—hint at " politics " and other irrational factors in economic development. Certain theorists look upon these as alien influences that only disturb the true working of the laws of pure economy. Or they consider this interplay of non-economic with economic facts as outside the research of the economist, whether he be analyst or historian. It is simply ostrich-like to overlook the great problem of the incentive " nationalism " as is frequently done by authors who dislike this motive. It is an issue which totally changes world and economic history if, for instance, near-Eastern States to-day develop their economic resources. Formerly the Western countries with their " earlier start," and sometimes assisted by the superiority of their arms, made use of these resources. Now countries such as Turkey, Persia, Saudi-Arabia make use of these resources in order to increase their own political and economic nationalist power, sometimes even with a hostile attitude towards the former dominant Western powers. And this process spreads all over the world.

From another angle, economic life appears to be a mere composite of the economies of the individual countries which make the economic system the servant of their individual political systems. Friedrich List condensed this policy into a theory. He was much impressed by Alexander Hamilton, the man who first created the National Economy of the U.S.A., which served as the great model for all countries ripe to develop their own economic resources. But List was far from being a mere " State-economist " or protectionist. He never overrated the temporary circumstances which made his system valid.

As long as patriarchal rule and self-sufficiency in agrarian countries allowed the working out of economic laws, economic life went on with only relatively small conflicts. With the interlocking of nations in the world market the great conflict begins ; in the 19th century in milder forms, because markets were available for industrial countries and political power and decisions were still based on small classes of the peoples. In the 20th century the political interest of individual national countries prevented the working out of an ideal exchange economy comprising all peoples, and the contrast became obvious : politics against economics, economics against politics. Here, the significance of internal social struggles can only be mentioned in passing. A quasi-general and international system of economy, however, presupposes—as already said—the existence of a like-minded and sympathetically inclined family of nations. This ideal has never reached maturity, and we do not know whether Nature or man, or the social and ethnological roots of Society will ever admit such a world State—to say nothing of the problem of its manageability. But, in spite of setbacks at a time of strong international differences, increasing understanding in certain spheres is progressing. This particularly refers to international cartelisation, by means of which the problems of the distribution of raw material, adjustment of production to consumption and currency co-operation might be tackled. Of course, these questions which in recent years come more to a head, will affect the problem of property relations of countries as well as of private people.

Thus, in reality, every economy of an individual country now lives in the compromise-state, which bridges the national will and economic laws, and the former shows itself in the general policy dependent on the strength of sectional political forces. In the more recent periods two main principles play their part, one " *national* "-*political* and the other " *international* "-*social*, which outstrips national borders.

There has never existed a Great Power—so long as it has kept its vital energies—be it liberal, socialist, or ethical in the political and economic sense—which did not make for national egoism and did not strive to enlarge and preserve its national unit. For the history of imperialism goes far back, and we find that it has not changed in principle, but has adapted itself to other forms, among which economic ones prevail. Both nations and World-Society subordinated economy to an instrument of power.

The period under review showed a changing parallelogram of incentives and forces which shaped history. We still see that history does not move upward or straight forward in one distinct line. There is still a change in the opposite forces dominating the movements. If this is a real symptom, then we cannot exclude it from our pre-conception. I do not, however, wish to class myself as an Hegelian logicist as opposed to the school of " *Historismus* " or of " irrationalists," supporters of which followed the inductive-organic method. I might use both as working hypotheses as, e.g., did Troeltsch who went even further and attempted to combine both methods.[10]

(c) ECONOMICS AND SOCIOLOGY

1.—The preceding paragraph surveyed some of the important data for the period under review which, through our " preconceived " views, became symptoms both economic and sociological of the approach to our subject. The recent analysis and conclusion of Professor A. Löwe's[11] masterly little book, " Economics and Sociology ; a plea for co-operation in the social sciences," with the argument of which I agree in the main, has made much of my original intention unnecessary. I have decided, therefore, to omit from the present volume a more detailed analysis and to follow Professor Löwe's main conclusions on the problem " Theory and Sociology." His analysis, especially of the significance and limits of pure economics and the " Society of Exchange," is based not on his own studies alone, but largely also on the writings of Professors Eduard Heimann and H. Neisser.[12] But I shall deal with these points only in so far as they are important for this investigation, which, after all, remains historical. I am mainly interested in the question whether the economic historian is not only justified in including the " sociological factor " in his pre-conception, but also even obliged to do so.

The validity of theories in general is a philosophical question. Theories are valid within the limits of their " institutional framework." Every theory of a particular branch of science, and every " deduction " (an inference from the general to the particular) must have connection with reality. It must be originally an abstraction from something concrete and so serve a corresponding purpose. Thus every deduction can be traced back to an induction (the general inference from a particular instance). Such a highly developed abstraction as mathematics, where the variables can be freely handled and are necessarily considered as "complex functions," is no longer capable of distinguishing the data from which conclusions originally derive. Where, however, these variables are real functions (i.e., by their very nature they become applicable to a *specific problem*) then they become determinant factors and they cannot in general terms be subjected to mathematical analysis. That can only be done if we deliberately pre-suppose certain elements as constant quantities. But biological and psychological science can never be segregated from their real starting points, whether they be the organs or the functions of the human and social organisms. Thus, if analogy furnishes a working conception, the organ or function to be examined *ought to be connected with its real starting points.* In this connection I recommend the reading of J. S. Haldane's thoughts on the "Philosophical Basis of Biology." Biology and psychology assume equilibria in their working hypotheses, but these equilibria can never dispose of the specific biological and psychological component parts which form the resultant. This holds good for social economics as well as for other sciences. Mathematical abstractions do not give more than quantitative relations between biological and psychological data.

If an economic analysis (based on the exchange economy) is the only way to get a true "construction"[13] or ideal scheme of economics then other ways must lead to wrong policies. Unfortunately, this economic "mono-analysis," being virtually the only guide to the liberal economic policy, repudiates all other non-liberal systems theoretically as well as practically. This school considers interference by the State or combined private forces as relics of the aberrations of less enlightened times. It is astonishing that this school, which has attracted many great minds, should exercise such great influence at a time when political liberalism is rapidly declining. This school also aims at impressing its authority on active economic policy with the same rigidity as its socialist counterpart. The liberal school blindly distrusts economic planning in much the same way as it distrusts anything savouring of socialism; while the "dictator-States"—and their theorists included—detest anything suspected to be liberal in tendency.

If the arguments of the liberal school are sound, then most of the economic measures carried out by active statesmen, politicians, and practical economists during the last century were based on fallacies, and that holds good particularly for Germany. If this theory is wrong it is dangerous, for it would lead not only to a misconception of former times but also rob us of a helpful guide to the understanding of future policy. Perhaps the solution of the great international problems of our time, such as the adjustment of world production to consumption and of the corresponding monetary processes, might be found in schemes similar to international cartelisation.

If we follow this exclusive road, then we shall have to explain the most distinctive features of recent economy by theories subordinated to the analysis of exchange economics. How faulty this conception may turn out to be, and how weighty the socio-psychological causes, may be illustrated by an example, the German stabilisation action of 1923, with which I have to deal (III(1)(b), §2) and which is illustrated by Professor Löwe in his account (p. 20-21). It is amusing that the foremost academic-economic association, the "*Verein für Sozialpolitik*," in its financial committee, just before the Government introduced the law, prophesied failure, some members with Cassandra-like forebodings. The only two dissenting members were of the bureaucracy which had prepared and was responsible for this law. Not only did German economists disagree with it, but so too did their colleagues in other countries. Later they attributed the obvious success of the law to the non-economic factors, the accidental influence of which made up for the bad effect of the monetary measures. Löwe asks: " . . . if the better argument was with the pessimists, what are we to think of a science the advice of which does not prove practical when most needed?"[14] If a certain "confidence" in a monetary transaction of a State is the necessary link in a chain of economic acts (i.e., it sets in motion a movement of currency-stabilisation) then the whole process cannot be explained by pure economics. For no monetary system can function without certain " definite ideologies or certain expectations as to future policy of the authorities and as to the behaviour of the members of the community." Löwe suggests that we may systematise the experiences into a sociology and psychology of money, credit, of inflation and deflation : If it is stated that rational monetary policy *must* be based on two pillars—on the economic as well as on the social psychology of money—why leave it to the amateurs in politics and administration to combine superficial economic ideas with every-day psychology, instead of rendering social science applicable by scientific co-operation? This holds good for a great number of psychological peculiarities of men or groups of men acting as component parts in economic processes. Among these the monopoly problem, especially expressed in the cartels and trusts, is deeply involved. I will not enumerate here those forms of conduct which are opposed to the great incentive of " pure " theory, " self-interest." This theory is valid only on the basis of this self-interest. If other incentives, of which we have enumerated some, form the basis for systems, then they lie outside the institutional framework of " pure " theory.

As I have stated, the theoretical problem in its essentials reveals two economic realities, which for the historian show themselves as two different worlds or epochs in which economics is only one component part. These two realities can hardly be measured by the same methods. Again we have to start inductively; the two deductions which arise when each reality is systematised disclose their own respective laws. Out of the first, the " smaller " world, the object of experience of the classicists and their followers in the 19th century to which their object of cognition was adapted—the static " pure " theory emerged. Out of the second reality, came the dynamic theory with its essentially new elements. Löwe compares the sociological pre-conceptions of these two epochs. He says that the first depicts more than some discontinuous and accidental features of the underlying social order, that the very structure of the corresponding Society can be read in the simple equations of the market laws. Analysis of the circular flow is more difficult. Classical economics " with the iron law of wages and the theory of saving, was the point where forces whose main field of co-operation is the transactions of exchange encroached on the social environment of the market." " That for some reason the spirit and order of the law of supply and demand are said to prevail also in the breeding of children, in the accumulation of private fortunes, connects the world of the market with the realm of social biology, with family life, ethical conventions, etc." (p. 103). How different is the system of equations expressing a simultaneous and stable order of prices and volumes, when this system has to be replaced by a fixed sequence of definable inequalities which describe typical and recurrent patterns of prices and volumes. Thus, with the dynamic theory, the course of the cycle, regulating supply of labour and capital in one phase by the extent of absorption or dissipation in the previous phase, provides the connecting link. This link will appear even closer when one considers that it is the objective patterns of the internal process of the market which control any relevant variations of the external social order. There is a constant and mutual interaction between the exchange process and the social environment. In such a case it is impossible to regard economic reasoning as dependent entirely on sociological pre-conceptions. Once sociological research begins to analyse a concrete social system, it must turn to economic middle principles. Sociology makes a fundamental contribution to economic reasoning. So too " realistic sociology " needs economic categories to describe industrial society.[15] Through the medium of the exchange process the primary causes of the trade cycle, themselves arising from the social environment of the exchange process, react upon the environment itself.

As to the static theory, it is the belief " in mobility and objective equilibrium as the true and permanent essence not only of the ideal but also of the real market process," an " essence that in the opinion of the ' *epigoni* ' has been obscured and perverted by influences arising exclusively from the non-economic aspects of Society."[16] As to the methods, which Löwe describes as confining themselves to instrumentalistic reasoning on hypothetical patterns—he says that it is obvious that the pure theorist as such could not contribute much to the illumination of a concrete economic system like modern industrialism . . . All he may properly deduce from his categories is, . . . " the durationless subjective equilibrium, a snapshot of individual position in which the continuity of objective processes is lost."[17]

Our second world is that which Marx visualised by the rise of the large scale organisation as the main expression of dynamical process. " The circular flow inspired the ' pure ' theorist to calculate the future point of rest in any market movement." But it is not, as Löwe says, " only the possibility of a clash between the actual point of rest and the calculated point of objective equilibrium which makes modern deduction less determinate than the classical laws. Even more important is the fact that the point of rest, as such, is no longer of primary interest." To Löwe, the essential difference between classical and modern reasoning consists in a shifting of research from state to process, from the lasting patterns of rest to the varying cause and shape of the movements. The classical pre-conception " was based on the supposition that all movements in the market are nothing but short run interruptions of a state of objective equilibrium, and, therefore, negligible if the fundamental order is to be studied. But the actual form and duration of the market movements prevents us from giving them the status of mere friction."[18] To these belong changes of the evolution of the social data without which the economic data cannot give a true picture. Löwe puts forward an argument which shows that, if one remembers the condition for the materialisation of objective equilibrium, " economic men and competition do not guarantee the existence and persistence of such an equilibrium as long as their efficacy merely relates to the process of exchange itself. Only if these principles are also valid for the process of social revolution as a whole, that is to say, for the changes in birth-rate, migration, saving incentive, technical order, etc., will the movements within the market be protected against distorting influences arising from the social environment ; only then will the forces making for equilibrium definitely prevail. In order to interpret the abstract possibility of a stable equilibrium as the concrete reality of the social order, we had to adopt the classical hypothesis that not only the transactions of exchange, but also the social data of these transactions, the supply of labour and capital and the technique of production, are subject to the law of supply and demand and to nothing else."[19] Without " dropping the classical misconception that objective equilibrium and states of rest are the true subjects of research," Löwe in common with other writers, sees no progress even through the methods of both supporters of dynamic theory who are found in the liberal camp.

2.—It is true that the dynamic process in its social and economic elements has not produced a clear-cut theory like that of static economics. Some of the experimenters in dynamics still stick to pure theory, which they combine with sociological elements. Schumpeter's theory of dynamic development is most interesting in this connection. He introduces a new type of entrepreneur—appropriating the common term—the man who has the will and the initiative to accomplish great alterations. Thus he evokes a boom but eventually the other phases of the trade cycle reappear and the former process is repeated. So Schumpeter's entrepreneur is the "mystical" dynamic element between two static periods. Other writers gave certain mystical functions to bankers or other human functionaries in the economic process. It is interesting that Schumpeter deliberately lifted, not the inventor or the discoverer, to his pedestal of dynamic agent, but the successful man who, through his will and initiative, carries through what other people may have invented or discovered. With the introduction of this sociological element Schumpeter left behind Böhm-Bawerk and his fellows of the Austrian school, from which Schumpeter himself sprang.

With this the exact methods of this school disappear, while on the other hand sociology is not ready to go on with comparable investigations. The " . . . analytical work only starts when he does with the complicated material of modern sociological investigation what the classical writers did with their simple pre-conceptions: transforming them into computable magnitudes and relations." " Only after having transformed that sociological finding into the concept of monopoly, thereby expressing a qualitative structure of social relations by means of a quantitative order of prices and volumes, do we understand the *economic* significance of social power."[20] But even with this Löwe does not arrive at the last word of wisdom. Our section (*d*) on individualism and socialism will, perhaps, show that it is not only lack of knowledge, but the very relativity of the subject itself, which would make it mere play to measure sociological facts in terms of magnitude and volume. The paragraph hinted at will discuss within the framework of this chapter how our present knowledge of this complex question influences our pre-conception.

3.—In *summarising* what I have said about Economics and Sociology, I have confined myself to stressing some major points of recent contributions such as that of A. Löwe. I have felt it necessary to clarify this point on which history as such is dependent, and so lay open the problem freed from the strait-jacket of the " pure " theorists. The next section may emphasise the two great motives of history in general, as well as in the period under review.

The connection between economics and sociology influenced every analysis of economic history, but much more economic theory itself. The historical view is clouded by the fact that in the science of economics everything is controversial, even the question of the purpose of economic theory, and in theory itself the question of its very subject. If economics is part of social science then one has to ask oneself whether economic theory is a mere appendix of sociology or is a theory of the mechanics of economic processes independent of sociology. On this point theorists strongly disagree. Most German economists, including the best, did not feel inclined to take up a definite position towards this question. For some Society shows a changeable form of human life in which the change of incentives changes economic processes and *vice versa*.

Within its limits, no scholar will ever deny the gigantic performances of exchange economics and its weighing of facts. But this method remains always only the first isolated scheme as a working conception and does not cover the whole economic ground. If economic Society is as complex a matter as Comte believed it to be—" the consensus of all social phenomena "—such an organism functioning only by the interplay of all these social phenomena must be scientifically investigated by methods appropriate to the component parts as well as by those suited to the resultant, which is a product of that co-operation.

I may quote here the fifth item of Löwe's summary of the relationship between economics and sociology. " Therefore the exact laws of the market have no deductive self-evidence at all but the mere probability which marks every empirical law. The degree of probability of their realisation depends upon how probable it is that the basic social conditions will themselves materialise, that is to say, on the historical fact whether and to what extent liberal society exists."

What has become after all of this " pure " theory ? " In principle he (Löwe here refers to those whom he calls the '*epigoni*') prefers instrumentalistic reasoning on possible individual patterns to outlining the general ground plan and the basic forces of an economic system. If he speaks in terms of a system at all he usually thinks of the logical arrangement of our analytical tools and of the unity of our machinery for the solution of problems (Schumpeter) rather than of the substantial reproduction of an historical reality."[21] By confining themselves to instrumentalistic reasoning on hypothetical constructions they cannot formulate the questions which seek an explanation of things outside the institutional framework, and they are led to the most extreme stages of abstraction in mathematical formulae. When I see such arguments coloured by pride in " exact " instruments, I am tempted to think of the time when chemistry tried to produce a human being, the homunculus of Paracelsus. I am reminded of the words of Goethe in " Faust "[22]:

To nature's portals ye should be the key ;
Cunning your words and yet the bolts ye fail to stir.
Inscrutable in broadest light,
She will not yield to force or disputations,
What she reveals not to thy mental sight
Thou wilt not wrest from her with curves and calculations.

(d) INDIVIDUALISM AND SOCIALISM

It is difficult to write on Germany at a time when her chairs of philosophy, history and political economy are occupied by men who express their deepest contempt for liberalism, which is yet one of the major philosophies of mankind. I feel it my duty, in a chapter dealing with the problem of social and economic history, to raise the essential points of argument; for the attitude towards individualism and liberalism (both political and economic) throws so much light on the German outlook. I shall touch on the matter more fully (p. 41).

No matter from which point I start or from which interpreter of the long row of philosophers who have dealt with the motives of human happenings, this province of science knows no generally approved principles. Every author throughout the ages gives his own. There are no " computable magnitudes " as in " pure " economic theory. In contrast to supporters of this doctrine, I cannot avoid revealing the influence of the great philosophies in the chain of effects and causes of Economic History. And these philosophies include ethical norms of human Society. With the acknowledgment of these influences authors introduce " teleology alongside of mechanism in the world."[23] In distinguishing between the world of spirit and the world of sense, both of which are necessary to explain the subject matter of social history, we see a twofold system of considerations which is common to most thinkers—that is, that both these worlds are functions of the human psyche and body and no abstraction can go so far as to loosen this original connection. Applied to history this means that the impulses of men and groups of men can never be anything else than human functions. Another point is that authors idealise what they see of the peculiar conditions of their time, including the social standard and their experiences in certain countries. I can select for this analysis the views of two such different thinkers as Adam Smith and Kant on freedom, ethics and the State.[24] Both, independently of one another, considered freedom and ethics as human functions and contemplated the moral law of individual freedom as limited by the moral function of Society as such or, as Kant saw it, expressed in the State. Therefore, it is interesting that Kant like Hegel, though to a much lesser degree, passed from the State of Plato to the Prussian State.

I might select also Professor R. H. Tawney's[25] " Functional Society," which " should be organised primarily for the performance of *duties*, not for the maintenance of *rights*, and that the rights which it protects should be those which are necessary to the discharge of social obligations. But duties, unlike rights, are relative to some end or purpose, for the sake of which they are imposed. The latter are a principle of division; they enable men to resist. The former are a principle of union; they lead men to co-operate. The essential thing, therefore, is that men should fix their mind upon the idea of purpose " . . . So, even this ideal, when applied, will reveal very different aspects of "social obligations" or "purposes" in 1000 B.C., in 1600, in 1800, 1900 and 1950 A.D. Thus there is no end to realities, through which the variable composition of the organs and functions of society show themselves. Man might recognise the ideas of previous times, for in turn their ideas will be, ten years hence, those of "previous times." Apart from the variable "time element" with its corresponding ideas—even if dogmatised—the great constant always remains, i.e., all impulses derive finally from the two main human characteristics : *Society consists of individuals and individuals make society. This is the reason why the borderline between Socialism and Individualism is in a state of flux. From no survey of human life can either of these elements be excluded. The ultimate form of society depends on which of these two the emphasis is laid. In the course of historical development tendencies change.* Marx himself never narrowed his ideas down to an all-inclusive socialism. The national socialist system despite its insistence that the nation as a whole is everything shows in the leader principle the peak of the individualist will. The former German types of social-democracy or liberal-Socialism were compromises varying in bias between the two principles. Of course, political philosophers stress the note of their leading principles especially strongly when fighting for recognition, but definition emphasised in the heat of the battle, must not be taken at its face value.

Professor Tawney's analysis, the "duty-Society" and the "duty-State" are opposed to the "right-Society" and the "right-State." Undoubtedly, if authors such as Tawney, Laski and Cole hint at "duties" they derive them from other "incentives" than those of other writers or politicians. When Professor Tawney wrote his essay shortly after the War, he felt that the general mind would not conceive the ideal of what he felt to be the contents of a functional Society and so he added a chapter on "the need of a new Economic Psychology." Even Kant's duty is something different. He lived at a time when the idea of the disappearance of private property could not be a topical problem and social and economic interdependence between individual States could only be conceived with the existing national countries as political units. Kant's idea included the moral right of the State to the conscription of its citizens. It is obvious that there is not *one* system of ethics, there are many according to the choice and the mixture of motives, to which in addition has to be added the consideration whether one regards the national State or an international formation as the bearer of the public authority. The national State grows automatically to the Power-State because it lives in competition with other States (which follow their self-interest). The political systems of all countries are still linked up in national States.

A general consideration of national-socialist ideology will be of interest, showing how, apart from the nationalist ideology the undoubtedly strong anti-capitalist movement paves the way for every kind of socialist action. But to what this undermining of the capitalist system in Germany will lead is not clear. Its ideology is still in the making; and as in the case of other states, such as Russia and Italy, which have undergone revolutions in recent times, it is hard to say whether certain measures are expressions of an ideology or are a continuation of tradition necessary during transition to frictionless government, or again, are actions forced upon them by the need of preserving power against hostile forces at home and abroad.

It will be my task to show in my analysis how the State in Germany during the period under review changed its functions. Although this State, in principle, did not change so much in the last 80 years as did others, yet in it also the spiritual incentives, social and technical progress, with their mutual interactions, were the main component parts in carrying through the great changes of our time. The old mercantilist State always appears in Germany's system. True, peculiar conditions such as geography and tradition produced a certain type. It is interesting to examine how the stage of development is reached which after the War gave the States of the World a new cloak. The incentives unearthed in the War, as in other great movements of world history, spread new ideas and with the ideas a certain set of instruments for their application. When in 1917 the revolution broke out in Russia, no model existed for forming a State and economic system on new lines. Germany in 1918 was confronted with a similar task, as was also Italy in 1922. To-day not only are there available models of how to make revolutions successfully or of how to carry through a modern non-democratic government; there exists also a certain " technique," like recipes in a cookery book, and one can carry things through in a " Power-State," in which objections on the side of the citizens are not permitted, by the same methods in almost every region of the world. Now even the ideology is ready which can easily be adjusted to peculiar conditions. But this ideology is far from mature: it is a propaganda-ideology which appeals to the masses because it attacks the ideology of the 19th century which took its general outline in the 18th century. It is this ideology, as expressed in the constitution of liberal capitalist states, which is challenged by the new dictator states. Though they differ in their replacement of former creative forces, they are alike in their contempt for the liberal state.

The world is still far removed from the ideal of a functional Society and its State as its propounders conceive it. And yet, however much ideas may differ in outward appearance, they are alike in fundamentals. Mankind is still caught between the two opposing natural forces. On the one hand there is *Individualism* in political and social as well as economic life, on the other hand there is *Socialism*—a contrast derived from the " harmony " of the classicists with self-regulation as opposed to " planning " by and for Society. And, although orthodox supporters of these opposing theories are prepared to wage war against each other to the death, both elements always exist side by side in any given period.

It is interesting to follow individualism as far as it participates in new stages of development. Individuals have mainly been responsible for inventions and discoveries. Politically and economically individuals are the levers of great movements. From this point of view Schumpeter's oft-quoted entrepreneur is not without interest. He is not the inventor or discoverer, but he is the dynamic element which leads things from one static period to another. So in social and economic history it is important to state that the so-called dictators and leaders did not bring with themselves something positively new either politically or economically. In fact they did what Schumpeter says; they had "the will and the initiative to carry through new things."

As far as the political province is concerned, Soviet-Russia's model, in which, as a non-democratic Power-State the one party system is everything, has been adopted elsewhere. Public administration, too, belongs to the party's functions. In tracing the idea of the economic system, it is indeed Marx's idea of the large scale organisation which shows us the way. I shall speak more fully about this idea later. The various forms of combines, above all the cartels (and their predecessors, the guilds), were from the first the organs of economic planning. The idea of setting up such "functional" groups—arising out of cartels—alongside of the parliamentary forms of "individual" democracy had already greatly impressed Bismarck before he attempted to establish a kind of economic parliament in 1881. The *Reichswirtschaftsrat* of Moellendorff (1919) was based on Bismarck's model. But the Germany of Cameralism and the Germany of Hegel always subjected " Functionalism " (as Cole calls it, loc. cit. p. 412) to the Authoritarian State. It must be remembered that it is rarely possible to decide whether the origin of important decisions is a functional group or an individual. In a State-socialist or neo-mercantilist country as Germany always was, there was a mutual system of assistance between State legislation and protection and private forces planning for the same ends. The mixed public and private enterprise became the missing link, not only in the pedigree of modern political and economic planning, but also between Liberalism (= Individualism) and Socialism. The system of control boards, which have been mixed enterprises (cartels subjected to State control) first arose as a typical feature of War organisation. In post-War times they have been extended to every political and economic sphere and have been combined in one great governmental scheme—as a new system of Public Administration. Marx did not know such systems in his time, but to-day he would recognise them as one of the stages of his vision of capitalist change. It is not without interest that Russia, Italy, and Germany show the foremost degree of designed development. In Germany, from Rathenau-Moellendorff's war economy, Wissell-Moellendorff's post-War plans, to the present economic system of the Third Reich, there is one line, starting with private cartelisation and government assistance in the pre-War period.

For in part the same people of the period of the war still hold office. It was only too obvious that when Lenin started he had to adopt the planned scheme of Germany's War economy which, to a certain degree, was not very different from the English War economy (Control Board system). In this latter economic system are to be found the instruments and the technique which I wish to describe. It is my task to show development and motivation.

Modern times identify much social and economic history with general history, and history is never at its end. It is development and change; the two opposite forces always fight for power and (history giving no computable magnitudes) the mere " speculation " of Hegel's dialectism shows itself always in the contrast of Individual versus Society, the ancient riddle of mankind.

My thesis is that Social and Economic Historiography gives an untrue picture if it bases economic policy solely on either the individualistic attitude to its economic outcome (economic liberalism or capitalism) or any kind of planned or socialist economy. To outline these two different systems as independent and unconnected seems to me an antinomy based both on false philosophical presuppositions and on an inadequate observation of facts. *It is not a question of individualism versus socialism, for both are inseparable parts of Economic Society and co-exist even if one is latent.* They are like molecules which are electrically loaded, both having positive and negative charges.

The pendulum swings between the two human characteristics of individualism (combined with economic liberalism) and socialism. Man is indeed a political animal; he is born a son, a brother, a cousin, a kinsman, a member of the community. On the other hand, this individual has, in the various epochs of history, achieved his will in defiance of the will and the power of the community. Even a community with a socialised economy could not dispense with the individual; the more so since, in fact, the system is dependent upon him for direction. This individual has shown that he is a " liber." And when he has possessed or created power then he has forced his will on other individuals and on the community as a whole. These tendencies all run in a curve up to a peak and once past this peak, they stop and fall. Thus it is with the individual. If he over-reaches himself, then counter-movements on the part of the other individuals or of Society supported by organised power come to the fore. Moreover, this is one of the leading views held by Hegel in his philosophy of history. It is on the balance of the tension between the individual and Society that progress in the history of mankind is principally based. During the long existence of the British Parliament, the idea of two opposing groups living in a state of tension was considered the root of public welfare and proved an impulse to progress. Sometimes an individual would master the parliamentary machine, and express the general will of the community when other individuals had proved incapable and the public in general had failed. When at a particular time neither element prevails then no major success can be reached. But the theorist who dispassionately strips off the outer covers of the political struggle and of propaganda and ideology will recognise that every system of government is always an incarnation of both these tendencies. Just as the individual man is always a compromise between individual and social elements, so the economic Society, whose task is production and satisfaction of wants, is a like mixture. Much has already been said about that by J. S. Mill.

I may digress here to show that actions described as individualist and socialist in the heat of the political struggle, are in reality both the one and the other. Thus, for example, some actions of a captain of industry, a real leader, are doubtless individual, often both initiated and executed in the main by himself. This individual, however, may perhaps command in the name of a mammoth trust which he may have founded himself, or even of the syndicate of a whole industry. But who is to decide the fate of this powerful social body when the individual leader has to leave the stage? The same " individualist " activity of this individual, continued by the plans and decisions of Society, or maybe of a board of directors or financial group, becomes social co-operative activity or " socialist."* Formerly they were considered individualist; now they may be considered socialist. If independent enterprises combine in big organs of power, in which the State may have partial or total control, it is difficult to decide to which element such a scheme belongs.

To give another example from history, those acts which themselves make for Liberalism, such as anti-trust laws and others, which protect the individual against combined interests, do not arise of themselves, but are normally planned, considered, and introduced by the most important groups of Society and of the State. Without the immense mass of governmental legislation no secure foundation could be found for any modern economy, including the liberal economy of the 19th century. And what is said here of Liberalism is likewise to be applied to Individualism, for in our time the individual is not a Robinson Crusoe on a desert island, but in all his actions is a representative of some social body or other, such as the State, a trust, an association. It is absurd to insist that only one of the two poles should be recognised. A purely socialist and planned management, excluding liberal principles of individualist interference and of self-regulating forces, seems to be impossible. The last is an outstanding factor, too; liberal economy does not only consist of individuals invading the sphere of economic forces,

* In the use of the term " socialist " there is an important difference of opinion which will be more easily understood later. To German eyes the distinctive mark of Capitalism or Socialism is not the private or public character of the ownership of the enterprise. For the system of public ownership in Germany, Cameralism is the better term. In my example the affairs of an enterprise can be decided not only by the individual " leader " but also by some social grouping, sometimes the representatives of finance-capitalism, sometimes joint boards of the representatives of public and private interests, and sometimes the executors of State regimentation.

liberal economy comprehends the self-regulation of these forces even when invading human forces are lacking. In his recognition of certain self-regulating economic forces, a parallel to the phenomena both of animate and inanimate Nature, man confesses that in many cases he cannot shape Nature. He can only, in such cases, influence the progress of the self-regulation of Nature. The Planner does not invent the activities of human working power with their ever conflicting interests. He is like the scientist and technician who do not invent fire, water and electricity. So planning does not mean inventing but *regulating* such elementary forces. These are the limits of planning. (The inroads of the State or combined private forces show clearly these activities which I mentioned above. Among them far-reaching interference in labour and currency problems, in the working out of the phases of the trade cycle, are instances of this kind. The guidance of saving and investing belongs to this problem.)

The economic system can, no doubt, proceed without the interference of the human mind or human planning, but the effects of letting it run uncontrolled and of leaving such forces to themselves is as dangerous as that of leaving natural forces like fire or electricity to themselves. It must be carefully handled, just as we insert a resistance into an electric circuit, in order to weaken its effects. Yet, individual, fallible men will not for a long time to come or, perhaps, will even never be able to "rule" so complicated an organism as an economy dependent on so many factors, mechanical as well as biological, or the incalculable changes of the trade cycle. These things will not be reduced by planning to the simplicity of an engineer's switchboard or of military commands. In trying to reduce to a formula for this transitional time the compromise, which we recommend, I may say that its main idea is still to preserve the price mechanism which is circumscribed by limitations of State and Society as by the rules of a game, i.e., the free competition of players limited by those rules.

There will always be good and bad plans. Hence, the effects, and particularly the social effects, may be disastrous. Other forces besides planning have, therefore, to play their part in diminishing the risk. An examination of the period after the War, which led to the greatest slump which the World has ever seen, reveals much bad planning and its effects. Certainly laisser faire depends on accident or as Mr. J. M. Keynes[26] once said : " It is neither clever, nor nice, nor just, nor moral and it gives only insufficient goods," but at least it offers to men more than one chance. The exaggerated economic nationalism of our period will one day surely decline and so offer again greater opportunity for competition. We still live at a time of a mixture of both systems, of individualistic Capitalism and Socialism ; systems separated by a gulf of motives without any common measure and which can only be bridged in practice by the most drastic compromise.

The fact itself does not alter but the force of incentives springs either from the Individual or Society and satisfies the needs of the one or the other. The struggle between the two ruling forces in human nature is eternal.

(2) FORCES THAT INFLUENCED THE TREND OF DEVELOPMENT.

(a) IDEOLOGY AND SOCIOLOGY I.

General Remarks.—To understand German Social and Economic History it is well to compare it with that of other nations. Perhaps it lends itself best of all to comparison with that of Britain, for in some outstanding fundamentals the two countries are very similar. These great countries bordering the North Sea have much in common in their ancestry and as followers of the Reformation, and there are no great differences in the way in which they formed their empires—by dynastic heritage or conquest in whatever form. Both are predominantly producers of industrial goods and as such dependent on their export markets. The divergencies in tendency arose from the difference in the spirit that animated them. This difference in outlook was conceivable in the days of poor communications. But how is it still possible in the small world of to-day? This dissimilarity of spirit and certain peculiar conditions in the actual fundamentals, accentuated in the course of their development from the beginning of the last century, prevented a convergence of ideas. These two great European neighbours kept apart for deep-rooted reasons. I shall attempt to show these divergencies from both aspects—materialist and ideological.

Mercantilism is the keynote of Prussian-Germany: Great Britain shook this off in the eighteenth century in a steady development of liberal ideas, which in 1846 were applied in the reality of economic liberalism. Meanwhile Germany's mercantilism developed into State socialism. Ultimately this difference is a difference of mind. We shall quote Troeltsch, the great German philosopher and theologian, who once showed that this difference possibly goes back to the time of the Reformation. It is true, it is a religious and ethical difference which extends from spiritual and moral issues to every province of practical life. Perhaps this difference is rooted in ethnological facts. This latter point of view is not to the liking of modern sociologists; my explanation will, however, be given with due reserve.

German liberalism was never one with English liberalism. Even staunch anti-socialists in Germany took a more or less strong dose of State-socialism for granted. Thus we find that the subdivision "municipal socialism" was generally accepted. German socialism in general was in the main of materialist character even amongst the majority of those who called themselves socialists. In a historical investigation there is no space for an elaborate treatise on the various politico-ideological systems, I have to limit myself to some mere brief remarks. Ideologies here will not be given as things in themselves, but as they might influence the motives of men, groups, and of a people. A comparative analysis of the history of ideas in both countries such as I attempt here is no new thing. Many

English writers have dealt with the subject. I feel it appropriate here to confine myself to quoting certain authors who have illustrated briefly and vividly these differences in ideology. The difficulty of our task is aggravated, for the German brand of socialism in its various forms, in fiction as well as in reality, was always a compromise. Undoubtedly, a strong element of opportunism, due to the necessity for meeting day to day problems and probably a mercantilist heritage, gives rise to such compromises in practical affairs.

One word more on *Ethics* in relation to the political and economic system (cf. I (a) (b), §4). Every system pretends to have its own ethical standard in its ideology though competing systems may most decidedly scorn it. At present the ideal of " Humanity," finding its peculiar expression in " Christianity," differs greatly from the ideal of " Nation " or the State as the leading ethical determinant. The ethical postulate of class consciousness or the ethics of class war may be denied by some systems and seriously condemned or punished as immoral by others. German doctrine often disliked submitting political and economic ideas to ethical principles. We find the distinguished German economist, Professor Diehl,[27] saying, in a well-known article: " It seems to me wrong to call all those schools socialist who desire to bring about a certain ethical fundamental norm in the social order." He refuses to stamp Kant's " moral laws " as socialist as they were so often considered. In this connection he quotes Marx who most emphatically declined to recognise any interpretation of socialism from an ethical fundamental norm, a point of view widely favoured in Germany (c.p. I (2)(b), §3).

I have mentioned that there are some peculiarities which have moulded the thoughts of the people and which have largely shaped Germany's destiny in social and economic affairs. These deep-rooted differences have first to be examined on an *ethnological* and *sociological* basis.

Prussianism: its ethnological derivation and its influence on the mind and on the social structure of Germany.—It is, of course, true that people of a similar station in life or with a similar environment develop common attitudes independent of race. So I do not wish to overestimate the ethnological influence upon a people's handling of problems. This is the more true because of the mixture which marks the composition of all living nations. But, however that may be, whether adaptations or ethnological peculiarities, if these show special characteristics in individual peoples, they may be emphasised in a history which has to give motives for actual happenings. I do not wish to enter into the controversy concerning the inheritance of acquired qualities. Neither, moreover, do I intend to give here even a brief ethnological survey of the German race. Germany's geographical situation made this nation a link between Western civilisation and the East. There is a relation that seems to exist between the culture of certain parts of Germany and their ethnological composition. Freedom has sometimes been taken as the characteristic expression of the minds of Western Europe while that of the East, especially Russia, is characterised by anti-individualism and a love of coercion and subservience. The need for individual liberty in Great Britain is proverbial. In Germany the liberal era was as short in duration as the general demand for individual liberty was small.

In Germany before the War, people of the Western districts, in touch with Roman and French culture, the Rhinelanders and some South German tribes, especially the Alemans, were for a long period free and democratic, in striking contrast to other parts of the Reich. The Low Saxon and other tribes near the Dutch and Danish border bear a similarity so far as they do not show the Prussian mixture. It is not without interest that this contrast is noticeably apparent when we consider the Germanised or colonised parts where Slavs and other Eastern races dwell and inter-marriage has been common for centuries. Here a few general observations on German history should be given before entering into the details of these ethnological problems. Surrounded by imperialist peoples and tribes, and themselves dominated by the will to conquest, the Germans from the beginning of recorded history followed expansionism. Where this was not marked only by border struggles, greater visions of a policy of conquest appear. The struggles of German Emperors show Germany's leaning towards the South and the West; but the tendency from early days was *towards the East*, the more so as the policy of the emperors declined and as the prospect of control over the mouth of the Rhine, conceived by the great Elector, receded. Hohenzollern and Habsburg were the rivals in this long fight. It represented a vision which has never faded from German eyes either during the time of the last Emperor or even to-day. The more German tribes, especially the Prussian element, conquered and Germanised regions with Slavonic population or even with a people of mixed Slavonic and Mongolian origin, the more they themselves reflected the racial and spiritual characteristics of the conquered people.

Germany's history developed the type of the colonised Slav and of other colonised Eastern races, showing the colonising master and the obedient colonised serf. Originally, the former was a German, later on a mongrel partly German and partly Slav. The feudal characteristics of the economic life at this time, agricultural in type—were transferred very early to the military life and later to the civil and public services. The Prussian State with its dominating military and bureaucratic class conquered and even Prussianised, step by step, the whole of Germany, in the North, the West and the South. We see this spirit in the typical militarist subordination of so many individual attitudes. This creates the machinery for a central command and an army of obedient subordinates expecting to be regimented. " Thoroughness " became the keynote of every system regulating the practice of men and things. Everything is coloured by the desire to organise. No wonder that this spirit placed the State on the highest pedestal in a country where the bulk of activities, private in other countries, is transferred to the State—where teachers, including professors, and numbers of professional officials were civil servants. The position of the Evangelical church as a State church from early times produced the type of clergymen, paid through Government offices, who did not differ greatly from a civil servant. They, as well as the industrialists and as the trade unionists, to take only a few examples, became imbued with this militarist spirit (cf. on " Militarism," chap. I (*a*) p. 39).

Ethnological derivation might perhaps explain some outstanding features of the German mentality which is so closely related to that of more Eastern nations of Slavonic or mixed Slavonic and Mongolian extraction. For example, Sir Arthur Keith[28] has thrown much light upon the heart of the problem. Perhaps his illuminating analysis may give us the ethnological background of the sociological phenomena. Sir Arthur, analysing the German race and especially the Prussian, quotes a French anthropologist's view after the Franco-Prussian War. This writer tried to show that there were two races in Germany—the true German or the Teuton, and the Prussian. In his view the Prussian race was not German at all, but a mongrel, round-headed mixture of Mongol and Slav. Sir Arthur goes on:

" The accusation from Paris was taken up by the leading anthropologist of Germany. He was a Prussian by birth and his name was Virchow. He said, our French colleague may be right for we know very little about the physical characters of the modern Prussians. Let us have a census made of their racial traits and see how Prussians compare with those who are accepted as true Germans—the people of Bavaria for example. Virchow, having great political power, had a survey made of the school children of Prussia and Bavaria. As every one admitted that the Germans of history—the Germans whom the Roman legions had to keep in check were blue-eyed and fair-haired, note was made of the proportion of children possessing these characteristics. It was found that Prussia was more German than Bavaria ; in colouring, Prussia resembled the headquarters of the Nordic race—Sweden and Norway. In colouring, Prussians can claim to be true Germans—or, to use the name which now finds favour, Nordics. But what about the shape of their heads ? As we know from the evidence of cemeteries, the Franks, Saxons, Angles, and Jutes were long-headed—almost exaggeratedly so. Very rarely did these early Germans have a flat occiput ; the opposite. The back of their heads usually projected as a prominent boss or cap—this projection adding to the length of the head. Virchow proceeded to have a census of heads taken. As long as he confined his attention to the people bordering on Holland and on the North Sea, things went well. The long Nordic head was found to abound. But when the survey was carried away from these Western lands it was found *that the vast majority of the German people had not the head of the North but the round head of the Slav.* It is known that round-headedness (brachycephaly) prevails in all parts of the German Empire excepting the extreme West and South-West."

During the War, Prof. F. G. Parsons measured the heads of soldiers from all parts of the German Empire. He summed up the result of his observations thus: "The more one thinks of it, the more one is convinced that since the sixth century the broad-headed Alpine (Slav) race has been slowly and steadily supplanting the long-headed Nordic type, not only in Prussia, but in every part of Germany." Sir Arthur goes on: " I have never understood the reluctance of Germany to accept brachycephaly as a national mark." He states that " Marshal von Hindenburg was a Prussian, and the flat vertical occiput was developed to an extreme degree," and he continues his anthropological analysis: "The spread of the round head in Europe—and also in Western Asia—is still an enigma. At the close of the ice age the entire population of Europe was long-headed. Now the opposite is the case ; Britain and Spain are the only strongholds of the long head now left. What has happened ? Have the various forms of round heads, which existed in Western Asia before they appeared in Europe, swept gradually over Europe, ousting and exterminating the long heads ? Or has something of a less tragic nature happened ? My belief is, that we may regard brachycephalism as a sort of infectious disorder. It cannot spread, of course, as diseases are spread ; *there must be invasion or colonisation with intermarriage*. But suppose only one round-headed man or woman were to enter a community, " roundness " is so dominant over " longness " that in a few generations it may be spread through the whole community. It is in some such manner, I suspect, that brachycephalism has spread through the population of Germany."

Admittedly, at the time of colonisation ,the German immigrant was more powerful, more intelligent and better educated than the native. Where the German knight or officer originally had had no more than equal rights in the agrarian community, he soon became the superior. His descendants made the natives bondsmen. This is typical of the manner in which the large estates in the Prussian East were founded. These knights who served as army officers to native Slavonic princes or as promoters or agents for land settlements of German peasants inter-married with the native nobility and peasantry. Sir Arthur Keith traces Marshal von Hindenburg's ethnological characteristics to a type of this kind. Thus the Prussian nobility developed on these lines and was not derived from the type common to Western and Southern Germany. This type, generally known as " Junker " became not only the mighty master over all his bondsmen but the dominating formative influence in the history of Prussia. Without doubt he fulfilled an important historical function at a time when the country was purely agrarian in structure and later played a part of the greatest significance in the financial development of his country. He was the greatest food provider as well as the producer of the most important export products such as cereals, wool, and wood, which were sent to Scandinavia, Holland, England, and North France, in this way enriching Germany's seaports. At a time when capitalism was merely agrarian capitalism, this Junker was the pillar of the realm. As land owner, as army officer and as official, he ruled with an iron fist. Western deomocracy was unknown to him and alien to his nature. Feudal allegiance to the State and its monarch was the expression of his soul. This type expected all actual subordinates, peasants, soldiers, officials, as well as the more fortunately placed of the nation to bow in subjection to him and those people descended from the serf-class willingly clicked their heels before these recognised masters. *Kadaver-Gehorsam* (implicit obedience, corpse-like), complete subordination in military as well as civilian life, was the distinguishing mark of their relationship. In time the master who colonised and his Slav serfs inter-married and similarities in ethnology made their appearance. This type of Prussian Junker appears in German literature and he is depicted in many novels, as in those of Sudermann, Clara Viebig (*Das schlafende Heer*) and others. Nowhere in history do we find the Westphalian peasants or the emotional Rhenish agriculturists or horticulturists or the Alemans showing the characteristics of this type of obedient servant. It is only recently, in fact during the course of this century, that the West and the South became Prussianised.

In the prototype of the old colonising master lies the root of the policy which Bismarck, himself a Junker, recommended as " *Machtpolitik* " (will-to-power policy). It is not without interest that Professor Ernest Barker in connection with this German power-philosophy once noted that two of the outstanding representatives of this policy, Nietzsche and Treitschke, were of Slavonic origin. Historically, the days of this Junker-caste, which without doubt gave to its country not only splendid army officers but also organising administrators and diplomatists of the highest level, ought perhaps to have been numbered, when American corn flooded the German market in the seventies of the last century. The agreement into which large estate owners and industrialists then entered and which under Bismarck's aegis initiated Protectionism (1879), artificially extended the power of this caste up to recent times. (As to Prussian Militarism and the outstanding part which it played in the whole structure; public and social as well as economic (cf. I (2) (*a*), p. 39).

There are doubtless other grounds for comparing Slavs and Germans of Slavonic extraction.

The systematic political planning of the German State (to which I drew attention on pp. 28-29) is often compared with the scientific planning of the civilisation of Soviet-Russia, her cult of exact science and technology. Beatrice Webb [29], throwing light on the Russian scientific planning, says : " One is tempted to wonder whether this Russian creed does not consist almost entirely of an insistent demand for the subordination of each individual to the ' working plan ' of the scientifically trained mind : Though, of course, the plan is assumed to be devised in the interest of the community as a whole." That could also have been said about German planning !

Another instance of the resemblance between the German and the Russian system may be given. The splendid Prussian soldier from the Eastern provinces is not very unlike his Slavonic brother in Russia, the Cossack, who also in border provinces fulfilled his task as a born soldier. The type of Prussianism which I wish to explain in the following chapters reveals this same interesting mixture of militarism and romanticism, the mystical emanation of the nationally minded. A certain ferocity and a certain sentimentality go hand in hand. These features are exactly the same as those shown by the Russian soldiery. Take e.g., Russian poetry, especially the Volga-songs still popular to-day. The enthusiasm for Stenjka Rasin the great Cossack Ataman, who in his famous campaign of 1667-71 destroyed the Russian Central local government in the provinces and formed in all captured towns " local nationalist " formations, has the same roots. Here we have a Slavonic kind of romanticism not unlike that of Herder—himself said to be of Slavonic derivation. Many authors, among them Nicolas Berdyaev and Professor Karl Meyer,[30] cite the lack of individual liberty in the great Slavonic Eastern empire. It is striking to see that the process of subjection and co-ordination into a class, into a collective, is as strong at the present time as it was 800 years ago. There is no Russian word which relates to the conception of the feeling of " personality," or of the " individual,". . . even the word " I " is seldom used . . . as Dr. Meyer continues: There is nobody who had a deeper perception of this mentality which " existed before Marx gave out his doctrine of the collective and of socialisation ; it belongs to East Slavonic mentality."[31] He continues by stating that there is nobody who had a keener perception of this mentality than the great poet of the Russian soil, Leo Tolstoi, who commends as the highest fortune of human nature, to lose one's individuality in the nation, to renounce individual wishes and give oneself over wholly to the will of the masses. Meyer continues by speaking of the outlook of Russians to-day—by which he means the inhabitants of the whole union—to whom the individual, as such, is nought.

But let us go back to some ethnological facts. Without any doubt, the Slav power of absorbing the German element, as mentioned by Sir Arthur Keith, was remarkable. But this phenomenon marked not only the period of colonisation from the Middle Ages to the time of the German princes of Eastern German territories in the eighteenth century. It is true, in this latter period, Frederick the Great gained dominions over enormous Slav areas by his wars and by the partitions of Poland (after 1772). The connection of Prussia and Saxony with Poland was close, e.g., Warsaw once became a Prussian town and the Elector of Saxony was for a long time the King of Poland as well.

More recently we find, however, the skilled Slavonic labourer settling for long periods of time in German textile centres everywhere. After the Industrial Revolution, streams of Slavs from foreign countries as well as from the Germanised Slavonic Eastern provinces inundated the German Western and Southern industrial districts.

The composition of the Slavonic population which amazed Sir Arthur Keith so much, springs not only from the Slav elements of the former Russian empire or their successor States, such as Russians, Poles, or even some Mongolian or other Eastern races, especially in Eastern Prussia, but also from Slavonic tribes, many of whom had lived in Germany since the sixth century and had dominated various districts. I may mention here, the Czechs, Croats, Kaschubes, Masures, Obotrites, Polabes, Liutizes, Pomerans, Rates, Sorbs and Wends, of whom some were of mixed Mongolian or Dinarian blood.

Some interesting statistics show how the rise of German industry was accompanied or only perhaps made possible by an internal migration from colonised Slavonic soil to Western and Southern industrial centres. Thus, it is no wonder, that before the Great War, Polish candidates contested constituencies in the Ruhr district for seats in the Prussian Diet. Intermarriage with pure Germans and other inhabitants of the West, made Slavonic blood more and more an essential feature of this racially mixed population. This movement became more accentuated by the numerous Roman Catholic immigrants with their higher birth-rate. A glance through directories of Essen, Dortmund, Bochum, Recklinghausen, Gelsenkirchen, will show the surprising number of Slav names and those of other Eastern races. Taking a longer survey,[32] during the period 1840 to 1905 there was a decline in the population of the province of East Prussia through migration of 633,500, in the province of Pomerania 668,900, in the Province of Posen 790,300, and in the Province of Silesia of 599,100. It is not without interest that during the last intercensual period before the Great War, the fall in population in the Province of West Prussia amounted to a yearly average of 10.7 per thousand as compared with 8.4 per thousand in the preceding five years. The fall in the Province of East Prussia was 9.4 per thousand (as against 8.8), in Pomerania 8.9 per thousand (as against 7.5) and in Posen 8.6 per thousand (as against 9.6).

The flight from the land was responsible for the increase in the populations of the industrial districts. During the period mentioned above, the population of Berlin increased by over a million, that of the kingdom of Saxony by 326,200, that of the Rhine Province by 343,000 and that of Westphalia by 246,100, over and above the statistical estimate of the natural increase. The official statistics illustrate the way in which population migrates from the agricultural formerly colonised districts to the industrial ones. The occupational census of 1907 showed that of 1,535,251 male industrial workers in the Prussian Provinces of Rhineland and Westphalia, 112,591 were born in Eastern Prussian Provinces of East Prussia, West Prussia, and Pomerania, and 102,341 in Posen and Silesia; while altogether 529,241, or one-third of the total were born in other parts of the country. The occupational census gives other interesting figures; thus without the Poles from the East of Prussia and the aliens from the West, East, and South of Germany, most of the collieries in Westphalia would have been closed. Of 387,000 miners employed before the War in the Düsseldorf, Münster, and Arnsberg Government districts alone, 135,000 came from the Eastern provinces of

Prussia and were overwhelmingly of Polish race, while 30,000 more came from foreign countries. In some districts before the War 50 to 60 per cent. of the mining population were either of Polish or foreign extraction, and there are collieries of whose work-people more than one-fourth are aliens.

The figures here given may illustrate how Slav migration influenced districts where the population was of pure German extraction before the second half of the last century. The great achievements of the German nation as evidenced by its history in the next chapters prove the mixture with its constituent races as sound. Imagination and self-discipline mark the type of the working German from inventors, discoverers, poets and artists, and the learned professions, to the manual worker and soldier, and explain the high degree of efficiency. And these seem to be presuppositions of a coming "synthetic age," an age which needs so much research and organisation. Furthermore we are led to believe by these considerations, that this inclination towards self-discipline will lessen that coercion which holds together all the planned systems of our day.

Taking all these figures of the high percentage of Slavonic and Mongolian blood in the German nation into account, some foundations of the new German ideology do not seem quite comprehensible. Out of the mass of literature, I propose to quote here one author, a well-known political economist, who says : " Europe shows a change of the *Bevölkerungsschwergewicht* (preponderance of the populations) which continues. The 20th century left the road of the 19th and now it develops on lines foreboding ill for the future.[33] In contrast to Western nations, including Germany,[34] Russia and the other Slavonic countries grow." And he draws the conclusion that the Slavs of Eastern Europe will outstrip in numbers the German people and that in a few decades more than half of Europe will be Slavonic. " So to the ' dis-Europising ' of the world the ' de-Nordicising' of Europe is added." " The change of the centre of gravity of populations turns in Europe from the Germans to the Slavs, from the West to the East. We are painfully compelled to recognise a parallel between the rise of population and the rise of foreign claims, in this case Slavonic, to a voice in economic and political affairs." These arguments show the basing of theories on racial grounds which are in themselves inconsistent, because there is not a real " German race " as against a Slavonic one. It is to a great extent itself as Slavonic as the Slavonic races which he cites, and which he refers to as " alien." Whilst the ideal of the Nordic race and its supposedly innate virtues still persist as a main point of ideology and is used as proof for the claim to dominate other races, some compromise has taken place. The obviously strong admixture with Slavonic and Mongolian blood compelled this compromise, especially in the legislation which " created " the racial type " of German blood and of blood of a certain affinity (*artgleiches Blut*) " to which latter the virtues of the German-Nordic race are evidently extended.

From the point of view of the analysis and figures given so far, in reference to and in defence of the leading ideas of the Third Reich, they culminate in showing the superiority of the German race as a Nordic master people and giving it the claim to its outstanding tasks in the world. This is the main principle which also puts forward the increase of birthrate as an essential in spite of which overpopulation and unemployment shall be justified by the tasks which a master people must undertake. Various official writers beginning with the leader and his lieutenant in all spiritual matters, Alfred Rosenberg, and numerous scientists such as Burgdoerffer, Haushofer, defend this argument. Professors who held chairs in German Universities of Law, History and Political Economy made this presupposition the foundation for explaining their philosophy and for exercising a practical policy and legislation. I cannot set out here innumerable quotations, and must confine myself to a few references. To give one example. Sometimes the race-characters become economic qualities. In writing of recent German economic history I find in a new book which attempts the same task an interesting treatment of motives of social and economic behaviour. Professor Wiskemann,[35] author of this latest economic history, says: "All in all, the German-Nordic race brought about the strongest progressive activity in the history of mankind." And he then exemplifies German enterprise as an expression of German race-characteristic as entirely different from that of other countries or races.

MERCANTILISM (CAMERALISM) AND THE "*Beamtenstaat.*"

Prussianism : its mercantilist economic expression in History, its influence on the mind and on the social structure of Germany.—There is no more conspicuous illustration of the German inclination to Mercantilism than the status of economics and the social sciences in University teaching. They were more or less squeezed into the Faculty of Law as an appendix to the Science of Jurisprudence. Significantly, professors of economics were appointed to chairs of the " Science of the State " (*Staatswissenschaft*) or the " Science of State Economics " (*wirtschaftliche Staatswissenschaft*). To the public administrative official who, except in technical branches, was always a lawyer, trained in the Schools, trade and industry meant a " service " which he could exchange any day for the administration of churches or schools or cattle markets or harbours and rivers. This " *Verwaltungsjurist,*" with his legal preoccupations was the main source of schemes relating to credit, finance and currency problems in their widest scope. This same type occupied sometimes the highest positions in private trade and industry. The " economist " who was not also a lawyer became common after the War, but was " *Ersatz,*" an inferior substitute, and only a few exceptional people reached high positions, such as Helfferich, Stresemann, Schacht. But even this type was educated differently from the British economist. The effect of this is clearly marked on the " theorists "

35

of the Science. Like the mercantilists, or especially the German cameralists (the servants of the prince's "camera") they did not undertake research with a preconceived deductive theory, a general law, as was done in Britain. Miss Warriner,[36] in describing German attitudes, especially towards monopoly theory, says: "The type of economic theory described as orthodox in this country, the analysis of the economic system with the aid of a general law of value based on the utility principle working through the consumer, was never generally accepted." Monopolistic formations, moreover, were the real bases of their economic system and were treated as axioms by the mercantilists. Therefore they were the precursors of Marx and various other authors in regarding these combinations as normal phenomena.

The conception of State interference and of State-monopoly as a mercantilist rule came into being in these early days and remained so strong through the ages, that the influence of the classical school was only episodic. To mercantilist investigation there was added as a fundamental study the unravelling of social and economic problems in the light of historical evolution and of general sociological considerations.[37] The Hegelian influence is here obvious. The ideas of the "*Cameralwissenschaft*" never died out among German scholars and their pupils who were the representatives of the "*Beamtenstaat*." The aim of these men was clear. They wished to build within the system of government and public administration the modern economic system, which they considered to be a temporary affair. I shall touch upon these questions when dealing with mercantilist ideology. Sir William Ashley's striking short survey on German theorists in contrast to British still holds good, to-day more than ever:

"In Germany there is a recognised distinction between the '*Grundlegung*' or '*Allgemeiner Teil*' and other departments of economics. The historical schools are in practice to be distinguished from various theoretical schools—

(1) by their insistence on the vital importance of thorough study of economic history after the '*Grundlegung*';

(2) by the comparatively small compass into which they would compress the '*Grundlegung*';

(3) by the comparatively slight attention they would give to the psychology of 'value' as a part of the '*Grundlegung*';

(4) by surrounding the individualist economics of self-interest there stated by general anthropological and historico-philosophical considerations."

There was a short period after the War when some younger scholars, among them curiously enough some of various Socialist tinges, the foremost coming from the Heidelberg School, based their investigations on the general law of liberal economics. Since 1933, most of them are scattered all over the world.

Although Mercantilism is a practice rather than an ideology there is, however, something in it which aims at an "idealised" practical policy. This spirit was always strongly expressed by the German Cameralism. The liberal view separated the State from the economic system. It is easy to trace how German political and economic scientists differed from the liberal view. The great Montesquieu built up the idea of his system (De l'esprit des lois, 1748) on the history, law and conditions of various countries which he investigated on the spot. The composition of governmental powers, whilst eminently suitable to his own age, seemed no longer valid to the German writers on political economy in the second half of the 19th century. Whilst on the one hand they were in agreement with him in subjecting ideas to practical policy, on the other hand they wished to build within the great constitutional framework a new social economy. In Montesquieu's age there could not be any constructive ideas on this subject since industrialisation, which created a new Society, was non-existent. *The modern world still awaits its Montesquieu.* The German historical school of economists—also called the socialists of the University chair—had as their goal the creation of a new system in which economics (called "social economics" by them) should be in subjection to a new political order. Schmoller, Wagner, Knapp, Bücher, Max Weber, and others, most of them "learned jurists," were among them. These men did not recognise a general law of economics valid throughout all time, but saw their "*eidos*" in the realisation of a political and economic system transferred to the needs of the citizen of our age. National-Socialist ideology, by combining State, People and Economy, seeks the same goal, though by different methods, as did other schools, including the Historical School. It was typical that the famous German economic periodical, "*Schmollers Jahrbuch*," carried in its title the word "for legislation and public administration." This "Public Administration" still retains its wide scope for economics in Germany. I shall show how a very extended economic organisation, the German Syndicate (starting from a private cartel), grew to be an important type of German Public Administration, a phenomenon no doubt not quite comprehensible to English readers.

Modern German economic policy is built up on Mercantilism. While Mercantilism was general throughout Europe it was widely modified, according to the peculiar conditions of individual countries and individual statesmen. That was because, as Karl Bücher says: "It was not a dead dogma, but a living policy of all statesmen of importance from Charles V up to Frederick the Great." In contrast to the British and Dutch type, in Germany eyes were turned in to the continent. Schmoller described Mercantilism as a creation of the State, and that means "a creation as much economic as political." From its early days, in Brandenburg-Prussia this policy was cut to the figure of the State. Since then it has supplied the backbone of

Prussian-German policy. Frederick the Great (1740-1786) was not a mere conqueror, he made a great nation from various isolated parts of a dismembered Germany which he tried to hold within an uniform trade policy. Moreover, he connected it with the world through communications with sea ports, by land, rivers and canals. He created manufactures, inaugurated a system of various types of credit and currency, made the State itself enter business as a banker for imports and exports or factories of various kinds—and established a thoroughgoing State policy of agriculture. Finally, he undertook a great policy of land settlement in the conquered Slavonic provinces. His great irrigation works were of outstanding character. To-day, one is accustomed to stamp schemes which cover many fields of political and economic activities and are planned by certain authorities with the name of "planned economy." But the mercantilist planning of Frederick the Great was not in essence different from that of, say, the Tennessee Valley Authority.

With the knitting together of formerly isolated districts to *one* country, national in administration, a common national feeling arose in general and economic policy, style of life, education and literature. During the time of the idealistic school this widened to "Nationalism" which rose slowly, but increased as it continued. The War of Liberation gave a fresh impulse to this development.

It is difficult to assign a place to Friedrich List in German Economic History. There were no socialists in his time—yet Oswald Spengler calls him a socialist in his book, "*Preussentum und Sozialismus.*" Was he a cameralist? This, he, as author of a national system which subordinated to the State all political and economic functions, most certainly was. But many of his sayings prove that he has well understood the interdependence of the economic systems for all individual countries. In this matter he was in advance of the representatives of a one-sided practical economic policy. His conception of the *Zollverein* and a modern transport system made him the great forerunner of Bismarck as founder of the German Empire.

In brief, expansionism, State protection in all great spheres of production and distribution, including State ownership of various undertakings, and general tutelage of the voluntarily obedient inhabitants, marked the development of Germany and especially Prussia from absolutism through constitutionalism up to totalitarianism. Step by step, these expressions of State interference and ownership of capital were intensified. It is noteworthy that when the Weimar Reich collapsed, more than 50 per cent. of the National Dividend belonged to the State, to say nothing of the fiscal power which could interfere intensively in every economic sphere. The ideological foundation of this policy is to be found in the philosophies of the State and in its function as social trustee of the community. Such a State is marked by a paramount bureaucracy performing many functions which elsewhere fall to private enterprise. The spirit of the dominating Prussian type of civil servant was for a long time enabled to spread over the whole nation from the Russian border to the French, from Denmark to Switzerland. This servant became a type akin to and generally belonging to the military, in most instances a reserve officer or former non-commissioned officer. In both public and private life to obey orders became second nature and made the national character strange to foreigners. The uniformity established in the great kingdom of Prussia, which at the accession of William II contained nearly forty million inhabitants, was transferred to all aspects of life in order to create a vast State machinery of army, trade and industry. Everything in the nation assumed a mass character, which lent itself to the creation of splendid organisations for making the best use of the poorer resources of the country as compared with those of other countries. Economy, piety,[38] solid and sober conduct in private life, were the hallmarks of the Prussian of those days in contrast to a certain decadence accompanied by luxury and snobbery in the succeeding reign of William II. But before dealing with the intrusion of a certain plutocrat spirit into the "*Beamtenstaat*," I shall give a glimpse of how pre-war German militarism appears to the eyes of a contemporary German philosopher. This reflects the relationship of this "militarism" to the other notable phenomena of William II's Reich. The significance of the great social revolution brought about by the Third Reich can only be understood by giving a picture of the traditional state which has been battered so much by the storm of this new movement.

Troeltsch on Pre-War Militarism.—It has been previously mentioned that it was one of the outstanding characteristics of German thoroughness that this idea of a military machine permeated the whole social life, public and private and even, to a certain degree, influenced German culture.

This militarism has rightly been called the cement that bound the whole structure of society into an entity. It was, and still is, an outstanding expression of the national efficiency of the Supreme State. In the greatest degree produced by constant drill, everything had to be as on the parade-ground, where thousands of soldiers monotonously repeated the same movement. This spirit of prompt obedience extended from the army to industrial life : the local units responded to the least word from headquarters. The giant industrial plants, large savings banks, local branches of the social democratic party, and even the trade unions, functioned through men of the type of captains or non-commissioned officers. The great philosopher, Ernst Troeltsch, has dealt so clearly with this subject that it would be wise to follow his exposition which I have summarised below.[39]

By militarism in this sense he does not mean the existence of an exceedingly strong army, the outlet for large masses of the population that were its mainstay, nor yet the pursuance of an imperialist policy, but rather a political institution. It is a peculiarly typical aspect of the Prussio-German constitution, a reflection of the mental outlook of the ruling classes in Germany. Herbert Spencer summarises the whole thing. He saw in the foundation of the Bismarckian empire the resurrection of the feudal and militaristic principle of State and Society, together with the moral and spiritual forces which were typical of them. He expected that this resurrection would lead to inevitable catastrophes in the path of the democratic spirit. Leopold von Ranke, too, forecast that the democratic spirit, almost omnipotent in the Western World, would inevitably arouse fierce opposition in the growing German empire. Politically, this empire had a dual personality. We find the civil government in the hands of the *Bundesrat* (Federal Council) and the Reichs-Chancellor subject, on the one hand, only to the supervision of Parliament, while on the other, it was subservient to the immediate and conditional military power of the Prussian King and the political desires of the general staff.

As we already know, from the outbreak of the Great War up to 1919 Parliament and the General Staff each had its own policy. This dualism was reconciled, first in the personality of the Kaiser, and later in the preponderance of the Prussian Diet, when the *Dreiklassen Wahlrecht* (the three-class franchise) of which the army officer class was so distinct a part, became dominant. This class dominated the *Bundesrat*, which became the decisive factor in the government of the Reich ("*durch den Reichskanzler ging der Riss mitten hindurch*"), in Troeltsch's words, the dividing line passed right through the Chancellor of the Reich. He was only able to formulate a policy agreeable both to the army and to the Prussian ruling class. The militarist group occupied this privileged position because, according to an old tradition of Prussian Society, a thorough-going system of patronage existed. The landed proprietor occupied posts in the army as well as in the bureaucracy. By these means, the landed nobility exercised a self-conscious control. The idea of the military machine permeated every aspect of life among the middle class—partly owing to the education of the army and reserve officers, partly owing to the dominating social position of the army officer, who took precedence over all other classes. Even the teaching of history in the school was carried out in this spirit. Before the War, admission into German society depended on this right to be recognised as a possible duellist (*satisfaktionsfaehige Gesellschaft*). This held good even for university students. In this way, this soldierly mode of life, into which other people were drawn, became the cement which bound the whole social system together. No career was possible without this outlook ("*die satisfaktionsfaehige Weltanschauung zog das Studententum in diese Ideenwelt hinein und wurde gesellschaftlich allmaechtig, Voraussetzung jeder Karriere und Massstab aller sozialen Gliederungen*"). To complete the picture, the newly-established big-business (*haute* finance as well as industry) followed the same pattern servilely. As Troeltsch goes on, these business men left no stone unturned, in business and society, to bring themselves into the machine. They joined noble calvary regiments and acquired landed property. This union between the powerful old nobility and these upstarts, anxious for assimilation into its ranks, stood actually and morally in the way of every democratic and socialist movement. (" *Industrie und Hochfinanz hatte sich auf diese Seite geschlagen. Diese Schicht hatte Geschaeft und Beziehungen auf den Fuss engster Gemeinschaft mit dieser Schicht gestellt, durch Grundbesitz und vornehmen Militaerdienst sich nobilitiert, Demokratie und Sozialismus im Bunde mit diesen Maechten faktisch und moralisch niedergehalten* "). It is extremely interesting to notice, too, that the Protestant Church willingly acquiesced and endeavoured to bring its philosophy into line with that of society in general. Socialism, Pacifism, the idea of a people-State were just an indecent and plebian expression of the subversive masses. (" *Sozialismus, Pazifismus, Volksstaat usw, waren auch fuer sie unanstaendige, plebejische Begriffe einer unbotmaessigen Masse* "). The new " Industrial State " and the great army and navy of the new German Empire demanded an enormous number of men. Therefore new principles for the selection of the army officers and the administrative group of the services were required. These were essential parts of Troeltsch's " *satisfaktionsfaehige Gesellschaft*." Before 1871, the nobility and upper middle classes (*Patriziat*) satisfied the demand, which, however, increased by thousands, since the State-Socialist State made public functionaries necessary where elsewhere private technical or commercial people held office. Schmoller once pointed out that especially the " *Era von Puttkamer*," who was the mighty Prussian Minister of the Interior (1881-1888), was largely responsible for introducing the system of regarding the men belonging to certain " student corps " and reserve officers of the army as a privileged class. Certain offices were completely reserved for it, and the marriage of this class with the plutocracy of either trade or industry marked a different type in the Reich and the Prussian highest bureaucracy. The end of this system, coupled with that of the federal state and the rebuff of both churches in the Nazi Reich marked a revolution in itself, not by the total destruction of these former leading groups, but by the supremacy of the National Socialist Party and its new principles of selection and its attempts to build up a new aristocracy.

Liberal Ideas.—From what angle did Germany view the conception of freedom and its translation into practice ? Why was Liberalism only of *episodic* significance in Germany ?

I tried to show in Chapter I (1) (*d*), in dealing with Individualism and Socialism, how these are but two aspects of human life, both ever-present, sometimes one in the ascendant, sometimes the other. It is natural, therefore, for a writer to be tempted to confuse not error for the truth but part of the truth for the whole truth. Many an antithesis may be exaggerated for the purposes of debate, whereas in fact, the nature of the object of study may, in the main, justify both contesting ideas. The student must, therefore, beware of the loose imputation of emphatic ideas to the great thinkers of the past by ardent partisans. Kant, Fichte, Hegel and others commonly suffer this treatment. Herder, for example, is treated thus by the exponents of the idea of the " nation." It is easy to make effective quotation from philosophers who, in a lifetime of writing, were bound to make apparent contradictions, now stressing one side of the truth, now another.

The idea of Liberalism was derived on the one side from a distinct school of thought, on the other from a distinct political environment. The liberal ideas of the period of enlightenment broke away from the conception of the interference of supernatural forces in every sphere of human life, while it insisted on explaining the world according to its own laws. Great astronomers proving that celestial bodies move without collision in obedience to well-defined laws drew general attention to a natural system which was soon applied to human society in its economic and political aspects. This was the root of Liberalism. Just as natural laws controlled the movements of celestial bodies, so the instinct of self-preservation governed the acts of men. Pursuing their own interests, they created a new order from which they expected a maximum of prosperity. State interference was condemned as obnoxious. Laisser faire was proclaimed as a rule of the State. The less State interference was felt the better. The more free play that was given, the greater the prosperity that would result. There would be a natural harmony between the interests of the individuals and the general welfare. The citizens of the 18th century felt that they had thrown off the shackles that trammelled private and public life while they were under the general tutelage of the State. They craved for individual mobility and freedom in production and trade: the French Revolution brought this long expected freedom.

Philosophers like Locke, economists like Adam Smith, and, later, scientists like Darwin, helped to lay the foundation of this doctrine and encouraged its development. It dominated men's minds from the middle of the 18th to the middle of the 19th century and its after-effect, even up to the end of the last century, was far-reaching. Liberalism remained the main internal and external policy of Europe up to this time, when social policy and protectionism appeared as signs of a new age. German professors of political economy up to the seventies of the last century taught this doctrine in the then undeveloped form, but it provoked a counter-movement. Later, the German historical schools sought conclusions in the investigation of the actual facts of a new age of technical and social progress.

It is interesting that in the two German countries, Germany and Austria, different attitudes toward the problem were held. The idea of harmony of the classical philosophers which contributed to the confusion of rational theory and economic liberalism, has been attacked by two methods. No doubt, the Austrians were more successful in formulating "theory" whilst the work of German historians crumbled into historical relativity. Both methods have their own justification; neither, however, made any real progress in formulating a law for the dynamic process. The one believed in the static scheme, whilst the other lost its way in generalisation and minute detail.

But this explanation of Liberalism does not wholly explain the conception. In Germany, as well as in Britain, the history of this system followed the development of religion. There is an immediate connection between the Reformation, the age of the Enlightenment, and the era during which the German School of Idealism prevailed (1790-1830).[40] The Christian principle of individual freedom, the great watchword of the Reformation, remained an essential factor with this school, influencing its development and at the same time being modified by it. The Christian idea of freedom merged with the Athenian ideal. It was only too natural that people brought up with the classical outlook should measure the new ideal of liberty against the old, a legacy from the time of the Renaissance and the age of the humanists.

At first Liberalism understood liberty as absence of restraint. At a later time it demanded general freedom from all restrictions. We see here an essential point of difference between the German ideas and those of Western nations which will be dealt with more thoroughly when we examine State philosophies and see how differently "ethics" appealed to individual nations. Liberal ideas can only be understood by an appreciation of these contrasts. In this connection it may be stated : no religious revival in Germany—such as, perhaps, was provided in England by "non-conformity"—was strong enough to contrast the individual Christian with the citizen whose church was characterised as an instrument of State policy.

But before turning to the ethical side I must explain some of the fundamental causes, material as well as spiritual, that made Germany's attitude so different from that of Britain.

The divergencies between Great Britain and Germany can be accounted for when we consider the difference in their positions. Great Britain was a wealthy empire, politically united, a world-financing power, dealing with its own possessions as well as with foreign countries. Moreover, the industrial revolution had taken place at an earlier time. Naturally, in such a country, unrivalled in the world market because of the cheapness of her productions, the free exercise of liberal economy was essential for its welfare. Germany on the other hand was a late-comer into the world market. She needed an outlet for her energies and wanted to take her share. She was politically and economically weak. As the poorer country she was obliged to economise her limited resources. And it was only natural that the State should become the controlling force in assisting a protecting economy, along the old mercantilist lines, since the idea of the State as general trustee was familiar to Germany.

Wherever German energies began to develop a more independent industrial life, they clashed with other nations, which were not willing to give opportunities for development to late-comers. In 1846, when Peel was successfully pursuing his policy of economic liberalism, when protectionism in Britain would have been madness, in Germany the creators of her industry would have considered economic liberalism even greater madness, as protection was necessary for their undeveloped trade. The German determination not to rest in the task of developing her natural energies as an industrial country may well be compared with the British determination to establish their Empire-policy during the Disraelian epoch.

During the golden age of liberalism evil effects might easily be overlooked or the brighter side turned always to the fore. It was a period of highly-contrasted change. The previous bondage such as that of feudalism was over. A process of long duration dissolved many economic and social ties. Personal initiative was considered essential for the building up of new forms. And these developed differently according to the peculiar conditions of the nations concerned. The private as well as the public will of the German people, curiously enough, mostly aimed at replacing old ties by new ones and that made liberalism inappropriate in their eyes. I might refer here to a spokesman of this German school (I might select others, for the opinion delivered is very widespread), who lends himself particularly well to quotation because he expresses the typical view of compromise which Germany has always shown in her active economic policy. The sociologist, A. Vierkandt,[41] once undertook to explain the German attitude towards this phenomenon. "It was owing to the peculiarity of historical circumstances, that this initial period of dissolution still possessed many assets in reserve. Liberalism asked for a free hand for individuals freed from every tie of community, society and State. But it could not be put to the test in every respect, for mankind was still bound by tradition, religion and custom. The dissolution of these 'reserves' lasted more than a century. Up to then many forces were active which liberalism did not take into account. Moreover, the destructive forces of the future could not at first be foreseen and these were the social groups hitherto unrecognised which gradually succeeded in coming to the fore."

To these destructive effects, Vierkandt adds those of the community of interests and the connection "with the soil of the homeland," which he stresses as *imponderabilia*, like so many other Germans, influenced by German Romanticism. His arguments continue : " The striking progress of technical science and economics hypnotised the world and this success was attributed to the liberal system without recognising the fact that the real cause was that the supply offered by the Western world could be easily absorbed. There were markets for all and it was only a matter of organising and exploiting them ; it was this age of expansion which gave liberalism its unique temporary significance. It was not only a negligence on the part of German authors that they did not prop up the doctrine of certain combines with the theory of competition and monopoly." For this they have been reproached. The difference of opinion goes far deeper, it goes to the root of the competition problem as conceived by both the British and the Austrian school. The main points are that the aspect of social psychology which served as a basis for exchange economy, self-interest, is not accepted. And then the scheme remains a static one : whilst dynamics create, to the eyes of German authors, a qualitatively new phenomenon which clearly cannot be conceived by methods appropriate to another philosophy. The continuation of the manner of thinking along mercantilist lines gives further psychological explanation of the German attitude.

Laisser faire theorists in Germany were very rare in recent times (cf. p. 36). The theories seemed contradictory to many Germans, who regarded the community as the essential factor, endangered if every individual member is absorbed in himself and is nonchalent towards the whole. There was no understanding of orthodox schools. Men considered heretics by the former were, therefore, abundantly quoted in Germany. Especially Mr. J. M. Keynes' lecture in Berlin University, 1926,[42] "The End of Laisser Faire," created a great sensation because his views coincided with the general feeling. "It is not true," as Mr. Keynes trenchantly declares, "that individuals possess a prescriptive Natural-Liberty in their economic activities. There is no 'compact' conferring perpetual rights on those who have or on those who acquire. The world is not so governed from above that private and social interest always coincide. It is not so managed here below, that in practice they coincide. It is not a correct deduction from the Principles of Economics that enlightened self-interest always operates in the public interest. Nor is it true that self-interest generally is enlightened ; more often individuals acting separately to promote their own ends are too ignorant or too weak to attain even these. Experience does not show that individuals, when they make up social units, are always less clear-sighted than when they act separately. We cannot settle, therefore, on abstract grounds, but must handle on its merits in detail, what Burke termed ' one of the finest problems in legislation, namely, to determine what the State ought to take itself to direct by the public wisdom, and what it ought to leave, with as little interference as possible, to individual exertion.' "[43]

Free competition, generally accepted in Germany as an ideal starting point from analysis, was no longer a sufficient interpretation of economic phenomena, and was not considered of any assistance in active policy. In this the British and German Schools will never see eye to eye. One interpreter whose textbook (at first written in German) was, perhaps, the most generally used in Germany after the War,[44] Gustav Cassel, expresses the view widely accepted in that country on this central problem in a way that I think cannot be improved upon. This quotation may also be the way to an understanding of the German attitude towards the theoretical foundations of the cartel problem : . . . " free competition," Cassel says, " is the means by which the exchange economy regulates itself. But there can be no free competition so long as the economic individuals are bound together by some organisation. Even the social intercourse of people in the same trade is injurious to free competition, as it easily leads to ' a conspiracy against the public,' an attempt to raise prices. The ideal is a society that we may call ' atomistic ' consisting of isolated individuals who only come into touch with each other economically and over whom there is merely a State which has nothing to do but see to the legal order of economy "[45] " It is thus quite intelligible that free competition was made the starting point for the whole of theoretical economy, and the work of the science was seen in the study of an exchange economy governed by free competition. This point of view is, however, only justified if free competition really has the effects which the theory assumes ; if, that is to say, at least in a general way it settles prices according to the principles of the cost, and does in fact predominantly rule our exchange economy. In fact, strictly speaking, even then it is only justified if free competition is an essential element in the process of pricing and in the regulation of the economy affected thereby."[46] . . . " This brief survey of the actual forms of the modern economic life will suffice to enable us to reach the following result. Free competition does not, as the theory supposes, guarantee that prices shall be fixed according to the principle of cost. Nor can it be said that free competition governs the modern exchange economy. In large and important spheres of our economic life recent developments have entirely abolished it. Competition still plays a very important part in modern economic life, but the forms it assumes are totally different from the ideal of free competition. The very idea of free competition is obscure. The negative definition of it as the absence of any regulation or organisation excludes the essential condition on which the modern community succeeds in certain spheres in creating a competition that helps us to realise the principle of cost. It would be very difficult to give a satisfactory positive definition of free competition. The idea of it is, in fact, quite irreconcilable with a matter of great importance in the modern economic life—the economic superiority of the *large business*." Here lies an outstanding point determining economics, as German economists see it (cf. II A (1) (c)). " In cases where this superiority makes itself felt, free competition is logically bound to bring about its own opposite—monopoly ; for, at what intermediate stage would the assumed superiority of the large business permit a state of equilibrium under free competition ? Such an issue cannot be prevented without forms of organisation acting on economic life in a severely regulatory fashion, which would therefore mean the end of free competition in the cases we are considering " . . . " we cannot make free competition the starting-point of the theory, for there is no doubt whatever that even without free competition prices can be fixed in accordance with the cost principle. Indeed, we (Cassel) shall see in the next section (The Socialist Community) that such pricing would have to be maintained in a community that rejected private enterprise and therefore excluded free competition. But even our actual society succeeds, as we saw, in many cases where free competition is impossible, in fixing approximately normal prices in other ways." Cassel, in this connection, said,[47] " free competition is, in consequence of the lack of mobility of fixed capital (and of labour, moreover) not capable of completely effecting this normal settlement of prices."[48] But this question will be dealt with in more detail elsewhere.

My brief reference to the attitude of German and other authors to the competition and monopoly problem and its treatment by foreign schools will undoubtedly not suffice for the more interested reader. For him I have added a special sub-chapter (II, A, (c), §3).

We may take it for granted that in Germany the general opinion gained ground that neither thoroughgoing individualism nor any pure form of socialism could meet the problem, for it demanded a solution by compromise. As Vierkandt puts it in his survey on compromise, in Germany as well as in other countries, the abyss separating Liberalism and Socialism no longer exists. He then gives instances very like those given in my previous chapter (p. 23). Characteristically, Vierkandt calls attention to the fact that even Mr. J. M. Keynes, lecturing in the University of Berlin, the native soil of these ideas, said : " I believe that the ideal extent for the unity of organisation and control lies somewhere between the individual and the modern State."[49] Keynes, in these words, hinted at corporative organisations : " Therefore, I believe that progress will be found in the direction of development and recognition of half-autonomous corporations in the frame of the State " (cf. what is said on the " mixed public and private enterprise " and the " war corporations "). Keynes' lectures were delivered immediately after a period of outstanding activity by these corporations and their successors in Germany.

The opposition to liberalism in Germany manifested itself not only against free competition, but was also directed against the ideal of freedom in national life, consciously as well as unconsciously. The two ideals which in the realm of thought have most influenced the development of mankind, the Christian ideal[50] of personal freedom and the Greek ideal of democracy and liberty, show the contrast emphatically between the two nations. It is an old argument which still reflects the present mind of the two nations. Once more the question is acute.

I find in Professor Ernest Barker,[51] a concise expression of English judgment which clearly shows how deep this difference goes. The Greek ideal of democracy and liberty, and the way in which it came to Europe with the rediscovery of Greek art and poetry at the time of the Renaissance in the 16th century, affected the two countries in significantly different ways. " The Renaissance, in matters other than those of scholarship and theology, was over two hundred years late in coming to Germany. It was only in the latter half of the 18th century that Greek art and poetry began to influence German literature. When their influence began, Romanticism was already a great power in German thought." The two diverging ideologies are contrasted in the following quotations from Dr. Ernest Barker who (in contrast to Miss E. M. Butler, who called a book "The Tyranny of Greece over Germany") argues that Germany never had any real perception of true Hellenism. " Germany broke with the Greek tradition, which is the common heritage of Western Europe, when she retired into a romantic cult of her own indigenous *Volkstum*. We may carry the break back to Herder; we may carry it back to Luther; we may even carry it back, as Troeltsch has suggested, to Eckhart and the Middle Ages." Professor Barker speaks of how falsely Germany romanticised Greece. He tries to show that this " romanticism " meant a tendency to see things in a golden haze—to indulge in a nebulous *historicism* (or as it might also be called) an antiquarian idealism— to return to a fabulous past and to see in that past the future. Dr. Barker summarises: "The relation between Hellenism and Teutonism is a matter of profound importance, not only for the interpretation of German literature from the birth of Winckelmann to the death of Stephan George, but also for the present and future of German thought and action. Some ingredient of the true and authentic Hellas is a necessary element in any sane and balanced culture. If Germany can drop the Märchen and learn the real lesson of the actual tradition of Greece—the lesson which her scholars are willing to teach, if her poets and prophets will hear—she will find liberation of her soul, and she will join the general comity of European culture. Hellas—and not only Hellas, but also Israel, united and married to Hellas in Christianity—these are parts of the long tradition which makes us civilised men; and with them Teutonism must make its peace—the peace of a true understanding, and not of a romantic perversion into the image of its own likeness." (As to the religious conception of freedom, cf. p. 60).

(b) Ideology and Sociology II

German Type of State Philosophy and of Socialism.—The terms " Socialist " and " Socialism " have been in use for the last hundred years. Originally they were closely linked up with the name of Robert Owen and were used both by his supporters and his opponents. Nobody at that time could have guessed how widely and variously the term " Socialism " would be some day applied. German Socialism is the outcome of two conceptions which mutually influenced each other—Prussian Mercantilism, a State philosophy with strong socialist tendencies, and the ideas of Marx and Lassalle. Both these thinkers influenced the mercantilist school, more particularly Lassalle. From them German party socialism derived; but this, in turn, was not able to tear itself away from mercantilist influence. It is, perhaps, an irony of history that the philosopher who laid the scientific foundations of this outstanding type of socialism can be claimed as godfather by certain liberal and other schools. This man is Hegel. He is the bridge which connected the different systems. His opponents, who, without doubt, underrate him, stated that this man who wrote as a revolutionary and also as a reactionary, could argue on all sides. Like so many of his South German Alemanic compatriots he began as a firebrand, glowing with ideas of unrestricted liberty. His mind reflected the first stages of the French revolution which he passionately admired in his young days. But the more he fell under Prussian influence, especially when he became a Prussian civil servant—as Fichte's successor to the chair of philosophy in Berlin—the more he became Prussianised. This process has often manifested itself in history. We find another example in the South German, Gustav Schmoller, whose democratic and socialist tendencies faded away under the shadow of the Prussian State when he became the " Historiographer of the Prussian Crown," and was ennobled by the king.

The oft-traced line of German State philosophers from Treitschke to Bernhardi, even those of National-Socialism, whose ideology is still in the making, may claim Hegel as godfather, as well as such democrats as Arnold Ruge and Ludwig Feuerbach—or Marx, Engels, and Lassalle. Thus, diverging ideas spring from Hegel's philosophy and assume strongly antagonistic forms. The deified ideas of " State " and " Nation " or " Statelessness " and " Internationalism " as well as the anarchistic streams of individualism, rise directly from this source. Neither the philosopher of the era of enlightenment nor Kant saw, as Hegel did, *the evolutionary process of History*. The graph of its development marked a curve. When it reaches a peak, there is perhaps the dissolution of the former stage. The more accentuated a system shows itself, the more it is doomed to disappear and its antithesis to take its place. Such a philosophy, applied to State and Society, ought to have its effects on the various schools of State philosophy mentioned here. But the history of ideas can only be understood when we consider the political and economic facts which follow or concur with corresponding features in the realm of thought.

§1 *Prussian Mercantilism (State Socialism)*

Mercantilism, unlike other driving forces of the policy of nations, emerged more from the flow of a practical development. So it is difficult to say whether it developed an ideology of its own. Experiences gained through centuries were systematised, State philosophies and other ideas, primarily of a socialist character, were interlocked with mercantilism. From early days a kind of State socialism developed. Most of its origin has been explained in preceding pages (p. 37). In these I have mentioned the recognition of combined action among competitors as the outcome of natural development and the use by the State itself of monopolistic formations and other measures interfering with the economic sphere as instruments of regulation. True, it also served fiscal ends but that was by no means the only purpose.

In unravelling the character of Prussian mercantilism, it was clearly seen that Nationalism, Imperialism, Expansionism and Militarism were successively mainsprings and products of this mercantilism. Therefore, I asked whether this policy developed its own ideology. Socialism, in turn, through mercantilist additions, became materialist. On the other hand, mercantilism became a most effective method of carrying out socialist ideas. Neo-mercantilism (then also finding expression as State-Socialism which was partly State-Capitalism) shows itself most in this form.

As social progress advanced, so the State and its economic organisation were permeated by a social spirit. The primitive feeling of social trusteeship of benevolent despots as well as that of great statesmen in early constitutional periods in the 19th century, as instanced in Bismarck's personality, did not satisfy a new world, conscious of equal rights of citizenship, especially States with outstanding working-class populations. Social ideas and the growth in power of the Labour Class began to break the chains of the Authoritarian State and to imbue it with this social spirit. The four periods under review from William I and William II to the Weimar and the Third Reich are remarkable and full of different forms of this State-Socialism.

The Prussian State had long recognised its position as the main bearer of social responsibility. A special philosophy expounded by Pastors R. Todt and Rud. Meyer, who edited the " State-Socialist periodical for social reform " (1877-82), adopted " State-Socialism " (which from then appears as a new political form) as the device of a doctrine and movement. This derived from K. Rodbertus' philosophy. Without doubt, this school, which fought against the Manchester school and the predominance of capital in general and economic policies, was important for future development.

Modern State-Socialism or Neo-Mercantilism, no doubt, was influenced by ideas of Marx and Lassalle. One of the items of Karl Marx's programme, the nationalisation of means of production, can easily correspond to cameralist development. The monopolies infiltrating the market overthrow free competition and with it economic and political liberalism. The monopolies likewise furnish bodies ready made for nationalisation and socialisation. The State need only replace the capitalist power in these monopolies, which had long ago ceased to be individualist. So State control and

State interference born of this development, no doubt a materialist issue, in its effect becomes a stronger force for socialism than pure socialist ideologies.

The German Social Democratic Party was, in fact, a "labour" party with only a very rough conception of socialist ideas. In the chapter on the Weimar Reich the consequences of this anaemia will be shown as leading to the downfall of this type of socialism which always had a strong materialist bias. The "revisionism" (see p. 62, and III (1) (b), §1), was not strong enough to be allowed by the party majority to inject a more powerful social spirit into the blood-stream of the State of the Imperial Germany.

§2 *The idealistic and later schools*

To understand German Liberalism we must compare it with its opposite which culminates in the conception of Society and State, the antithesis of which the German historian, Professor F. Meinecke[52] described as "National State and Cosmopolitanism." Owing to the strength of the opposing force, the idea of liberty was doomed to mediocre success. German thought throughout the centuries was moulded and fashioned to a great extent by external European influences of various and even conflicting kinds. Most German State philosophers, statesmen as well as scholars, were to a certain degree pupils of Machiavelli, Thomas More, of the leaders of the Reformation, and of exponents of natural law like Hugo Grotius and Christian Wolff. Spinoza and Leibniz, too, influenced them; sometimes they approved their teaching, sometimes they opposed it. Rousseau, in a certain sense following Plato's idea of the State, influenced Kant and Hegel greatly. Kant born in one reactionary period and dying in another, was deeply affected by the French Revolution and he gave expression to varying ideas of the State. As the philosopher Vorlaender[53] puts it, it is remarkable that he should have combined in his philosophy of the State the ideas of the liberal-democratic, the conservative and the socialist schools. This conflict between the ideas of the rationalist period of enlightenment and those of the idealistic periods of romanticism moulded the minds of such German State philosophers as Fichte, Hegel and Schelling. Their precursors and their contemporaries, among them the great thinkers of classical literature, had been brought up to some extent in the atmosphere of conflict. From among them Herder became the genius of romanticism. His influence (whether rightly understood or not) still governs the German mind in its Prussianised form. This theologian and classical scholar (1744-1803), born near the Russian frontier and alleged to be of Slavonic origin,[54] was, as a well-known philosopher says, "a man not in the least politically minded, weak and sentimental like a woman."[55] Politics and matters of State did not appeal to him. Nature, as he saw it, was a decisive element in the creation of families and peoples, not States. Peoples, or as he says, fatherlands, not States, inspired him. For him a people had the historic qualities of organic personality and he believed in the historic mission of peoples and their place in the unfolding of the creative plans of Providence. In his "*Humanitätsbriefe*" (1797), Herder refused to accept the whole of Machiavelli's doctrine of the State, but he is prepared to recognise it in so far as it aimed at the national State—the State as conceived according to the political means of that period. To his way of thinking " national State and cosmopolitanism " were indissolubly allied and Lessing, Goethe and Schiller also accepted this ideal. But Herder was the product of a time which did not distinguish nationalism clearly and only so can he be understood. Much mischief has been done recently by contrasting Herder the nationalist with Goethe the cosmopolitan.

J. G. Fichte, who held the chair of philosophy at Berlin shortly after the foundation of the University, has been similarly worshipped as a hero of nationalism. This man, too, belongs to the Slavonic borderland. He himself was born in the Lausitz—the home of some of Germany's great thinkers, among them Lessing. Fichte was one of many other outstanding reformers as historian, philosopher and educationalist. In 1800 he published a complete draft for the socialist State (*der geschlossene Handelsstaat*). This is still, no doubt, a most reactionary conception, resembling very much that of the " police " State of the 18th century, at least in its external organisation. Yet it is an Utopian dream, in which we see Fichte as Germany's first socialist. His doctrine of the State is the work of a desperate patriot, deeply moved by the breakdown of his country. He advocated violent means of salvation, hitherto undreamed of by a civilized community. Meinecke states that Fichte in his book "*Grundzüge des gegenwärtigen Zeitalters*" (1804) condemned patriotism which " clung to soil, river, hill." Moreover as he says, " the sun-loving spirit has to turn its back on the State if it collapsed and face light and right." In the "*Dialog über den Patriotismus*," the first of which was published in 1806 he, like Kant, identifies patriotism and cosmopolitanism. It is true that in his pamphlet on Machiavelli he has advanced beyond his previous opinions as, on the collapse of the fatherland, he is anxious to resort to *Realpolitik*. He did not repudiate coercion as a method of acquiring freedom (Vorländer). But as Meinecke states,[56] " he did not incline to following the rule of the *Machstaat*. The revolutionary of 1793, the socialist of 1800, never sacrificed the ideal of the Rational State." In the three following periods through which he passed— enlightenment, classical idealism, romanticism—he identified the German spirit with that which creates in the State the sublimest ideal of culture. It is interesting to note that his ideas which agree with Machiavelli's will-to-power policy and his patriotic claim, as the task of the German people, made him rightly or wrongly the medium which led to the idea of the *Machtstaat*.

Hegel, his successor in the chair at Berlin, is considered a further kiln. He expressly agreed with Machiavelli and distinguished between private and State morality. As a State philosopher he based his theory on the objective spirit. This manifests itself in the law which determines the will of man, an objective spiritual power from without rather than a power where the mind controls the will from within. The whole system finds its culminating expression here where the subjective mind is embodied in an objective reality. This shows itself first of all in the family, later in formal public institutions of civic Society, and ultimately as a consciously formed and developed organic reality, in the State. This is for Hegel the sublimest appearance on earth of the objective spirit, the incarnation of the earthly-divine, which reveals itself in the internal and external law of the State and in the history of the world. The external law of the State springs from its individual moral law. Hegel repeatedly glorified the State; he even deified it. Already in his " System of Morality " (1802), in his progressive investigations he considered it the highest manifestation of the spirit. He called it " the realisation of the moral idea or of liberty, as a thing absolute in itself." The climax of this wild exaggeration is the State as " the complete realisation of the spirit on earth, indeed, of the divine idea as it appears on earth."

It is no wonder that the Prussian subject has to venerate this sublime manifestation of God on earth, whereas the State itself showed a godlike indifference to the individual.[57] Such words spoken by a man as influential as Hegel in the intellectual life of Germany, passing through a period of revolution in thought, had enormous effects. It was just what all Prussianised Germans, brought up in the conception of State service or State mercantilism, wanted.

Hegel, no doubt, had many adversaries in his time, but not because of his deification of the State. The Prussian feudal conservatives followed Haller and Stahl. It is a peculiar phenomenon that what we may call a Prussianisation of thought sprang from many causes.

Some romanticists, such as Gentz and Adam Müller, became later the spiritual godfathers of Fascism. These men were widely influenced by Edmund Burke, the great hater of the French Revolution, whose work Gentz translated into German. It was Otmar Spann who, during the ten years following the War, created an imaginary ideology of Fascism of his own : he exhumed Adam Müller and made him the hero of the romantic creed of the totalitarian State. The State is to Müller " not a mere collection of governmental institutions—such as factories, dairy farms, State insurance or mercantilist company," but " the most solid combination of the entire physical and spiritual demands of the people, of the entire physical and spiritual wealth of the internal and external life of the nation to a totalitarian unit, great, energetic and indefinite in motion and life." As shown by this verbosity, the conception of this sentimentalist, like those of Herder, had no stable basis. The State was to him an " individuality," a vivid personality only to be understood in the light of its own soil and according to its own internal laws. Even War is an institution of the State. " War gives the State first of all stability, individuality and personality . . . " Adam Müller makes no mention of a philosophy, such for instance as Fichte gives, of the evolution of the State through reason and moral power.

As Meinecke[58] shows, Adam Müller, the romanticist of the State, " recognises neither the ethical nor the modern thought of evolution in the province of the life of the State." It is true that at the time when Müller wrote his doctrine, the idea of the State was not at all well conceived. Conceptions that are widely accepted to-day by the majority of thinking men, were then expressed in a very nebulous manner, among them his conception of " nature." His main idea lies in the word " Nationality " which gave rise to the great slogan of the 19th and 20th century. Nationality is to Adam Müller not a community of culture as Fichte claimed it, but an indigenous growth, such as the romanticists Novalis and Friedrich Schlegel, conceived it to be. The Prussian nation for example, is such a State community. Before the Third Reich appeared Adam Müller had become a heroic figure in the ideology of the party. Later he and O. Spann, who had revived interest in him, were pushed into the background.[59] No great weight can be given to the romanticists Novalis and F. Schlegel as theorists of the State, even though they speak much of it. Their nebulous manner of symbolising the conception State and Nation gave them a certain significance.[60] Their contemporary Schleiermacher was more independent. In contrast to Kant and Fichte he wished the State to be an ideal of which the ethics have to be embodied in some material things. He sees, not unlike his adversary Hegel, the ideal type in the modern national State of the great countries which had to be identified with the spirit of the community.

Tendencies mentioned as reactionary against the spirit of the French Revolution found a spiritual centre in the personality of Friedrich Julius Stahl, who as a scholar and leader of the conservatives in the Prussian House of Lords, showed a certain romanticism up to his death in 1861. He was the representative of this romantic king, Friedrich Wilhelm IV, who called Stahl in 1840 to the chair of Constitutional Law in the University of Berlin. He translated the claims of the landed nobility into scientific language. As a skilful advocate of these ideas he influenced politics widely. He combated Hegel and opposed liberalism which he feared might lead to democracy and socialism. He inclined more to the theories of Haller, who detested English parliamentarism in his love for an absolute kingdom founded on divine right, " authority not majority." His conception was a religious and a reactionary one. Kelsen[61] very clearly explains Stahl's significance : " . . . the relativity of the value based on a certain political professional creed compels the negation of political absolutism as well as the impossibility of claiming absolute value for a political programme and ideal. This holds good for every subjective attachment and personal conviction. This holds good for the absolutism of a monarch or the domination of priests, of nobles, of warriors, or of protected classes or groups that exclude others. He who is inclined to rely on the Divinity and his calling turns a deaf ear to the voice of men. He imposes his will in an absolute fashion in a world of men unbelieving and deluded because they are inarticulate. The Christian monarchy therefore could only be the watchword of the divine right, authority not majority. This phrase of Stahl became the mainspring for everything that was directed against spiritual liberty and science, freed of miracles and dogmas and based on democratic tendencies." There was no successor to Stahl in the consequent absolutist theory.

The so-called theorists of power sprang from other roots. On the philosophical side Nietzsche is claimed as godfather. No doubt Nietzsche's influence on German intellectuals was very strong. Some of his ideas became a kind of creed and are even reflected in the latest German ideology: thus there came into existence the idea that all impulses can be reduced to one original impulse, that is, the will for power. It is not reasoning power (*Vernunft*) which decides what is true and what is good. The comparison of the moral laws of various countries shows that there are two fundamental types of morality, that of the master and that of the slave. Greek, Roman, and German culture originated from the conquering of other peoples by " master " peoples. The conquerors are the aristocrats of the new countries who fix the values which have to be generally acceded to. The master-man is like his God who is the personified " will to power." Opposite the master is the subjected or the slave, and this is the inferior man. The slave despises everything that is master-like, violent or cruel and which is the cause of fear. His virtues are sympathy, patience, mildness of temper and benevolence. According to Nietzsche the religion and morals which made our culture originated amongst the Jews who were a typical people of slaves. Jews were at the same time the priestly people of the world. It is the duty of the priest to suppress the will to power which exists also among the slaves as a resentment against the master. The priest turns the slave's will to power into a depreciation of his earthly life, and an elevation of the salvation after death and thereby changing the orientation of his inner life. The idea of Christ, according to Nietzsche, took over all these Jewish values and falsified still further the nature of man through the doctrines of immortality and freedom of will, and by his emphasis on sin. Consciousness of sin and the persistent bad conscience is the most important peculiarity of the slave who now connects his feeling and moral inferiority not with his master but with God Himself. The ideal of humanity, democracy and socialism presents merely modern types of the Christian-Jewish morality of the slave.

So far Nietzsche. He has often been quoted in connection with the historian, von Treitschke. One of the most outstanding followers of Nietzsche and Treitschke was General von Bernhardi. Probably they are linked closely with romanticism and with Hegel's philosophy of the State which had other foundations both in theory and in fact. Of both the latter schools Schmoller once said that had these theorists not existed there would have been no German Empire. As for the historian, Treitschke (1834-1896), it must be said that he had immense propagandist influence on German youth. He made it quite clear that it is *power*, or as he puts it in his pamphlet, " *Bundesstaat und Einheitsstaat*" (1864), repeated in his German History IV, p. 204, F, three times over, "power first, power second, and yet again power that makes the State." There are thousands who crave the opportunity to follow a master with such a stirring watchword. Thus the worship of force became the animating idea of even the educated classes in Germany. A type of this kind, but not of such scientific importance, was the historian, Dietrich Schaefer, who held the chair of history at the University of Berlin. Similar ideas are to be found in his book, " *Staat und Welt.*"[62] General Friedrich von Bernhardi, who popularised the *Machttheorie* was one of the most energetic spokesmen of this class. I quote here : " Force is the sublimest law, the law suit is decided by the yardstick of war, which is the biological judge because its decisions spring from things themselves ; . . . whereas consciousness of law is only a very vague and subjective conception."[63]

§3 *Certain socialist schools*

State-Socialism, into which Prussian-German Mercantilism developed, and the socialism of the leading socialist party, were greatly influenced by the doctrines of Marx and Lassalle. It is true that the genius of Marx, who first gave socialism as a body of political and economic doctrine a definite form and was the creator of a world-wide movement, is not bounded by time and place. Both doctrine and movement found in his homeland, Germany, with her traditional strong tendencies of State-Socialism, a different soil for development than in his adopted fatherland, England, with her traditional liberal and religious-ethical tendencies—or in Russia.

As shown above, Marx and Lassalle were followers of Hegel, in so far as they were educated in his idealistic philosophy and made his doctrine of the constant process of evolutionary development their starting point. In contrast to Hegel, however, Marx's development was a purely materialistic one, influenced by economic facts. Notwithstanding the fact that Marx's books became a kind of Bible to his followers, it was not a guide to positive policy and so they differ widely in their interpretations of his doctrines. These differences and contradictions in his publications (which cover nearly 40 years of rapid development), split the Marxists into several sects which differ in their beliefs in regard to the tempo and the methods of carrying out the movement, whether by slow evolution or radical revolution—whether on democratic or anti-democratic lines.

In contrast to Lassalle who built up his movement on national lines, Marx already in the Communist Manifesto, gave his Socialism an international character. The economic fact on which the theory was based was "the class struggle in Society." This he pursued through a long course of historical development. Feudalism, itself a product of class war, was replaced by the rule of the middle classes. The conflict between Capital and Labour was the problem his own age had to face. The property-less worker was forced to sell his labour to the capitalist for a bare subsistence wage. According to his doctrine, capitalists received the surplus which really belonged to the insufficiently paid worker as well as the profits which arose from inventions and economics. It was Lassalle who, in his "brazen law of wages," amplifying Ricardo's theory, declared that the value of a good, which is not a monopoly, is fixed by the price of labour—the wage allowed being no more than enough to keep the workman alive. Another point is the tendency of Big Business to swallow up the small. This fact, resulting in combinations and the increase of the working population, would lead to the collapse of capitalism. The working class would realise its own strength and the means of production would eventually belong to the community.

Marx pointed out that this revolution, marking a new stage of development, like the overcoming of Feudalism, had to take place as a consequence of facts, independent of human will, due to conditions inherent in the capitalist system. This view of the position of capital and labour was widely accepted by German socialists in the second half of the 19th century—who were, however, also greatly influenced by the schools of State philosophy (as mentioned I (*b*), §1). Lassalle proposed to the Prussian State to form co-operative associations of labourers, governed by dictatorial power, which would rule through a centralised body. In contrast to Schulze-Delitzsch, who established his co-operative societies with the funds of their members, Lassalle characteristically wished to reach this goal through the State, and, moreover, his device was a national one. With the failure of the revolution of 1848, the form of organisation suggested by Marx and Engels receded and it was Lassalle who finally formed the first worker's union. The internationally-minded Marx established in 1864 the first International Union of Workers. In 1869, the German Social Democratic workers party was formed in Eisenach, twenty years after Marx left Germany and five years after Lassalle's death in a duel. However, as its name shows, in that it was a democratic party it was characteristically opposed to Marx's later principles. From this time Marx ruled in London as a dogmatic pope or adviser for the propagation of his gospel. In contrast to active politicians and statesmen he thought in terms of centuries, while they were obliged to reconcile their ideas with the political expediencies of the moment. Marx's German followers of both wings, the national and democratic and the international radicals, decided to unite at the Party Congress of Gotha in 1875, owing to the impending common danger of persecution by the Government. But, with this decision, the problem which dealt with the former controversy was not solved; it is still the outstanding problem of socialist ideology as well as of the practical movement. The difference between Marx, who visualised the fulfilment of his religion in stages of a long course of historical development, and the active parliamentary parties preoccupied with the conditions of their own time, can be seen even to-day.

The first party which adopted this creed, the German Social Democratic party, consisted mostly of workmen. There was only a small sprinkling of intellectuals, among whom without doubt there were some who believed in Marx's creed in full. The others were bound to adapt this creed to the management of everyday problems in an individual State. Thus, they cut Marxism to suit the body of Prussia-Germany, the State as well as the Nation. So, in many ways, they followed the ideas of the German State philosophers and preferred Lassalle to Marx. Their ideal of Society was not that envisaged by Marx in its ultimate development. They were democrats, esteeming and tolerating minorities in every relationship, including parliament. They would not give the community greater rights, as they did not wish to suppress the individual liberty of its members; they were opposed to terrorism. Neither did they want the rule of one party—such a system as exists at present in Italy and Germany—nor of one class, as realised in Soviet Russia. In Germany, the idea of the rule of the Proletariat, the identification of socialism with the working-class movement, belonged more to a handful of intellectuals and few other members of the social democratic party. The vast majority refused to recognise this principle, involving anti-parliamentary and international planks in their platform. Franz Oppenheimer, who once occupied a chair of sociology in Frankfort, a socialist of this democratic type, constructed a system of Social Liberalism or Liberal Socialism, which, in fact, was not far removed from the creed of most supporters of the German labour party. This general feeling did not exclude the more radical attitude for propaganda purposes, especially for elections. The Communist party at a later phase drew away from the former, adopting the whole range of extreme ideas.

Despite their democratic principles the German Social Democrats organised their party in the characteristically Prussian manner, which favours mass organisations regulated like an army, such as, e.g., August Bebel's workers' battalions. He, himself the son of a non-commissioned officer, in some official speeches leaves no doubt that, as he said, every member of his party would take his rifle on his shoulder to defend the fatherland. He died long before the Great

War in which his party followed his nationalist line by marching in rank and file with the other parties of the German Reichstag and swearing its allegiance to the belligerent Imperial Government. Party leaders joined the army as enthusiastic volunteers during the Great War and one of their best men, Dr. Frank, was killed in the first days. I may mention in passing, that from its early days Trade Unionism in its organisation also showed a strongly militarist note in the manner of centralising disciplined and obedient masses under a supreme command. The differences between trade union organisations in Britain and Germany were outstanding.

A former socialist of the German Reichstag, Arthur Rosenberg,[64] in his book, " A History of the German Republic," mentions this enthusiasm for " mass-numbers," in the craving to secure for themselves powerful representation in the Parliament. With regard to the lack of interest of this huge party in the great social and economic problems of our time and to the " spurious radical formulae " which served more as mere propaganda than the masses could conceive, Rosenberg says : " A certain element of danger nevertheless lay concealed in this cult of elections and electoral successes in consequence of the purely academic Radicalism that dominated the Party up to the outbreak of War. It is true that the cult was never given formal expression, and that every Party official would have rejected it with contumely. Nevertheless, German Socialists as a whole up to 1914 unconsciously regarded social policy and the suffrage as the most important things in the world, and let all other questions sink into the background. This one-sided education of the German working class by the Social Democrat Party was destined to bear bitter fruit in the course of the Revolution after November 9th, 1918."

One historical event had great influence in consolidating the ideas and the party in Germany. From the end of the seventies up to the beginning of the nineties special anti-socialist laws proscribed the party and its propaganda. The contact of the hidden living party with foreign labour movements, mainly of British extraction, brought a feeling for a gradual evolution of their doctrines. Thus when the party appeared again in the open, opinions clashed. Eduard Bernstein and others, the " revisionists," worked for a step-by-step transformation of the Capitalist Society. This group wished to abandon the radical phrases of the majority of the party which believed in the survival of capitalism for a long time and so did not wish to present the masses with an active policy. The revisionists " prophesied a great war in the immediate future, and arising out of it, vast revolutionary movements. Hence they demanded that the Social Democratic Party should adjust its policy to prepare for the future. The working class must train itself in readiness for the seizure of power " (Rosenberg). They sought a collaboration with the existing State and its administration, so preparing the way for the replacement of the capitalist system. The radicalism of the majority was more formal; it exhausted itself in staunch opposition to the middle-class government and objected, as a matter of course, to the budgets and to the foreign and military policy. However, they had no constructive methods by which to achieve their own policy.

It is true the " revisionists " were defeated in the Party Congress in 1903, but their ideas were the more important for the future of the party until its end in 1933. The complete unpreparedness to transfer ideas into active policy and to carry them through in administrative work showed itself strikingly when the party in 1918 took over the government. The adherence of party followers to more evolutionary procedure and the revisionist desire to collaborate with the middle classes were greatly strengthened by the fact that during the preceding thirty years the general welfare of the population—an expression of the social trusteeship of the State which had mitigated the disadvantages of the capitalist system—had greatly improved.

After the revolution in 1919 (see Chapter III) at the party congress in Goerlitz, the party presented the picture of an assembly of patriotic " petit-bourgeois " with some socialist ideas. One delegate said of the Social-Democrats in contrast to the wild and furiously working Independent Socialists, Communists and Spartakists, " we realise we are growing older." The more advanced groups became the more Marxist. But, if we say " Marxist," we must indicate the aspect or phase of Marx's thought to which they adhered. Did they follow Marx and Engels, the democratic revolutionaries of 1848, or the stage of their development in which they conceived State and Society as a unity? One must ask, indeed, what then was Marx's fundamental idea, adopted or not adopted by such different types of followers? H. Kelsen,[65] once condensed the whole doctrine so well that I cannot do better than quote him: " The Class State of Capitalism will be followed, after a violent revolution, by the Class State of Proletarians." This stage still presupposes the State, as opposed to a world State, as a unit to settle human affairs socially, economically and administratively. At this stage socialisation meant nationalisation. " Then the Stateless Society of complete Communism would consequently develop." Kelsen continues: that Engels, even more clearly than Marx, pointed out that the " individualistic anarchy of the future would be the last consequence of the socialist idea." Marx was far more interested in the struggle than in the goal; the draft of a socialist community seemed to him mere Utopianism.

§4 *Differing Views on Ethics*

These few words on ethics may be given more as an appendix than as a proper analysis. They continue what I have said on ideals, both the Greek and the Christian and those of other ideologies, but they are necessary to make German social and economic history comprehensible to the English reader. To select a simple example, individual liberty and the " Sacredness of Personality "—emphasised by the great reformers of the 16th century and by non-conformity—are commonplaces of English thought in all classes and types of society. There is not a fraction of one per cent. of the German population which has ever heard a word of non-conformity and its various sects ; to say nothing of having an understanding of its meaning. On the other hand, the training of the German mind is likewise unknown to the Englishman.

To repeat what I have stated elsewhere in this book, moral ideas of conduct are highly subjective in character, and the followers of different creeds wage war against each other. Conceptions of Christianity, humanity, class struggle, nation and homeland, are accompanied by the greatest moral fervour.

No doubt the systems outlined earlier in this chapter are not to be described as being without ethics. Their ethics, however, are founded in the light of the final goal of an ideology, which has first to pass through various stages. If nationalisation of the means of production could be carried through, or if a stateless society could be reached, then according to the vision of certain Marxists the individual, purified and unselfish, will lead a moral life. State-Socialism puts forward mercantilist methods and leaves it to the State to decide the share of welfare outside material things that it will give to its individual subjects.

Socialism, as a party creed in Germany, has always been irreligious. It is true, there were at times movements which tried to de-materialise the spirit of Socialism or to Christianise it. Therefore, evangelical pastors like Stoecker established the evangelical-social movement to create Socialist Christianity or Christian Socialism. The *Evangelisch Sozialer Kongress* survived the War but hardly succeeded in creating widespread movements. Another pastor and leader of some successful social movements, Friedrich Naumann, who, at times, professed strong sympathies with the Socialist Party in their endeavours to support such movements, combated strongly its hostile attitude towards Christianity. It was an exception, indeed, when a member of the Social Democratic Party in Germany did not describe himself in the official directory of the Reichstag, as being " without religious confession." This fact, in itself, did not mark the difference between the democratic socialists in Britain and Germany ; these are far more deep-rooted. It is a matter of different religious feelings. The relationship of the church to its individual following and to social legislation, inspired by ecclesiastical circles, must be distinguished. Dr. W. Temple, now Archbishop of York, puts forward an essential point, throwing light on this difference in enumerating some principles which he says, are " inherent in the Christian view of life for which social application is demanded." Amongst these principles he gives first place to " the Sacredness of Personality."[66] He says that this principle lies very deep in the Gospel. " It is rooted in the conception of God's universal Fatherhood, which carries with it the corollary that every man is a child of God, and has worth accordingly. Kant reaches this same position when he gave us one formulation of the Categorical Imperative, the requirement that we should treat humanity in ourselves and in others always as an end and never only as a means." The Archbishop continues, " this principle is at once the root and a criterion of Democracy. It is its root, because belief in personality and the right of personality to express itself, is historically the motive behind the great democratic movements ; and it is also its criterion, for Democracy is only true to this its root principle, when it shows a great respect for minorities, in as much as they have just as much right to their opinions as any majority. . . But Democracy left to itself is liable to betray its own principle, and the definite religious concern for the Sacredness of Personality is needed, not so much now to advance the cause of Democracy, but rather to keep Democracy true to its own root principle." What an unbridgeable gulf divides British and German Christianity in so far as this personal sacredness is concerned ! What a difference, again, between British and German socialism, including the socialism now existing in the Third Reich !

History and mentality developed different types of Christians among the two nations. British non-conformity, for instance, from early beginnings, linked up with religious as well as political freedom, maintained all its peculiarities up to the present time. Everything is centred around the layman whose active life in his religious community reflects his relation to the personal God. Chapel after chapel, of the same denomination, or of denominations of little real difference, draws a picture of the rich religious life of men, women and children who prefer congregating in smaller groups. They know each other more or less intimately and are interested in mutual welfare and social life. Non-conformity, without doubt, gave a stamp to British socialism, given from the pulpit as well as from the pew. This socialism did not exhaust itself in rationalist principles, in cold-blooded considerations or practical applications of this kind. Thus this type of British socialism has always remained as moral, as religious, and anxious to further brotherhood. It is all the same whether this socialism, which had affinities to non-conformity, ends in a general socialism, perhaps forming strong groups in the Labour Party, or is confined to Christian socialism. This latter British type differs from the German in spirit rather more than in socialist and social institutions. The difference may best be described by stating that British socialism is, or was ethical, as compared with the strongly materialist character of the German kind. Thus, so many English socialists are consciously or unconsciously not followers of Karl Marx. Without doubt, his rich arsenal of thoughts provided and clarified a good deal of the paraphernalia of their creed, but they do not follow Marx to his final conclusions, repudiating other creeds, creeds of minorities, which they wish to tolerate. They never liked the " one-class system," like that foreshadowed by Marx, the working proletariat. They would not dream of compelling people of other creeds to follow them by terrorism, even by murder. Non-conformity leaves freedom of thought and creed to the individual member of the community as well as to small groups of movements combined in small chapels as their cell of spiritual and social life.

Why could the German evangelical church not gain a similar influence on social life and the socialist movement? This question is the more justified because roughly two-thirds, say, in round figures, some 45 million inhabitants, are evangelical. In the first place, founders of German protestantism succeeded through the assistance of German princes, and did not begin by satisfying the religious and ethical needs of the ordinary man. The German evangelical church always remained from this time onwards a State-church. The individual was not consulted: "*Cujus regio ejus religio*" had not only temporary significance. German pastors and leading Protestant figures were themselves never of this conciliatory temper so inherent in the British character. The German evangelical church, like other German institutions, found to some degree a mass expression. As against the many small chapels there were a few big churches in greater communities, to which whole districts, consisting often of thousands, even tens of thousands of members, belonged. Not knowing each other, unknown to the pastor, they had no other connection with him than listening occasionally to his sermons, which, with few exceptions, did not move their feelings very much. The layman, unlike his English counterpart, had no say. As far as the upper classes, including learned people, were concerned, the number of churchgoers from their ranks was very small and youth in these circles lacked religious feeling. But this youth was craving to satisfy its metaphysical needs and so, unfamiliar with an individual creed of Christianity, sought for other Gods who would attract them more. The God of Love had not penetrated into their souls; in his place was the spirit of the nation and the spirit of war; for this is not a new invention, it has a long history in the Germany of the 19th century. Having left school, hundreds of thousands lacked any connection with the church and the ideas of Christianity. No doubt Roman Catholicism had a greater appeal to the feelings of the congregation.

The German Youth Movement,[67] undoubtedly an idealistic movement at its inception, offered an escape from this materialism—but how did it end? As a movement subjected to the idea of thoroughness inculcated in the State, Nation and Army: a movement instrumental in preparing for these organisations.

Even at the opening of the 19th century Goethe hinted at weakness of religious feeling in explaining the defiance of creed in the evangelical church. "It is not much in its service and it is not direct enough to appeal to the congregation." There has been a wide discussion for the last hundred years and more around this point. In addition to Troeltsch whom I mentioned, I may instance a distinguished Professor of Theology, once at the University of Berlin, W. Luetgert,[68] who gives an interesting analysis of the decay in a vast investigation on "*Die Religion des deutschen Idealismus und ihr Ende*" in which the religious crisis, the different movements of awakening and their ultimate failure are described. Professor Luetgert carefully traces how the thought of liberty, as expressed in the classic ideal and in the meaning of a Christian, as given in the doctrines during the era of the Reformation, was unable to resist certain counter movements from the time of the Renaissance, namely romanticism and mysticism. These counter movements were expressed in the decay of belief in the creed and in education through centuries from the time of the humanists in an era of materialism conscious of the achievements of science and technique and last but not least the atheism dating from the time of idealistic thought. Luetgert shows the close parallelism between the last phases of German idealism and the movements of religious revival in this period (e.g., Hamann, Jacobi, von Baader and others, but also earlier prominent figures of the Pietist type). He also shows very clearly in Vol. III the relationship between the religious awakening of the early 19th century and the nationalist impulse which characterised the period of the War of Liberation.

Unlike comparable movements in England, almost all German movements of religious revival eventually grew into expressions of purely nationalist development. The attitude of the German nation towards these questions has been made clearer by the earlier discussion of Herder, Fichte, Hegel and others. The evangelical pastor, like his younger evangelical followers, devoted himself more to " force-worship " and more materialist incentives. Dr. Troeltsch, an evangelical theologian himself, often mentioned this militaristic character of evangelical pastors and their following and how these circles inserted themselves into the traditional system of militarism, which dominated, as I have shown, the whole public life as well as focussing spiritual life and culture. Before National Socialism came into power, pastors and teachers of all kinds supported its ascent. Even pastors who called themselves outspoken liberals and democrats set the God-Nation besides Christ. Pastor Friedrich Naumann, a man with influence over hundreds of thousands of souls, who belonged to the German liberal and democratic parties through many sessions of the Parliament, placed the Nation and the spirit of the national community, the spirit of the national State, higher than any feeling of Christian individualism. This speaker and writer was a nationalist of pure blood, who founded his periodical, the " National Socialist " " *Hilfe* " in 1895. He based his creed on the recognition of the existing State as the presupposition and foundation of all social reform. From henceforth he proclaims not a " Christian " but a " practical patriotic " or " National Socialism." This " early " national socialism must not be confused with the national socialism of to-day. He combined with his devotion to the poor and the outcasts the strongest note of militarism. Jesus had before only been seen in the international Empire of the Romans, in the little Jewish corner. We have, then, to transfer him from Galilee to other conditions. These are the duties to the State and nation. "Militarism," he says, "is the foundation of all order in the State and of all prosperity in the society of Europe." "A State not built up around a skeleton of militarism does not exist[5]." "Hence we do not consult Jesus when we are concerned with things which belong to the domain of the construction of the State and Political Economy. This sounds hard and abrupt for every human being brought up a Christian, but appears to be sound Lutheranism, etc." All this was said long before the rise of the Third Reich. I must add that Naumann was not an eccentric, he was a milder kind of fighting evangelical parson and was typical of his kind in the Weimar Reich in which he was once a Secretary of State. If even the preachers of the creed did not understand what Dr. Temple calls the "Sacredness of Personality" as the embodiment of true Democracy, which he puts forward as the first principle ruling Christian and social life, how could it be expected that the practical man who collaborated in the rise of German industry and trade could create or carry out individual schemes in an individual liberal economy?

In summary, history shows periods of pronounced decay of religions and culture. Jacob Burckhardt, the great Swiss philosopher and historian, once assumed this stage as a natural one. He speaks[69] of the spiritual defiance of individual categories of the peoples and especially enumerates the educated class. No doubt, in the 18th century, at the time of development of liberal ideas, there was everywhere a period of decay in religious life. It is of the greatest importance that Britain found in John Wesley the man who lifted the masses and gave the creed a new life. The Oxford movements have to be mentioned in this connection. Germany, from the era of the Reformation up to the present, however, showed no religious leader able to imbue the masses with new religious spirit. From the 18th century onwards the two nations followed various roads. Their souls formed themselves according to peculiar traditions and characteristically in Germany without any outstanding religious leadership. Here lies the root of the difference of mentality as far as liberty and democracy as ethical categories are concerned. It has to be added that from the very beginning the connection between moral philosophy and State philosophy in Germany was never so strong as in Scotland or England. No doubt, the period of classicism and idealism and romanticism especially revolutionised people in Germany, but it was only a certain part of the population of this period which was attracted by the religious outcome of these movements. Significantly, at the time when John Wesley reawakened and deepened the creed of his countrymen, romanticism in connection with a certain nationalism started in Germany, an influence directing German thoughts for two centuries, as non-conformity and the classic liberal ideal formed the new British mind. It is true that "movements of awakening" often started in Germany, and also in the period to be described, but their influence on the religious life never showed any great vigour.

(c) SOME ASPECTS OF THE PERIOD BEFORE WILLIAM II IN THEIR RELATION TO LATER DEVELOPMENT
(The main features of the Economic System)

The Reich of Bismarck—as he left it—was merely a political and economic framework. Before its establishment, Germany's development had been restricted throughout the centuries when the great countries of Europe were extending their influence over large areas and establishing their empires, partly in Europe, partly overseas. When the Spaniards, the Portuguese, the Dutch and the Danes receded from the world stage, the other Western powers spread around the Atlantic, and there was no room for the restoration of a mighty German empire. So from a medley of many states Bismarck evolved this framework. He himself began as the political descendant of a long line of Brandenburger and Prussian imperialists. Earlier plans, based on attempts to give Germany control over the territories of the mouth of the Rhine, inhabited for centuries by German tribes, had failed to create an overseas empire. Possessing only a short coast-line, Germany found imperialistic overseas expansion of the Western European type impossible. Her imperialism was therefore of necessity Prussian and Continental in character. When Bismarck was dismissed, capitalism had already passed its youth. Industrialism had grown rapidly, while at the same time agriculture was steadily advancing, owing to the efforts of a clever and industrious population, and the encouragement given by every kind of protection. Trade and industry tended to approach the level reached by the older countries, who resented the growing powers of this new competitor, whom they regarded as an upstart, elbowing her way into their economic field.

All that could be done to cripple the child and prevent her from becoming dangerous had been done. It is a problem of world history whether this method was right or not. It is true that it under-estimated the vital necessities of this competitor, and the methods applied against her ultimately proved ineffective. On the other hand, it is questionable whether a partnership conceded in time would have had better results. No confidence was placed in the newcomer. Perhaps her imperialist desires would not have stopped short at a share, especially at a time when the world re-echoed with the news of conquest. In the 19th century, of which the Napoleons were characteristic figures, Britain acquired a greater share of the world's surface, Russia aimed at Asiatic imperialism, and Italian plans looked to the formation of a united kingdom beginning with the revival of the Roman Empire; the U.S.A. consolidated her power in South America and occupied an Asiatic island, and even the decrepit Austrian conglomerate, uneasily held together by the Habsburgs, showed signs of a second summer. It may have been that the Prussian-German rival of the " Have's " would have fought for a bigger partnership or even for supremacy, in the militarist spirit which also animated its industrialists. Thus, the trend of history tended to alienate Germany from the West, while her historical background made for a State eastern in body but inoculated with the western spirit. Bismarck's policy moulded the character of the German of his time, but it did not altogether prove adequate over a longer span of years. The principle animating his policy may perhaps be traced to his ancestry. His father was a Prussian Junker. His mother, on the other hand, was the daughter of a high civil servant who was something of a scholar, a liberal-minded official who made many vain attempts to introduce reforms under the reactionary King Frederick William III. In Bismarck we find the union of two opposing ideas. He was not the kind of German militaristic imperialist he is often considered to be. He repeatedly called attention to the division of labour between statesman and soldier.

His foreign policy after the Franco-Prussian War aimed at doing everything to avoid a deepening of hostility against old and new adversaries. His statesmanship, rather, hinted at engaging these powers in great political and economic undertakings in colonial territories, hoping that this addition to their prestige might divert them from plans of revenge. That did not prevent his policy from influencing the balance of European powers by strengthening the conflicts of interest between them. These tendencies especially inspired his policy in the Mediterranean and the Black Sea. His policy was opposed to a provocative naval and foreign policy: his imperialism was of another conception. No one can say whether, if he had held power for a longer time, his genius might have been equal to the task of smoothing things out diplomatically till the young Reich was consolidated. He left the Reich an unwieldy mass of strong federal States in which there already existed the elements—dynastic, ecclesiastical and political—which made for its disintegration. Moreover, in Bismarck's time, German trade and industry developed into Big Business and large-scale capitalism. The thrust of these new industrial forces not only destroyed the older tradition, but, as in other countries, created immense problems. These were only just beginning to be felt towards the end of Bismarck's rule, but they ultimately involved the new Reich externally in a great imperialistic struggle for power, and internally in a bitter fight for a new social order. The rapid development of science and of its technical application led inevitably to the growth of the industrial spirit which then sought predominance.

The mass character of capital, goods and men did not show itself conspicuously till the post-Bismarckian phase. But even during his period of power, the rapid industrial development was giving rise to the problem of the massing of the people in the towns. We shall consider in the next chapter how this happened, and how the whole development of industry came to rest on the banking and financing system characteristic of Germany's national temperament.

There is no doubt that Bismarck saw the social problems developing. He foresaw the crises of the latter forties, of 1857 and 1873 ; he recognised that his " exceptional " law against the socialists of 1877 was an error. He tried to meet the problem by his policy of the social insurance acts of the eighties, which was the first effort of the kind that had ever been made. But the man who gave the general franchise to his country (1867), against the will of his own class, did not perhaps recognise the social spirit of a new time, which proved such a mighty factor in general policy, nationally and internationally. He could not see that the mass of men, inarticulate for some thousand years and politically insignificant, would now take a decisive part in politics. It is true, he once admitted : " Even the slight progress in the field of social reform has been accomplished only by reason of the existence of the Social Democratic party and of those who feared it."[70]

But Bismarck never imagined that the ordinary citizen, and especially the working man, would one day acquire rights equal to those of the traditional castes, the services and forces which had constituted the Prussian government. Let us not forget that he was already in his manhood when Prussia was granted its constitution which, however, set up the franchise on an income basis and excluded the whole working class from participation in public affairs. This limited parliamentary privilege came into being at a time when the English system had already gone far along the democratic road. Then there were many citizens who were brought up in the time when feudalism, serfdom and trade and craft restrictions were the ruling forces in large territories in Prussia. Owing to G. F. Knapp's[71] brilliant investigation, it is now realised that the so-called liberation of peasants in Eastern Prussia worked out largely in the interest of the big estate owners. It is estimated that sixty thousand small peasant holdings disappeared through incorporation in the estates of the big landowners. The peasant thus ostensibly freed, formed a class of agricultural workers, very many of whom later on joined the ranks of industrial labour.

Bismarck subordinated all social and economic problems, such as the rights of man, individual liberty, free competition, protection, the struggle between capital and labour, to the idea of the authoritarian and monarchist State of Prussian temper. Capital, labour, trade and industry did not touch any deep-rooted convictions of the first chancellor. These were things to be dealt with just as any other departmental work of the administration, not according to any theory or conviction, but according to the opportunity of the moment. Thus, these problems were of subsidiary importance in the greater policy of the Reich—and as custodian of the " *Staatsraison*," he was in all these matters an opportunist. He himself was brought up, more or less, in the free-trade ideas of the translators and successors of Adam Smith, such as J. B. Say, about whom he wrote a paper for his first service examination. Yet he dropped Free Trade, not because of any change in ideals, but rather in order to foster the revenues of the Reich. At a time when the first preparations to suppress the Social Democratic party were already taking place, he was secretly represented by a confidential agent, Wagner, in the meeting of Marxists (1874). The philosophy of the sixties which led to the general franchise gave way to one which relatively weakened the liberal middle classes and their parties and strengthened the growing working class. But later, as their ambitions grew too fast, he reversed the helm and ultimately suppressed the whole party by legislation.

He found his attempted suppression a failure and, therefore, introduced the great social insurance act as a means of reconciliation, rather than as a conscious expression of social obligation. The words which introduce the famous " Imperial Message " of 1881, announcing the new Social Policy, are characteristic. " The cure of social evils must not be sought exclusively by way of repressions of Social Democratic excesses, but equally by positively promoting the welfare of the workmen." In II A (3) I shall give more details of this in a wider connection.

In Bismarck's time it was by no means only the worker who had no say in affairs ; this new Society as a whole did not have a free hand in exercising its functions. The government took care to keep control of its actions and its welfare. In the second quarter of the 18th century the big estate owners were aided by a credit organisation (the *Landschaft* of Frederick the Great's time). The credit demands of the small man, peasant as well as small tradesman and craftsman, were met at a later date by private efforts on their own part (the agricultural co-operative societies being founded by *Raiffeisen*, and the urban co-operative societies by *Schulze Delitzsch*). The provision of credit for the small man by means of savings banks was not at first to the liking of the Government, and does not appear until the Prussian Savings Bank Act of 1838. The municipal savings bank system suffered greatly at first from the distrust of the civil service, which scented the approach of revolution in the spectacle of the small man helping himself : they considered this an encroachment on their rights. Self-government began with the Stein-Hardenberg reforms (from 1807), the outcome of an infiltration of Western ideas, but they affected political institutions only. In the first semi-public companies formed during the Great War, we see the use and growth of a more marked self-government in trade.

Bismarck's policy always remained that of a conservative bureaucracy built up on agrarian interests, to which were added in his own day the more thrustful capitalist interests. In the year 1879, the propertied classes were consolidated into one force. Agriculturalists and industrialists from this time combined to keep power in the State. This first found expression in the law of the autonomous duty tariff system which made German trade policy a protectionist one in 1879. An important element in this protectionism was the bargaining for the spoils of political power: the well organised heavy industries and certain others consented to agricultural protection on condition that they secured higher tariffs for their own products. This was a corner-stone in Bismarck's national economic policy. The liberal-minded Minister of Economic Affairs, Rudolph von Delbrueck, who had been one of Bismarck's ablest collaborators, dissociated himself from him (1876). This brought Germany's short period of economic liberalism to an end, and so with Bismarck's conversion to protectionism, the whole outlook changed fundamentally. Hitherto Bismarck, like other big estate owners, had aimed at an unhampered export of their products, grain, wool, wood, etc. Owing to developments in world trade, they were faced with totally different problems (II A (2) (*a*)). But Bismarck was often opposed to a conservative policy and leaned for a long time towards the National Liberal group, which by this union between leadership and bureaucracy were transformed into a kind of left wing conservative group, comprising the representatives of the more important elements in trade and industry, public servants, professors, etc. Certain very small liberal and democratic groups remained outside and retained a certain modicum of public influence. On the whole, they were looked upon by the pre-war ruling groups as disgruntled people to whom the State could not allot posts in the services. The decline of party liberalism thus began very early in Germany.

Bismarck while in power kept an iron control over the individual political and economic groups which later became independent forces and contributed to the disintegration. It was the clash of opposing ideas which brought about this new order; the traditional spirit of the military and of the civil service, which had in it something religious and humanist, had to unite with the spirit of materialism of the new technical and capitalist age.

The result was the emergence of a new society. Out of a genuine agrarian nation, there sprang an industrial and mercantile nation with a majority of townspeople.

The empire soon found its power restricted by some of the federal States whose policies ran contrary to general empire policy. Bismarck, therefore, had to strengthen the power of the Prussian State, which was the medium through which he and his successors controlled the empire. (See Troeltsch's remarks, p. 39).

The finances of the Reich during Bismarck's time reflected many political motives. However, although the system appeared complicated, it amounted to no more than the acceptance by his national Empire State of alms from its federal States. Being jealous of the Empire, they kept the assessment of direct taxation to themselves. Thus Prussia with her limited franchise could easily protect her landed property. The absence of representatives of the working class in the Diet safeguarded her from experiments in social problems. But even here, good use was made of the big income derived from the State railways in building up a good system of elementary schools and in developing the industry-less East. Apart from the income it derived from the federal States, the Reich lived on duties and a few indirect taxes. It also held the Post Office. The financial arrangement, here outlined, enabled the Reich to carry out its obligations, but it was already becoming a source of trouble in the years just before the Great War. Expenditure on the Army and Navy, on the colonies, on old age and health insurance was in the province of the Reich. The enormous budget for social purposes adopted in the later days of semi-socialism was not a feature of the Reich of this period. Bismarck's transport policy was of outstanding significance. Besides being part of his " national economy " his nationalised transport undertaking became the biggest enterprise of this kind in the world. He, the Prussian mercantilist, made a State undertaking alike of all waterways, canals, etc. The railways served various general and governmental purposes. Thus, they contributed largely to the budget. At a later time, it was the railways that served as pledge for the loans which Germany received in the chaotic after-War period.

A few figures may illustrate the relation of the problem of population to that of industrialisation and the growth of big towns. These problems had, of course, the same social and economic effects elsewhere.

A hundred years ago, Germany was an agrarian country. Prussia, where roughly two-thirds of the population lived, had in 1800 only seventeen towns with a population of over ten thousand inhabitants. The process of industrialisation, which mainly began with the German *Zollverein* (1834) and Friedrich List's propaganda for economic nationalism, caused the rise of certain industrial centres, among the first of which were the Rhineland, Westphalia, the kingdom of Saxony and the Berlin district. With the *Zollverein* came Germany's first wave of protectionism.

The relation between the urban and rural population in the fifty years between 1875 and 1925 was entirely reversed. In 1875 two-thirds of the German population still lived in rural communities and one-third in towns. The actual rural population figure of roughly twenty-six million had not, generally speaking, changed much in the decades before the War. The increase in total population of more than twenty millions during the fifty years referred to is found in the towns, and especially in the big towns. By 1925 we find that the urban population of Westphalia had increased by 84 per cent., Rhineland by 82 per cent. and in the former kingdom of Saxony by 76 per cent.[72]

The connection between density of population and industrial progress is shown by the following figures according to the census of 16/6/1933. The average density of population was 140 per square kilometre, but in Westphalia the figure was 249, in the Rhineland (excluding the Saar) 318, in Saxony 347, whereas in rural districts such as Pomerania and East Prussia the number was 63, in Mecklenburg 50, in the border territory of Posen only 43. England and Wales showed in the same period a density of 265 (cf. figures on the flight from the land to the industrial centres, p. 33).

The population of the area included in the German Empire grew during Bismarck's lifetime (1815-1898) as follows[73]:

	million inhabitants
1816	24.8
1850	35.3
1870	40.8
1904	46.5

On the rise of industry, the birthrate in Germany was 42 per thousand in 1875. In the decades 1871-1880 it was 39.1

1881-1890	36.8
1891-1900	36.1
1901-1910	33.0
in 1913	27.5
1924-1929	19.3
in 1933	14.7

The big towns especially showed the lowest figures:

Berlin 1931	8.8
Dresden	9.6
Frankfort	10.2
Leipzig	10.6

As in other countries, the effect of a decreased birthrate was to some extent counteracted by the heavy fall in the general death rate. The figures in 1861-1870 of 27.0 per thousand, and of 27.2 in the next decade, fell to 15 in 1913, and to 11.1 in 1930. Owing to improvements in living conditions, the advance of knowledge, the growth of curative and preventive medicine, the improvement in nutrition and hygiene, infant mortality fell notably. The length of life increased. The German Statistical Office[74] mentions that the decrease in the deathrate led to a considerable increase in the average duration of life. From 1924-26 the expectation of life increased to 57.4. According to the Table of 1891-1900 it was 42.2, and from 1871 to 1880 only 37.0 years.

Chapter II
THE ERA OF WILLIAM II

A. UP TO THE GREAT WAR.

(1) FACTS AND FORCES OF A NEW CAPITALIST AGE

It was not until William II's reign that the third stage of 19th century economic policy was reached. At the beginning of the century Germany depended mainly on her own agriculture. Ancient crafts and primitive mechanised industrial production satisfied the scanty demands of her twenty million inhabitants. Germany was still rather isolated and imported only a little foreign produce. The second period set in with the arrival of the machine age, some decades later than in Britain. The development of transport, which made time and distance of less consequence, changed the position of isolated self-sufficient countries. Every nation became a participant in a world-wide circulation of goods and money and so became more dependent upon others as far as certain vital goods were concerned. Thus in Germany, some important goods were no longer produced at home, as for example, the whole supply of textile raw material. *Autarky* was not yet an urgent problem.

The second phase, the Bismarckian era, saw the first real organisation of the new industrialism, while during the third phase, the reign of William II up to the War, all the tendencies of this new economy, which has been called large scale capitalism, are seen in full development. This system only achieved success through a legacy of the Mercantilist days, that is, the system of *export industrialism* (as German authors call a certain international division of labour). For the highly developed Western nations obtained a great deal of food and raw material from the overseas countries and from the agrarian European countries, while they themselves manufactured goods and exported them on a large scale to the countries furnishing the raw materials. This system of export-industrialism, arising out of the transport revolution, brought about a transformation in the structure of supply and demand and made possible mass supply and mass demand. New methods to perform these tasks had to be created ; for primitive production, finance and distribution were not sufficient for the needs of the second period. H. Levy[1] is doubtless right in saying : " The economic history of modern times shows that it was not individual competition which stood on the threshold of modern industrial capitalism. On the contrary, the early period of modern industrial capitalism was characterised by monopolies in many of the ' new ' trades, and by a capitalist domination over the guilds through some sort of putting-out system." Before giving further details on this economic problem the political aspect has to be discussed.

The system of export industrialism, which brought so much wealth and prosperity to Western nations, has been identified with the system of capitalism that prevailed at this particular period. It allowed a relatively free play of forces. This "liberalism" became a faith complete with its dogma. People forget that it was only a reflection of temporary circumstances, the circumstances of a special economic and political epoch. Production, suddenly increased as the result of machinery, found, besides the enlarged home market, additional markets overseas and in agricultural European countries (Era of Expansion). The followers of economic liberalism did not believe that the Western nations could ever reach a state of saturation when the world markets would be unable to absorb their home production. Reasons of a political as well as of an economic nature played a part. The theories derived from these temporary economic events are valid, if markets and employment are available. If free trade had continued to prevail after the sixties, the consequences would have been pernicious for both importing and exporting countries. First of all, the predominance of Great Britain, which was the only large European producer of industrial goods, could not have been maintained in the long run. The ideal system in which countries exchanged those goods in the production of which Nature gave them an advantage or perhaps even a monopoly did not exist. Great Britain's predominance in producing industrial goods was the result of her early start. But even if this predominance were to be taken for granted, the natural economic development would not have been the success assumed by the liberal school. Here the political side of the problem must not be ignored. The revolt of the American colonies gave them the right to establish their own industrialism and ultimately to dispute the markets with the great world industrialist and world trader which was in a fortunate position and was able to cripple the infant industries of other nations. If, for instance, Germany had not developed its own industry and had been a mere tributary as an importer of British goods and furnishing Britain with rye, potatoes, flax, wood, very soon a disproportion would have arisen in the mutual trade balance, unfavourable to German eyes. On the one hand there would have been an omnipotent creditor, on the other hand a debtor-nation politically as well as economically dependent. Furthermore, had she followed free trade, Germany with her doors open to all cheaper producing agricultural nations, as early as the seventies, would not even have been able to compete with Eastern Europe and America either on her agricultural home market or outside. She was then a country without important industry and without profitable agriculture. Great Britain would not have remained the exploiter of all nations in the world. First she would have lost customers who were unable to pay because of bankruptcy, secondly she herself would have been compelled to stop the export of tools and other machines which developed industrialisation in other countries. For unprotected countries this import would have been of little use, for they were faced with the powerful competition of both Great Britain and those countries which protected their own industry.

The way which most of the nations took in order to develop an industrial system like Britain's was bound to lead to misgivings, which, indeed, clearly showed themselves later. Both ways have clearly their evils, but the second sprang from natural political feelings with which Great Britain had been familiar since the breakaway of the U.S.A. Germany developed a national system of economy, following old traditions based on Mercantilist lines. This chapter will show how this national policy was in truth an essay in " planning."

Germany's imports in the period under review provided work and wages for enormous numbers. This system of export-industrialism was responsible for the rapid economic development of the nations. Such countries as Great Britain and Germany were able, in less than a century, approximately to treble their population, and the number of the inhabitants in the United States increased tenfold. The population of Germany now numbers sixty-eight millions, showing an increase of forty millions during a period of roughly ninety years. In the fourth stage it is seen how economic conditions changed. Sombart calls this stage late Capitalism. This system held sway from the period just before the War to the end of the Weimar Reich. In our third phase all the tendencies which are characteristic of the capitalism of our time are already visible. We may here pick out some of the more remarkable tendencies.

(a) Large Scale Enterprise

The first distinguishing feature of the units working to satisfy the demands of hundreds and thousands or millions of consumers of a multifarious nature is their size. Sometimes they have as many employees as some countries had inhabitants a century ago. In some branches of industry, the units are growing into large scale enterprises. It is of the essence of private economy, that this great apparatus should not only achieve the prime task of satisfying demand but also that the units themselves should be stable in their structure and should show a regular profit. These private enterprises have to reckon with risk and uncertainty. Thus, in spite of some interesting theories that the entrepreneur's function is that of a dynamic factor between two static economic phases (Schumpeter), as long as the capitalist system prevails, it is the enterprise which remains the " business unit " to meet and bear the risk. But the vital interests of enormous masses of men are directly or indirectly affected by the risk of these undertakings. Therefore, from the public point of view, it is the social risk which is most important in this modern type of capitalism.

"The economic superiority of the large business in the modern economic life," in Cassel's[2] eyes, demands a revision of theory. "In cases where this superiority makes itself felt, free competition is logically bound to bring about its own opposite—monopoly; for, at what intermediate stage would the assumed superiority of large business permit a state of equilibrium under free competition? Such an issue cannot be prevented without forms of organisation acting on economic life in a severely regulatory fashion, which would therefore mean the end of free competition in the case we are considering." Professor H. Schmalenbach[3], in examining the problem of the large business, draws conclusions which go even further. In his exposition, the increase of fixed costs arising from the increased use of fixed capital involved in technical progress is the cause of a new economic order. This increase of fixed costs makes a constant market even more important, and attempts are made by the formation of cartels to satisfy this need. Pushed to its conclusion, this would mean the end of free competition—Socialism. "What is the process which we now witness but the fulfilment of the prophecies of the great Socialist, Marx?" (Schmalenbach). That may be, as far as the trend is concerned; but Marx in his visions laid down not only the trend but also more or less certain definite stages of which the first, the nationalisation of the means of production, is not yet accomplished. No doubt, the contradictions of the various capitalist systems which Marx attempted to describe are already clearly visible. The influence of fixed charges may provoke a new system, but it is first a creation of capitalists and not of socialists. It is true that State and communal action in our period, up to 1933, shows socialist ideas rapidly on the march but capitalism did not die. To these transitional conditions monopolist and monopoloid formations adapt themselves in astonishing forms. Pre-war Germany, the Weimar Reich and the Third Reich, all show an evolution in which Capitalism compromises with Socialism, self-regulation with planning. And this road will be followed for a long time to come. In order to fulfil the two tasks of meeting private risk and social risk, new forces were fashioned. "Planning" comes again to the fore as a new device. The planned system of the new finance capitalism and the new forms of dominating the whole economic sphere originated in Germany. That was first seen there in the seventies of last century. Large scale enterprise now simply appears as one form of this system, in which associations of enterprises work in various degrees of combination, from loose agreements through cartels up to the strictest form of monopolies (see II, A (1) (c), §3).

German industry never questioned the necessity of cartels and trusts. Even at the beginning of this century, when Germany took second place as a producer of pig-iron, and Great Britain receded into third place, Germany's commercial and technical organisation was recognised as an outstanding advantage. This was thought to be one of the main reasons why she produced so cheaply and was so successful in every market. The integration of the various stages of production was introduced very early in German iron works. Several outstanding undertakings worked not only horizontally in the same trust, but also in connection with local collieries, coke-ovens and various chemical works. Chemical works originated from the utilisation of coal by-products and thus the great dyestuff and pharmaceutical industry began. Then, again, gas produced in one of the integrated works was used for power in another. The production of pig-iron, steel, rolled iron and of various finished products, formed part of an unbroken process. A general feature of integrated works was the construction of blast furnaces, rolling mills, etc., in such a manner that metal could be passed hot from one process to another. Several German trusts owned their own deposits of iron-ore, limestone, coal, and other raw materials. The history of combines and amalgamations has been so often described that details of technical and commercial organisation need not be repeated. It is interesting to note that Herr A. Kirdorf, the managing director of the Steel Syndicate, pointed out at the beginning of the century : " The entire economic development necessarily leads to integrated undertakings, for a company can only prosper permanently when, besides manufacturing finished goods, it also produces its own raw material."[4]

This conception is widely approved, not only by representatives of heavy industry, but also by those of the engineering industries and of refining works. Walther Rathenau,[5] once chairman of the General Electricity Works, emphasised the fact that " the competitive ability of some industries is based on the cohesion of great groups covering production from the raw material up to the refining and finishing stages. The law of mass production demands organised decentralisation of markets." Rathenau dealt briefly with some points which showed the attempt to bring legislation into line with technical and economic progress. " The emergence of by-products calls for plants which must be formed into companies perhaps independent of the parent company in the legal sense. Advancing technique compels the organisation of wavering demand. Each task of establishing works, which are to be consumers of the electrical enterprise, leads to new undertakings—in other words, independent joint stock companies, because the peculiarity of objects, diversity of geographical conditions, the special forms of plant, and the provision of capital, are not suited to legal centralisation. The undertaking extends into a group, a trust, and propagates itself to the third and fourth generation. The unity of administration, however, has to be maintained by a personal tie. It is true that the supervision of minor and more remote sections may be carried out by mandatories, but these again have to be watched in certain combinations. Thus administrative work may accumulate like that of central offices and ministries of the Government services." Sometimes the undertakings have been tied together by the holding company system. The German law never clearly defined these types of combinations of undertakings, of which the key company would take the legal form of Joint Stock Company or G.m.b.H. (*Gesellschaften mit beschränkter Haftung*—comparable to the English private limited company). From the theoretical point of view, the large scale undertaking has the novel feature of organising demand as well as supply. It is no longer a mere competitor with other undertakings of production on the supply side. It is the mark of a modern industrial State that the big undertakings of production have to create their own markets, with all the corollaries such as the financing of the producer and consumer. If a German undertaking which produces amongst other things, gasworks, had waited for demand, it would never have got as many orders as it needed and would never have shown a profit. It does not produce for an already existing demand. It creates consumers and then supplies them. So in the State-and-municipal-socialist Germany the undertaking "planned" a distinct new market; it drew up a plan for the consumer, a town corporation or the like, enabling it to provide capital and interest over a long period for the purpose of building a gasworks. That required a great financial apparatus on the part of the enterprise. It would often organise a combination of consumers and sub-consumers; for in supplying one want profitably, it would find it necessary to supply a number of subsidiary wants, and so its tentacles would spread over new trades and industries even in foreign countries. Sometimes gas alone would not sell because electricity is a complementary power for fuel and a competitor. So the undertaking would work with the electricity industry, by agreement or by amalgamation which meant division of labour or co-operation in one unit of enterprise. Even when combined, the undertakings of production would feel that many circumstances still hindered profit-making. Such were the proportionately high fixed costs, certain assurances against risk and compensation for works of the same trust which temporarily did not bring sufficient profit. So they had to establish such consumer undertakings abroad and overseas. This system once established continuously produced offspring of the new gas or electricity works which had to be financed or set in operation. It is only too clear that this system presupposes an interlocking with financial interests. The history of more than half-a-century showed that the appearance of the same undertaking on both sides, supply and demand, expresses itself in various and changing forms.

It is only a matter of adaptation and not of principle that, at a certain time, enterprises fulfil economic tasks through agreements (cartels) or in tied combinations, or by pure amalgamations or by undertakings comprised in a certain financial connection (holding companies or the like). So financial groups, undertakings of production or combined consumer-establishments have various forms and are produced for a variety of reasons. Amongst these I briefly enumerate the fluctuations of the trade cycle, legislation at home and abroad, and influences affecting the powers representing the financial side, whether they be produced by currency problems (viz., inflation problems, III (2) (a)) or political or economic power groupings. Therefore, there were changes in the nature of the component parts of such supply-demand enterprises. But I must emphasise this point again : that *joint control of supply and demand* is, under these new conditions, one of the most essential innovations of the age of large scale enterprise. The adaptability of these organisations to quickly changing conditions is characteristic : cartels as well as " trust " enterprises come and go, and appear and reappear in new forms. Some undertakings changed often during this period, as for instance, the Siemens electrical firm, which, as an undertaking of production and consumption—once it was even linked with coal, iron and shiping—appeared as a part of the Stinnes trust. Then it again achieved independence by the dissolution of this community of interest. Later as a member of electrical producer-cartels the firm again took part in an invisible and unofficial electricity monopoly. The great Siemens-Schuckert firm sometimes appeared as the holding and financing company of its many daughter companies.

It is always difficult to be sure of independence or dependence. If an individual undertaker receives credit from an institution, one never knows how far he becomes dependent on the financing body.

The only permanent issue is that the modern economy is mastered by these institutions, which maintain their power by certain monopolistic positions which they possess or create *ad hoc*. It is very difficult to say what size is best for these " Joint supply-demand " enterprises, which are partly in competition with similar institutions, and are partly united by agreements with others in a wider field. False expectations and gross speculation (including promoters' profits) sometimes led to unhealthy exaggerations of size.

It is quite useless to judge the quality of an undertaking, or industrial or financial transactions, without considering the whole network of threads which they are held. So many irrational as well as rational influences are decisive in a particular judgment, that it is difficult to find a reliable measure. There will be differences according as they are in the hands of the State or municipal authorities or private owners, and sometimes there may be a big difference between financial and industrial power, or in the influence of outstanding personalities. So it appears naive to believe that one can decide whether the transactions of a joint supply-demand undertaking could be better carried out by free competition. The size of the member undertakings is always changing, and outlay takes place in times of experiment and speculation. Yet the natural selection of the form most suited to the conditions is always discernible.

We are now able to see how the new system emerged in its German form.

(b) Finance Capitalism

§1 *Banks and Industrialisation*

The fact should be brought into the foreground that the Joint Stock bank in Germany was not merely a credit organisation but a politico-economic instrument. It was an instrument of German power-policy, part of Germany's economic front, and became an economic expression as typical of German mentality as the large scale enterprises, trade unions, or cartel-syndicates. These banks created the German Industrial State and developed concurrently with it. As a famous German scholar says in a textbook on Banking : "Banking policy was long regarded as being independent of State economic policy, as that in turn was regarded as being independent of diplomacy. But unconsciously the political element streamed in, as, for example, when the ideal of low discount rates receded behind that of a stable currency . . . Let us be frank, for Germany the final criterion is *Power and Security, economic as well as political* . . . In order to attain these objectives we must concur with the large scale activities of the banks and their activities in bringing about the industrialised State ; for how could Germany have met the competition of the Anglo-Saxon world, with a small and unorganised banking system ? "[6] (Schulze-Gävernitz).

The German deposit bank, developing according to laws of its own, was destined to grow formidable and powerful. It was, as Somary[7] says, " the most important characteristic in the process of organising economic life, because it made it possible for the banks to dominate the money and capital market and to carry out their own private economic policy." Thus, the movement of amalgamation which created mammoth formations at later stages became inevitable. The political and economic activities of the banks made it possible " to introduce national and cultural points of view into the economic life " (Riesser), an opinion which has also been shared by such banking experts as Goeppert, Schulze-Gävernitz and others. Somary, hinting at the contrast between the larger central banks and the smaller provincial ones, says that the central banks " which are not compelled to live from hand to mouth, can concern themselves with national issues in so far as these conform with their profit-making. Their boards grow less commercial and more governmental as compared with provincial banks."[8] Or as Schulze-Gävernitz puts it : " Bismarck's so-called national economic policy (1879), i.e., the agreement between the large East Prussian estates and the Rhenish-Westphalian blast furnaces, created the division of labour—the political leadership remained in the hands of the former, while the economic centre of gravity was transferred to the mining industry in the West. The industrialisation of the banking system in conjunction with cartels of the heavy industry is rooted in Bismarck's policy." " Bismarck, the great Junker—but at the same time as great a mercantilist as Colbert—became also the obstetrician of a new age."[9]

This author is not wrong in referring to the banks as the most important economic medium for national unification.[10] There is another point in connection with the German banks. Their power grew to a point at which they became almost States within the State. As such they were forms of private finance capitalism. Their potentialities as instruments of State capitalism will be dealt with later.

British industry was able to gain its world power through individual private enterprise. The Joint Stock Company came later, and even the principle of limited liability was not introduced until 1856. Germany's industrialisation, especially in the heavy industries, coming after the Franco-Prussian War, began almost immediately with the system of stocks and shares. Lacking the great financial resources of Great Britain this was the only possible means of raising the enormous amount of capital for fixed investment to establish all the big industries. Moreover, the cheque system and the City's foreign bill market, which latter contributed so much to Britain's credit cover, were both undeveloped in Germany.

The establishment of the German banks and the principles that governed them contradicted every tradition of banking venerated in England then and now. This late-comer into world economics created its own system, developing its institutions according to the peculiar conditions of the country and profiting from other countries' experiences.

Unlike the deposit banks in Britain, German banks (in addition to their regular banking business) have been the *main-financiers* of industries. Professor Adolf Weber once stigmatised the German type as " deposit and speculative banks." This comparatively poor country, progressing from the agrarian State to the highly industrialised, needed a spirit of speculation as a stimulant for industrial investment. In the interest of their industrial debtors, banks exercised the double function, beginning mainly as financiers and consequently becoming bankers. For their activities in connection with industry, they built up a special stock exchange business. Thus it is generally recognised that Germany's gigantic iron works and shipping companies could never have materialised without the "*Reportgeschäft*," the speculative advances on collateral security made by the banks.* The former State Commissioner of the Stock Exchange in Berlin, Professor Goeppert, emphasises that the rise of industry depended in no small measure on the public's participation in stock and share speculation.

It is, no doubt, true that the actions of German banks were always accompanied by a greater risk than those of the sister establishments in England. The rapidity with which German industry developed was certainly due to this system; but creditor and debtor were always exposed to risk. English and German banking organisations reflect in their nature the difference in the

* See footnote p. 83.

amount of capital available for direct investment in financing industrial and commercial activities. Wide distribution of risks led the German deposit bank into activities upon which the English bank, with its ideal of liquidity, would never have dreamed to venture.

In Germany the development of the Joint Stock bank and industrialisation were locked together. The period for some three or more decades after the Napoleonic wars was one of unprecedented peace in Germany. It was accompanied by a marked development in agriculture, an increase of population and much accumulation of capital. Owing to agricultural exports, partly as a consequence of the abolition of the British corn duties, the balance of payments was favourable. The import of precious metals, especially after the gold discoveries in California, made possible an increase of bank deposits. Eventually the Bank of Prussia, the predecessor of the Reichsbank, had to find an outlet for the accumulated deposits. The demand for capital caused by the technical changes in industry met this need. Factories for building steam engines, steam boats and locomotives, blast furnaces using coke in the Ruhr district, and then the boom in railways and the basic industries enlarged banking activities. The capital issues in industrial stocks exceeded the usual business in State loans and made speculation possible. From the beginning of the 19th century private bankers had been advancing relatively small amounts of capital, but as soon as large demands were made, new institutions had to be formed. The combination of deposit banking and speculative investment in the German institutions sprang from the principle of the " freedom of banks," proclaimed in the middle of the century. This meant there was no restriction whatever on the manner of investment by the banks of sums deposited with them. To meet the demand for credit which greatly exceeded the amount of its own capital, deposits (in the nature of loans) had to be raised. In Germany these deposits did not flow only to the deposit banks as in England. They ran into two other channels as well, the co-operative credit institutions and the savings banks.[11]

The deposit banks (with their own capital and with the funds of their customers) stepped into the breach and themselves subscribed the whole issue, subsequently " placing " it upon the market. This type of bank was the actual guarantor of the success of the loan. Most of the new issues went to the market through a group or " consortium " of banks, which took over at " fixed " price the loan or the capital issue, in order to place it on the market at a higher price. The British system of promotion through merchant bankers, foreign banks, brokers and underwriters, was unknown in Germany. In the second half of the last century the Joint Stock banks, in order to carry out their issue and the " consortial " activities, were compelled to increase their own capital greatly. As one example, the Essener Kreditanstalt (which was situated in the centre of the mining and iron industry) trebled its own capital in the short space of six years

82

(1894-1900) in order to advance capital for industry (1893 saw the establishment of the Rheno-Westphalian coal syndicate in Essen). This bank was able to diminish the risk by receiving the support of the Deutsche Bank, with which it amalgamated some time later. With its backing, the risk was distributed among a group of leading German banks.

Next to the traditional business of issuing State loans, railway issues were the main flotation business up to the seventies, but after the development of a system of State railways banks were deprived of this important activity. Later the transfer of Public Utilities and tramway lines to the municipal authorities lost them further business of great speculative value. An extension of the banks' activities into industries to some extent filled the gap. Formerly the railways were big borrowers from the banks—now, however, the substitution of industrial securities made a great demand for investment credit (cf. p. 89). That meant for the Joint Stock banks a long period of immobilisation until they could succeed in turning the long term loans of industry into shares or debentures of the works promoted or financed by them, and then dispose of the stocks on the market. Very often banks, as a possible means of liquidating their loans, reserved the right, where necessary, to change the industrial undertaking into a Joint Stock Company or to demand the issue of new capital. All this replaced their former activities in issuing railway stock. But banks, in order to get rid of the shares and debentures of the undertaking financed by them, succeeded in attracting the interest of the general public and were able to utilise the deposits of their customers. Thus their activities in providing the public stocks and in offering " Report and Lombard " credit,* gave them great influence, amounting sometimes to almost complete control, over the administration of their customers' resources. Certainly the clientele was sometimes made the rubbish dump for such securities as the bank wished to dispose of.

When a credit account with a bank was opened, there were unobtrusively included agreements that the customer would buy his shares through this bank and that he would allow the bank to act as his proxy at company meetings. If the customer's account was overdrawn, the bank in normal times would extend credit freely, and the customer in general would be willing enough to allow the bank to administer his activities. Thus at the general meetings of industrial concerns the bank would exercise great influence by utilising the votes attached to the shares of their customers.

* " Reports and Lombards " are closely connected with speculative activity on the Stock Exchange. The latter is an advance covered, usually exclusively, by the pledge of Stock Exchange securities. The former corresponds to the process on the London Stock Exchange where a " bull " or " bear " speculator might wish to " carry over " his transaction from one settlement date to another by payment of " contango " (Report) or " backwardation " (Deport).

§2 Technicalities in Banking and Exchanges

If we consider the activities of German banks over a long period it can be seen that the promotion side of the business was decidedly in the centre of the stage. It influenced the whole range of their relations with their industrial customers and their depositors (from whom was drawn the necessary capital for industry) and their attitude towards professional and amateur speculators. The bank regulated the extent of credit (in various forms) offered to industries, according to its estimate of their future prosperity. Thus the bank, and with it the industrial company, became involved in a vicious circle. If the industrial debtor's loan increased too much, another issue had to be floated; if ordinary shares at the time were not to the liking of the public, debentures had to be issued. The industrial debtor, on the other hand, if he needed loan-capital, had no choice but to approach the bank. The consequences might easily involve loss of his independence. Experience shows that the great metamorphosis bringing about giant impersonal trusts and finance capitalism with all their economic and social problems, could never have come about without the acceptance of grave risks. The industrial State would never have materialised without the risky engagements in which all the participants were involved. Banks, in order to diminish risk and to enlarge at the same time their basis of profitmaking, were always seeking for new activities. As the integration of industrial works proceeded, so the need for credit increased; as the process of production lengthened, so the period of credit had to be extended. Banks, as direct creditors for these activities, now took the place of the individuals who formerly supplied funds. After integration and cartelisation had developed, the old methods of financing the provision of materials by commercial bills largely fell into disuse, and the banks would directly finance the now combined companies. As Th. Vogelstein, writing at the beginning of the Great War, says,[12] " The industry used to borrow as much as it could from every side, with every method, for every purpose. Loans from ten to twenty million Marks were a regular thing; but in some cases they reached thirty and fifty millions. These measures were not necessarily unsound." The banks had very wide opportunities to serve their industrial customers—as issuing firms, as banking creditors, as holders of large blocks of shares and as members of directorates. They accompanied them from the cradle to the grave. They floated them, issued new shares, gave credit accounts and manifold loans, delivered them of daughter companies, performed surgical operations in crises and provided for decent obsequies at the liquidation.

In order to clarify the close connection between banks and industry, it is necessary to go into further detail. The peculiarity of the German system lies in the investment credit system already mentioned, a form of credit " which passed the bounds of liquid investment." It was characteristically different from money market credit where the advance is regarded as being covered by floating assets. The investment creditor on the other hand, was more deeply involved and in case of trouble had to try to save his capital by participating in the management of the enterprise or by negotiating its sale. Money market loans are fungible. They are acquired without a close investigation of the enterprise. Investment credits, however, are individual. The affairs of each company have to be examined with regard to its management and profitableness. Thus the money market debtor may—except in periods of crisis—change his bank fairly easily. Conditions are otherwise in the case of investment credit. Naturally, a concern would be reluctant to disclose to a second bank, the state of its affairs and, in addition, the dissolution of old relations would often give rise to a certain suspicion and prove a cause of trouble. Again, banks were able easily to liquidate money market credit, but not so easily (sometimes not at all) investment credit. In the case of investment credits, the bank would be closely interested in the fate of the enterprise; the bank might, and did, suffer serious loss in the event of its collapse. It was in the vital interest of the banks to supervise the management of the undertaking.

In contrast to the state of affairs in Great Britain, it was a normal thing to find the banks participating in the affairs of industry.[13] Banks often became the prisoners of their debtors. This system was against the main principle of credit banking which implied short term loans where the bank would not become an industrial entrepreneur itself. When we study the history of the banks it becomes clear that after the period of the first great crisis (1857) when the banks had no precedents upon which to work, this fault tended over a long period to be gradually eliminated. But in later periods, particularly during the Weimar Reich, this close relationship between banks and industry re-established itself. A certain cautiousness prevailed when giving investment credit to the more powerful undertakings and, before the War, bankers clung to the principle that investment credit should not exceed the enterprise's capital. Banks often refused to give short term credit to companies which they already supported in the " consortial " business. Clearly, between the time of taking over an issue of shares and the time of disposing of them to the public, they were bearing a large part of the risk of the enterprise. The big banks in Berlin, therefore, distinguished as far as possible between financing and short term credit business. The disposal of the shares in the bank's own portfolio to their general customers throughout the Reich by means of their system of branches, was as extensive as it was pernicious, and at this time, many of Germany's favoured industrials were notorious gambling securities in stock exchanges all over the world. This issuing system often gave rise to unscrupulous transactions. Banks sometimes remained in possession of industrial issues, partly deliberately, and partly involuntarily. Experience showed that the burden of this issuing business became one of the reasons why the banks created daughter companies to whom, in addition to other nominees, shares could nominally be sold.

In spite of the difference between the short term and the long term credits, both forms were offered in the same way, i.e., as loans " at short notice." But this essential condition was a mere formality.

The system of investment credit, nominally at short notice, gave to the banks a powerful influence over industrial undertakings. Credit would be augmented in a period of scarcity in the capital market, when capital from other sources was not to be obtained, and industrial companies became quite dependent upon the banks in this connection. German *cartels* and *syndicates* developed vigorously under the stimulation of the Big Banks. The connections which banks had with different undertakings in the same branch of industry often gave them the power to coerce their customers into joining cartels or special combinations (coal, iron, cement, etc.). The cartel was, in the eyes of the banks, an instrument against cut-throat competition, maintaining the stability of prices, which protected the works promoted by them. A report of the Darmstädter Bank in 1900 (immediately after a crisis) states : " The community of interests of great industrial groups, as expressed in cartels, protects industry from expenses and sudden collapses, such as occasionally happened before their establishment."[14] So banks often succeeded in breaking the resistance of individual undertakings to a combination.

The promoting activities of the banks gave them opportunities to obtain seats on the *Aufsichtsrat* (Supervisory Board) either for their own directors or for those of other industrial trusts in which the bank was also interested. In this way, also, influential members of cartels became, by the will of the banks, members of the *Vorstand* (Managing Board) of certain industrial enterprises, and, on the other hand, industrialists dependent upon the banks could be forced into the cartels. Leading personalities thus found themselves holding a variety of key positions, for example, Emil Kirdorf, among many other positions in banking and industry, was at the same time Chairman of Germany's greatest coal cartel (*Rheinisch Westfälisches Kohlensyndikat*), general manager of one of Germany's coal trusts (Gelsenkirchen) and vice-chairman of one of the greatest deposit banks (Diskonto Gesellschaft). The banks had also an almost dominant control over the Stock Exchange. Handling their customers' money, they possessed great influence both as buyers and sellers. Moreover they were able to profit by the knowledge which they were able to obtain from the fact that the bulk of Stock Exchange engagements would pass through their hands. Further, loans on collateral security (" Lombards ")* brought them into close touch with the more speculative activities of the general public, activities which the bank itself often inspired.

* See footnote p. 83.

Writing at the beginning of the Great War, Schulze-Gävernitz rightly says,[15] : " In the seventies, a young and over-exuberant Stock Exchange laid the foundation of Germany's industrialisation by using shares as a medium for gambling. But, to-day, the domination of the exchange by the Big Banks through their " Report " business (but not through that alone) is an expression of the fully organised German industrial State. Certainly the province of free economic laws was narrowed down by that activity, and conscious regulation by the banks came to the fore. The responsibility of a few ruling heads was infinitely increased. By means of collateral advances, banks were able to assist in overcoming economic and political troubles and in avoiding catastrophic falls in stock prices. And on the other hand they could counter artificial rises in stock prices by offering for sale stocks from their own portfolios. The enormous influence on the trade cycle through the ' report ' business revealed the power of the banks." Thus, it was possible to speak of a certain domination over the Stock Exchange by the Big Banks. " When the ' report ' business started, the big banks only wanted to use this channel as a means of making money. Later, when the bulk of ' report ' capital accumulated more and more with them, they exercised a conscious ' report ' policy. The big independent speculator disappeared, the smaller ' proletarian ' helped to increase the power of the big Joint Stock bank."[16] The big banks patronised most of the industrial stocks on the market.

" The Joint Stock Company was the characteristic form of the newcomer, and such joint stock companies were especially successful, their shares being dealt with extensively in the ' report ' business. Thus the banks were able to contribute to the predominance of large scale enterprises. The Joint Stock Company was the legal form best adapted to modern requirements. The large amounts of capital necessary to establish such enterprises as blast furnaces, great power stations and large chemical works, could be financed in no other way than by gathering in the scattered resources of many individuals. The accumulation of capital outgrew English standards and became comparable to those of America. Such was the origin of the giant works of German large scale industry."[17] More recent methods of financing certain undertakings related to the Trusts will be dealt with in §13.

We may now turn to a brief history of the German Joint Stock Banks. These arose at the end of the forties, that is to say, some years before the establishment of the Credit mobilier. This fact shows that they were not an imitation of the French principle although, later, this widely influenced their activities. The Joint Stock bank owes its origin to Cologne bankers who wished to develop the Rhenish-Westphalian industry by exploiting its treasures of coal and iron ore. The principle of the joint stock share either changed the character of the older private banks or gave rise to the establishment of new ones. The A. Schaffhausen Bank at Cologne became the first private institution which changed into a Joint Stock bank (1848). Cologne bankers founded the Darmstädter Bank mainly to deal in railway and industrial stocks (1853). The Diskonto-Gesellschaft in Berlin, precursor of the Schulze Delitzsch type of co-operative institution, was organised for the new banking business in 1856. In this decade other establishments, such as the Berliner Handelsgesellschaft were set up. In 1871 the Deutsche Bank, and a short time later, the Dresdner Bank were established. The activities of the provincial banks became centralised in Berlin and a process of concentration and amalgamation followed. This centralisation was a visible expression of developing economic power in the imperialistic Wilhelmian period.

All these banks came into being in a period of rapid development when there existed no knowledge of the management of such giant formations and when no one knew what their consequences would be. Their early experiences in the crisis of 1857 and 1873 yielded empirical knowledge of trade fluctuations which slowly grew into a theory of the trade cycle. There were not a few academicians who considered the activities of Joint Stock banks to be a swindle.

Joint Stock banks early acquired an international character. The Deutsche Bank which, under its virtual founder, Georg von Siemens, was in its earlier days indifferent to promotion and issue business, developed step by step a considerable business overseas. Branches of the big German banks were established in London.

International contacts were facilitated as a result of the Franco-Prussian War. Austrian securities from France went to Germany, mining undertakings in Rhineland-Westphalia were transferred from French to German ownership. Two-fifths of the War indemnity came to Germany through the sale of foreign securities by French people, the purchasers often being Germans. In a still greater measure, international speculation (for instance, the Roumanian transactions of the large scale speculator, Strousberg) stimulated enormously the whole banking business and the Stock Exchange of Berlin grew into a market with an international reputation.

After the Franco-Prussian War, the Reichsbank was established. In addition to its tasks as central note institution, it became, through its activities in rediscounting industrial bills, one of the mightiest supporting institutions of the Joint Stock banks and was known as the "industrialist banker's bank." Thus the Reichsbank became a link in the chain of the industrial State.

§3 *New Forms*

Banks and industry faced entirely new problems during the era of William II, when branches of industries, in particular the electricity industry and local railways, brought new and large demands for investment and credit. The risk—as it is said by Riesser[18]—of providing the greater part of the long or short term capital invested in industry, was taken by banks, beginning with the flotation. The need to limit the risk engendered new forms. The demand for capital by individual industries became so great that the Joint Stock banks whose activities had to be subject to a certain degree of liquidity could no longer cope with it. How then, were the new forms of technical organisation to be financed? As industries pressed towards integration (cf. p. 184). the financial as well as the technical requirements had to be " planned." The task was to make the best use of the poor financial resources of Germany on behalf of industrial borrowers. It is clear that such a system arising out of, and conceived in, the spirit of capitalism, was dependent on the promoting specialist of the bank, and, with him, came the opportunity for the profiteer. Many things were done contrary to any preconceived ideas of general or national welfare, and this new system was, indeed, accompanied by no small measure of criminal offences. But in spite of them, a new economy arose by quite empirical methods ; a missing link between banking and industry was forged. It was now not possible to tell to which of the two component parts the link belonged. To this kind of capitalism, some authors, even before the War, gave special names, such as " Finance Capitalism " (R. Hilferding) or " *Effekten-Kapitalismus* " (=Joint Stock Capitalism). Liefmann used the latter word to express the fact that a mutual exchange of blocks of shares in the various enterprises, namely Joint Stock Companies, had been the binding force of this new interdependence. The achievement of "Vertical Integration " of various groups of commerce, industry, and transport, became an outstanding activity of the German Joint Stock bank. Inside the framework of cartels, new giant companies were formed which eventually outgrew the cartels themselves. The movement proceeded rapidly to the greatest dimensions. The combines and amalgamations covered all stages of a divided production, from the supply of the raw material to the manufacture and sale of the finished product. From the mining of coal and iron ore, through the manufacture of semi-finished iron and steel goods, and railway and engineering material, such trusts advanced as far as shipbuilding and even held interests in shipping companies. To write the history of Germany's great banks, one would have to write the history of her big industrial trusts. Germany's greatest modern trust of the coal, iron and steel industry, the Vereinigte Stahlwerke, which is so closely connected with chemical and other industries, emerged from trusts directly established by banks. An important instance of this kind is the Deutsch-Luxemburg A.G., which was later to be the spring-board for Hugo Stinnes' ill-omened industrial trust, and which is still one of the essential parts of the present Vereinigte Stahlwerke. The Gelsenkirchner Bergwerksgesellschaft, a famous undertaking which now also belongs to the Vereinigte Stahlwerke, added blast furnaces and iron works in Lorraine to their coal resources and iron and steel organisation. Another giant German industrial unit, the " Lothringer steelworks," owed its enormous expansion in the Ruhr to the support of the banks. For the purpose of industrial amalgamation, the banks by which the component parts had formerly been financed, usually acted jointly and after the amalgamation had been completed, these same banks continued to finance the new concern. Moreover, this type of contact between the banks accelerated the process of amalgamations among the banks themselves. A few large banks, the result of such concentration, were the godfathers of the major part of the heavy industry. With their support, Germany's iron and steel industry in the early years of this century outstripped that of Britain. One step farther and the competition between the big trusts themselves will diminish, and many examples of this development can be seen. Mutual understanding between these industrial forces was brought about by the impersonal financial power which guided the masses of capital for all trade and industry. Our next section will show that the newcomers in large scale industry (electricity, etc.) were soon squeezed into the framework of these powers. Monopolies, developed inevitably out of competition, first penetrated into the market and then dominated it. What forces will eventually dominate these monopolies ? Already, other than private forces began to shape themselves vaguely in this period. The visions of Marx as well as of Saint Simon seemed likely to find their partial fulfilment in the trend of this development.

In the period under review the form of the industrial trust and of certain financial institutions began to mould itself into an interesting pattern, modelled partly on English and American lines. Various means served the same ends. The essential point for large German deposit banks at the commencement of the new century was to depart from the principle of promoting directly the new and giant undertakings of certain industries. Their conceptions of liquidity and spreading of risk meant that they could not risk too much capital in one individual industry in a fixed form. From this time, banking and industrial activities became interlocked to a further degree. The innovation at this time was the modern " concern," the main type of which is in Germany called " Trust." (It should be noted that the word " trust " has a different significance in other countries). The new methods of industrial financing were not, as is sometimes suggested, a creation of the post-war period. At this time it became more generalised and covered a wider field of industry. During this time of unrest, when attempts were being made to bring about industrial recovery, both during a time of inflation and after the inflation, by means of artificial and unsound borrowing, it became clear how unsound had been the methods by which German industry had been developed. With only small resources available, risky methods of finance had to be undertaken. They succeeded in the less troubled pre-War days. The strain and unrest of the post-War years were to prove their weakness.

A distinction must be drawn between the trust and an outright amalgamation or fusion. In the former, the individual concerns do not lose their separate identities. In the latter the amalgamated concerns lose their identity in the newly-created concern. In the Trust, a net-like organisation usually joins together a collection of separate enterprises which may themselves take various legal forms. The strands of the net usually lead to one key organisation which may be concerned either solely with financial activities or with both financial and productive activity. Sometimes the Trust is financed by one of its constituent organisations (*Konzernbanken*, see pp. 92 and 178), sometimes by one of the big banks, sometimes by a financing company set up especially for the purpose by one of the big banks. For one undertaking to control another it was necessary to hold at the very utmost only 51 per cent. of the capital. Often, indeed, very much less would be required to obtain practical control. The controlled company itself might control, in the same manner, a third company, and the third a fourth, etc. Thus the original undertaking might dominate a pyramidal structure although holding perhaps only a small proportion of the total capital (*Verschachtelung*). The system has grave potential dangers. While the constituent parts of the Trust are legal entities the Trust as a whole is not. It is rather an *economic* entity. Every component company of the trust has its own general meeting, supervisory board and managing committee, but the concern as a whole has neither a general meeting nor supervisory board. Nobody is responsible for the concern as a whole. Every part, being in reality nothing else than a dependent organ of the concern, bears its own responsibility. In Chapter III the abuses of this period which led to legislation will be mentioned. Great branches of industry, in particular the electrical industry (beginning about fifty years ago), were built up in this manner. The few big manufacturers in the heavy electrical industry can virtually be said to have financed their own customers. From the early days of this industry these consumers were not only sought at home but everywhere in European countries such as Spain and Russia, and in South America. All these measures required financial transactions. The following would be the typical procedure. If, e.g., a power station were required in a provincial district or abroad, where there was little likelihood of the necessary capital being raised locally, the finance institution of the Trust would bridge the gap. A company would be established, its shares would be taken up by the finance institution of the Trust, which would pay for them with money received from a new issue of its own shares. It would be impossible to make a direct issue to the public of the shares of the new company. For such shares would not be mature for issue. The name and prospects of the new company would be unknown and a long period of construction, exploitation and development would have to be expected. Thus arose the principle of what is called " *Effektensubstitution*." The finance institution would thus advance investment capital to new industries and mobilise it through the issue of shares or debentures of its own, thus, in effect, substituting its own issue for that of the new company. A matter of great importance in this connection was that the finance institution carrying out these activities might at the same time combine ordinary deposit banking. Borrowing on short term and lending on long, these banks contradicted the fundamental principle of banking. The insecurity grew in cases where financing institutions established companies which covered a wider field of various branches of trade and industry. Therefore, some of these financing institutions became exaggerated into a kind of institution which speculated in stocks and shares. The finance institutions of the Trusts might take a variety of forms. It might be a subsidiary company of the Trust carrying on the financing activities of the Trust alone, or it might combine financing with the dominant interest. Banks of industrial Trusts were known as "*Konzernbanken.*" A famous institution was Merton's Metallbank and Metallurgische Gesellschaft in Frankfort-Main and, later, the Westbank of the Sichel Konzern, and the Röchlingbank of the Röchling Trust.

In addition to the aforementioned branches such as local railways and metal trades, big banks were interested in special financing banks, those for gold mines and for the oil industry. In this branch, the Deutsche Petroleum A.G. and the Deutsche Erdölgesellschaft which gained profits from valuable establishments outside Germany, were formed by the Deutsche Bank, the Diskonto-Gesellschaft, the Bleichröder Bank and other banks. A whole network of financing holding and daughter companies was woven around these establishments. After the inflation the importance of the banking institutions developed even further. Hugo Stinnes, for example, held interests in some of the big deposit banks.

During the trustification the proceedings sometimes took an unexpected turn. Firms hitherto engaged in production might abandon their productive activities to subsidiary companies and continue as administrative and financial bodies only. For example, the Siemens & Halske and the Schuckert works once formed the Siemens-Schuckert Co. which took over the bulk of the productive activities of the two firms, leaving to the two firms only the financial and administrative side of the business.[19]

(c) LARGE SCALE ENTERPRISE (CARTELISATION, TRUSTIFICATION).
A further consideration of the subject will be found in
Chapters III and IV.

§1 *General outlines of combines in German history.*

From the loose agreements of independent entrepreneurs (aiming at an improvement of their market situation) to those of more legal standing, written on a "*charta,*" *cartels* developed into powerful organisations of still independent enterprises which ruled whole industries. In the course of development the grip of strong private or public forces changed these cartels into formations of a different character. Trusts, socialist co-operative societies of production, State enforced cartels or even public departments might derive from them. Thus cartels begin in a competitive Society, they end in a socialist one. During this long development not only do their original functions undergo essential changes but naturally their forms of expression are subjected to corresponding changes. *Tempora mutantur, chartellae mutantur in illis.* One can divide their history into three periods.

(1) The first is the period which lasted from ancient times up to the Great War. In the last stage of this development we see cartels in an age when private capitalism was relatively unrestricted. *Private enterprises, which were then the units of the economy, mainly followed the laws of profit of private economy.* From early days competitors tried to exclude competition either in the form of combines of undertakers or of co-operative societies and these came under the control of public authorities when their private interests conflicted with those of the public. Schmoller,[20] " in unravelling the elements of the structure of trade through the ages in a cursory survey," once described this development, ". . . the commerce-guild from the 9th to the 12th century, the craftsmen's guild from the 13th to the 15th century, and the new commercial corporation from the 14th to the 17th century, showed mainly the same principle as the cartels and trade unions of our period. Again and again Economic Society must try to dominate the side of supply by combined forces. After all attempts to proceed with a free play of forces without these measures, Economic Society returns to them. Again and again compromises take place, corresponding to the state of production, trade and transport, between free competition and the *Staatliche Marktordnung* (market control of public authorities). Again and again this control has to admit as much free competition as is useful for the total development, and this control has to tolerate as many and as strong combines, as serve public welfare or the profits of their members without abusing their monopoly."

As far as modern cartels are concerned, they are a German invention and still remain in their homeland dependent on its peculiar conditions. They came to the fore in the " seventies " during the great depression following the crisis of 1873 (therefore they are called offspring of poverty)—and they gained their special significance after 1879 when the German economic system made the transition to protective duties. The connection between these duties and cartels is evident (see p. 185). The exclusion of foreign competition is an essential foundation of cartelisation, therefore Professor Schumpeter adapted the saying mentioned above to " cartels are the offspring of protection." Where exclusion of foreign competition was obtained by control of railway and other transport rates, there was no need for protective duties. These policies introduced by the State combined with banking policy, and with the overseas and colonial policy of public and private forces, to form what has been called Germany's "national economic policy." This was clearly the formation of a planned economy. So, in a wider sense, the transition from the exchange economy to the planned served purposes of preservation as well as of power, because planning meant promoting effectively all the energies of the rapidly growing people, and thereby raising the standard of living to a considerable extent for the individual.

Cartels, as combines of formerly isolated entrepreneurs, were looked upon as part of a system in which organisations and unions such as amalgamations, trusts, trade unions and co-operative societies expanded. Rightly or wrongly the " collectivist " and " corporate " note of this period was therefore stressed. It must be remembered that cartels remained associations of independent entrepreneurs, who united themselves by legal agreements for certain purposes.

The inroads made by cartels into free competition reached a certain climax. Cartels simply covering delivery and conditions of payment were frequently found in the textile and certain finishing trades. They were the most numerous of cartels. Other cartels fixed prices, especially minimum prices. An old type, but recently again prominent, is the "*Kalkulation*" cartel, which involves supervision of the costing records of the individual concerns, and uniformity of costing methods throughout the group, and which thus prescribes the basis upon which selling price is to be determined. More advanced cartels combine the fixing of prices with the fixing of output. These "*Produktion*" cartels sometimes fix quotas, and sometimes establish a system of regional markets among their individual members. Where the sale of the production of member firms is transferred to a general selling office, the "Syndicate," the cartel of the highest order, emerges. Even at this stage, the association is still one of independent entrepreneurs. This type of cartel frequently combines in itself a variety of cartel purposes. Controlled prices through all the many stages of production up to the stage of retail sale often lead to coercive domination of the market by these monopolies. This higher form of business organisation establishes its own premises for these purposes. Later, centralised drawing offices and showrooms come under the control of these syndicates, which are formed as public or private limited companies. The post-War period developed these syndicates into a final form of monopoly organisations, of which a few examples have already existed for thirty or forty years. Basic industries dealing with relatively few and uniform products such as coal, iron and steel, cement, sugar, and alcoholic spirits frequently took this form. This form spread later to include machine-tools, locomotives, wagons, artificial silk, etc. The development was of special significance where the members of these cartels were a few large amalgamations, such as in coal mining. Miss Warriner,[21] in summarising the German point of view, distinguishes the important difference in objective between trusts and these forms of cartels, " that of the trust being independence of the market, that of the cartel, market control; the trust studies the possibilities of reorganising industry in order to adjust costs to prices; the cartel studies market conditions in order to adjust prices to costs." There is, no doubt, a great difference between the syndicates and those cartels which never advanced to a higher degree of organisation.

An instance of the extensive control of the larger cartels is given by the transport arrangements of the iron and steel cartels. These have a general transport scheme (transport scheme Oberhausen, named after a coal town on the Rhine), whereby the cost of transport from place of production to point of delivery is uniform throughout Germany. Thus, the central German consumer of iron and steel pays for transport more than would be the actual costs of transport under an unrestricted economy, while a consumer in a remote part pays considerably less. Thus at least one of the conditions which contribute to the localisation of industries can be influenced to a remarkable extent by such a cartel. Where members enter cartels voluntarily, some advantages must be offered to them and in this way even certain marginal entrepreneurs who by free competition would have been gradually excluded, have been protected by the cartel and have been permitted to gain profits. On the other hand, the syndicates obtained rationalisation by closing down unprofitable plants, thus restricting production to the more efficient plants of their members. The concerns whose plants were closed down received a certain share of the total profit, and this factor would tend to establish a price level higher than would have been the case under free competition. By differentiation of prices, in spite of the fact that this might mean higher average prices, the monopoly position would make it possible to increase the output of the works. Either certain consumers at home will be subjected to different prices according to their different capacities to pay, or high prices internally will compensate for losses incurred in the world market by dumping. In the case where goods dumped in the world market are raw materials, the internal manufacturer who has to pay the high home-price for his raw material becomes weakened in his capacity to compete with foreign producers. This differentiation between the two prices at home and abroad is only possible if the home market is protected. Without protection, formation of cartels of such a high order is never possible. For example, the German iron and steel producers, in exchange for the protection offered to them, were forced to give the inland consumers of their goods a rebate on goods, which they, in turn, exported. Even so, this rebate was sometimes not enough to compensate the actual damage inflicted upon the home finishing industry. The removal of the price-struggle into the field of foreign markets frequently led to international cartelisation. The industries dealing with iron and steel, potash, and in post-War time, nitrogenous products, are typical examples of this international development. Cartels also differentiated prices regionally at home. In Germany a distinction was made between "*unbestrittenes Gebiet*," which is a district which comes under the control of a cartel policy with regard to a certain commodity, and "*bestrittenes Gebiet*," which is a district in which competition is continued. A good example of this type of arrangement was furnished by certain agreements between the large cement syndicates, that of North-West and that of South Germany. These would agree upon prices in certain controlled districts. Other districts would be reserved to one or other of the syndicates, while yet other areas would be subject to the uncontrolled competition of the various syndicates.[22]

Cartels, however, cannot prevent new and independent producers commencing production. So the price policy of cartels regularly leads to outsiders who use for themselves the so-called cartel shadow, i.e., the difference between cost of production and the cartel price. They enjoy the special advantage that they are not limited as far as the amount of production is concerned. The cartel into whose field these independent producers encroach, regularly seeks to buy up the undertakings of these intruders or to bind them by the cartel arrangement, offering them as an inducement a high quota of cartel production. More than once, independent works have been established solely for this purpose, in spite of a general over-capacity in the industry. Such operations involve a prodigious use of capital and result in increased costs of production. The existence of the cartels controlling key industries was of great consequence by reason of their influence on all other following industries. This fact has to be mentioned especially with reference to a country in which the industries are so much concerned with finishing and exporting. In this first period, the phenomenon of combines was not so generally developed as to deserve treatment as an essential economic and political problem of its own. Especially in Great Britain free competition was less restricted. In Britain, the combine was considered to be a mere method of profit-making, and an aberration from recognised economic principles. In Germany, combines in this period were already regularly used in certain industries. The German attitude tended, therefore, to frown upon exaggerations but not upon the principle of combination as opposed to free competition.

The German State in this first period took an ambiguous attitude towards cartels, which, in practice, it supported or even occasionally enforced (the Potash syndicate and, later, the Rhenish-Westphalian Coal syndicate), whilst in theory its representatives proclaimed free competition. The support of public authorities was mainly directed towards influencing trade by general commercial and transport policy, while in other respects leaving private enterprise alone. The period before the War is one in which the State was making nothing more than a tentative move towards interference with private capitalism.

(2) The second period is one of marked transition. It shows cartels (which previously had been only occasional institutions) and State control (which previously had been no more than tentative), spreading generally and becoming more intense in their activities (as the development of syndicates exemplified). This tendency was not confined to Germany. In Germany, both cartelisation and trustification, at least in dominant trades and industries, become typical and State interference in various forms becomes the normal condition of the economic system. The decline of economic liberalism shows itself in different degrees of intensity in individual countries according to their peculiar conditions. Cartels, formerly regulating forces planned by private capitalism, are now used by governments as a medium to " put order in the market," or as an instrument of self-sufficiency. In themselves a piece of planning, cartels where they appear, transform an unplanned economy into a planned one. But they are never more than a part, though an important one, of economic planning. Cartels are no longer national institutions; the world market begins to be infiltrated with international cartels. No doubt the maintenance of prices beyond the frontiers often motivated German cartelised industries in this development. But another cause is that in times of a shrinking world market an understanding upon the international distribution of certain important commodities seems necessary in order to alleviate the distress of areas dependent upon export. The establishment of these international associations leads to the organisation of cartels in individual countries, in order that their trades and industries might be able to become partners of the international institution.

In this and the following period the new order of things shows itself by the springing up of another criterion—what has been called " *profitableness of public economy* " or " productivity of national economy "—which at this stage finds itself in existence alongside the still existing criterion of private profitableness. (The term " public profitableness " is only to be understood in connection with organisations of economic planning, see p. 98). In this second period, Schmoller's " compromise " (see p. 93), a certain combination of two divergent systems—laisser faire and planning—is evident. (Chapter III and IV will give a detailed analysis of this period).

This second period shows that in certain countries, including Germany, the problem is no longer free competition versus monopoly or partial monopoly. By this time, combines were so long established and so widespread that the problem, no matter how it originated, became a problem of its own, which produced further qualitatively new problems in economics and politics.

(3) In the third stage, experiments on a large scale are made in certain countries. There appears the semi-public economy, or pure public economy of which nationalisation or socialisation and State control of trade are essential foundations or aims. These systems

abandon in part or whole the order of private capitalism. Even in these two last periods, cartels exist or survive, but their functions and forms of expression change. In certain countries private entrepreneurs still exist but their private character is greatly limited. They are part of a system where public enterprises, mixed public and private enterprises of various kinds, and individual departments of public administration (or unions of departments) exercise functions which were formerly the prerogatives of individual entrepreneurs. " Public profitableness " is no longer concerned with the welfare of private enterprises, but takes national economy as a whole. In order to organise so vast a field of economy, this public profitableness needs a special regulating machinery (see Chapter IV) to balance the various interests (especially losses and profits) of the economic system, which at this stage may be carried out partly by public means and partly private. This machinery has to be exercised through a superior organ and that can only be the State or local authorities. Here again, the influence of " syndicates "* (associations of still independent companies) can be traced. Before the War they already regulated production and distribution, fixed prices, pooled profits, etc., so that their organisations in certain cases reached the point where they might be regarded as the brain and backbone of the whole industrial group. In War-time the State used these syndicates or even established them under its control (see Chapter III) and at this time the scheme was enlarged to include the whole of agriculture as well as the whole of trade and industry. After the Great War, in the " laws of socialisation " (1919) the same scheme of cartelisation (with still independent entrepreneurs) was utilised for heavy industry and others. A few provisions safeguarding the interests of workers and consumers were inserted in this scheme, which never justified its name.

Soviet Russia very early in her attempts to regulate trade by the Centro-textil and Centro-metal and other autonomous bodies adopted the German War-cartel-scheme. The exclusive right of selling abroad of the foreign trade monopoly also finds its closest analogy in the syndicate which exercises this right for all its member firms.

Where monopoly is nearly complete, the transition of these developed cartels into public departments is easy to trace. The Third Reich utilises cartels in connection with other associations to manage her economy according to a comprehensive plan. The word " *Staatsraison*" (action in the interest of the State), abundantly used by Prussian statesmen for 200 years, serves as the foundation of reasoning in an arbitrarily managed economy.

It has been suggested that cartels and other forms of monopolistic organisations and extension of State control tend to grow in times of

* These are very different from the anarcho-syndicalist regimentation of individual enterprises, a system which, except in times of temporary revolution, has nowhere been reached.

shrinking markets and political distress. The question then arises whether these organisations are likely to be permanent or not. Professor D. H. MacGregor[23] stresses the transitional character of all these types of combination, which he considers will tend to break up upon the approach of more prosperous conditions. In this question attitudes are clearly the expression of one's general way of thinking about economics, and argument can only be conducted on very shifty ground. The essence of the problem is this. If monopolies inevitably form out of the flow of development (resulting even from free competition) then there will be no permanent return to free competition such as has been assumed. Certain phases of the trade cycle may, perhaps, show a decline in agreement-activities and perhaps a rise both in outright amalgamation and in free competition. Then again with a new swing the cartel and associated forms will come to the fore. The particular form of cartels or trusts may be temporary, there may be new types of formations. But these considerations still presuppose the prevalence of a competitive Society. In a Society where the State plays an outstanding part, the socialist society, the management which now rules labour policy and monetary policy, will spread over to further provinces. Our present economy in a transitional and experimental time, caught between two epochs, cannot show clear ways or clear devices. So it is largely temperament which decides whether the economist sees these things as temporary aberrations or as the precursors of a new epoch. Political philosophy rather than economics is now the battlefield of these controversial opinions.

There is one thing which of itself again and again produces irrational influences which weigh heavily on economic problems. In spite of the decline of the birthrate of the Western nations, for the next two or three decades, the number of people of employable age will grow and flood the labour market. The solution of this problem alone demands planning, and this planning is widely subject to non-economic influences. There lies a monumental problem, beyond the power of exchange economics to solve, the more so at a time when the world is sharply separated into national States which want to decide their destiny, each in its own way. Unfortunately, when existence is at stake, an " essay in persuasion " to an economic religion, which is ignored by all present governments, is futile.

The transition from the second to the third period (see p. 97) can be shown by the fact that socialists and planners now find themselves opposed. One group still agrees that socialism, like capitalism, is a market economy, in which the demand of consumers decides what is to be produced. Not only must the market for consumption goods be preserved, but, in general, also the market for production goods. In both, the competition of the buyers of these goods must be considered. Thus, this group still links up price as an index of the relative importance of goods with " economic calculation." Planners of this kind try to trace their theories from those of exchange economy and work with conclusions taken by analogy from the latter. The followers of both schools, self regulation and planning, aim at the same end, i.e., the best satisfaction of human wants. But their different starting points result in different ideas as to what is the " best " or the " most just " satisfaction.

A more advanced group of planners believes in an order which decides price by public regimentation independent of exchange regulations. Even Professor Cassel seems to believe in the possibility of such an economic system.

There is a twofold difficulty in comparing or understanding the cartel problem in two countries with different attitudes towards the main problems, or in comparing the same industry in two different countries when in one it is cartelised and in the other not cartelised. First, a regimented economy which works arbitrarily, can only be compared with an exchange economy if there are commensurable elements of the former. Secondly, one must guard against comparing what appears to be the same industry in two countries, when, in fact, the industries are subject to entirely different conditions, a consideration which would involve the whole theory of complementary goods. This occurs especially when a substitute competes on the same market as the original commodity. But I shall deal with the value of comparisons of free and monopolised systems in the next section.

§2 *Cartels in German Theory.*

Where cartels unite competitors in order to interfere with a self-regulating price formation, the process will find its explanation in the theory of competition and monopoly as far as the state of research permits. Where the market situations are influenced by non-economic factors, pure theory can only investigate their effects on the economic mechanism, but not their causes, which are mainly sociological.

Cartel-theory and cartel-sociology derive from these two starting points.

Where cartels survive in a managed economy, one has to distinguish between the residue of a market-economy and the introduction of an arbitrarily directed economy. The former is still a fit subject for competition-theory, the latter only so when human efforts fail to direct, and things again take to regulating themselves.

Managed economy was faced with great problems by State interference, affecting both cartel-theory and cartel-sociology, The causes of State interference belong to sociology as well as to economic theory. This is most clearly seen if and when the development of private forces leads to a strong monopoly, which affects the political and social conditions of the community, and the State has to react. So far as the effects of State interference on economic mechanism are concerned, the problem primarily belongs to economic theory. The rapporteur of the Enquiry Committee on cartels of the *Verein für Sozialpolitik* (1931), Dr. Wolfers, summarises his judgment on the German cartel literature[24]: " German cartel doctrine never supported theoretically the empirical material of the monopoly position held by German cartels. Thus the economic consequences of termination or limitation of such monopoly-position (if possible) were never dealt with." At another place he stated : " In spite of a lot of good work done to tackle the problem by practical experience, the sociological and psychological phenomena of the establishment of a cartel, or of the cartel in itself, or of the relation of cartels to other groups, are in no way sufficiently expounded."

That is all true ; moreover, a good deal of German cartel literature is a collection of generalised individual cases ; for example, where conclusions gained by experience with raw material or heavy industries (highly organised syndicates) were extended to finishing industries or cartels serving certain special purposes, which were much more loosely knit organisations.

The German attitude towards the monopoly problem in general and the cartel problem in particular, needs a certain explanation or an apology. Certain arguments have already been given in various places in the first chapter which show the German disinclination to submit the " body economic " to an all-embracing theory.

In this important particular problem, the conscious or unconscious heirs of schools such as the " historical," the " neo-mercantilist," or the " professorial socialist " were and are opposed to those of the Vienna school which is closely connected with the modern liberal school in England. The rapporteur of the Enquiry of the *Verein für Sozialpolitik* says[25]: " If from the social aspect, the ' association ' has been looked upon as progress as against individualistic competition, it did not necessarily follow that cartelisation represented a higher principle in economic relations. But this was the consequence in Germany because their doctrine of cartelisation considers ' free competition ' to be economic anarchy. . . . As far as the German doctrine is concerned, cartelisation is considered to be a transition from anarchy to planning, order and regulation of the market. The abolition of free competition (i.e., monopolisation) may also, theoretically, under certain conditions, guarantee a higher degree of order than free competition." This point of view is, for instance, expressed by Schaeffle, Brentano, Bücher, and Liefmann. German authors consider—and this is the most decisive point of difference from orthodox schools—monopolies and cartels to be phenomena, originating from and growing out of the normal flow of development. Gustav Cassel's[26] argument has been given already. Carl Landauer,[27] in his analysis, on which I shall dwell in the next section, considers the establishment of monopolies as an inevitable development of free exchange not only in reality but also in abstract theory. Miss D. Warriner[28] throws some light on the proper understanding of German schools. " A law of competition, comprehending the combine problem, as it was assumed by the classical school, has been generally opposed in Germany." It was argued that this law was valid " so long as inter-firm competition was the rule rather than the exception." Since important phenomena cannot be looked at as mere " friction " in the competition problem, but as essential deviations from the rule, " there can be no analysis on the old lines : there are too many unknowns. The motive power of the old system itself cannot be treated as friction, yet any theory which analyses the capitalist system with the assistance of a general law of value is obliged to regard the combination movement as nothing more than affecting the surfaces of friction ; it must base its final judgment on the extent to which increases in some relation offset reduction in others. Even if such effects admitted of quantitative measurement, they could not be compared, because this type of theory can only calculate the effects of trustification by taking one effect at a ' time ' . . . ' Late ' or ' managed ' capitalism cannot be analysed as if it were a ' market ' regulated system " (cf. p. 3 in my introduction, on " the validity of theory throughout all times "). " A theory which treats capitalism as a system tending towards a position of equilibrium, self-regulated through the adjustment of costs and utilities cannot see the necessity of stabilisation or conscious direction."[29] The positive progress against the former doctrine shown by Schumpeter's theory of economic development, Miss Warriner continues, lay in its criticism of the anti-combine prejudice based on orthodox theory, but did not bring out a new combination-theory. In any case it is of interest that his analysis is built up so largely on a non-economic psychological issue. That is the conception of the entrepreneur as a dynamic force between two static periods.

The presentations of free competition and its opposite (derived from different starting points, the one from the standpoint of the general law of the exchange economy, the other from that of conscious direction) are irreconcilable. The economic politician is compelled to *form a working hypothesis*. From this expedient he can weigh the problem which he has to treat practically. He cannot ignore an economic policy which put its stamp on the period of more than half-a-century in various countries, because one school of thought denies its necessity or its right to exist. And this economic policy was the rule, with the one exception of the " Era of Expansion " in Britain from 1846-1914. To the German mind such a basis is necessary so that legal action may settle controversial disputes in economic life. From Mercantilist times, German administration has been accustomed to prescribe rules and codify laws. Free competition as such was still assumed, but the legal practice did not wish by its " interpretations " to interfere with monopolies. Since the time of the great Enquiry Committees and *Deutsche Juristen Tagungen* (conferences of jurists), the establishment of monopolies was supposed to be an inevitable development from free exchange. The legislation which admitted free exchange consequently could not prevent the formation of monopolies. In addition, the futility of the

U.S.A. legislation which attempted to prohibit every kind of combination did not encourage restrictive legislation. Later legislation in the Weimar and the Nazi Reich did not prohibit monopolies. The Third Reich, creator of enforced cartels, inserted the association system as part of a planned economic system intended to create a governmental control of markets (see IV (2) & (3) (a)). True, the German method is the reverse of the British—the former is inductive, the latter deductive. If one argues: "According to my mind, the ideal scheme of free competition shows the best or the only way to act, and I refuse to recognise any deviations," then there will be no understanding of German necessities. Monopolies in Germany are as frequent as motorcars in modern traffic.[30] Legal control of monopolies is as urgently needed as traffic regulation, but it needs a theoretical basis. Are the conclusions of deductive monopoly theory strong enough to act as this basis? If not, inductive conceptions must support the law. The more State-managed production and consumption are jointly subjected to regimentation, the truer this becomes.

No doubt, the majority of German investigations were based on working hypotheses, on "institutions," and not on a general law. The free competition theory embodied as a general law a process of exchange which, to the German mind, was in practice no more than an unusual case which, however, formed a good starting point for analysis. The procedure of determining the doctrine of free competition philosophically originated from inductive observations, as did most general laws, and later deductions were drawn from it. But our days furnish situations in the market which were not present when the theory of free competition was originally propounded and they could not be comprised in this scheme because the real facts from which a "general inference from particular instances" (induction) could be gained did not exist in complete clearness at that time. In Germany certain economists made a generalisation of these distinct market-positions of more recent appearance, exactly as the "free-competition-scheme" was a generalisation some generations ago. Further instances of market systems which differ from this scheme will explain the more inductive German attitude (see § 4). If we start with the derivation of such monopolies such as cartels and trusts, this attitude will become clearer (see next § 3).

The abandonment of the free competition doctrine as shown in Britain by Mr. Keynes and the socialist school of thought, was at all times much more general in Germany. German literature on the cogent reasons for the inevitable rise of combined action or monopoly situations is voluminous. In it the role of large amounts of fixed capital invested in highly rationalised industries has always been emphasised. Professors Cassel[31] and Schmalenbach[32] and others conclude also from this argument the futility of a general law. If inductive method can be justified, it will be easier to understand how present-day Germany is tackling the problem. Private interest as the fundamental principle was always strange to the German Mercantilist and State-Socialist mind. The idea of State interference was always congenial. Following the law of continuity, where State control begins there is no stopping, and with the passing of time it develops hypertrophic forms and makes its own laws. At this time again opinions diverge. The one side rages furiously for all-round regimentation, the other waits for the time when things will fall back and regulate themselves as far as possible. To the eyes of these moderate men, further control of prices and more extensive State control would clearly hamper technical progress and rob the economy of its necessary elasticity. It is true, however, that peculiar conditions deriving from the neo-mercantilist attitude are noticeable. There are numerous markets at home where the State possesses a total or partial monopoly of demand and the formation of prices is seriously influenced by these monopolies, which produce counter-movements of combined action on the side of supply (see § 4 and what I have said about the joint supply-demand enterprise). And there is the case in which the State subjects the whole economic policy to its will, identifying itself with the community of producers and consumers.

§3 *A short account of how cartels and trusts originate and of their position as monopolies*

It is part of the theory of price formation that the more completely a particular want is satisfied, the less will be the price offered for the further satisfaction of it. Beyond a certain point the producer may have a great interest in restricting supply. The fall in price may be such that there will be more profit in a smaller turnover than there is in the larger one. Among many competitors an individual producer cannot benefit from this. If he slackens production, others will take it up. If he can oust all his competitors from the market, he can begin to make extra profit by restricting supply. Where this cannot be done the next best thing is for the competitors to combine. *Here lies the origin of cartels (Landauer).*

Some German authors deny that cartels tend to increase prices or to fix a rigid price, and say that they aim at price-stability in order to mitigate the fluctuations of the trade cycle (Liefmann, Wiedenfeld and others). There is no doubt that, over long periods, most cartels, especially in heavy industry, tend to avoid rapid alterations of prices; for they would risk losing control of the organisation, which is better preserved by a certain stability. And this aim frequently finds support among the producers who depend upon the cartel product for the manufacturing of their goods, the dealers in the finished articles and the wage earners, who are all interested in the maintenance of a relatively stable price level. The steadying of prices in times of boom may serve to avoid setbacks in times of slump. Therefore they do not take advantage of all the possibilities of increasing prices during booms. The various enquiry committees mention this fact. The maintenance of prices during slumps seems to be the chief purpose of cartelisation, for it is the great protection against the too well-known cut-throat struggle in distinct phases of depression. But when it comes to the keeping of prices relatively low in the upswing, a fact contradictory to the self-interest of entrepreneurs, the acumen of cartel leaders is frequently praised. It is certainly a fact that some industries succeeded in their policy of price stabilisation, but it is open to question whether, in fact, for over half-a-century all the syndicates adopted this strategy of stabilising prices, and it is doubtful to what extent the other cartels followed.

German literature is full of the "pros" and "cons" of the question whether monopolistic price is or is not the main objective of cartelisation. Nevertheless, it seems clear that the purpose of a cartel is finally to increase the average price above the level which would result from free competition. Heavy industry in Germany before the War succeeded in restricting supply in order to get higher prices. The relatively small number of producers (coal, iron and steel) could more easily agree to a price-scheme, and furthermore, their produce was fairly uniform, a fact especially conducive to the formation of syndicates. Much depends on the technique of organisation. In recent development, even finishing industries show a high degree of cartelisation, with great effect no doubt on the formation of prices. Certainly there were special conditions that favoured this development after the War. The new establishment of plants was nearly excluded by the higher cost of building up companies as compared with the costs of existing companies. It does not require great powers of prophecy to predict that a progressive cartelisation will continue, and that it will invade many more industries in which to-day a certain free competition exists (see development of cartelisation in the Third Reich, IV(3)(a)§2). Experience has shown that a branch of production resists cartelisation as long as one section of the producers still hopes to exclude the other section. If they succeed, then the victorious undertakings will remain masters of the field. Then they will have to ask themselves whether they wish to continue competition against one another. On the other hand, if the attempt at domination fails, i.e., if the strong, or the would-be strong cannot destroy the weak, then they will soon learn the advantages of reconciliation. In either case the struggle will end in a cartel. Thus, as Landauer puts it—in expressing a general opinion[33]—*the tendency to monopoly is not an occasional aberration but an inevitable process* which extends further and further with the progress of technique or organisation all over the vast field of economy. This process will be temporarily arrested by transitional stages of competition brought about by new circumstances such as new industries, technical discoveries, etc., the consequences of which have yet to be experienced by the parties concerned.

In practice not all goods can be equally monopolised, and thus extensive differential profits go to certain producers. To this point Landauer,[34] whom I here follow in his further deduction, argues that " a thoroughgoing perception of the economic relations, such as might be conceivable under the ideal (exchange) scheme is not attainable in reality " (in the ideal free market the exchange relations and the factors that strike a particular price can be read off as easily as one reads a thermometer). " Thus, in general there will be no well-differentiated formation of price but limitation of production. In practice, in the whole of economic development, we cannot trace conditions which could end the indeterminateness of the processes." Thus Landauer[35] argues that the producer would not have any other choice than to limit the production of the goods. The only opposing argument that could be advanced is that an expansion of production would be justified, if costs were sharply to decline, in order that there might be a saving on overhead charges. With the increasing proportion of fixed capital to the total amount of the capital, the importance of fixed charges increases as against that of the variable charges. The stimulus in favour of a bigger turnover increases and this at least tends to weaken the controlling power of the monopoly. Free competition may expand production as long as a price can still be obtained which covers the costs of the " last " unit to be produced. If costs fall as production expands, this point will be reached later than if costs are constant. The monopolist then, will not expand production beyond the point at which the curve of the possible prices cuts the curve of the costs. So as nearly as possible he chooses a certain degree of production which represents the mathematical result derived from the gain achieved through the difference between price and cost. Thus he must also endeavour, if the curve of costs tends to decrease, to have a greater aggregate result than he would have if the curve of costs were to run horizontally. The advantages of decreasing costs tend to the amalgamation of producing firms. The cartel is primarily concerned with the maintenance of its member plants. Therefore it is compelled to adjust its policy of prices to the cost of the marginal plant. But in the case of a cartel a more extensive limitation of production is almost always carried out than corresponds to the monopolistic optimum where there is an exploitation of declining costs. This optimum can therefore only be obtained by the *trust*, which is no longer an organisation to protect independent enterprises but one to protect hitherto independent undertakings amalgamated in a single new and great enterprise. Inasmuch as the optimum-production of a monopoly, in the case of decreasing costs, approximates more closely to the result of free competition than in the case of the cartel, Landauer concludes: " The development from cartel to trust marks an economic progress. The two greatest German trusts, those of chemicals and iron and steel, were indicative of this development."

There is an interesting transitional form between cartels and trusts, the *Interessengemeinschaft* (community of interests) which since the eighties at certain times became prominent but is not now of much significance. The present name of Germany's paramount chemical trust "*Interessengemeinschaft Farbstoffwerke A.G.*" (I.G. Dyestuff Ltd.) reflects the great past of this form of undertaking, as well as the history of this individual trust. This form was once a substitute for cartels or an auxiliary means to achieve certain combination activities by undertakings which were already combined. Liefmann[36] says: "These are contractual agreements between two or three, but not frequently more, enterprises which remain independent (i.e., from the legal point of view), in order to distribute the profits according to an agreed key." Their affinity with the pool cartels is obvious. As Liefmann says, the community of interests becomes a cartel if it comprises a whole industry and with it aims at a monopolistic position. The *Deutsche Pulver-und Dynamit-Gruppe* was an example of this type. The big chemical works since 1904 made especial use of this form, which became the transition to amalgamation. Other industries and trades, such as electricity, shipping and also banking, used this form. The undertakings which formed communities of interest and were before mainly combined used the form as a kind of substitute for a fusion, in order to pursue monopolistic purposes. Frequently fusions in fact were the consequence; if not, then conflict and dissolution ensued.

To the general remarks on the problem I may add that in a State-managed economy there has taken place a metamorphosis of cartels and trusts as instruments of a "market order," subjecting cartels to new laws. The dilemma arises that the transitional stage of an economy—partly planned and partly self-regulated—does not allow the consideration of things other than along two different lines of investigation. Finally, the inductive method of the mercantilists (see p. 2) still remains the only way. The time has not yet arrived where one can combine both "monopoly theory" and the "theory of imperfect competition" with that working hypothesis gathered by inductive means. This hypothesis does not consider "imperfect competition" but "imperfect monopoly." Thus, to these economists, the combines and new formations developed from them are the normal market figures of our modern economy.

Even where monopoly theory deals with forms of markets, solutions are far from final and authors may, after their positive results, employ their imagination. No doubt, German and British writers on the monopoly theory, following their different general conceptions, differ in conclusions. H. von Stackelberg[37], for example, in a treatise on market-forms and equilibrium, investigating the form of duopoly, leads us to the conclusion that the only way can be a total price control and ultimately a corporate State!

§4 *Market systems outside free competition*

It is a German peculiarity that the consumer's influence, above all represented by the State, organised production to a great extent.

" Free competition " implies that a market price, in a pure sense, can only exist if the demanders and suppliers are proportionate to the extent of the market ; in other words, where none of the persons concerned in the market can alone influence the price to an appreciable degree. These presuppositions are not valid in modern business, where cases of pure " free competition " are the exception rather than the rule. In cases where the supply side, as well as the demand side, is organised monopolistically, conclusions drawn on the assumption of free competition must be modified. The same holds good if, on either side, a partial monopoly, or so-called oligopoly (i.e., a small number of great sellers and buyers), prevails. Under these circumstances, some suppliers can be seen attempting to decrease the price below cost in the hope of displacing others or of forcing them to a price agreement. Similar cases occur if, in spite of a great number of suppliers, one of them dominates the market. The analysis of Dr. Miksch[38], whose method of investigating new monopolies differs from that of Anglo-Saxon authors, may be introduced. He attempts a more realistic approach. He systematises a wide and expert knowledge of cartels and distinguishes two forms of " limited competition " between the two extreme cases of free competition and full monopoly. These four cases exist on both supply and demand sides. Thus, following this analysis, suppliers and demanders of the different types can link up in sixteen possible relationships. The relationships which on both sides do not comply with free competition are the result of natural conditions, as well as of inroads by the State. In transport and public utilities, the service of the supplier for technical reasons is tied up with a certain network of rails, or power lines. Thus, it is quite clear that the competition among railways or supply undertakings can rarely be completely free. At most there can exist only restricted competition. The railway tracks, and power grid and electric mains offer a situation of monopoly to the supplier, although there may be a form of restricted competition (as may happen when individual places are served by different lines, or if individual consumers can be linked up with various power grids, or if road transport competes with rail transport, or if the consumers' private supply stations compete with municipal power stations). The State may facilitate the restriction of competition, e.g., when protective duties cut off supplies from abroad, and thus narrow the market artificially, a factor regularly supporting the formation of cartels. The supply side lends itself to the creation of monopolistic positions more readily than the demand side. The development of monopoly on the side of demand made enormous strides after the War when the State and certain consumers' co-operative organisations step by step took up a predominant position—in the case of certain commodities and services, an exclusive position.

Not only is the economic structure of Germany affected by these developments, but the whole problem of competition takes a new turn as a result of this expression of national economic planning. Further details on this matter will be found in Chapter IV (3) (a), §3. The market forms mentioned above and in Chapter IV give a new conception of the market system. These conclusions gained by inductive methods do not give a monopoly theory, but they do furnish relationships which provide a basis for practical work. It is doubtful whether the good work done upon "imperfect competition" by writers such as Mrs. Joan Robinson[39] and Professor Chamberlin can provide as much. Indeed, Mrs. Robinson herself does not claim that her diagrammatic market schemes are devised for "tool users" who are in haste to set to work. Instances in this and the last chapter evidently show a great variety of forms serving practical needs: from a quasi free competition through one-sided monopolies (either of supply or demand) till one monopolist, the State in general policy, or great combined private enterprise (both again in various degrees of development), dominate production and consumption. These latter stages show the exclusion of self-regulating forces on either side, supply or demand, bringing to the fore far-reaching planning. How far the well-considered cases of the authors mentioned, or such as are contained in Professor A. Pigou's fine book, "Economics of Stationary States" (1935) may suffice to explain the latter systems, is open to question.

If the growth of combination is inevitable, then the fiction of free competition embodied in the German legislation has to be given up, and the Law must be expanded to recognise the combination principle. If combinations are superfluous, they must not be permitted to undermine a rule of Law based on free competition. In this event the formation of cartels must be forbidden. The fact that neither one nor the other has occurred indicates an uncertainty, in contrast to the old faith in competition. The daily legal controversies of business life cry out for a new code of law to cover the new conditions where combines of both sides of the market are normal. Thus in Germany for many years an adaptation of the law to cope with combination has been sought.

A second point, closely connected with the first, derives from the German mentality with its predilection rigidly to codify acts of social and economic life. With the legal recognition of an economic system which is not free competition, a stage of complete organisation, the "*Marktordnung*" (order of the market) emerges. It seems to be clear that where free competition only exists in one of the above-mentioned transitional forms, the State is compelled to supervise or control the fixation of prices. Where this state is reached, the automatism by which free competition provides the optimum of production, employment of capital, price formation and distribution, is at least partially excluded. To preserve this automatism, if possible, seems no doubt to be a healthy economic policy, and here again may be grounds for compromise between laisser-faire and planning, i.e., laisser-faire set into action by Governmental planning, which would not be in essential principle different from the holding of the ring by the Government, deputed to it even in the freest system. But this case cannot exist, of course, where natural impediments forbid, or where other cogent reasons compel a more autocratic interference.

(2) COMMERCIAL POLICY, WORLD AND COLONIAL POLICY.

William II's reign saw Germany's rise to an economic power of the first rank. Her industrial development in her basic as well as her finishing industries was outstanding. Germany, having displaced Britain as foremost producer of iron and steel in Europe, after the U.S.A. held the second position in the world. There is no need to repeat here other instances of rapid growth. One fact, however, has to be stressed which emerged from the advance of the heavy industry. A growing instability caused by the fluctuating demand endangered great amounts of fixed capital invested in industry and made insecure the lives of innumerable workers. Of course, Germany's impetuous, young and unentrenched industry needed for this purpose an elaborate system of private and State support which had to be built up, ultimately dragging the whole nation into the whirlpool of its interests. Inevitably its activities were to grow immensely in its hold over both men and capital and widened the field of conflict between private foreign competitors as well as between imperialist rivals. Germany's fate was now closely linked up with the world market. The maintenance of exports and imports became the most decisive element from the material side in her national policy, and still is. A vast number of her people found their livelihood in manufacturing goods mainly from foreign raw material and semi-finished products which were not available in the homeland. Her population far exceeded that of either Great Britain or France and grew at a more rapid rate than either. This increase was to a large extent made possible by the imports of goods which gave work to millions. The imports were paid for mainly by the exports of manufactured goods, which in their turn cheapened the process of manufacture through a full utilisation of fixed capital. Since then, Germany has been an exporting country comparable with Great Britain and the U.S.A. A few figures from Germany's trade balance will show the increase in manufactured goods produced by her industrial population.

(In 1,000 million marks.)

	1873	1883	1893	1903	1913
Total Export	2.5	3.3	3.2	5.1	10.1
Manufactured goods thereof	0.9	1.8	2.0	3.3	6.4
Total Import	4.3	3.2	4.1	6.3	10.8
Raw material thereof	1.8	1.6	1.7	2.8	6.2

Between 1873 and the Great War Germany's total export quadrupled, while the manufactured goods grew sevenfold. Imports increased by two-and-a-half and the raw material for industry by three-and-a-half.

When Germany began to play the part of exporter of manufactured goods (1913, roughly 64 per cent. of her total export), she entered the danger zone. As the capacity of foreign markets to absorb products varies, so economic equilibrium suffers shattering variations. By every considerable shrinkage of these markets the country was faced with great problems, and the growing pressure of competition with other exporting countries (as happened during the last two decades before the Great War) was bound to lead to catastrophe. The close interlocking of industry and finance made it necessary for the latter to seek for expanding business all over the world. The need for the profitable investment of its free money and the risk of being dependent on the home markets only, compelled it to distribute the risk over a wider field. Ultimately industry itself, of which finance became so important a part, needed such activities. New markets, overseas and elsewhere, for the great industrial producers had first to be financially developed, to make consumption possible, and cheaper provision of raw material stimulated business abroad as well.

It was not economic considerations alone that weighted the scale. On the psychological side a Great Power must remember prestige. A great nation, the embodiment of Prussianism and Militarism, could no longer be expected to accept a position of world inferiority, such as had been her lot in the past. The question of how widespread these feelings were in Germany is so often dealt with in English literature that I can restrict myself to a brief quotation showing how even a well-known socialist writer of the Wilhelmian epoch saw things: "To-day, when Germany is the equal, economically, of England and the U.S.A., and is compelled to take up an attitude towards all questions of world-politics in the interest of her industry, the naval policy of modern industrial States may indeed be severely condemned, but it cannot be expected of one's own country that it shall take up an exceptional position which might be fatal; as matters are to-day the prestige of a State abroad depends on its readiness for war both on sea and land " (R. Calver[40]).

But here, as elsewhere in German policy, State policy expressed the view of the most important classes which then dominated the State. It was all the same whether State departments, or the staff of the army and navy or the dominant groups of the Empire carried out the policy which combined foreign, military, commercial, industrial or colonial affairs. One spirit united all their activities in a complex whole. The marriage of militarism and capitalism at this time had no opponents who could seriously disturb it.

In so far as agricultural policy has not been included in the general history of trade policy, it will be given in brief in IV (3) (c).

(a) COMMERCIAL POLICY

After the early sixties, Prussia took the initiative towards a liberal policy in the German Customs Union. In the space of half-a-century internal tariff barriers had disappeared, and external barriers were now kept extremely low. The Union mainly followed the British lead in forming a system of liberal trade agreements. Thus, in 1862 and in 1867, such treaties were concluded with France, England and Belgium. They did not entirely renounce protective duties but followed unconditionally the " most-favoured-nation " treatment. There were always, however, opponents of such a policy. Thus Austria still remained largely protectionist and the German iron and steel industrialists and certain other groups, such as the spinning section of the textile industry, never agreed with these liberal tendencies. Just as in France, these industrialists and agriculturists began to stir up a certain opposition. On the other hand, semi-finishing and finishing industries, such as weaving mills or engineering works, benefiting from the liberal treatment of imports of certain iron and steel goods or yarn, were always staunch supporters of free trade. The trading interest in the big towns, and above all in the ports of Hamburg and Bremen, supported the tendencies making for economic liberalism. The Franco-Prussian War was, to a certain degree, the turning point in the commercial policy so far pursued on the continent. Consequently, it became clear that the liberal ideas were never deeply rooted there. The French treasury after the War was anxious to get new sources of income. A direct income tax such as existed in England was there extremely unpopular, thus import duties and taxes on consumption became the more important. It is known that M. Thiers agreed to a clause in the peace treaty which provided for the eternal most-favoured-nation treatment between Germany and France, because he opposed a treaty of long duration which would counteract such a protective policy as was certainly planned at this time. The new Republic required new sources of revenue; an income tax on the English model was not feasible, and therefore high protection was stimulated.

After the Franco-Prussian War, Germany held a better position, mainly owing to the war indemnity loan. But Bismarck's policy wavered. On the one hand the prevailing influence of Prussia in the *Bundesrat* (federal council) gave him many advantages. In a certain sense he welcomed the dead weight of a more conservative policy which Prussia, through the composition of her Diet, guaranteed as against the Reichstag with its growing left opposition. On the other hand, the dependence of the Reich on the federal States aggravated the difficulty of consolidating the then not even stable structure of the Reich. So he conceived that the great task of the national and central government had to be supported by giving the Reich more sources of revenue of its own. But the constitution of the Reich in the loose form which was the most that could be obtained in 1871, offered few chances of thoroughgoing reform of the revenue system such as would give preference to the Reich. From a fiscal point of view, import duties might thus have been welcomed, but that could only be a secondary consideration. Furthermore, the whole province of economics, as Bismarck saw it in the middle seventies, demanded a new system able to fill his great framework, the establishment of the Reich, with more life. Instinctively Bismarck finally based his policy on the economic forces, the outstanding agrarian and industrialist groups. It is true the problem arose whether there would result from the tariff (1879), an increase of the profitableness of the protected industries and landed estates, or a decrease of the economic productivity of the whole population.

In the eighties, the French bounties on iron exports, and in the early nineties, the rise of high protection in Austria, challenged Germany to make a definite change in her commercial course. The measure found a more willing ear in the Reichstag and federal council than it would have done if only the big land owners had moved the bill. Their complaints had long before opened a discussion which has engaged statesmen, politicians, and scholars till to-day. The then topical problem was a protection desired by the landed aristocracy for their main produce. I repeatedly mentioned parts of the problem (e.g., see financial policy in Bismarck's time, p. 71).

As far as agricultural competition from overseas[41] is concerned, the wheat production area in the U.S.A. in 1869 was 20,000 acres, which was doubled ten years later. The yearly export from the U.S.A., which in the average of the years 1851-1860 was only 5.5 million bushels, was in 1880 150 million bushels. The average price for wheat in Prussia in 1871-1875 was 235.2 Marks per ton, decreased in 1878-1880 to 211.2 Marks and showed falling tendencies. The problem was aggravated at this time because Germany, an old exporter of cereals, had become an importing country.[42] The cost of production in U.S.A. was low owing to the cheapness of agricultural land, which was largely given free or very cheaply by the government, which subsidised every development including transport for settlers and their products. The success of railways and trans-Atlantic transport played an enormous part in this development. Inventions such as, in the steel industry, the Bessemer process in the sixties and the Gilchrist-Thomas process of 1876, opened wide fields for easy and profitable long-distance transport of perishable goods. Large scale industry was able to provide all that was necessary for promoting the world-wide supply of foodstuffs which now set in. The American advance could not be expected to last for ever. It was a fact that after a generation, with advancing civilisation and increase of population in the U.S.A., these advantages would change. As a free trader, Professor Adolf Weber, says: "We know from theoretical considerations that protective duties, imposed in the case of the transitory advance of a certain country, are justified. They safeguard against adaptations which frequently changing conditions would otherwise demand, and which unhindered would make the trend of development unstable."[43]

But, finally, there were at this time other countries such as Russia and certain Balkan States, also growing agricultural competitors, which necessarily aroused the suspicion that West-European production would long be menaced, a suspicion which later proved well-founded. There were other reasons which made for protection such as the growing general over-production which always ended in a kind of dumping in continental markets. Continental countries such as Germany and France had to risk their independence in food supply. They did not wish to ruin their peasantry, an asset to their armies, so they dyked up against the flood. So, France, too, moved at this time towards a stronger protective policy. Whilst in Germany, duties on cereals, vegetables and malt in 1885 were 12.5 per cent. of the total German duties, by 1889 they reached 27-28 per cent. of their total import duties. As shown above, this was largely a fiscal policy; but gradually Bismarck became convinced of the imminent danger of growing world competition, which could ruin Germany's Eastern agriculture. The Prussian power depended to a great extent on the traditional ruling class of Eastern land owners; but smaller land owners also built up the stronghold of conservative elements (see Troeltsch's words, p. 40). Bismarck's policy began rather tentatively with a very low duty on cereals, of only one mark per 100 kilograms, but already by 1885 the duty was increased to three marks and by 1887 to five marks. Even by 1881 the duty on flour mill products was increased by 50 per cent. Other duties were imposed upon oats, turnips, vegetables, etc.

But a policy of this importance once established—in many countries moreover—became of symptomatic significance. In 1891 the Russian system increased the small protective duties introduced in 1877: in 1892 France passed a strongly protective act.

When he commenced his protective policy, Bismarck was lukewarm towards industrial duties. He suspected that increases in the rates would provoke retaliation and so diminish the German export trade. Thus, when Bismarck left the scene, there was in commercial policy, a fight of each against all among the various countries. Germany with her growing industrial power was very much affected by this state of affairs. Bismarck once said: "The stronghold of our industry is export. Any harm pressed upon it would involve all other industries in troubles which would no longer enable them to compete abroad." Foreign countries, indeed, did everything they could to weaken Germany's export industry; moreover, their trade policy was very changeable. Bismarck, in 1887, considered changing this state of affairs by stimulating the interest of agrarian countries to buy German industrial export goods. This could only be done by reducing agricultural duties in compensation, a bold step at a time when Prussian landlords held political power.

Bismarck's successor, von Caprivi, was courageous enough to tackle the problem. Germany's export industry should be enabled to obtain reductions of foreign import duties; and agreements as regards duties should be negotiated. This could be attained only through reductions of agrarian duties, which had been increased repeatedly within a short space of time. So the most important point of Caprivi's bill was the reduction of the agricultural duties from five marks to 3.50 marks.

It has been stated that the German economy at no time made more progress than in the period of the commercial treaties negotiated by Caprivi from 1892-1906 and also that German agriculture then experienced technical and organisational development.[44] Germany's protective policy was greatly influenced by other nations, such as the U.S.A. which never thought of changing its protectionist system. The Americans rather overtrumped with MacKinley's second tariff in 1897 which was called highly protectionist.

The attempts of great countries with large colonial possessions to give commercial preference to their colonies, such as were begun in England by J. Chamberlain or in France in 1892, compelled the continental competitors to show the greatest caution.[45]

The roots of all these attempts are to be found in a generally held view of this particular period, that commercial policy should be instrumental for a wider policy of imperialism. I shall go into this question in detail in the next section. The use of economic forces, such as commercial treaties, was one strong political means to attach other countries to their centre of power. " Protection for national resources and labour," once the great watchword of Friedrich List and part of the national power-policy, was a German conception widely accepted by the various imperialisms. The leaders of German policy were strong enough to make the State the cloak of these aims. In the general competition for great sovereign empires Germany took an inevitable part. In the shadow of this competition the Bülow tariff bill (decreed 1902) came into operation on January 1st, 1906. Some duties were greatly increased. Minimum-duties for cereals protected agriculture against the effects of commercial treaties. Wheat thus received a minimum duty of 5.50 marks, rye and oats 5.00 marks, malt barley 4.00 marks, and a certain maximum tariff was provided for in case international agreements were to fail. An elaborate tariff consisting of 946 headings with certain subheadings for commodities, thus comprising 5,400 designations was published. In spite of the "most-favoured-nation" clause which was still assumed as a basis, this highly specialised treaty tended to indicate that special agreements with separate countries had to be concluded. Subsequent negotiations led to treaties with Bulgaria, Belgium, Italy, Austria-Hungary, Rumania, Switzerland and Servia in 1906. Treaties with Sweden, Portugal and Japan followed later. The result of this trade system showed itself in increased figures of output and value and the welfare of the population appeared to be improved. It is true that German industry was restricted in certain relations by the tariff. But in spite of some transitory setbacks by the great crisis in the early years of the century, the rise of industry again continued.

Tariff agreements and the " most-favoured-nation " clause, were the two pillars of the German system of foreign trade policy. The " most-favoured-nation " scheme dominated relations with Denmark, Norway, Holland, France, Great Britain, Montenegro, Turkey; in Africa : Egypt, Ethoipia, Liberia, Morocco ; in Asia : British-India, Persia ; in America : the U.S.A., Mexico, Argentina, Bolivia, Chile, Ecuador, Paraguay, Venezuela. In some of the latter countries the system was valid only in part as also in Spain and certain Central American countries. The British colonies, except India, gave preference to imports from Great Britain; for the rest the " most-favoured-nation " clause was valid.[46]

It seems to be clear that the general tariff was instrumental in bringing about trade agreements or in changing or renewing the " most-favoured-nation " clause.

From the time of the Bülow tariff till the War the German trade balance showed the following figures (in millions of Marks) :

Year	Import	Export
1906	8,021.9	6,359.0
1910	8,934.1	7,574.7
1912	10,791.8	8,956.8
1913	10,870.3	10,196.5

The comparison between trade balance figures with countries bound to Germany only by tariff agreements and with the most favoured nations may be shown by the following statistics :

Years	1901	1904	1907	1910	1913
Import million Marks	2,138.5	2,410.2	3,164.2	3,282.8	3,593.8
% of total import	37.4	35.1	36.3	36.5	33.3
Export, million Marks	1,695.3	1,999.2	2,741.3	3,041.0	4,181.6
% of total export	37.6	37.6	40.0	39.0	41.4

The development of export absolutely or relatively is favourable to treaty policy. The trade balance of most favoured nations is shown by the following figures :

Years	1901	1904	1907	1910	1913
Import million Marks	3,181.1	3,957.2	4,975.9	4,786.9	6,005.0
% of total import	55.7	57.6	56.5	53.7	57.7
Export million Marks	2,507.8	2,935.5	3,641.1	3,948.7	5,165.9
% of total export	55.5	55.1	53.0	52.7	51.5[47]

Imports and exports of the most favoured nations exceeded those shown by the "tariff agreement" countries.[48] They show a considerable absolute increase; in the case of imports there is a relative increase, in the case of exports a relative decrease. Although Great Britain and America, throughout the whole period, exported goods worth 800 million marks more into Germany, yet their proportion decreases by about five per cent., which is a proof that Germany had penetrated further into the world markets. This point will be dealt with again later.

Germany's trade policy has so far been dealt with by considering certain decisive acts of legislation. Of the political significance of these something has now to be said.

It must be recalled that through the War of 1866 Prussia's supremacy in the union of the German peoples was definitely achieved. After 1871, two independent German empires stood abreast. Austria-Hungary was a great continental block but, compared to its extent, had a relatively small outlet in the Adriatic. But it was a ramshackle empire, held together with great difficulty; for its various parts were attracted by political and ethnological ties to its various surrounding neighbours. Irredentist movements spread for a long time. Every act of trade policy reflected these conditions. The Crown and religion were the cement of these mixtures of races, to which, however, the policy of conquest in the Balkans, Bosnia and Herzegowina added Mahomedan subjects. Some politicians in Germany as well as in Austria-Hungary put forward at various times a plan for a customs union between the two empires which would take certain neighbouring countries into its ambit. This Middle European Customs Union found many followers in the years between the seventies and the beginning of the century. In 1903 an association to promote this idea was established. The Great War produced a revival of this idea. No doubt, it was the tendency to a greater Germany in the middle of Europe. As such this idea has not lost its historical and economic significance even in our time. Bismarck objected to the Union because of the great disparity in economic development between the two main countries; for Austria would be the main beneficiary, while certain powerful German interests might suffer; political reasons also played their part. Thus, the trade agreements were a matter of great diplomacy as well as of commerce. One result is not without interest; German exports into Austria-Hungary from 1903-1912 rose from 649.3 to 1,036.3 and imports from 754.8 to 829.6 million marks despite mutually increased import duties according to the bill of 1906.

I turn to *France*. In 1913 France's share of Germany's trade balance was only one-seventeenth. Since the Treaty of Francfort (1871), Germany and France were linked in their trade policy, under " eternal " " most-favoured-nation " clause. As long as liberal treaties were valid, i.e., till 1879, France had some advantages from this clause whereas Germany, especially during the period of crisis, was flooded with French imports. Then Bismarck's autonomous policy repulsed French imports, whilst the Caprivi policy of tariff reductions made the French trade balance again favourable (1892). The French minimum tariff of this year was one of the causes of this. The Bülow tariff again repulsed France. Great trade relations were important in the conflict which subsequently arose. The standstill in the French population and in technical progress on the one hand, and Germany's impetuous advance to the world market on the other, were contributory factors to the antagonism.

German-*Russian* relations were characterised by Russia's high exports of agricultural produce and industrial raw material and by Germany's export of industrial commodities and her financing business, which, however, followed far behind that of France. But Russia was characteristically a debtor country, which at the same time shared greatly in the railway debt and loans to banks and industrial undertakings. As far as German-Russian trade balance is concerned, Germany's export to Russia was in 1894, 194.8; in 1904, 315.5; in 1913, 880.0; her imports from Russia were in 1894, 543.9; in 1904, 818.7; in 1913, 1,426.6 million marks.

Trade relations with the *U.S.A.* were the expression of a far-reaching dependence on certain goods which Germany urgently needed, such as cotton, copper, oil and foodstuffs. This dependence was aggravated by monopoly and the cornering of prices by American producers and business men. Increasingly the U.S.A. became not only the exporter of important raw materials but also of manufactured goods. Her ruthless trade policy has been mentioned already. Germany could only compensate for her enormously unfavourable trade balance (her imports from U.S.A. reached in 1913 1,000 million marks over Germany's exports into that country), by profits and dividends of capital enterprises, profits from her transport undertakings, transfers from German emigrants and travellers' expenses in Germany, etc. The great number of emigrants did not improve Germany's position in U.S.A.

The conflict between Great Britain and Germany, in so far as competition in foreign markets was concerned, was marked by a certain division of labour. Germany repulsed Great Britain step by step from certain European markets, leaving her the bulk of the overseas' markets in which she had some natural or traditional position of domination.

In this connection it is not without interest to survey Germany's exports into the various continents. In 1889 she imported 79.5 per cent. and in 1912 56.2 per cent. of all her imports from non-European countries, and exported in 1889 77.1 per cent. and in 1912 75.4 per cent of all her exports to non-European countries. The American imports and exports from total trade in the same two years were 15.6 per cent. and 27.0 per cent.; 18.9 per cent. and 16.7 per cent. From Asia Germany imported in 1912 9.4 per cent. and exported to Asia 4.8 per cent. (Sartorius).[49]

Where competition between England and Germany was conspicuous, the latter's position was marked by her considerable staple products whereas England saw herself involuntarily restricted to her quality products.

When the two countries, Germany (at this time the Customs Union) and Great Britain, concluded the trade treaty in 1865, which was based on the most favoured nation clause, Germany was a beginner as a large scale industrial producer and exporter. In 1897 under the auspices of Mr. Joseph Chamberlain's policy this treaty, which was valid for the whole British Empire, was terminated.

In these three decades the two countries showed different development. Free trade in England caused England's decline in agriculture. If industry first profited from this system, so its influence gradually receded behind trade and finance. It is true, there were still progressive figures of increase, but England's share in the world trade receded from 24 per cent. in 1867-68 to 18 per cent. in 1893, and her export of coals, which amounted in 1868 to 53.6 per cent. of the world production, diminished in 1893 to 35 per cent., whereas cotton, of which England manufactured 50 per cent. of world production in 1860-1861, decreased to about 30 per cent. in 1895. U.S.A. and Germany were the most pertinacious competitors of England (Sartorius)[50]. Especially in other markets their competition clashed violently with each other. Iron and steel, constructional and other work of the engineering trade, ships, cables, textile manufactures, glass, and paper, were the main commodities involved in the struggle.

As far as the mutual exchange of trade between the two countries was concerned, there a strong basis of understanding could have existed, because Germany was finally the best customer of England and her empire. From 1909 to 1912 British exports to Germany increased from 1,505 million marks to 2,000.5 million marks, whereas the German export to Britain and her overseas possession increased from 1,255.3 million marks to 1,510 million marks. Germany overcame this passivity of her trade balance through financial and transport achievements. These included the progress of the German mercantile marine. In 1911 5,058 British ships (comprising 5.79 million register tons) landed in German seaports, whereas 5,357 German ships (comprising 7,01 million register tons) arrived in the British Isles.[51]

Whereas Germany, since the beginning of the century up to the world War, could easily absorb an increase of her population of more than eight million inhabitants, and showed very low figures of emigration, Great Britain's emigrants rose at this time to about half-a-million of her inhabitants yearly. It is known that among these emigrants the number of industrial workers belonging to certain branches endangered by foreign competition was very high, especially as far as unskilled labour was concerned.

(b) World and Colonial Policy
§1 General

The penetration of German industry and transport in European and overseas countries through the banks helped greatly to obtain a favourable balance of payments, since the trade balance with some great countries was unfavourable. During the second half of the last century the idea of intensifying foreign trade relations was everywhere revived; there is no need to give further reasons for such activities by Germany. An active colonial policy, a policy of acquiring influence in less developed countries was begun.

As to colonial policy, I briefly state here that since 1884 Germany acquired colonies in Africa and in certain South Sea Islands of Australasia. When the Great War broke out Germany's colonies covered 2.9 million square kilometres or six times the area of the homeland. The white population amounted to 24,389 people, whereas the coloured people numbered approximately twelve million.

The capital invested in companies in German colonies was in 1896 62 million, in 1904 185 million, and in 1912 505 million Marks. The length of railway tracks amounted in 1913 to 4,176 kilometres. The export of cotton from German East Africa and Togoland was in 1913 2,695 tons (= roughly three million Marks). Rubber exported from German East Africa, the Cameroons and Togoland amounted in 1912 to 4,180 tons (=28.2 million Marks). The output and value of sisal hemp from German East Africa were in 1913 approximately 21,000 tons and 10.7 million Marks respectively. Oil products from various colonies were in 1912 roughly 780,000 tons (=roughly 25 million Marks). Exports of timber and tanning products in 1913 had a value of 6.5 million Marks; coffee and cocoa export reached approximately two million and six million Marks respectively. Copper export amounted in 1913 to 47,345 tons (=7.7 million Marks); diamond exports in 1912 from South-West Africa, 30.4 million Marks. The figures of trade between Germany and her colonies run as follows: German Total Import in 1913, 10,800 million Marks; Import from German Colonies, 52.8 million Marks. German Total Export in 1913 amounted to 10,100 million Marks; Export from German Colonies, 54.6 million Marks. The import into Germany in 1913 amounted from German East Africa 14.6, Cameroon 13.1, Togoland 7.3, German South-West Africa 7.5, New Guinea 7.0 and Samoa 3.3 million Marks, whereas Germany exported to German East Africa 16.5, Cameroon 12.0, Togoland 2.6, German South Africa 20.9, New Guinea 1.9, and Samoa 0.6 million Marks. If the share of products gained in her colonies was still very small in comparison to the total amount, it was still steadily progressing. In 1897 Germany established a naval base at Shantung in China. This was subsequently fortified and colonised.

Moreover, Germany was deeply interested in a policy for the building of railways, the colonisation and the expansion of trade in Turkey. This was part of an extensive and far-reaching plan, a plank in the platform of the propagandists of a greater Germany: The Deutsche Bank especially developed in this region great activities. There is no need to discuss this so-called " imperialist " policy further. It is well-known that the division of some Near-East countries into power spheres was under consideration by Great Britain, Russia and Germany, just when the Great War broke out. The rapid growth of the Navy and the mercantile marine is another aspect of the imperialist tendencies general among all great Powers at this time.

§2 *German Banking Policy in foreign Countries*

Shortly before the Great War, Germany possessed deposits abroad amounting to approximately £1,000 millions,[52] but this sum was small compared with British foreign investments of which, for instance, railways in the Argentine amounted to £200 millions, while those in railways and mining in South America were only estimated at £375 millions. Figures given of the total foreign investments show for Great Britain £3,500 millions and for France £1,750 millions.[53]

The limited amount of German capital did not allow the investment of such vast amounts all over the world. The urgent needs of home industry took premier place. As Helfferich stated, investments in foreign countries changed according to the greater demand in home industry. The ratio between German and foreign investments was 2 to 1 in the period 1886 to 1890 while it was 9 to 1 between 1906 and 1910.[54]

But before giving the different reasons why and how German resources available for foreign purposes were distributed, I must mention some brief historical facts. It was at the end of the 'eighties that a new period of issuing first set in; it followed the period of stagnation which was accompanied by a low rate of interest and a conversion of State loans. As it is sometimes stated, what other nations did not take on the revived foreign market, German banks acquired. Their quota available for this business at this time could only be small. The State loans of European and certain American countries of partly obscure character played a great part during this phase. The blessing of Caprivi's commercial treaties showed itself in an unprecedented rise of industry. Joint Stock banks shared greatly in these activities. Their strength increased when certain private banking undertakings collapsed at the beginning of the nineties. The attitude of the public now changed, and its deposits were placed with the big banks which then assumed a leading role in the administration of the greater capital to be invested in stocks and shares through their agency.

Very early in their history German Big Banks began to invest abroad. The Diskonto-Gesellschaft, even from the middle of the last century, stressed such an activity which it shared above all with the Deutsche Bank. Already in 1854, the Darmstaedter Bank shared in the ownership of a New York house and, for instance, in 1871 it became instrumental in the establishment of the Amsterdamer Bank. Middle and East Europe were the natural fields for German investment. Germany never could rival the leading capital lenders in the West. Her banking not being of the rentier-investor kind worked primarily as an instrument for her industry. Certain outstanding events, at times, gave a greater impetus to the business, as, for instance, when on the nationalisation of the German Railway system, a large amount of investors' capital was set free. Again on another occasion the German Stock Exchange Bill of 1896 was directed against the markets in futures. Speculation, hampered in its activities, turned to the spot and to foreign markets. The bill was the outcome of the hostile attitude of the general public towards the stock exchange and banking, but achieved the exact opposite of its promoter's wishes. The speculator, now pushed to the spot market, which demanded much greater capital than the market in futures, applied for credit to the Big Banks, which thus became the money lenders of an extended speculation in stocks and shares. This risky business ultimately proved very remunerative for the banks. The former speculator in futures was always able to carry through the whole business by a contrary transaction of the same date ; he risked only the difference of the rate. The same commodity at the date of liquidation changed hands frequently. Thus an enormous turn-over could be carried on relatively small capital. The market in cash caused by the bill of 1896, however, needed ampler amounts of capital, which could only be offered by the big banks, which inspired by this new chance of profitmaking had no objection to lending. The share capital of all the German banks increased between 1890 and 1901 from 1,573 to 2,792 million Marks.[55] This new kind of banking, with the greatly strengthened issuing activities, brought about a new era of company-promotion.

As far as big banks were concerned, the Deutsche Bank established a system of branches abroad. Shortly after its establishment this great institution included in its programme an attempt at international business. Credits in advance for exporters of German goods and foreign bills for importers of raw and other material without the interference of foreign banks were stated as some of its principles. A foreign bill market, the instrument of the financing business of exports and imports of raw material, was thus intended. There was a certain success in popularizing the market in bills drawn in German Marks, especially in Russia and South American countries. Branches in the Far East which were first established proved unsuccessful, but the " Deutsche Bank, London Agency," established 1873 in London, became a great success. Dresdner Bank and Diskonto-Gesellschaft followed its example, and in 1895 and 1899 respectively, by the establishment of branches in London, it became evident that German investors avoided foreign bank influences. Moreover, the German banks saw in London the centre of gravity of world-trade, political neutrality and stability of currency. The Deutsche Bank likewise established branches in Belgium and Turkey, all mainly instruments of their big industrial interests.

I do not wish to enumerate all the independent banks established by Germany's big banks abroad. In addition to the already mentioned activities of certain Berlin banks, the Berliner Handelsgesellschaft, a typical instrument of industrial enterprise, the Nationalbank fuer Deutschland, the v.d. Heydtbank, whose activities took place between the two wars which Germany fought, must be mentioned. The Balkans, Turkey, the Far East, and South America joined in Germany's business abroad which was at first carried out mainly with her neighbouring States.

Great private banks, also carrying out various banking functions abroad, had their origin in Germany, some of them moving their headquarters to foreign countries. Such houses existed in London, Paris and elsewhere. The house of Mendelsohn in Berlin became a great creditor for Russia, and bankers from other places, principally from Francfort and its neighbourhood, spread over the whole world, finally establishing their headquarters in various foreign countries. Speyer-Elissen, Hallgarten, Kuhn Loeb und Co., Warburg, Ladenburg Thalmann und Co. may here be mentioned. These institutions became agents for the whole credit and payment traffic of German trade, because foreign legislation prevented the direct activity of branches of banks.

Preoccupation with the foreign interests of German industry remained one of their main features. There is no need to dwell on the fact that an increase of investment capital which was not sufficiently available was important for these banking activities. Likewise the finding and keeping of foreign markets in all ways possible for export industries was the decisive factor in this banking abroad.

As independent institutions, the big German banks, described as Germany's main industrial financiers, had for their own sake to spread over the whole world the risk which was always great, owing to the internal methods of financing and banking in the homeland. At the same time, new business abroad in connection with export activities attached to industry or provisioning of raw material, widened the field of banking. Other activities which helped to open up new countries such as the building of railways, harbours and bridges, provision of electricity, oil, public utilities, and the creation and preparation of agricultural areas and other kinds of colonisation work in relation to seaports and transport, were tasks which German banks or their auxiliary branches performed abroad. At the same time the growing population of these regions became increasingly important customers.

No doubt, material reasons outgrew themselves and so indirectly set the pace for other, especially political, tasks. Like other countries, Germany possessed in her banking institutions an instrument willing to serve general political purposes. So Schulze-Gaevernitz, whose description of banking I followed in this chapter, introduced a paragraph in his book with the words " export of capital is instrumental for the purposes of foreign politics. The success of either of these endeavours, capital investment abroad and foreign policy, is mutually dependent." Thus, this chapter again deals with the wider aspects of German foreign and power policy.

(3) Social Policy

Social policy not only from the Wilhelmian period, but also up to the present time, is best described as a policy of social reform. There is no upheaval here, breaking the capitalist system and suddenly establishing something quite new. If we compare the beginning and the end of the period with which we are concerned, there is certainly evident an ascent from primitive and inhuman social methods to more humanitarian ones. And yet these problems can hardly go beyond the framework of the political and economic constitution to which they are submitted. And then again, the social question was not the primary concern; as frequently shown, British and German industry here disclose remarkable difference. As Miss Warriner[56] says, " discussion of British industrial affairs usually begins and ends with the relations of capital and labour, and in Germany that has never been a primary problem; labour costs have never been so important as costs of capital and transport . . . "

The root of all the social problems of our time lies in the fact that the personal factor of production is the working capacity of a human being. This factor, however, appears in the books of capitalist enterprise as costs under the title " expenditure for wages and salaries." The close alliance between human fate and economic problems which we find in the labour market, is nowhere more obvious than in the debate, so passionately argued, on the relation between price and wage. For centuries these things were considered merely matters of trade, belonging to the private enterprise. During the liberal period price was considered a medium to enlarge markets; wages as part of costs had to be kept as low as possible while hours must be as long as possible. Thus, interference with the free exchange of labour by the State or by unions of workers was condemned as an offence against a sacred theory. Certainly the Wilhelmian State showed an enormous advance on the " Police " State of a generation ago. Social problems were, during the latter, one of the obligations of the State, which, anxious to keep law and order, was merely interested in the care of the poor.

Yet the State, the main agent of society in the carrying out of social policy, was supported by capitalist forces and reciprocally these forces were supported by the State. But this State by degrees became more socially minded, as its socio-political acts proved. Following a regime which drew its strength from landed proprietors and a military and bureaucratic class, industrialists and business men appear as a new active force; William II's era marked the culmination of this change. Doubtless, through it, a system of great economic power and potential assets for the country emerged, but a certain snobbism came into the foreground. The new elements of finance capitalism, great and small industrialists, business men, bankers, and an army of higher officials of a bureaucratised trade, as well as the rapidly increasing number of State servants, came from ascending social classes. These new elements were assimilated to the former dominating group only as far as politics were concerned; they were not fundamentally influenced by its ethical values and culture. One must, however, emphasise that these cultural elements, including religious ones, were at this time themselves in a marked stage of decline.

No wonder that the strongly materialist note of the newcomer strengthened the materialist tendencies already in existence among the former ruling classes. Still the spirit which animated even the excellent work of social legislation in the 'eighties was far less the expression of an intrinsic understanding of humanitarian obligations towards one's neighbour, whether he were workman or poor man, than a form of political opportunism. The State thought itself compelled to ally itself with a new force in order to have a freer hand for what it believed to be its main political aims. It was a marriage prompted by reason. This new combination was the outcome of the impetuous march of the Third Estate which at this phase was vigorously coming to the fore and could no longer be kept back. This new power in the State was best counterbalanced by certain sedatives. The traditional wisdom of Prussian statesmen that met a problem—which they could not hinder—by a constructive practical policy and the masters of mass-organisation again set up a new link in the chain of governmental care. I recall here what I said about Bismarck's Social and Economic Policy (pp. 68-69). Once this work was vigorously taken in hand, it developed into a great achievement of social progress. It began a quarter of a century before Mr. Lloyd George was to follow in the same path and, at least ten years before Mr. Joseph Chamberlain boldly drew up schemes for social legislation. It was first reserved to the Weimar Reich to widen the social trusteeship of the State by enactments of outstanding significance. This I say without wishing to do injustice to the accomplishments of the previous forty years. I do not wish in this section to draw attention to mercantilist tendencies of the State which, by way of State capitalism, led to socialisation. I shall only deal with direct measures of social policy.

We must briefly survey the distribution of incomes in the State, as this distribution is so intimately linked up with the capitalist system. We are handicapped by the inadequacy of statistical data on this subject but an examination is necessary for the exact understanding of the social welfare of the individuals living under this economic constitution. Furthermore, this special analysis allows us to draw conclusions as to the limits of socio-political measures in a still capitalist community. Sombart[57] cautiously draws some interesting conclusions when he examines German conditions throughout the last century. In general he states " the change in the distribution of income during the 19th century is not very remarkable from the point of view of the increase of wealth, which is assumed to be several times greater than the increase in the population—millionaires or millionaire-aspirants were bred in greater numbers. Formerly, only a few of this type were to be found. Moreover, the lowest classes of income disappeared and the slums of society were abolished. There resulted a greater differentiation between the income classes in comparison with those of a hundred or fifty years previously. The disparity between the poorest and the richest people appears greater, not because the poorest became poorer (in reality they were less poor), but because the richest increased their properties much more quickly " . . ." in 1900 only 6.1 per cent. of the Prussian population received an income of more than 3,000 Marks (=£150 p.a.*), whereas not even 1.0 per cent. received more than 9,500 Marks (=£475 p.a.)." In principle these figures of taxable income remained the same before and after the War. In 1913 only 5.4 per cent. of people whose incomes were taxed had more than 3,000 Marks ; they did not possess one-third of the total income of the population (31.9 per cent.). After the War new groups of incomes were created so that statistics before and after the War are not comparable with each other. But figures show that in 1926 2.9 per cent. of all people whose incomes were taxed had more than one-fifth of the income of the people (21.7 per cent.). Only 1.6 per cent. of all people paying income tax in 1913 received more than 6,000 Marks (=£300), 21.7 per cent. of the total income. In 1926 only 0.9 per cent. of all people paying income tax had an income of over 9,000 RM (£450), their share of the total income of the population was 12.8 per cent. In 1913 the average income was 1,530 Marks (=£76 10s. 0d.), in 1926 1,440 Marks (=£72).

C. Landauer[58] who quoted these figures gives some very reasonable interpretations of them. Even if necessary corrections could be made, the result is quite clear ; only a very small proportion of the population which enjoys a life of a certain modest comfort, and the biggest proportion of the income of the population belongs, even to-day, to the lower groups which are comparably greater in number than the others. Even a complete levelling of all income could not enable the lower groups to enjoy much more than a typical proletarian standard of life. But—in the case of this levelling—even the skilled workman would run the risk of a considerable decrease in his standard of life. Evidently there is not much to be got from the top of the income pyramid. Landauer continues by stating that the levelling of money incomes corresponds exactly to a certain structure of production. By lowering luxury-production in a wider sense not much was to be gained for mass production. The total picture

* Pre-War par.

would not be very much changed even by a complete levelling of income.[59] The approximately twenty million people included in the income class below 1,200 Marks (=£60 p.a.) would—with their large families—live mainly on the same goods which they consume at present. There is no need to give more detail of Landauer's analysis which concludes that general equality of income could not effect any changes in the process of economics "neither in an exchange economy nor in a planned one." No order of economics which wants to satisfy "productivity" (which, according to this author, is the only measuring rod of economy) can ever completely level incomes into an average. So far Landauer; but there may be planned economics in which productivity (which he evidently thought was built up on individual processes similar to the exchange economy) may follow other lines. There may be attempts to attain a productvity of the whole community and to distribute the social dividend by an authoritative regimentation. Still, living under a capitalist system, even if strongly restricted, Landauer's conclusions are valid. That shows that all socio-political measures in the framework of the existing economic order are limited. Assuming this, the social measures which Germany carried through were, no doubt, the most developed in a non-socialist world.

The Social Insurance Acts inaugurated in 1881 occupied the Legislature for nearly three decades. They mainly comprised insurances against accident, old age, disablement (invalidity) and sickness. The work of social insurance legislation was generally appreciated in Germany. As to the costs of contributions, employers paid the major part of accident insurance. Two-thirds of the cost of sickness insurance fell upon the worker, one-third upon the employer, whereas in the cost of disablement and old age insurance, both parties shared in equal proportions, while the Reich contributed £2 10s. 0d. p.a. to every pension granted. A short survey illuminates the significance of social insurance. In 1913 workers were insured against sickness to the amount of £14,500,000, whereas both parties paid £23.1 millions, equal to 31/6d. per member p.a. The amount given to the members in benefit of all kinds amounted to £21,500,000, of which £8,900,000 represented sickness pay. Workers (including agricultural) who paid insurance against accident in 1913 paid £25,800,000; contributions of employers were £9,700,000, and the value of the compensation (mainly in the form of pension) and benefits awarded to the victims of accidents or their dependents, £7,900,000. Workpeople insured against disablement and old age paid £16,200,000; the amount of the contributions paid in moieties by the employers and the workpeople was £14,447,600, and the amount awarded in pensions and other benefits was £10,400,000. Average pensions granted were: for disablement, £9 15s. 0d.; and for old age, £8 7s. 0d.; for widows and widowers, £3 18s. 0d.; for orphans, £4. In the case of disablement and old age, the Imperial Government contributed £2 10s. 0d. At the beginning of 1915 nearly a million and a quarter pensions were being paid, whereas those of the year 1914 amounted to 193,000.[60]

While Bismarck was successful in social insurance[61] he was not favourably inclined towards protective legislation for the workers ; by tradition he appreciated the " master in one's own house " outlook and was influenced by his careful efforts not to disturb the export interests of the industry. So, during this period, the State was neither able nor ready to improve the protection of women and children and to bring about " Sunday rest." The after-effects of the law against socialists which, since his decree of 1878 had to be renewed periodically, intensified still further the clash between capital and labour. Trade unions, even their " Christian " divisions, were faced with such chicanery and brutality that they had to dissolve and did not reappear until the end of the 'eighties, when they were supported by men like Professor Hitze, a parliamentarian of the Roman Catholic Party. Still, in 1886, the decree of the reactionary Prussian Minister, von Puttkamer, tried to destroy the labour movements by submitting strikes to the anti-socialist law. It is well-known that Bismarck's dismissal was to a certain extent due to his attitude to the labour problem. The young emperor, although his tendencies changed later in his reign, was, during his early years, a fervent supporter of social policy, and was strongly opposed to repressions and inclined to more positive social work. He still cherished the dream of creating a " Social Monarchy." The problem of the protection of the worker, hitherto neglected, inspired him to interfere personally. The Prussian Deputy Premier and Secretary of the Home Office of the Reich at the time, Boetticher, supported him. This Bismarck resented as disloyal to him as Chancellor of the Reich. Bismarck's Anti-Socialist Law (not being renewed by Parliament) receded ingloriously into the background. The new Reichstag of 1890 saw twice the former number of Socialist voters. Since 1887 they had increased to 1.4 millions. Shortly before the election in 1890, William II enacted the so-called February decrees, one of which bore the strong influence of Bismarck. With it he wished to divert the Emperor from active social undertakings, and so he launched the International Conference of Workmen's Protection with the intention of showing that the standard was higher in Germany than in other countries. The conference took place in March, 1890, in Berlin. The new Minister of the Prussian Ministry of Commerce, von Berlepsch, who had hitherto prepared all the splendid social legislative work, became its president. No doubt, this man belonged to the best type of leading official, who understood the essence of the labour problem and saw in the humanitarian State and its social trusteeship towards labour and the poor the great ideal of public leadership and administration. The effects of the Conference did not follow immediately, but they were significant. The second decree, drafted under the Secretary of State, Boetticher, whom Bismarck suspected as his rival, did not receive the Chancellor's official countersignature. This decree shows Boetticher also as the type of official of the humanitarian State. The significance of Berlepsch's and Boetticher's activities increases when viewed against a background of a reactionary anti-labour minded officialdom and all the propertied classes and their paid representatives in the various parliaments of the Reich and the federal States. The main idea of Boetticher's decree was the modernisation of the Prussian Industrial Code which would then be transferred to the entire Empire as an Imperial Law. The State assumed its task of supervising hours of work and kind of work in the interests of the health, morality and economic needs of the workers. Methods of representation of workers to settle disputes between employer and employees were already provided. This was almost a revolutionary move in comparison with former custom. It was a disadvantage that the Prussian *Staatsrat*, a council of generals and great industrialists and a few intimidated workmen had to prepare the law.[62] It is not without interest to record that there were among them splendid characters, such as the Undersecretary of the State, von Rottenburg, and Lohmann and others, who were convinced supporters of the ideal of the State as social trustee. They fought for this ideal even at a time when William II had lost his interest in labour. In 1891 the Industrial Code, following the conclusion of the International Workers' Protection Conference, became an Imperial Law.

Among the main items of the new law were a Sunday rest of 24 hours in industry, and a maximum occupation of 5 hours work in certain trades according to local regulations; a tightening up of truck acts and protection of workers' wages; conditions for healthier working places which could be enlarged by the *Bundesrat* (Federal Council) for special trades; protection for women and children, the 11-hour day for women, care for women in labour, the 10-hours day for juveniles, and a strict prohibition of child-labour under 14 years of age, and of night-work for women and children, and regulations for working intervals. The competence of inspectors of factories was widely extended. Before this law came into operation, a law court to deal with trade cases was the first stage of arbitrational work between employers and employees (1890).

Moreover, at this period private intellectual and clerical forces organised themselves to support the great social work. The *Verein für Sozialpolitik*, already in existence since 1872, was widely engaged in this matter. In 1890 the Evangelical Social Congress was founded. In 1897, one of the founders, Pastor Stoecker, left it to form his own ecclesiastical social conference. Later followed the Evangelical Workers Union (Pastor Weber) and the National Socialists of Pastor Naumann and a social democrat, Pastor Goehre (who it is interesting to note, was once Undersecretary of the War Office during the Weimar Reich). There is no need to add that most of the leading members of these associations were representatives of the humanitarian State, some of them later on inclined to combine this ideal with the Prussian militarist viewpoint.

The Roman Catholic Church spread a network of social institutions over the community and some outstanding work was done by individual clergymen and also laymen. The Peoples Union of the Roman Catholic Germany was the corresponding foundation.

The Social Democratic Party, after the anti-socialist law became invalid, did not recognise the striking successes of social reform (Heyde). The attitude of the party which distrusted the Emperor, who was continually making disparaging utterance against labour and the socialist party, stressed far-reaching political and economico-political ideas. The party, deriving its inspirations from Marxian creeds, showed in 1891 at a party meeting in Erfurt two sharply opposed tendencies; a radical one, which refused to collaborate with the other, and propagated all extreme claims; and an opportunist wing which wanted influence in State affairs through a close collaboration. Their evolutionary exponents (von Vollmar, Bernstein, David) clashed frequently with the revolutionary supporters. A group of compromisers, consisting of the most influential leaders, among whom were Bebel and Liebknecht, gravitated gradually from the left to the right wing which was strongly under trade unionist influence. Trade unions at this time made slow progress, being then and later to a certain extent in rivalry with the party members. The more evolutionary revisionists, who were mainly intellectuals, had no contact with the unionists, who came from the ranks of the workers. One of their groups, the " Christians," founded in 1894, comprising Evangelicals as well as Catholics, declined to follow Social Democratic principles as did the democratic trade unions following their founders, Hirsch and Duncker. Certain other organisations of commercial officials and some few of Government officials were established at this time. The *" Deutschnationaler Handlungsgehilfen Verband "* survived from 1893 until in recent times trade unions and similar organisations were dissolved. No doubt, trade unionist influence was not even strong. It was a later time which gave trade unionists a predominant influence, first of all in the Social Democratic Party.

A few figures show the growth of membership of trade unions:

MEMBERSHIP IN 1,000's.

Type of Union	1891	1912
Socialist	277.6	2,553.1
Christian	65.6	109.2
Hirsch-Duncker		814.7
Yellow		231.0
Total	343.2	4,052.0
Confessional: Protestant and Roman Catholic		765.0
Total		4,817.9 [63]

"Yellow" or "Pacific" meant organisations which were promoted and subsidised by the employers. In the Rhineland and Westphalia there was a significant special group formed by Poles who, in spite of being Roman Catholics, showed a greater social affinity to the Social Democrats.

The whole movement for social reform suffered great setbacks from the counter-attacks of big industry, which were mainly directed against trade unions (Heyde). Rhenish-Westphalian industrialists, of whom Emil Kirdorf was very successful in organising the counter movement, and the Saar industrialist, von Stumm-Halbach, were in the autocratic forefront of the masters of heavy industry. The socially-minded professors of economics and social science mainly fought in the framework of the *Verein fuer Sozial Politik*, which led to their being nicknamed " *Kathedersozialists* " by the reactionaries. But these tendencies against bureaucracy and in industry were so small that the reactionary movement became dominant. This was so strong that after 1894, when the French President, Carnot was murdered by an anarchist, it closed its ranks against organised labour, in order to create an exceptional bill (*Umsturzvorlage*—bill against revolution). Chancellor von Caprivi, who did not follow the spokesman of the reactionary group, the Prussian Premier, Graf Eulenburg, fell from power. Caprivi's successor, Prinz Hohenlohe, presented the bill to the Reichstag which rejected it. The bitter fight greatly alienated the Kaiser from the Labour Group and Party, against which he publicly raged. Minister von Berlepsch, the protagonist of the social reform, was dismissed in 1896. In 1897 von Boetticher followed. The group of industrialists through their various instruments was keener than ever in influencing the Kaiser against organised labour. The new socially reactionary era was brought about by the man who was soon to become one of the foremost social reformers, Count Posadowsky, Boetticher's successor (Heyde). He still combined in the Imperial Home Office many functions to which economics and social policies belonged. A new bill, which again tried to counteract some achievements of the social reform, received the name " *Zuchthausvorlage*," because, as personally announced by William II, it threatened all strike agitators with penal servitude. The bill failed to pass Parliament, but circumstances revealed some embarrassing facts for Graf Posadowsky. It became clear that the government of the Reich had accepted 12,000 Marks from heavy industry for propagating the bill by leaflets, etc. It is true, the greatest party in the Reichstag, as well as the greatest representative body of labour (1898, 2.1 ; 1903, three million votes—or 81 members in the Reichstag—every member of which was stamped as an outcast) had no say and were prevented from any positive collaboration. During the first five years the party met in an atmosphere of oppression and was menaced by exceptional laws against it. The party shared this treatment with the trade unions which in its socialist sector grew at this time to approximately 1.9 millions and the " Christians " to 274,000 members. The latter objected to the strike as an economico-political instrument (Heyde).

Almost all the officials of the great German Reich, at the moment when industry reached its highest peak, were strongly opposed to settling seriously the problem of capital and labour. There seemed to be no understanding of this vital problem which might have led to the passing of a law of association and a law governing strikes and lockouts. The socialist party with a negative and defensive policy offered no ideas for a constructive policy. A small group of intellectuals who were not Social Democrats fought against insurmountable difficulties. At first Posadowsky showed enmity towards them, but they were to become later his strongest supporters. They had to face the fact that they were considered as outcasts, and yet they formed the nucleus of that body which later brought about the acts for the protection of the worker. The " *Soziale Praxis* " founded in 1892 by Dr. Heinrich Braun, continued in 1895 by Professor Jastrow, and in 1897 by Professor Franke, was the periodical which dealt with the foremost problems. A group developed, to which v. Berlepsch, v. Rottenburg, a very small number of professors, such as *Kathedersozialists* and other intellectuals, belonged. This, after the establishment of the International Union for Legal Protection of the Worker (founded at the time of the World Exhibition in Paris in 1900) established a German branch, the " *Gesellschaft für Soziale Reform*," in 1901. It lasted for about 15 years till the socialist party and the socialist trade unions could be persuaded to collaborate with these elements which really prepared social legislative work. After certain improvements in the social insurance legislation had been brought about, Posadowsky grew to feel a very deep understanding of the rights of the personality of the worker which was expressed in the spirit which the totally revised Code of Industry showed. Codes for the commercial employees, technicians, sailors and a host of smaller groups in section after section of industry, were worked out. In 1903 there came the law for the protection of children which, to a certain degree, also tackled the problems of homework. Altogether during his more than 10 years of social service, Posadowsky proved a sincere and very able representative of the leading bureaucracy who intimately understood the great problems of the humanitarian State. Buelow's chancellorship followed in which Bethmann-Hollweg succeeded Posadowsky as Home Secretary. In this and the following period in which Bethmann became Chancellor, and Clemens Delbrueck, Home Secretary, there were promoted some important acts of social legislation, such as the new law of association, the collection of all insurance laws into an Imperial Insurance, a house-workers law, control of agents of labour exchange, facilitation of previous restrictions in trade-competition and promulgation of extension classes (Heyde).

Shortly before the War broke out, there was a sinister reaction against these attempts at social reform and against the freedom of the workers movement, especially against their organisations.

A certain weariness towards social reform, partly an outcome of terrorist acts among strikers and partly due to the above-mentioned propaganda was significant in middle-class Germany. But the political as well as the trade unionist movement was as strong as ever. In the election to the Reichstag in 1912 there were $4\frac{1}{2}$ million Social Democratic voters and 110 members. The socialist trade unions counted over 2 million members. Just before the War, no doubt, a tense atmosphere prevailed.

Trade unionism during approximately two decades before the Great War became a microcosm in itself, a great contrast to its British sister organisations from which the whole movement had once originated. The same spirit of militarist organisation underlay the Social Democratic Party as well as the trade unions. There was a head with a departmental organisation and headquarters which centralised the whole army of trade unionists in certain large towns, and again central offices of subordinated federations controlled masses of well-disciplined men and women, whose activities worked like clockwork. Central as well as subcentral provincial offices worked in combination. These included individual unions, certain enquiry agencies, labour registries, reading rooms and libraries, lodging houses, restaurants, etc. Every unit obeyed a secretary, a man of a certain military stamp. The whole represented an instrument which was likewise trained in attack and defence, in strikes and lockouts, marshalled in orderly ranks when marching for propaganda or any other purpose commanded by the headquarters. A spirit of order seemed the outstanding characteristic of the German worker. He received the best available elementary education, which was continued in extension classes and in the military service. Employers praised it very much; for they stated that this training made men efficient as workers, since they learned obedience, discipline and regular habits, and it was pointed out that as a result they were more alert, quicker in the uptake, smarter in every way.[64] On the other hand, in spite of exceptions, the average worker liked his service as a private soldier, which extended to two years in the infantry and three in the cavalry. German workers, gifted with a strong solidarity feeling, liked to show it in a military manner. Professor Robert Michels[65] once said : " Spontaneously with the proletario-socialist philosophy grew in a completely apodictic manner the claim of class solidarity as an ethical postulate. The law of duty ran : the individual must be subordinated under the whole of the workmen, whether it be those of a factory or another actual unit . . . " " The strikebreaker thus became the most contemptible among the workers, following the moral code . . . " The military predisposition of the German worker gave his struggles occasionally a characteristic note. Certainly the present National-Socialist government with its strong military and police forces benefited from the German worker's peculiarities. As long as the dictating forces are strong and use their power ruthlessly, there will be an ordered army, but the everlasting latent forces may use the same methods of military mass organisations in other directions. History will show whether this one-time strongest feeling of the worker, his class feeling, ceased to exist and with it what Michels calls "the postulate of self-determination."

Tidiness and cleanliness were the outstanding characteristics of the German working class. The German worker's wife was generally the typical German housewife whose domestic virtues covered a wide field. Wherever possible, vegetable gardens and the keeping of small domestic animals were encouraged. Factories which provided houses with small stables and gardens were very wise in doing so. After the War, public building societies were anxious to create an atmosphere of semi-town and agricultural life. The system of allotment gardens grew at a rapid rate from the beginning of the century. In the period between the two wars which Germany fought, the conditions of the labouring classes were in a transitional stage; after years of bitter experience there followed a period of undeniable well-being which helped to wipe out Proletarianism and made the worker a kind of petit bourgeois. When trade unions became at times dominant in labour politics this characteristic was conspicuous. Working-class districts in the German industrial areas presented a very different appearance from those of Britain. These differences sprang not only from the material side but also from differences in mind and character. Since the separation of the left socialist wing took place, the Social Democratic party took on more and more bourgeois features. The proletarian type of slum or the tenements such as called " *Mietskaserne* "—workers' barracks— lacking in elementary hygienic provisions, were steadily disappearing. More (as regards social policy) has to be said about the Weimar Reich's achievements later.

B. WAR-TIME ECONOMY

During the War all the belligerent countries adopted similar economic systems. The normal supply of industrial goods and foodstuffs, as regulated by the world market, was interrupted. In addition, there was a preponderance of such goods as are only required in war time, such as war goods proper and substitutes for those goods which were no longer available. But there were differences between countries which were cut off from regular supplies and those which were still able to import most of their requirements for the conduct of war and for domestic consumption. In this way Germany's economic system differed from that of the other nations because the country was a besieged fortress and soon had to face the issue of an enforced self-sufficiency. If the war should be prolonged by other methods even after the declaration of peace, then this self-sufficiency might still survive if the country, with its small capital resources, did not want to be economically or politically dependent upon other countries. On the other hand, if the country could return after the war to its place in the world market system, then self-sufficiency might pass away more or less completely.

Germany's trend from 1914 to the present day is governed by this struggle as of a besieged fortress. Self-sufficiency, therefore, as an emergency measure, remained in the forefront, except during the boom of 1924-29, when imports were enormously swollen by extravagant borrowing. Given time, every economic policy, including that of self-sufficiency, will establish forms of its own, particularly if other countries adopt a similar scheme and so give the opportunity of exchanging experiences. It is for the historian to reveal that the economic system of the War was not only significant as the outcome of a temporary event, the War, but that it developed into a scheme in and for itself. The free market economy, so far as it existed before the War, changed to a large degree into a planned economy such as had formerly existed only in certain countries and there to a lesser degree. The need to make ends meet with scanty means, which was mainly the cause of former planned systems, now appears in modified forms. The economic system of the War not only becomes a stage in the trend of an economic system dominated by planning, especially through self-sufficiency, but it appears as a new type of socialist economy. Not laisser-faire but conscious direction by Society or by the State regulates the exchange of goods and services under a general plan and is influenced by motives of national interest and national efficiency. The forms of organisation formerly used as making for a planned efficient economy now become transferred and inserted into the new system: the guild, the cartel and other forms of combined action appear in a new guise. They develop to organs of Public Administration.

The Prussian War Ministry, the official representative of the national German army, at the moment the War broke out, turned to a man who knew much about economic problems and was known to be a patriot and to have a feeling for the social needs of the community. This was Walther Rathenau, who was officially appointed organiser of German trade and industry at the outset of the War. His appointment was a sudden decision of the rulers of the War Office and this was reflected in the hostile attitude of the other departments concerned with economics, both national and federal. Rathenau, then already a middle-aged man, combined in himself the ideas and the will to act as a captain of industry. But, since he came from the second generation of industrialists, everything took in him a more refined and critical form. His father was the founder and managing director of one of the two greatest electricity trusts in Germany, of which he himself became the chairman. He started his activities in one small room in the War Office in close collaboration with von Moellendorff, a young engineer attached to his trust, and some of his friends, also drawn in the main from his trust. It is not quite clear how far there might have been a coincidence of thought between Rathenau and Moellendorff. If so, it is easily to be understood; for the main features of such a system as would be dictated by war would be in the air. That is shown, for instance, by the war organisation of a liberal country like England which, serving the same purposes, was not unlike the organisation of State-socialist Germany.

Throughout his lifetime Rathenau had seen expanding the system of finance capitalism, of which he was an exponent and which I have described in Chapter II. He saw the new electricity industry growing and becoming the model of modern industrial organisation, combining production and consumption through the financier. He knew the regulation of industries by understandings and by cartels supported also by the banks, in which, too, he had had experience. It was a mind prepared on these lines that formed the idea of the economic system of the War period, and so, too, that of the post-War period. If even in liberal England the State became an important factor in settling economic affairs during the War period, how much stronger would State interference show itself in State-socialist Germany! The system became a mixed growth springing from three roots, the mercantilist, the planned, and the socialist systems. This new system was by no means dominated by a preconceived plan; it developed by degrees—a fact not yet fully realised by historians. In this small room in the Prussian War Office they started to group the individual branches of industries concerned with warfare. Rathenau's collaborators became the heads of the departmental work for these industries. A few years later this small room had expanded into blocks of buildings. Certainly a plan, however indefinite, existed, but the growth of these departments and their combination in a general scheme came later. Rathenau began his work with the war organisation of iron and steel, metals, chemicals, leather, and rubber—following in this the order of war needs. In time and by degrees the other groups of industries were slowly and hesitatingly organised in governmental departments, or achieved self-government under the supervision of a government " *Kommissar*." Among Rathenau's collaborators there were organisers, who later became prominent. One of them was Hermann Schmitz who now with Carl Bosch (the man who carried through Fritz Haber's synthesis of nitrogen) heads Germany's gigantic Chemical Trust. The War organisations grew, like mercantilist institutions, not according to any clear principle, but from individual opportunities. The prototypes of these groups—the revived guilds and the revived cartels—at this time assumed forms which were closely connected with the period of finance capitalism and so the banks took their part. With these War cartels all cartel activities were resumed, such as quota and price fixing, pooling and compensating etc.

So from an accumulation of divided activities in departments dealing with individual groups of industries arose a new interim solution for a planned system which remains in principle the same in Nazi Germany, in Fascist Italy and in other countries, so far as the economic organisation is concerned. What is different in the newer systems as against those of the War period is the attitude towards the various stages of development from capitalism to socialism as Marx and Engels visualised them. It was political and economic self-defence which formed the incentives in individual states, considered as units of economy. It is the idea of the nation to which all political and economic ideas were subjected. It is the War system continued and adapted.

An inside view of the organisation, especially the organs established for war purposes, will reflect their functions. I have stressed the fact that for Germany the War period was a time of economic restrictions and compulsory control of resources: these conditions precipitated the system of planning through associations. It was a relatively simple task to build the War cartels where cartels already existed. Take the German steel industry, for instance: the companies of this industry had been united for a long time in cartels such as the *Stahlwerksverband*, steel syndicate (p. 186). This was a framework of cartels including most of the branches of the iron and steel industry and embracing most of the works of the country. The War Office had an easy task in bringing the outsiders into an existing cartel and so regulating production, prices, and distribution. But it was much more difficult to form a cartel combining so many heterogeneous and specialised industries as the different branches of the textile trade. Certain War-time companies were created for particular functions. The demand for materials for gun powder, for example, had formerly been met by certain cheap kinds of cotton which could no longer be imported. For some time, until the wood-pulp industry was able to meet this need, cotton rags had to be used. This entailed linking together three sections—the rag collectors, the manufacturers of cotton shoddy and the chemical works which carried out the process of nitrification—before they could satisfy the demands of the munition department of the War Office for the quota of gunpowder. And there were certain types of War associations serving distinct purposes. The building of War companies was, in general, bounded by the same difficulties which aided or hindered the formation of cartels during peace-time. Cartels were rare in industries with a great variety of branches and of finished products, except for regulating payments. This made it a considerable task to bring into cartel combination firms which were never combined by agreements. This task became all the more involved, e.g., where in the cotton trade the process of production was divided into separate industries which were formerly only linked in the market by the factor system through commercial agents. No doubt, the experience of these middlemen could not be dispensed with in War-time.

The economising of resources soon led to a selection of those plants which were allowed to work for War purposes and for civilian needs. Finally the Government selected the so-called *Höchstleistungsbetriebe*, or those plants working in the most highly rationalised manner and with a maximum of efficiency. In this they followed old models, in the distributing activities of cartels which decided to which works orders should be given and in many cases gave compensation to the others. The selection of plants or companies for this work caused great difficulties, protests and claims from closed works, presented through channels of every kind, political and even military. The capitalist system wrapped all the commercial activities of an individual undertaking in clouds of secrecy, beginning with the cost of production, manners of financing certain transactions, etc. The close collaboration of all these works under Government control lifted the veil, and so activities began at this time which made visible their working as it is shown now by the so-called " *Kalkulation* " norms which are the foundations of compulsory auditing in present-day Germany. The member firms of such War associations came for the first time to know the strength and the weakness of every other company and its capacity of production, etc. Accordingly steps were sometimes taken by powerful works to stifle the weaker and to begin an era of combinations that was the beginning of strong trustification which was unknown to it before the War, e.g., in the textile industry. Not only was production regulated, but also the distribution of finished goods. Every citizen received special allowances for different types of articles, viz., for housekeeping and for clothes. An army of officials of both sexes registered the permits for everybody by an elaborate system of book-keeping, and issued the corresponding permit certificate. Food and other necessities were distributed in this way and so in the time of war one branch of industry was completely organised, i.e., the leather industry. From the cow to the shoe, the process of leather manufacture was strictly controlled up to the last year of the War and for some time after it.

The organisation which controlled the War-time economy was divided into two parts, first the Government chiefly represented by the War Office or its special delegates, the " *Kommissars*," and, secondly, the representatives of the cartels of each industry. These became more and more a self-governing union of all the member firms (or their representatives), though they were never legally independent and completely self-governing. In all leading industries in Germany, the so-called *Kriegsgesellschaften* (companies for War purposes) came into being. Existing ones were changed for War purposes or new ones established; and they became consulting boards for the Government. The Government closely supervised operations through officials of the corresponding Ministry and partly through special " *Kommissars*." Officially these War companies figured as consultative and executive boards of the Government;

in reality, however, their influence predominated—except in such rare cases as where the "*Kommissars*" were independent and capable men unbiassed by industrial associations.

It is not a contradiction to call these bodies self-governing in spite of the fact that they were legally controlled. They may be compared with political self-governing bodies, such as the Prussian municipal councils, after the Stein-Hardenberg Reforms of 1808 and later; it must be born in mind that these also never operated without State control. These War cartels for the first time united a whole economic system for joint action. They were interesting foundations both from the point of view of War purposes and even more from that of the development of administrative marketing organs in a planned economy. The two different influences in these organisations and their joint occurrence in the time of War economy provide the missing link between the planned economy of yesterday—as I may call it—and modern forms of development. Both the cartel and this form of enterprise were originally private institutions. Henceforth, their joint form becomes a State institution. Furthermore, it becomes a new system of planned economy, that is, the economic division of public administration. I once gave these institutions the name *Gemischtwirtschaftliche Kartelle*[66] (cartels of mixed public and private composition) and called them the transitional link between capitalist and socialist forms of management. This organisation of administration derives on the one hand from the system of the German *Gemischtwirtschaftliche Unternehmung* (mixed public and private enterprise), and on the other from the transformed cartels often mentioned before.

I attempted to show the tasks of the component parts of this compromise institution which represent different economic systems, the one competitive, the other planned. It was only too clear that this type was adopted in War time by the men who saw it working splendidly, especially with public utilities a long time before the War (see p. 200). Most of the new mixed enterprises (War companies) have been established in the form of limited liability companies (comparable to the English private limited companies) or as joint stock companies. The War companies which, as we saw, were the cartels of certain trades, were amalgamated with banking offices, established as special departments by Germany's great deposit banks, so that any possible losses should be guaranteed but we must notice that, in reality, no risk existed, since these companies carried on their activities at a time when the demand was greater than the supply. Through these channels, the Government, which completely controlled the foundation of these companies, was also the only supervisor of production and consumption for both military and civil purposes. The State fixed the small dividends as the earnings of the War cartel. The insertion of the banks into this economic system resulted from the knowledge which a man like Walther Rathenau had collected over many years as a member of the system of finance capitalism.

Having laid down the principles of a modern war economic system, Rathenau resigned, not quite voluntarily. The work that had been inspired by genial imagination was continued by army officers, a partly civilian staff and a machinery that became increasingly bureaucratic. It is well-known that this system ended in the blind alley of bureaucratism—not even free from corruption. Thus, it foreshadowed all the follies to which later planned systems were exposed: in periods of emergency they provide a higher degree of efficiency by bringing all forces under command and coercion. But in periods such as we have perhaps entered and which I have called a "synthetic era," then the forces of routine work must be assisted or guided by stronger forces of initiative. This does not affect the principle. Mankind can no longer expose the fate of hundreds of millions to accident. So young a system, compared with methods which we can trace through centuries, cannot be free from growing pains. All these events were clear to Rathenau and his collaborators, as will be shown later.

In this chapter the principles of the industrial system during the War have been described. The agricultural system at this time did not differ essentially from the industrial. It will suffice to say that all agricultural products for both human and industrial consumption were subjected to marketing schemes exercised by special boards. In these schemes we have the forerunners of the organisations of the Third Reich described in Chapter IV.

According to estimates by Eulenburg, roughly 20 per cent. of the population before the War received their food from abroad. These 20 per cent. (=roughly $13\frac{1}{2}$ millions) had to be fed mainly by home production during the War and, in addition, the army proved a very great consumer. Like industry, agriculture had some very interesting cartels which operated in connection with the producers' associations and consumers' associations, the most important of the latter being the municipal authorities. Besides these organisations, certain offices regulated the "examination of prices" (*Preispruefungsstelle*) very strictly. A whole network of these offices became a system in itself, reaching throughout the country down to the smallest village, and its principles provided experience for the establishments of later times. There is no doubt that from 1916 a central planned food economy existed throughout Germany. Prices fixed at all stages from the producers to the ultimate consumers marked this system, in conjunction with regional regulation.

As far as both Germany's trade and agriculture were concerned, there had been no previous consideration of how they could be provided and carried on during a modern war, so all the institutions worked without precedents. The War Ministry at the outset of the War had no plan for providing industrial materials or food and feeding stuffs. The so-called "*Schweinemord*" (murder of pigs) was an example of actions which were decided by the Government in default of the necessary statistics. Roughly 25 million pigs in

Germany consumed mainly imported foodstuffs. As these were cut off, nine million pigs were slaughtered, because the competition between men and pigs as consumers of home produced food seemed to be dangerous. The War system showed itself very clearly in import promotion and export regulation. In connection with the Home Office an organisation of "*Reichseinkauf*" (official purchase) became established, which, in the long run, developed vast chains of great associations, mixed public and private enterprises, which were under Government control. During the War a Ministry of Food was established, with v. Batocki as its gifted chief.

By 1916 the demands of the War brought about, mainly through the influence of the High Command, a new and tremendous armaments programme and a general service law. All that could be done to mobilise the German people and their economic resources was done. The "auxiliary service law in the interest of the Fatherland," *Hilfsdienstgesetz* of December 5th, 1916, was decreed for this purpose. The programme of action of the army, which was extended from Flanders to Egypt and Mesopotamia, had become greater and greater.

Material and human efforts would hardly have sufficed even if the fortunes of War had been more favourable. So this chapter of economic history ends in the strategical history of the War. Moellendorff, who was Economic Adviser to the *Generalfeldzeugmeister* (controller for armament) at the end of the War, and who might have been the only man who could have written a history of the relation between supply and demand of War materials, often regretted that the records officially composed by him disappeared after the War. His outlook, based on his profound knowledge of the supply of materials, was very pessimistic. That, however, has no connection with the fact that certain War appliances, such as tanks, the necessity of which was recognised later, had not been built sufficiently.

Here we are not so much interested in factual detail as in the schemes so far as they are stages in socialist and planned systems. Rathenau, as well as Moellendorff, revealed their schemes even at the time of the War.[67] From administrative measures for temporary needs they came to a more general approach. In one of his pamphlets, published as the first of the series "*Deutsche Gemeinwirtschaft*," Moellendorff chose as his motto one phrase of Walther Rathenau[68]: "*Wirtschaft ist nicht mehr Sache des einzelnen, sondern Sache der Gesamtheit*" (The economic task is no longer a private one, it is the task of the community). This sentence reveals the manner in which the men who laid their stamp on the new planned economy conceived their programme. So it was not a new invention or a difference of ideology when national-socialism later put its economic principles in the words "common weal before public interest." Curiously enough, the schemes of Rathenau and Moellendorff were the only available socialist schemes which had any hope of execution when socialists demanded socialisation after the War. There is no doubt that both authors revolted against the opinion that a return to pre-War economy in a liberal system was possible. But, in fact, this obsolete point of view dominated nearly all practical economists and many theoreticians. When in 1917 the Imperial Government opened the " Department for transforming War- to Peace-economy " (i.e., the office which later developed into an independent Cabinet Ministry of Economic Affairs) the man who was appointed its head, Dr. Helfferich, said : " This office will understand its task best if it returns as soon as possible to pre-War economic conditions "(!)

Rathenau who visualised the transformation of the economic system into a drastic socialism recognised, however, the great part played by the joint stock capitalism. In dealing with the secret reserves of the joint stock banks—a feature of private capitalism, strongly criticised by jurists and politicians—Rathenau said that they were the decisive elements in Germany's enormous technical achievements during the War.[69] In another place he makes it clear that there is no " reason for following the quack prescription of certain socialists and for destroying the edifice of organic achievements of a thousand years, in order to replace it by police bureaucracy and the War ration system, and to replace the liberty of the citizen by improved poor laws." So Rathenau, who aimed at the complete transformation of the organs or functions of an economic system built upon private enterprise and the private entrepreneur, like Moellendorff in his plans or schemes which were carried through, did not believe in dispensing with the entrepreneur in a transitional system. Rathenau has expressed his opinion thus[70] : " We are confronted by significant upheavals in economic structure and thought. The War, which, since in its nature it was political, was an event of world revolutionary character, shattered the economic and social order of Europe. In a few months destruction was wrought such as would not have resulted from the same number of aeons of peace. From the ruins will arise neither a Communist State nor a system allowing free play to the economic forces. In enterprise the individual will not be given greater latitude ; on the other hand, individualistic activity will be consciously accorded a part in an economic structure working for Society as a whole ; it will be infused with a spirit of communal responsibility and common weal." Nevertheless, the programme foreshadowed in Rathenau's various pamphlets leaves no room for doubt as to his trend : as when he says : " A more equal distribution of possessions and income is a commandment of ethics and economy. Only one in the State is allowed to be immeasurably rich : that is the State itself. Through its means it has to provide for the abolition of the distress of all. Differences of income and property may be allowed but no longer for a one-sided distribution of power which may be abused. The present sources of wealth are monopolies, speculation and inheritance. The monopolist, the speculator and the millionaire heir have no longer a place in the new order of economy."[71]

Chapter III

THE WEIMAR REICH

(1) DEVELOPMENT, 1918-1933

(a) The Chaos

The history of the Weimar Reich may well be called a stage of tentative experiments in social progress. These experiments were destined to be made at a time when the infant republic was still convulsed by the consequences of the War and the Peace Treaty. Recovery was only possible by means of interim-solutions bringing temporary relief, the drawbacks of which again involved the Reich in considerable difficulties. These attempts ranged over all aspects of human life, political as well as social and economic. The reforms were, in fact, a continuation of former systems, while they endeavoured to put into practice ideas which had developed during the 19th century in politics, constitutional law, and economics.

In the political field the strengthening of sectional interests brought about the gradual dissolution of Bismarck's legacy, the centrally-governed Reich. The national State was checked by the growing anti-centralist feeling in the federal States, particularly in Bavaria. The old governing classes, the army, the land owners, and the industrialists still played a leading part in the ruling of the country and the domination of its economic forces and strove for the support of all those who were dissatisfied with the new régime and weary of the chaos it had to face. They opposed the government vigorously since the Third Estate had come to the fore in it. After Bismarck's dismissal, the reins of government were no longer held in one mighty fist. To use a mathematical simile, the political and economic forces had taken converging lines whose point of convergence was in the hand of the political ruler. On the other hand, under Bismarck's successors convergence gave way to parallel forces fighting one another for power or joining strength with other forces. In the time of the Weimar Reich the power of these sectional interests grew, and Parliament became the field where all these manoeuvres were executed. Perhaps the greatest misfortune of the period was the scarcity of strong men able to give a strong lead to the nation.

The new elements which temporarily ruled in the Weimar Reich breathed the spirit which hoped to form the New Age after the fall of Feudalism and Capitalism. But the leaders of the Left Wing opposition did not achieve power by conquest; it passed inevitably to them after the Armistice in default of any other heirs of the Hohenzollern rule. History will decide whether it was really a social revolution which broke out after the German army collapsed in 1918 and the High Command asked the Government to enter into negotiations with the allies.

Not very long after the War extremists disappeared from the field. Nevertheless, a strong working class movement, although in no way prepared to take office as a government, began to take control amid the chaotic conditions. Experienced as they were in certain provinces of social policy, their lack of training in foreign and home political affairs compelled them to become subservient to the bureaucracy, the heads of which thus regained the real government. To overcome temporary difficulties, to win over individual groups, especially the Roman Catholic Centre Party, and to pacify their own followers, political bargaining and the sharing of the spoils of office with other groups became the general practice. Socialist leaders busied themselves with daily expediencies at the expense of carrying out their programme. These men, who faced the task of carrying on the government during the difficult 1918-1919 period, had sprung mainly from the former opposition. They were workers and intellectuals, on whose crutches the workers leaned and limped, together with a middle class group hostile to the old régime for humanitarian reasons or because of allegiance to some form or other of liberalism or socialism.

The results achieved by the Weimar Reich were partly due to a natural development which discarded anachronisms, and partly due to the ideas of the intellectuals whose differences of opinion, however, were as great as their ideologies were unready for translation into practice. The new leading group was doomed to failure from the first by its lack of power. This is also true of those non-socialist elements who, in the 14 years after the Great War, held some of the highest offices in the Reich.

Resistance to the dictates of the victorious Allied Powers was big with risk as well as with serious social repercussions in the Reich itself. The statesmen knew that their power was limited, and their plans aimed at a gradual revival at home and abroad. A certain decency among the various Social Democratic leaders must be mentioned, for they never attempted to get rid of their opponents by wholesale murder, with or without mock trials, though they saw their enemies growing. No doubt, in many groups extending from the middle classes to the ranks of the Social Democratic Party, a feeling for democracy existed. But among the population in general such feeling was very weak. The average German received this suddenly-acquired individual liberty with indifference. For the many who were hitherto not accustomed to have any say in public affairs, democratic ideals did not mean much. A time of widespread ruin and demoralisation was not suitable for the growth of the new moral forces which advanced the ideal of humanity. And as far as these ideals were an import from the West, expressed in President Wilson's doctrines and those of the League of Nations, they and the whole idea of the humanitarian World State were damned in German eyes by the manner of their execution. Traditional nationalism and romanticism survived as the strongest feelings, and offended national pride produced disgust with the compliance of the German statesmen towards foreign pressure. No doubt, the widespread distress prompted the opposition of great numbers who later on became the followers of the Third Reich. It is not without interest to read the historian, Arthur Rosenberg, who, in spite of his being once a left wing socialist member of the German Parliament, shows very impartially how sparing the socialist groups were in constructive ideas and what destructive effects on socialism and democracy were promoted by the Communist Party which took orders directly from Moscow. Everything from abroad, from Versailles through Poincaré to Barthou's policy of encirclement, worked more or less to hinder Germany's economic recovery. The injections of the Dawes Loan and the submission to foreign financial control could only bring about a short pseudo-prosperity, which, however, made the Reich more resistant to the new blows to come.

The economic situation of the Weimar Reich was that of a great empire collapsed owing to the losses of the War and covered with the penalties of Versailles. The statistics of the belligerents differ widely. As far as Germany's payments after the War are concerned, neutral American estimates are available; the disparity between those and other estimates we shall quote in another connection (pp. 174-175). The figure mentioned officially from the German side amounts to 67,673 million marks, which are alleged to have been paid up to the 30th June, 1931, the commencement of the "Hoover Moratorium." German economists say that roughly 90,000 million marks were wasted in the War. The total of these sums (=157,700,000,000 marks) would mean a loss corresponding to nine-tenths of all taxable income over 10,000 marks (according to the estimate of the "*Wehrbeitrag*," 1913[1]). Even if these estimates were too high, 50 per cent. of these amounts would show a disastrous breakdown of the economic system of a country with roughly 67 million inhabitants. The main sources of work and food were destroyed, to say nothing of the effects on the political mind.

I shall touch only lightly upon the losses which Germany suffered by the Treaty of Versailles. The German government had asked the President of the United States, in a note of October 3rd, 1918, for an Armistice in order to organise a peace based upon his 14 points and his later manifestoes (Wilson Programme). The Entente had agreed through the U.S.A. to enter into peace negotiations on this basis (November 5th, Lansing Note) with the exception of two items—the freedom of the seas was refused and the rebuilding of the War zones was extended to include the entire damage imposed upon the civilian population. Following this agreement of November 5th, the German Reich was prepared to make certain sacrifices as regards "undoubtedly Polish districts" in her Eastern country, and an unimpeded entrance to the sea for the new Polish state which did not, however, presuppose a partition of the German country. At this time even for Alsace Lorraine, a vote of the population was mooted, and, perhaps, also as regards one or more of the German colonies. A limitation of Germany's armaments was agreed on "mutual guarantees." An amount of War indemnity did not belong to the obligations, but only the recovery of the damage done to the civilian population through the German attacks. On the other side the Allies agreed to conclude all agreements in the spirit of justice, of the self-determination of peoples—including the German people—and of the abolition of all economic barriers and the establishment of a League of Nations in which Germany would receive a seat. The Armistice of November 11th, 1918, anticipated in certain points the conditions of the peace, and already contained provisions which reached beyond the earlier agreement, but the Allies indicated that these conditions were only preliminary. The Peace Conference, however, abandoned the basis of the earlier agreement and ultimately dictated the peace. I do not dwell upon the motives of these acts which were based on the "War Guilt" Clauses, and gave the peace agreement the character of a penalty. First of all, Germany lost enormous parts of her territory. The colonies were taken away under mandates but no recompense was made for land, railways, seaports and other public and private works. The indemnification of shareholders was left to the German government. Germany lost one-eighth of her territory and the whole East was cut off from the Reich by the Polish Corridor. Alsace Lorraine and nearly the whole Province of West Prussia and the Province of Posen and parts of East Prussia and Silesia had to be given away. Danzig became a Free City outside Germany. Territory was also lost to Belgium and Denmark. The loss of important industrial and agricultural areas in Upper-Silesia was strongly resented in Germany as an injustice. In spite of the majority of 707,000 German votes against 479,000 Polish votes, the Conference of Ambassadors, following the report of the League of Nations, made an award favourable to Poland. The Saar-Basin went for 15 years, officially under the administration of the League of Nations, in reality to France, which immediately took over the great German State works of the mining and iron industries and also transferred private enterprises from German into French hands. The internationalisation of German waterways and restrictions on military and civilian air power stunted the development of German transport. I only wish to mention some few more facts, such as the delivery of material left behind in the war zones and the cession as indemnity of the bulk of the German navy and mercantile marine, as well as great quantities of railway material, either already in use or to be manufactured.

The losses through the Treaty, which humiliated German pride by a control of sovereign rights, broke up the well-established trade connections between the different regions of the empire which had formerly made it one.

The problem became the more dangerous for Germany, as it now became surrounded by the Succession States, which were hostile to her and followed the French lead in the policy of the encirclement. East Prussia thus became a political and economic problem in itself. Completely cut off from the Reich it yet remained dependent upon it; for it was not possible for it to be self-sufficient. Emigration from East Prussia into the West had been going on for a long time, augmenting the prospects of their neighbours, especially the Poles, who still had the high birthrate of the Germany of some forty years ago. The separation of East Prussia, together with the loss of other parts, diminished Germany's food supply. In this way she lost 15.4 per cent. of her cultivated area (16.4 per cent. of the wheat area and an important potato area). The Eastern parts, now cut off, brought new political and economic problems to add to the difficulties of the home politics facing the statesmen of the Weimar Reich. The agricultural structure in East German provinces will be described in Chapter IV. The big landowners living in the isolated parts were strong enough to re-establish the old political influence which they had always had in the German Reich and in their co-operation with the army and industry. The disastrous conditions emerging from the War and the Peace Treaty now brought thousands of millions of marks to East Prussia, in various forms of recovery funds or subsidies from the treasury to the big estate owners. The land settlement problem was early tackled at this time in order to recover and re-Germanise these provinces, a policy which the uneasy Polish neighbour watched carefully. The big landowners did everything to prevent land settlement for small farmers coming from the class of the unemployed. It is significant that at a later stage of the Weimar Reich, Chancellor Brüning's dismissal was closely connected with his policy of claiming a large part of the property of the big estates for land settlement (which was called "Agrarian Bolshevism"). Army circles, to which Hindenburg (who was himself a landowner in the East) belonged, had a strong interest in the preservation of this kind of pampered agriculture and the class which benefited therefrom.

The great industrial centre of the Ruhr with its coal deposits was now cut off from the ores of Lorraine, the Saar, Luxemburg, etc. By this loss Germany, one of the greatest exporters of finished iron and steel goods, lost nearly 74.5 per cent. of its iron-ore basis, 26 per cent. of its coal and 68.3 per cent. of its zinc deposits. With the transfer of Lorraine to France the German potash monopoly was destroyed by the cession of the potash deposits. The loss of important parts of the industrial area of Upper Silesia meant the loss of great coal mines, iron works, and zinc works. With this, at the same time, Poland became a strong commercial competitor of Germany on the world coal market. These troubles culminated in the complete decay of the currency when inflation was at its peak, and this coincided with the Ruhr invasion. This invasion, the frustration of the popular vote in Upper Silesia, and other things, going beyond the Lansing Note, were generally resented in Germany as unjust and offensive to national pride. Already at this time nationalism had become very strong and with it hatred against the men and the parties which had to rule the country and against the parties which made for internationalism. The assent of the national assembly to the signing of the Treaty of Versailles was given on June 22nd, 1919. Revolts, sometimes equivalent to regular civil wars, marked the tense atmosphere which was always present during the period of the Weimar Reich.

The War debt, which turned out to be the greatest obstacle to economic peace and to the natural exchange of goods and money, gave the German statesmen in the first post-War years a herculean task. It was almost impossible to estimate for a Budget for the Reich, or for the federal States and municipal corporations, or even for the ordinary citizen. War loans and the inflation which swept away middle class property had created an army of malcontents who, backed by their strong national feelings, soon became the natural opponents of the Government parties. The instability of the currency, both at this date and at later times, afflicted every part of social and economic life and caused a flight to durable goods, wherever they were to be found. The care of the Government to prevent the alienation of German trade and industry, which was to be got cheaply by foreigners, made its position more difficult. Some mercantilist measures, such as the taking over of the properties and stocks of banking and industrial companies by the State, arose in this connection. Inroads of the State with increasing variety, both of kind and of degree, into every sphere of economic life, grew as the Weimar Reich approached its close. Foreign bill control, various acts of industrial legislation, loans creating work for the unemployed, housing and land settlement policy, and labour camp schemes, were among the measures which later became important elements of the economic system of the Third Reich. The State became more and more the great provider for the mass of the population.

During the Weimar period industry itself was filled with a spirit of new adventure, aiming to promote economic recovery. According to the character of Germany's industry which, after the War had exhausted its stocks, with outworn machinery and refractory labour, certain new methods came to the fore. I shall deal later with " rationalisation " and its consequences and the share of German finance in the new activities aiming at recovery. Efficiency was needed to reduce costs in order to compete on the world market; for Germany's important export trades were destroyed, her export markets artificially blocked, her navy and mercantile marine dissolved by the Treaty of Versailles. Difficulties in financing industries at this time brought the middleman to the fore who, as financier and supplier of foreign credits, strengthened the old ties which had always existed between finance and industry. The sudden disappearance of regular business on the money market from the time of inflation led to rapid investment in industry, which resulted in over-capitalisation. Big business of this kind showed extravagant features. It was led by those great entrepreneurs of industry itself, often transient figures, and by various groups of middlemen, among whom new and undesirable types appeared, who largely contributed to the great depression.

Such was the general picture of the political and economic chaos of post-War Germany. Before I return to complete my account of German pre-War finance capitalism I should like to sketch in more detail the inroads of foreign countries into Germany's economy and the measures taken to preserve the currency, and to outline the structure of Germany's industry and her export trade.

(*b*) RECOVERY, CRISIS AND RELAPSE

§1 *Socialism in the Weimar Reich*

With the description of the Treaty of Versailles we have proceeded too far; for between the Armistice and the Treaty much was done to bring order out of the chaos which was a legacy of the War; and, in addition, the first experiments in carrying one or the other of socialist ideologies into practice were begun. What was done in this direction in the 19th century was never more than social reform and never overstepped the framework of the old conservative Power State. The old tradition, though momentarily weakened, was still sufficiently strong to offer opposition to the new ideals of the Weimar reformers. Models to be copied, apart from the Russian movement which was not yet two years old, were not available. And at this time the new socialist republic in Russia was compelled, in order to consolidate its forces, to slow down its advance by temporary truce with the capitalism of other nations.

Socialism, as it showed itself in the German Reich, has been described in Chapter I. The socialists, in keeping with their general attitude, gave special support to the War; the Social Democratic party adapted itself to the policy of the nation of which it always felt itself a part.

The new socialist movement, as it showed itself after the Armistice, had three roots.

(1) There was a foundation consisting of what was created in the last century by Marx, Engels, Lassalle, Bebel, Liebknecht the elder, and the old guard of Social Democrats of the Reichstag. In addition there was the circle centred around certain periodicals, among them the " *Sozialistische Monatshefte*," to which latter group the intellectuals, David, Bernstein, Kautsky, belonged. Other men, like Legien, coming from the trade unions, had a strongly-organised power in the party behind them.

(2) The State socialist or neo-mercantilist movement which gave impulse to a practical socialism, a movement inclined to dethrone private capitalism by slow degrees and to establish the State as an " organised economic society " in the place of the individual enterprise. This developed to an extraordinary degree during the War.

(3) The influence of Soviet Russia also was obvious. There was a small group of intellectuals to whom, elements, which in Russia prepared the way for a communist ideology, were not strange. Their ideas, too, were derived from Marx : Capitalism would come to an end as the result of the contradictions inherent in its very nature. The socialists had to concentrate a class-conscious proletariat in such a way as to organise it for victory over the capitalism that created it. The capitalists were driven, by the growing disparity between an ever-increasing production and the home consumption, to look out for new markets abroad, and to combine at the same time in ever larger trusts, which by degrees would eliminate the small capitalist and secure monopoly. The rush to exploit and appropriate undeveloped territories led capitalism through the stages of imperialism and world war. The followers of this Marxist theory thought his predictions notably verified by the Great War, the origin of which they considered to be economic. War was the inevitable result of increasing competition for fresh markets under the guise of imperialism. As Lenin declared: " Imperialism is capitalism in that stage of development in which monopolies and financial capital have reached a preponderating influence, the export of capital has acquired great importance, the international trusts have begun the partition of the world, and the biggest capitalist countries have completed the division of the entire territorial globe among themselves."[2]

Russian intellectuals, as well as some supporters of these ideas in Germany, considered that the time had come to overthrow capitalism, and to transfer the social ownership of property to the militant workers. The upholders of this creed believed that the victory of the working class carried with it the emancipation of humanity.[3] The revolution was to be carried out on a class basis but the Society which would emerge from the revolution was to be based on the abolition of classes. Communist ideology saw in its fight on behalf of the dispossessed class, a battle for the whole of mankind. Their supporters were of the opinion that these ideas could not be realised except after a long period of time. The road to Utopia was designed by Marx himself who conceived of two distinct stages of revolutionary progress. One was a transitional revolutionary stage which was based on the domination of the State by the working class. The second stage was a classless Society in which the State as the repository of authority had also vanished. Engels once said : " Since the State is only a temporary institution which is to be made use of in the revolution in order forcibly to suppress the opponents, it is perfectly absurd to talk about a free, popular State: as long as the proletariat needs the State, it needs it not in the interest of freedom, but in order to suppress its opponents; and when it becomes possible to speak of freedom, the State as such ceases to exist."[4]

How did the majority of the people look upon the various socialist goals? In Germany for a long time Socialism developed in its State-socialist form even among Conservatives and Liberals, but the propertied classes scorned a socialist ideology. The monarchical idea and attitude, favourable to the former governmental system, had suffered enormously under the blow of the loss of the War and there was a widespread feeling among the people that they had been misled both by the administration and by the army. To many of the middle class the collapse came as a thunderbolt owing to the misleading reports issued daily by the army headquarters. So the former Imperial government had lost most of its supporters, and the bulk of the population after the War was in a state of agony and disappointment. Large sections of the population which had never before known any contact with democracy, now even seemed inclined to look forward to a more democratic system. Middle class people in general were also inspired, by their terror of a communist revolution, to make every concession, beginning with beflagging their houses in red. The great landowning families, from which the high bureaucracy and the army were partly recruited, and the industrialists were hostile to a revolutionary movement which had been widely joined by the working classes, and the supporters of the old system feared that the movement would follow Soviet lines and result in a socialisation of either industry or landed property. The industrialists feared a policy of increasing wages together with a far-reaching social policy. The attitude of the middle class parties was cautious, waiting upon events and in any case unwilling to follow the workers' programmes. In the Centre Party, which comprised the bulk of the Roman Catholic workers, the Left Wing grew stronger, but it was not at all revolutionary.

With the disappearance of the Hohenzollerns and as a result of recent experiences a great step towards Socialism had undeniably been taken in Germany. But the Weimar Reich, handicapped by the difficulties of the time, was only one stage along the road of these ideas and their translation into practice. Thus social progress in the light of history was only modest. National-Socialism as a form of socialism or neo-cameralism, continues this history under another cloak. It is significant that this movement could not arise in a State having roughly 20 million employees, as national " conservatism " or national " capitalism " under a liberal cloak. Undoubtedly it was conceived as a people's movement, but it is a stage and not the end.

It is possible for the historian to trace the sources from which originated the stages of this development and to distinguish it from the effects of the actions and conditions of the moment.

On November 10th, 1918, the Workers' and Soldiers' Councils in Berlin, acting as the representatives of all revolutionary workers and soldiers in Germany, elected the first Republican Government. Six representatives of the people—Ebert, Scheidemann and their four colleagues at the head, virtually combined the duties of the President and the Chancellor of the Reich. At its birth the new government found itself saddled with a legacy: there was but little change in the public service which held office under these six men. All important departments were continued under the same type of high officials. It is true that there had been a slight change since the time when, shortly before the Armistice, under Prince Max von Baden as Chancellor, the Reichstag and the Government had outlined a democratic régime, in which Social Democrat leaders such as Ebert and Scheidemann had a seat in the Cabinet. So it was these socialists, as former official leaders of the Imperial Government, who set up the republic. Of the six representatives, some were Majority Socialists and some Independent Socialists, and so the balance swung to the side of the socialist workmen. But this did not change the general composition of the Government. In the highest government offices the members of the old bureaucracy, parliamentarians of the Centre Party and the Left Wing Liberals sat side by side. The new régime had behind it the rank and file of the German army and navy who were the initiators of this change of leadership in the country. These had revolted against their officers, chosen councils of soldiers and expelled the various federal royal families. The councils of workers joined those of the soldiers, for the workers could never have carried through the revolution if the military forces had resisted them. The collapse of the army was the beginning of the upheaval.

There is no need to trace all the phases of the social revolution. There were frequent changes in the strength and position of the various political influences. The description of these events would be rather the task of political history. The description of the dominant social and economic ideas and motives is more relevant for our purposes. The three tendencies, the roots of which we described earlier, were strongly divergent and results were obtained only by compromise. In addition, the influence of foreign dictation modified the acts that the government projected.

The Russian model was itself in a state of metamorphosis. Arising out of very primitive groupings of workmen at the time when the Czarist régime allowed neither socialist parties nor socialist trade unions, the councils of workmen (Soviets) emerged. They originated from the revolution of 1905, so that it was only natural that the new upheaval in 1917 adopted the scheme of these councils which were composed of delegates from various factories in some of the bigger industrial towns. Councils of soldiers and of peasants joined the movement. The organs of the Czarist public service at the beginning of Lenin's régime still carried out the functions of the administration. The first Soviets were a kind of primitive democracy of the masses of the working class. But this picture soon changed when Lenin, in the spring of 1917, recognised that only the Soviet councils were able to destroy the feudal and middle-class Russian State bureaucracy. " All Power to the Soviets "![5] I can only show briefly how at this time these bodies were in the midst of a state of metamorphosis, for, meanwhile, the power of the Bolshevist party developed rapidly. It was a strongly disciplined party in which the authority of the leaders was imposed upon every party member. This party was to rule the entire country; first of all it penetrated the Soviets not least in their capacity as instruments of administration. The original Soviet democracy was now completely swept aside by the power of the Bolshevists. " And as early as 1918 Russia was ruled by the Bolshevist Party dictatorship. According to the Constitution the Soviets were omnipotent. In reality, they were miserable shadows lacking all power and authority."[6] With this the model was created which became the prototype for the non-democratic political systems of our time. The rôle of the party in the " one-party-system " as the organ of liaison and control in the Public Administration was founded. The leader of the party became dominant. Stalin, for example, has been general secretary of the party and not the president of the government. Like the old German " *Herzog* " or " *dux* " who took the leading position in wartime besides the king, the duces and leaders arose. The new principle abandoned the doctrine of " the enlightenment," the division of governmental powers as outlined by Montesquieu, and combined all governmental powers in the totalitarian State, under the Party leadership.

But the Soviet ideal of the German movement in 1918 never included the principle of such party dictatorship over the proletariat; even the extreme Spartacist leader, Rosa Luxemburg, rejected this principle. From November 10th, 1918, the workmen's and soldiers' councils wielded the actual power throughout Germany, both in the town and in the country, supported by the revolutionary groups in the army and by the working men who, in many places, also furnished themselves with arms. As in the early days of Soviet Russia, the previous authorities of the State and the municipalities still existed besides these new bodies. Officially, the bureaucracy carried out its work under the supervision of the councils which still kept democratic tendencies. In contrast to Russia, in the fight between bureaucracy and council, the " revolutionary " councils were defeated. Here is the borderline where the Russian system separates itself from the German system of that time. In cameralist Germany he who has his grip on public administration is the stronger, but the Weimar Reich did not attempt seriously to attack the pre-War bureaucracy, as the " party " has done in the Third Reich. The mentality and tradition of the bulk of the Left of the Weimar parties decided this attitude, together with the complete lack of administrative control on the part of the workers, who had no training in such things either in the State or in their party organisations. This lack of experience justified the warnings of the " revisionists " long before the War. With the disappearance of the soldiers in the councils and later on, of the councils themselves, much of the ideology which animated the Soviet movement disappeared. The idea of a parliament of such revolutionary councils, to a certain extent based upon the principle of corporate organisation, soon faded away. It is true, there was a widespread feeling in Germany after the War that the capitalist order had outlived its time, and the desire to convert this system into a socialist one was strong. Middle-class people, too—anti-capitalist always—sympathised with such ideas as they did later at the time of the Third Reich. But radical plans among the divided socialists, soon caused the middle-class elements to cool off. This was one main reason why the old officialdom was again triumphant. The official opposition parties which were brought together in 1917 by the Roman Catholic Centrist member of the Reichstag, Erzberger, and to which liberal democrats also belonged, were far removed from any revolutionary spirit. That was one of the reasons why Socialists were able to take the reins after the disappearance of the Hohenzollerns and the old system. The Majority Socialists kept their old battle cries, but they took fright at their own ideas and while crying with the masses on the streets and with their own left wing, they had, in reality, very little desire for socialisation. The German trade unions especially felt uneasy about the newcomers of radical mind who threatened to destroy the work which they had built up for over half-a-century. The " majority socialist party " saw in the workmen's and soldiers' councils a transitory symptom of revolutionary disorder, which had to disappear. If real socialisation was to be carried out, these councils, of course, would have to play an outstanding part. The main Socialist group in the post-War government felt that the time was ripe for a return to democratic parliamentarism, i.e., by a transitional National Assembly leading to a new Reichstag. I may add that despite strong Socialist feelings in the German working class population, Communist ideas, and far less, Communist political methods, were never deeply rooted. One should not be mislead on this point by the high figures of Communist votes recorded in periods of extreme distress.

The strength of the socialist movement was handicapped by its own main political group. These Majority Socialists might have been satisfied with the mere socialisation of certain branches of industries, but also that is not clear. It is no wonder that the result of all these endeavours which were made by socialist groups, as far as this item of the programme was concerned, ended in a piece of bluff, the so-called laws of socialisation !

When the councils of the peoples' delegates (*Rat der Volksbeauftragten*), Germany's highest authority, began its work, it was happy

enough to shunt its economic anxieties on to committees. So the
"*Sozialisierungskommission*" was established in 1918 to which
politicians and economists of various shades belonged. Among
them were Hué and Umbreit as former workers' representatives,
some outspoken socialist theoreticians such as Kautsky, Lederer,
and Hilferding, and people of liberal standards like Franke and
Vogelstein. This committee sometimes co-opted other men of
high reputation as thinkers or practical men ; in this way Professor
Schumpeter joined the commission. The then leader of the
Ministry of Economic Affairs, Dr. August Müller, very soon separated
himself from the work of this commission which, contrary to his
wishes, did not choose him but Kautsky as its chairman. From this
time separate action occurred in the matter of " socialisation," still
the slogan of socialists (both those who were good workers in social
policy in official party bodies), and of the men in the street. This
Enquiry Committee had a shadow existence from its very beginning.
Partly it followed academic lines in investigating the whole material
thoroughly, partly its more political-minded members felt themselves impelled to get on more quickly because the workmen's
revolution seemed to them to be waiting. But for the committee
it was a tragedy that the ministry of August Müller-Moellendorff
passed some laws on its own initiative without consulting the
committee in any way.

Socialisation was the magic formula for socialists of every kind
at this time, but no attempt at immediate realisation showed any
preparedness to deal with the question. The belief that the transition
from the capitalist to the socialist Society would take place automatically in consequence of the capitalist development was a chimera.
The extensive industrial concentration which made it easier to
supervise and manage from one centre was regarded as " ripeness
for socialisation." The degree of stability and of economic technique
attained was assumed to make unnecessary the pioneer work of
dealing with new industries, a process always involving great risk.
The possibility of creating this manageability was decisive for the
realisation of socialisation. Eduard Heimann,[7] who as a young man
was the official assistant to the members of the *Sozialisierungskommission*, revealed the great difficulties of this committee when
faced with a translation of these ideas into practice, a state of affairs
which was as true for the socialist government department which
later decreed the first laws of socialisation. The results of so finely
adjusted a network of big enterprises, a miracle of planned composition (as described in my chapter on Finance Capitalism) could
not be achieved by a rough and ready scheme of socialised production
and consumption. All, that was thought possible, was a repetition
of the transitional period from craft to factory system when the
division into sections very often frustrated technical and organisational progress, which developed easily in the highly planned
enterprise.

But how could groups of industries be made ripe for a socialised organisation? First of all the committee and others argued that socialisation could be achieved only in a flourishing economy, such as was absent at that time. Heimann goes behind the theoretical veil. The problem of surplus value played an outstanding part. Marx's axiom that only labour, dependent on capital and exploited by it, created surplus value could no longer be maintained, since the socialists themselves recognised two different elements of surplus value. As Heimann says, Marx's doctrine dealing with value and price theory was strictly static.[8] After that time attempts have been made to explain the dynamic forces of development by the "dynamic profit theory"; and whether the dynamic factor be the entrepreneur or some other agent—and on this point theories differ—his labour does not belong to Marx's surplus labour. In practice, the pre-War capitalist system was based upon this second factor, of which Heimann says[9]: "This factor or its class fulfils a social function in so far as it in no way consumes the surplus value completely. For the greater part it is saved and again invested in enterprise. Moreover, it dispenses large sums in taxes and in partly legal, partly voluntary, social obligations. Ultimately the incomes of those workers who are not engaged in production and distribution of economic goods (partly in the form of luxury consumption, e.g., Art) are paid out of the surplus value of the capitalists. All these expenses, besides social and cultural expenditure which cannot be overlooked, had to be covered by the profits of the production in a socialist economy also, i.e., by the community." If, however, the amounts arising from investments and taxes are subtracted, only about one-third would remain at the disposal of the workers, according to various estimates, when distributed. The *per capita* quota for the individual worker would be very small; for profits in a concentrated production with relatively few profit-sharers would, if distributed amongst all the workers, be mere crumbs. The extra-surplus value of the intellectual work of the entrepreneur, undoubtedly not profits of exploitation, had to reappear in one form or another also in a socialised economy. Heimann[10], summarising his various arguments, states that a survey of the nature of surplus value shows that the capitalist net profit is a complicated formation and not as simple as the surplus-value of Marx. Heimann from this point hints at the "vain hopes of socialisation"; but as a socialist still regards distribution and not production as the main task in achieving economic progress. The great break from the capitalist system to socialisation, by distribution of surplus value, appeared to be impossible when tested. As no other "socialist" plan offered itself at this time, Rathenau's War-economy in its refined form was the only plan available. The War-economy, specially adjusted to the distinct conditions which arose from the War was, however, adapted to the development of the economic system. I described in Chapter II (*b*) Rathenau's ideas, which proved to be very socialistic in their attitude towards the laws of inheritance and towards monopolists. But Rathenau was aware that the changes suggested would necessitate a very long development before they were carried into practice. What remained of his plans for a practical scheme was the organisation of all economic groups under a general plan. Here again we find the mixture between socialist and liberal elements. In one form or another, the State has the general supervision or ownership of the means of production, but the economic activities have to be run by private organisations. In carrying out the principle, greater emphasis will be laid now upon points of ideology, now upon points of practice. As far as the latter are concerned, the principle of the old guilds and corporations again comes to the fore—whether they are transformed into co-operative societies for trade (among them guild socialism) or whether cartels are used (the guilds of the machine age). It was only too clear that the new scheme was connected with the War-time economy. Little more was heard of the abolition of the laws of inheritance or of the State as the universal provider: these belonged to ideology. The entrepreneur of the capitalist system was preserved and so transferred into a socialist system. I shall return to this compromise when I go into the details of Moellendorff's system.

At this time, W. von Moellendorff was the permanent secretary in August Müller's Ministry. He was really foremost with these ideas which were concentrated around what has been called " economic planning." It is remarkable how little is known about his influence and the work he carried through. An able historian such as Arthur Rosenberg, to say nothing of investigators in Britain, did not even mention him. As far as I know, the word " *Planwirtschaft* " (economic planning) was coined by Moellendorff and conceived by him long before the end of the War. From the early days of the War, Moellendorff, in co-operation with Walther Rathenau in the War Office, carried through the first organisations of industry under State influence and collaboration. As shown on p. 137 *inter alia*, War-cartels were used—by adding to them outside companies in a kind of economic self-government—to carry out governmental plans; and where War-cartels did not exist, by creating new ones. Moellendorff, who knew how to handle governmental and industrial apparatus, and the possibilities of what could be achieved at this unsettled time, used this kind of thorough-going cartelisation by the State as a first stage of development to a socialist planned economy. He was, without doubt, a socialist and had advanced ideas, but he wished, like Rathenau, to work within the framework of the possible. An electrical engineer by profession, he found systematic economic organisation, divided into groups and their sub-divisions, working like an elaborate switchboard, greatly to his extreme liking. From this time on the analogy with the " bringing in line " of electric current—*Gleichschaltung*—became a term in economic organisation. And so in the ministry under his aegis plans were developed, which he comprehended under the two names of economic planning and " *Gemeinwirtschaft*," which means an economic system in which the common weal and not private interest regulated policy. This system is undoubtedly a type of socialism and was called alternatively " constructive socialism " or " centralising socialism." Later Moellendorff himself, fusing the ideological and practical roots of his system, gave it the name of " conservative socialism." In this, perhaps, he wished to express the combined force of romanticist ideas and Prussian-mercantilist measures.

Moellendorff's energy was as strong as his influence in the ministry which he dominated. He succeeded in anchoring his ideas of " *Gemeinwirtschaft* " in the Constitution of the Weimar Reich (§156 and §165) which foreshadowed socialisation (though of what kind was not stated), in the establishment of the *Reichswirtschaftsrat* (Reich Economic Council) and in the main laws of socialisation mentioned above. The idea of this council was also conceived by Moellendorff long before the end of the War in a certain leaning towards a council similar to that for which Bismarck failed to receive parliamentary approval in 1881. The laws of socialisation did not exclude entrepreneurs and did not transfer the means of production to State or other bodies of Society, in any form, but used the War organisations, which were a kind of cartel under the supervision or command of the State, to regulate certain big industries. First of all a framework of law (March 23rd, 1919) was set up for such regulated " socialisation." The organisation of the coal industry was decreed on the same date, the law for regulating potash on the 24th April, 1919, and later on the regulation of the iron and steel industry, which, however, never proved to be successful. Coal and potash were brought together in their own organisations representing employers, employees and consumers, and placed under State supervision. The law regulating the coal industry divided the country into ten special districts, each of which was placed under the control of a special cartel. Among these ten, the Rhenish-Westphalian Coal Syndicate was pre-eminent, dwarfing the nine others. So this powerful institution of the old typical capitalist mining industry, with their strong masters, survived. The syndicates were then combined into a national cartel, called the " *Reichskohlenverband Ltd.*," endowed (1) to accept, reject, or modify the recommendations of the regional cartels concerning production, sale, and prices of fuel; (2) to fix maximum prices and determine the amount to be produced by members of the syndicates for their own consumption; (3) to assign production quotas to the cartels and to divide market territories among them; (4) to regulate the granting of rebates and discounts and to inspect the books and correspondence of the cartel members. The *Reichskohlenrat* was thought to be a kind of coal parliament, made up of representatives of mineowners, consumers, and technical experts. While this later body was originally empowered with but little real authority, its power has been somewhat enhanced by the assumption of the price-regulation functions formerly belonging to the *Reichskohlenverband*. Extensive veto powers and some initiatory powers (through emergency interpretation) were entrusted to the Ministry of Economic Affairs.[11]

With the laws relating to coal and potash and iron and steel, there should have been made a beginning of socialisation. Electricity, in certain connections, certain branches of the chemical industry, flour mills and others were taken into consideration in Moellendorff's plan. A law concerning electricity supply was decreed in another ministry; for the union of all economic functions in one ministry as designed by Moellendorff could not be achieved. Before I discuss Moellendorff's work from the point of view of principles (see p. 161), some more details of his programme and the position of the socialist leaders of this time towards " *Planwirtschaft* " should be given. It cannot be said Moellendorff's plan meant, in fact socialisation, or nationalisation of the means of production, but only by degrees. His beginning to carry out such far-reaching plans aimed at lifting Germany out of chaos and building up a new system. The first aim, of course, made the fulfilment of an economic programme difficult; but it is the lot of all active reformers to carry out their plans at the height of the tempest. I may add here that even the most ardent followers of Marx could not tackle the problem otherwise than by such a planned system. Wherever for the last twenty years State socialist plans in various countries were taking shape, they had to use schemes of economic planning. In our transitional time the economic system naturally is composed of both constituents, laisser-faire and planning. However these " planned " schemes may differ, socialist to a great degree as they are, they are the only practical schemes of States which wish to rule their economic systems by conscious direction under social control. Undoubtedly the socialism of these schemes was severely materialist, and so Moellendorff followed a strong mercantilist line. His was nothing if not an anti-capitalist mind. That romanticism which now infuses the ideology of the Third Reich was strong in him, and the Third Reich is now absorbing those ideas of Spengler ("Prussianism and Socialism"), Moellendorff and others. Apart from every ideological point of view, practical considerations demanded continuity, so all the existing " associations " of trade, industry and agriculture (including mainly certain cartels) which once derived, no doubt, as a consequence of a capitalist competitive system, *should be preserved for establishing bodies of self-government. Here one followed simply the administration of the economic system of the War period.* With the road trodden in this manner, planning, where it necessarily encroached in neighbouring districts grew enormously. Planning once begun never ends. This was all the more clear to people who followed this course during the long War period. To fulfil these tasks without friction or red tape was the task with which the Ministry of Economic Affairs was confronted after 1918. The War economy ended in the blind alley of bureaucracy which had carried red tape into a new sphere. The old belief, proved everywhere, that bureaucracy in the economic field will quickly be accompanied by corruption, showed itself conspicuously at the end of the War. It was difficult to act under the given conditions, because a " socially-minded " bureaucracy did not exist. What was good in the traditional civil servant was now frequently diluted by new War officials biassed with other views. So it was obvious that it was simplest to preserve the " association system " that private economy had built up through long years. But it is obvious, too, that such a system—as a system of State or Government control—shows different features if led and exercised by a spirit of private capitalism or by socially conscious agents of the community. That was the crux of the War period which showed various types of peoples operating the system. At the end of one epoch and at the dawn of a new one, Rathenau, Moellendorff and others saw clearly that only a very slow process of changing two different mentalities was possible, and for that very reason the work was especially risky in the turbulent time of transition.

Moellendorff's plans are laid down in some very interesting documents which he, in his capacity of Under-Secretary of State for Economic Affairs, submitted to the leaders of the government of the Reich (of 28/11/1918, of 3/12/1918, of 7/5/1919).[12] They contain a complete economic programme within the constitutional framework of the Reich. First of all an all-embracing economic policy of the Reich was suggested with one central organ to deal with the regulation of production, distribution and corresponding money processes. (Hitherto the handling of economic problems was scattered over various departments without any connection, in which every diversity of opinion was possible). A thorough system of groups of all trades (not unlike the War cartels under central government supervision) organised in a kind of self-government, had to consult and assist the central economic government office. Moellendorff made definite suggestions as to how to start work by public orders. First of all he wished to make use of all hitherto private companies connected with the Reich and for this purpose a bank belonging to the Reich had to be established.[13] His suggestions were rather radical, and proposed, e.g., that the State should take part in the industrial enterprise by a planned taxation of property. This and the death duties were to give the Reich the means by which it could acquire a great part of German stocks and shares or other kinds of property. For instance, the companies, instead of paying taxes, would have to give shares to the Government. So a kind of expropriation would result, while the management would remain with the companies. The above-mentioned bank would also have to take over a great part of the stocks and shares.[14]

A certain *Reichsfund* consisting of some thousand million marks was to be formed and managed by the afore-mentioned plan. This was to operate in close connection with the self-governing economic associations, which were to promote production of goods and so create employment. Comparison with the loans floated in later times—the advance taxes loan when Papen was Chancellor and the employment creation loan in 1933—shows many similarities. There is another idea which was later adopted : if the government provides work to completely unemployed industries, then the government must take its share of the profits with the industries. So Moellendorff in his official report to the government suggested that the profits of the companies concerned should be limited, and any excess above a certain amount should be transferred to a Reich fund. Moellendorff's plan not only provided a list of preferences according to which the restricted resources of capital and material had to be used most efficiently for the most urgent purposes, but, under his personal supervision, these plans were worked out in detail in the Ministry of Economic Affairs, in close collaboration with the corresponding associations and other representative groups of trades and industries. Moellendorff in his programme provided a complete system of groups, which were divided according to subject and region, and in which employers, employees and consumers had formally an equal share.[15] It was already realised how difficult it would be at this time of chaos to provide the necessary raw material and foodstuff without foreign bills or gold. The beginnings of regulation of the foreign bill business—an important element in Nazi Germany—were made in these plans.[16]

It is very difficult to examine the problem under the aspect of how far this decline of a competitive system had to be considered as an emergency measure or as a complete change of principles. A war lost under the German conditions certainly necessitated a longer wait for the general recovery ! The attitude of the Allied Powers was so obviously hostile that it was not difficult to predict that Germany was dependent on self-help for a long time to come. So the policy was nothing other than the continuation of the War economy. The country was still a besieged fortress, which had to economise means and distribute them according to their scarcity. History must record that if Germany wanted to keep her independence, she had no other choice. If the nations really intended to bring economic conditions back to the lines of free competition, especially on the world market, they had to do everything to animate the vanquished enemy to go on with his work, so that he could meet his problems. The plan of self-sufficiency was conceived by many economists and politicians at this time but was especially put forward by Moellendorff. He felt it the weapon of the weaker nation against its powerful oppressors, who were dominated by the mania of "sanctions" and conquest. The affinities between economic nationalism and political nationalism laid in this period the seeds of the systems, the consequences of which are now conspicuous.

Political and economic self-defence was the answer of the vanquished. In a book[17] containing Moellendorff's pamphlets and documents, his policy is described by the editor as conscious *Binnenmarktpolitik*, i.e., national home policy, certainly presupposing self-sufficiency. If this were Moellendorff's work, then it was that of an active statesman with a temporary goal which he realised would take a long time to reach. Moellendorff himself described his system as a type of constructive socialism, thus going further than his interpreters. From the point of view of the economic historian, self-sufficiency (comprehensible as a necessary emergency measure) is a throw-back which (as often stated in this history) creates abnormal conditions of production and distribution among the peoples of the world. Peoples begin production of goods which are outside their natural field, whilst peoples with a natural monopoly for these goods are impoverished. They, as the normal customers of the now self-sufficient peoples, cannot buy from them because of their falling purchasing power. So, the whole period, which no doubt is typical for the world, stamps itself as transitional until the time will come when world production and consumption are more normally adjusted; perhaps without aggressive nationalism which has to use violence even upon its own subjects to carry out the economic task. The disciple of laisser-faire and the planner both aim at an optimal economy.

With Moellendorff's short but impressive appearance, the socialist period of the Weimar Reich reached its peak. On 8th July, 1919, the Cabinet unanimously rejected Moellendorff's plans, " *Aufbau der Gemeinwirtschaft* " (Germany's economic planning) which Minister Wissell submitted to the Cabinet. A Cabinet which was preponderantly socialist rejected with it many socialist plans influenced by the Marxian and other schools. Amongst these plans were the restriction of the entrepreneurs and State partnership in or complete ownership of the means of production and even the centralised economic guidance of the community. Neither the committees of socialisation, which led a shadowy existence in Germany, nor yet the various socialists in high government offices produced hardly any constructive socialist idea.

The historian's interest is attracted by the fact that the Third Reich followed directly in its social and economic system the model given by the Weimar Reich, most noticeably in its ideas of planning; it again depends on the mercantilist State. *Natura non facit saltum.*

§2 *Stabilisation*

The year 1923 was, perhaps, the most critical for the Weimar Reich. At a time when the pressure from abroad upon the changing German governments was at its height, the existing chaos at home paralysed every attempt to set the house in order. In 1922, Dr. Cuno, a former high civil servant in the Reichs-Finance Ministry, later managing director of the Hamburg Amerika Line, followed Dr. Wirth of the Centre Party as Chancellor of the Reich. His Cabinet was intended to be a non-party body, including members of different views, with the aim of organising national resistance to the demands of the Entente. Opinions differ as to whether Big Business was too selfish to support Cuno,[18] or whether the variety of conflicts with which Germany was faced at home and abroad did not allow him to carry through such a policy. The words of Clausewitz, " peace is the continuation of war by other means," were more than true as regards Poincaré's policy after the Great War, and especially in 1922-23. Cuno demanded that a final estimate of reparations should be calculated according to Germany's capacity to pay. He rebelled against the methods of his predecessors who, by compliance with every ultimatum, were reduced to successive demands for respite and so carried Germany from one date of payment to another without offering her any hope of solution (Rosenberg). If his plans for a definite solution were refused and the Entente continued pressure, there was no other way than a resistance to the occupation of the Ruhr and any other coercive measures insisted upon by France. Unless inflation, which destroyed any combined action by the mass of the people was brought to an end, such a national policy was not possible. Cuno found support among the middle-class parties and among the Social Democrats. Whilst the Communists refused to enter into a political truce with the government, they agreed to a policy of national resistance to France. Poincaré refused Cuno's suggestions and asked for the fulfilment of all payments and insisted that sanctions had to be enforced upon Germany. It was not difficult to establish Germany's default and asserting that Germany had not delivered the agreed quantities of coal and timber, France occupied the Ruhr in order to confiscate coal. On January 11th, 1923, a Franco-Belgian army occupied the Ruhr district whilst England and Italy made no attempt to interfere with Poincaré's plans. (Rosenberg.)

The Cuno government responded by stopping all further payments or deliveries to the Powers that had sent their troops to the Ruhr. Passive resistance, in fact, began. Civil servants, police forces, officials and managers of the mines and other industries were removed by the French army, which soon pursued a policy of terrorism against the population of the occupied zone. French soldiers fired on German demonstrators. The historian, Arthur Rosenberg, says[19] that the only sphere in which a really successful resistance could be made was the economic one. He accuses the industrialists of making a mockery of passive resistance. They prevented the general strike with which the workers of the Ruhr district proposed to meet the invasion. The industrialists kept the pits open, fearing the loss which cessation of production would bring, and disregarding the compensation offered by the Government. The French, on entering, forbade the export of coal into the unoccupied districts of Germany. The German mine-owners begged to produce coal for the local inhabitants and industries and for a reserve of coal for delivery to the unoccupied areas in case a compromise with France was found. " Thus, the production of coal, though it was much restricted by the abnormal conditions, never actually came to a standstill."[20] The miners worked the coal and piled it at the pit mouth. When the French approached, they left the spot indignantly and did not return until the French, assisted by foreign labourers whom they brought with them, had taken away the coal with great difficulty. The process was repeated time after time, and was known as "national passive resistance."[21] I do not know whether Rosenberg is right in saying that the Cuno government should not have permitted the German mine-owners to play this game but should have ordered cessation of work in all industries in the occupied area. He asserts that the German workers, at that time ready to make any sacrifice, were prohibited by the great industrialists, and Cuno who, as he says, was not imbued with the spirit of Robespierre of 1793, did not feel inclined to take strong measures against the German capitalist class of which he was a member. Another opinion is that all the events which had occurred since the beginning of the War had had such a demoralising effect on the working class of Germany's biggest industrial area that they were no longer capable of a national resistance. Lack of space prohibits me from giving an account of the low real wages and the terrible state of nutrition among these workers, and of the consequences, especially of the disastrous moral and physical consequences on youth.

It was not Cuno's fault that his plan to act with an all-embracing policy to deal with Germany's recovery failed, as far as foreign policy was concerned. The only way to carry on an economic policy would have been to stop inflation, a measure which Cuno and some of his supporters and some experts contemplated seriously at this time. The breathing space obtained by the refusal to pay reparations after the Ruhr invasion, gave Germany an opportunity to stabilise her currency through her own efforts. I shall describe later on the events leading to stabilisation. I need only mention here that in January, 1923, the government fixed a rate of exchange that made the dollar worth about 20,000 Marks. This measure only had the effect of stabilising currency until April, and then " the patience of the speculating financiers and industrialists gave way " (Rosenberg). The dams broke " and during the next few months the paper Mark literally vanished into the void." Here again Rosenberg accuses " the capitalist class " and Cuno, who, as a prisoner of his own class, did not take the necessary measures. "When the dollar exchange crept up into the region of milliards, passive resistance was brought to an end and Cuno's plan had failed." It was only too clear that under these conditions the process of demoralisation must grow rapidly. " For a loaf of bread, notes were paid the face value of which ran into milliards or even billions. The German currency had, in fact, lost all value."[22] Alone the financial speculators, great industrialists, and estate owners reaped a rich harvest. Goods were produced at absurdly low costs and Germany could sell at a cheaper price than any other country. So production rose in 1923, and goods were dumped upon foreign markets./ The inflation hit most at the German lower middle class, the wage and salary earners, and swept away all the savings of the thrifty. Rosenberg ends with these words: "The systematic expropriation of the German middle classes, not by a Socialist Government but by a bourgeois State whose motto was the preservation of private property, is an unprecedented occurrence. It was one of the biggest robberies known to history." And in this connection he quotes Stresemann (Nobel peace prize meeting, June 29th, 1927, Oslo): " . . . the intellectual and productive middle class, which was traditionally the backbone of the country, has been paid for the utter sacrifice of itself to the State during the War by being deprived of all its property and being proletarianized. How far reasons of State could justify the demand of such sacrifice of a whole generation—a sacrifice that consisted in the total devaluation of money issued by the State, . . .—is a question upon which the minds and, perhaps, also the practice of the legislature have hitherto been mainly exercised."[23] The working classes had similar losses. In spite of the fact that the number of unemployed in Germany was relatively small in 1923, real wages were falling lower and lower between April and October. Rosenberg quotes a statement " that in October of this terrible year the wages of a trained and skilled worker for one week were just about sufficient to buy a hundred-weight of potatoes. Nine or ten hours of work were necessary to pay for a pound of margarine. For a pound of butter a man would have to work for several days. A hundred-weight of fuel briquettes cost the pay of twelve hours work. A pair of ordinary boots took six weeks' pay, and a suit of clothes that for twenty weeks."[24] We have to bear these facts in mind as a background for the fearful convulsions in which Germany was involved at this time. She was shaken by the fear of revolutions by both Communists and national extremists. At this time mass-psychology and ideology were shaping themselves into the antagonistic ideas which clashed during the next period and came to a head in January, 1933.

The fight of German governments against inflation goes back to the year 1919, when the then Reichsfinanzminister Erzberger, failed to stabilise the German Mark, a step seriously contemplated by him and his supporters, in order to stop the War inflation. The connection between reparations (direct payments and indirect burdens) and the inflation of German currency is evident. The unknown amounts of obligations towards the Entente hung like a sword of Damocles over the German head and prevented or postponed every necessary solution. In the spring of 1922 the Entente answered Germany's demand for a moratorium in her current reparation payments with a demand for making the Reichsbank independent of the Reich. This was based on the conviction that the Reichsbank, in complying with the demands of the Germany treasury for money, hindered the fulfilment of the reparation obligations. In fact, in May, 1922, a decree made the German currency bank " autonomous." The German tragedy was heightened by the fact that the governor of the bank, Herr Havenstein, was hardly suited to these exceptional times. He could not produce constructive plans for a general policy, which required a sound knowledge of monetary theory. During the summer of 1923 the German government, and also financiers and industrialists, recognised the impossibility of carrying on affairs without a stable currency. A speedy decision was necessary before it was too late, and before all that remained of the existing order was swept away by a social revolution. On 12th August, 1923, the Cuno government resigned, leaving behind the destruction of the German currency, economic dissolution and political chaos. Stresemann, formerly a secretary of employers' associations in the finishing industries, and at the same time one of the best speakers in the Reichstag, became Chancellor. During his period of office, stabilisation schemes suggested to the government and to the currency bank were seriously discussed. One such scheme was suggested to the government by Dr. Helfferich. He began his career as a University lecturer and a pupil of G. F. Knapp, who first influenced him in his work on monetary problems. After a short period as a civil servant, he joined subsidiary companies of the Deutsche Bank, such as its railway companies in the Near East, and then held a seat on the board of this greatest German deposit and financing bank. During the War, he became, among other things, the Cabinet Minister for the Treasury which financed the War by loans and which prepared the way for all those later inflationary measures of issuing treasury bills with the help of the Reichbank. After the Great War, Helfferich became a member of the German Nationalist Party (Conservative) in the Reichstag. He was an outstanding figure of his party and was fully expected to lead it, but met his death in a tragic accident.

An historical investigation is not the place for a thorough examination of monetary theories. Their application cannot be enforced in a uniform manner at all times. Confidence of creditors is called for, without which no scheme can work, and the inducements offered will vary with the development of experience. A stabilisation scheme in the year 2000 will not be the same as one in 1923. When the political and economic chaos demanded strong action, the state of knowledge at that time could find no other ultimate solution than a currency founded on a medium independent of changes in the political scene. Confidence at home and abroad towards a German currency was certainly best brought about through one medium, and that was gold. Therefore, as I shall show, even with the interim-solution of the Rentenmark, the connection with gold has never been abandoned. Germany was at this time more than ever dependent on international economic relations and needed this general confidence. French policy was not governed by the belief that ultimately economic ends could only be solved by economic means. The policy aiming at the prevention of German recovery did everything to increase the chaos. At a time when the Ruhr invasion coincided with a widespread revolutionary atmosphere at home, a stabilisation scheme could not be devised in the academic seclusion of a study.

Troubles had to be overcome in order to convince foreign countries of Germany's still existing political and economic strength, and, particularly when one of the strongest Powers was politically biassed in its decisions, this could only be achieved by a currency as independent as possible of political influences. At a time when a German party immediately under Soviet Russian command planned to overthrow the existing system, the fear of monetary improvisations did much to deflect the support of capitalist nations. There was, too, a variety of expert opinion. Knapp's nominal theory exerted a strong influence. A final solution on nominalist lines was, however, not possible; for it under-estimated the factor of confidence, especially in those unbalanced times. In fact, non-economic, and above all, psychological, factors were decisive in restoring the confidence of the masses—directly by their effect on national economy, and indirectly through that on the confidence of foreign creditors. A gold basis was imperative, but the country's lack of gold prevented an outright return to it; an interim solution was all that could be found. To stop inflation meant primarily to stop the issue of notes and this, in turn, involved the diminution of budget expenditure as well as other measures of deflationary character. But every interim solution led to mistakes which involved it with a more or less unstable currency, the very end which the final solution sought to avoid. Seen retrospectively, this end would never have been accomplished had it not been for the Dawes Loan. Perhaps the judgment of history will recognise the necessarily experimental character of the German stabilisation. The historian Arthur Rosenberg calls the stabilisation through the Rentenmark a bluff. If so, then it was a successful bluff and the value of decisions in history depends on success more than on other things. The ill-omened Loan raised in August, 1923, and intended to be one of stable character based on gold value, was to be the first step towards stabilisation. The Loan amounted to 500 millions of gold Marks, which could be subscribed for either in foreign currencies or in paper Marks. The Loan was allotted in units which corresponded to dollar values, and was, therefore, in Germany called the " Dollar Loan." It was intended to cover the budget deficit by this loan, and taxes were to be based on stable value. But this plan failed because these two means were not sufficiently far-reaching to arrest inflation. That could, perhaps, have been achieved if some measures had been carried through, such as the increase of the bank rate, thorough-going restrictions of credit to trade and industry and continuation of a rigid foreign bill control. An expected deflationary phase was supposed to bring about exports which in turn would have provided Germany with foreign bills. Since the issue of notes was not stopped, a more complicated route, involving the so-called Rentenmark, was followed. Dr. Schacht[25] called that part of the plan which purported to reconcile the powerful German agrarian group with the Government's currency policy (to which the group was opposed, as it was opposed to all its measures) a work of genius. According to the plan the currency was to be backed by the German landed property. Dr. Helfferich suggested a plan to stabilise the currency by the introduction of a " rye-Mark." This was a currency whereby the value of money was to depend upon the value of the grain. It was fortunate for Germany that this suggestion was never put into practice, for that would have based a currency upon a completely unstable standard of value, to say nothing of the impossibility of adjusting the new German currency to the stable foreign currencies. Dr. Helfferich explained (*Reichswirtschaftsrat*, September 6th, 1923) that, at the time of the French Revolution the attempt of the Republic to stop inflation by issuing currency, backed by the ecclesiastical property and the national lands only failed because this money was not convertible. Gold, however, for this purpose was not available, so some other backing had to be found. To Helfferich, money could be kept stable only if convertible and that was to be arranged by means of certificates based on rye, and managed by a bank similar to the German mortgage and landed property banks. Here Helfferich's point of view on this convertibility corresponded with that of many of his German colleagues who wrote on the currency problem before the War. But the restriction of note issue and not its convertibility was the factor which was to effect stability. Certainly, if his opinion were true, rye-Mark certificates were preferable to notes ostensibly convertible into gold, for this was not available at the time. The political effect of gaining the confidence of land owners, as expressed in Helfferich's and Dr. Luther's plans, was dubious in character. First, the inducement offered, which was the stabilisation of rye prices, was in itself doubtful and even then only the big estate owners would benefit while the smaller owners were not interested in rigid and high prices of rye. At that period, the price of rye was very high as compared with industrial products. The convertibility of certificates based on rye or on landed property is highly complicated and is accompanied by many shortcomings. But Helfferich also wished to stop the tremendous discounting of treasury bills by the Reichsbank. Helfferich's plan had at least one good aspect, namely, the fixing of the total amount of notes at four thousand million Marks. This corresponded roughly to the average circulation of notes in the preceding years. It is true, a certain disadvantage might be involved in the rigid upper limit of the amount of the issue.

Helfferich's plan, which was based on the consideration that no big gold cover was necessary and upon the anticipation that foreign bills would come in, had to make provision for the urgent import of goods. He was of the opinion that the Rentenbank, which was later established to carry through the government's plan, was only a transitional organisation and that foreign relations would require another organisation for which he visualised the plan of a bank of gold or foreign bills. Schacht, although accepting the idea of an interim plan, was strongly in favour of the reintroduction of gold currency and was opposed to Helfferich's plan to introduce the rye-Mark certificates. It is to the credit of the then Finance Minister, Dr. Hilferding (known for a treatise—very Marxian in outlook—on finance capitalism which he had written as a young Austrian physician before the War) that he very properly refused to adopt so speculative a scheme as the rye-Mark, and supported the idea of gold as a basis for the new currency. The government at first determined to create a special gold note bank which was to be completely independent of the Reich finances by possessing legal autonomy, although working in conjunction with the currency bank. It was Helfferich's intention that the Rentenbank was to be established by private enterprise through its centralised organisations only, which he felt would appear more trustworthy to foreign creditors than the Reich. His slogan, and that of Big Business, was "hands off" as far as the State was concerned. The new bank ultimately did become established by these organisations, but the new Finance Minister, Dr. Luther, and other members of the high bureaucracy rejected a direct dependence on these economic groups. In the deflation crisis the readiness of such groups to return to the policy of increasing money tokens was to justify the rejection of their influence. Dr. Luther brought a certain influence to bear on the scheme which finally came into being. He had made his name as a local government official and was for a long time secretary of the German association of town corporations. During the War he was associated with the War food board, and later he was appointed Minister of Food in Stresemann's Cabinet, which office he subsequently changed for that of Chancellor of the Reich, Governor of the Reichsbank and Ambassador to the United States. He suggested a "land-Mark," the cover for which was to be German landed property (debt certificates on mortgages of landed property were of old standing in German law).

The new Mark, final plans for which had been conceived by Hilferding, ultimately materialised as a mixture of the various conflicting suggestions. At this time the South of Germany had more or less cut itself away from the North, fighting was taking place in Middle Germany—a real civil war—and on the 8th and 9th of November came the revolt in Munich of Ludendorff and Hitler with their plan of a march on Berlin.

When Hilferding was suddenly overthrown in the same year, he had already prepared the way for the end of the German inflation. The Cabinet decree which created the new currency bank, the Rentenbank and its establishment, came into being in autumn of 1923. The decisive factor in the stabilisation was the balancing of the budget, in other words, the continuous inflationary note issue, by means of which it was financed, was to cease. Stringent reduction of the State's expenditure, increased taxation, and restriction of credit were the main means adopted to attain this objective. No doubt, additional note issue could not be completely stopped until normal income could be expected to cover vital demands. Halm[26] says that the problem would never have been solved in this late stage of inflation if the increase of the amount of money had been the decisive cause of the fall in the value of money; but, in fact, this was not the decisive cause. It could be proved that the increase of money did not correspond to the fall in value of the currency and occasionally a great shortage of money tokens was observed. Furthermore, the value of the mark fell fifteen times more than the amount by which the money was increased. The amount of money, expressed in gold Marks was only one-fifteenth of the amount of the money circulating before the War. An explanation for these facts can only be supplied by the enormous increase in the velocity of circulation which was the necessary psychological consequence of the continuous fall in the value of money. This was one force intensifying the fall in value. If it was possible to decrease this velocity of circulation, then the amount of money had to be increased if, at a given price level, the normal amount of monetary transactions were to be possible. This increase of money (which, of course, was not allowed to outstrip certain limits) again enabled the vital demand for credit by the State and by private enterprise to be satisfied for a transitional period. It is clear that the diminution of this velocity of circulation was a *sine qua non* if confidence in the stability of the new currency was to be given.

In these circumstances it was psychologically sound to maintain a certain fiction that the Rentenmark was really backed by Germany's landed property and by a guarantee of her corporate organisations. The new money was backed by "*Rentenbriefe*," certificates based on gold value and bearing six per cent. interest, which pledged the whole of German agricultural property. The Rentenmark was based on gold but was not convertible into it. It is true that with this procedure every amount of money issued could be "backed." The real advantage was the limitation upon the total amount of Rentenmarks to be issued. The government issued only 2,400 millions of the authorised 3,200 million Rentenmarks. These were allotted in equal parts to the public administration and to private economic forces. The new law did not forbid the Reichsbank to issue notes, but the issue of notes backed by treasury bills was prevented, while issues backed by commercial bills were still allowed. The conversion of notes into gold was again suspended, but the Reichsbank received the privilege of issuing notes backed by gold, a measure which presaged the return to gold. The new Rentenmark rested on the same weight of gold as the former gold

Mark. Thus, the exchange relation of the dollar to the Rentenmark was fixed and a basis was given for the stabilisation of foreign bills. On November 15th, 1923, the new issue came into the hands of the public. On November 20th, 1923, the exchange relation of one billion paper marks to one Rentenmark was fixed. The stabilisation took place without any legislative act, through the readiness of the Reichsbank to exchange the new token at the indicated rate, but there were still many difficulties to be overcome. Dr. Schacht, the currency commissioner, felt it his first duty to inspire the commissioner for foreign bills to raise the arbitrarily fixed dollar rate on the Berlin Stock Exchange to the free quotation on the Stock Exchanges of the world. From the beginning of the War, foreign bill control had been in fact exercised, with the intention of avoiding fluctuations of the foreign bill rates in critical times. Schacht was appointed currency commissioner on November 12th, 1923, when the official exchange rate was 630 thousand million marks to the dollar. On November 12th it was raised to 840, on November 14th to 1,260, on November 15th to 2,520, on November 20th to 4,200 (all expressed in thousand millions of Marks). That was the rate in dollars at which the Rentenmark was stabilised. For various reasons there was, up to April, 1924, a certain small inflation. There were still some different money tokens in circulation besides the new Mark, and the unification of the currency was accompanied by considerable difficulties. Among these money tokens, the " emergency " money issued by individual works and by municipal authorities had to be exchanged into the new Mark, but the commander-in-chief of the French army of occupation ordered the continued acceptance of this " emergency " money.[27] In Western Germany, and in particular from the Stock Exchange in Cologne, there was a strong and not unexpected resistance[28] to this attempt of the Reichsbank to regain control over the German currency. The Cologne Stock Exchange was protected by the occupation army and was free from foreign bill control and did not care much about stabilisation policy. Speculation there was continued beyond November 15th. Even on November 20th, the date on which the dollar rate in Berlin was fixed at 4.2 billion, speculation reached the rate of 11.7 billion Marks to the dollar. With stabilisation, the way was open for an improvement of German economic conditions. Retrospectively, it is easy to appreciate the mirage-like appearance which the future must have then presented. The interim stabilisation was followed by the Dawes plan which ended inflation but did not solve the problem of recovery. Outwardly it was a recovery but it was only a " borrowed " one, resting on enormous debts from abroad. Neither the political nor the social and economic Germany was sufficiently consolidated to suffer the blows to come—once the trend of the trade cycle changed. The Dawes plan, and Stresemann's policy connected with it, have been judged harshly by the divergent political wings in Germany. National politicians regarded it as the enslavement of

Germany under the yoke of international capital and under disruptive elements in the State. The Left saw in it a resurrection of the power of army generals, junkers, and the capitalist group, which from 1879 had constituted the Prusso-German domination. But nobody can say what would have become of the country if it had not received at least relative security of its political organism from the foundation of a more solid currency, even if that was achieved only by external debts. The absence of such security has been declared the cause of the over-capitalisation, over-production and under-consumption (which necessarily had to follow the Dawes-Stresemann policy which, in turn, has been emphasised as a cause of the Great Depression).

Laisser-faire has often been praised as the only means of recovery for all concerned. Germany's desire to retain her sovereignty as a nation and State which survived at least as a framework, was natural enough. What could laisser-faire have achieved in Germany? Would other nations of their own free will have given to this people of 67 millions the standard of living which again existed after 1924? Germany's peculiar condition lay in her dependence upon her gigantic export trade, production for which is carried on in only a few very densely-populated centres. Any setbacks which these export industries meet must reflect on the very existence of the people. Even before the War, Germany's resources of raw material were relatively small. The Treaty of Versailles, as a further handicap, took away roughly three-quarters of Germany's deposits of iron-ore and other metals—and Germany was the greatest producer of steel in pre-War Europe! Nearly a quarter of those provinces which provided her with corn and potatoes were lost. The most decisive means to prevent Germany's recovery was the destruction of all ties which linked together for the purposes of efficient production the various complementary and supplementary industries as well as the destruction of transport facilities. How could this country live, dependent as it was on export? Where has history since 1924 shown a single instance of a European industrial State which lived or wished to live under a system of laisser-faire? Instead of that, a vast system of protective duties, preference protection, quotas and so on, has been evolved throughout the world. Where were the markets for Germany? What were the possibilities for German existence if she was to be the only country left adhering to laisser-faire? She would have become the cockpit for other nations' quarrels, a dumping ground for their debris, a hotbed of revolutions which would have spread over the whole world involving both the vanquished and the victorious peoples of the Great War. The end of this chaos for Germany would not have been uncertain for him who knows the historical trend of German development. Did the policy of the Treaty of Versailles from Clemenceau and Poincaré to Barthou break in any way the vital energies of a people which continually demonstrated its " will to live," its militarism and its gift of organisation? If things had been left in a state of chaos, National Socialism would have been reached and it would have been reached earlier. The statesman who at this time directed Germany's destiny took the road which might not have led necessarily to collapse although in fact it did so later. The Germany that Stresemann left when he died in 1929 was a convalescent who relapsed. But how would the patient have fared without Stresemann and the Dawes Plan?

When the interim stabilisation had reached a certain maturity an alteration was seen in the policies which hitherto had been directed against Germany. The French elections in May, 1924, revealed the willingness of a great part of the French people to liquidate the Ruhr adventure and the new Premier, M. Herriot, promised an attitude of reconciliation. At this time, the United States, abundant in financial and economic power, considered that Germany offered splendid potentialities. The economic history of Western nations has shown many more risky markets than that of the industrious and eager German people. How the exhausted country was provided through diplomatic and financial channels with new capital cannot be described in this book. During these negotiations, in which the American Ambassador Houghton played an important part, Great Britain, through her Ambassador, Lord d'Abernon, was the great intermediary. In the spring of 1924 a foreign inquiry committee was set up in Germany which reported on Germany's political, financial and economic situation. This commission was led by Mr. Dawes, an American financier. It put forward a constructive plan to transform the political reparation question into an immense financial deal. The scheme was to provide Germany with a foreign loan amounting to 800 million gold marks. That was Act II of the stabilisation drama. The German Reichsbank received so substantial a backing for its currency that it was enabled to abandon the transitional currency and to return to gold. He who knew Germany's financial situation at the end of November, 1923, cannot but feel that a solution giving an effective basis for commercial transactions was little short of a miracle.

The purpose, as far as the diplomatic financial side of the scheme was concerned, was to enable Germany to raise taxes from her population, which, it was thought, would become more prosperous as a result of the new loan. In this way, the payment of reparations was thought to be possible. The Dawes Plan came into force on September 1st, 1924. It did not fix the total sum which Germany had to pay as reparations but specified annual payments for the years to come. The scheme provided for smaller amounts during the first period of four years, to permit economic development. In the final year of the period an amount of 2,500 million gold marks was to be paid. In the plan a welfare index and a gold index were provided for, and possible increases in the amount of the annuities were envisaged in the event of increasing German prosperity. In the first year, 1,000 million gold marks were to be paid as reparations, of which the greater part (roughly 800 million gold marks) was to be raised by an international loan to Germany—the Dawes Loan. The Dawes Plan remained in force for five years. The total of Germany's payments in these five years amounted to 7,970 million gold marks, and they were raised according to the regulations of the plan as follows[29]:

From the Reich budget	30.3%
Payment of German State railways (debentures and transport duties)	47.5%
Debentures of German industry	12.2%
From the Dawes Loan	10.0%

This set of figures shows that the plan involved, as a measure of security for the creditors, a system of control and supervision of figures mortifying to Germany's pride and usurping her rights of sovereignty. The State railways, the greatest individual railway undertaking of the world as well as the greatest State socialist experiment, were removed from the control of the government. An autonomous company was established, which exercised financial control as well as technical supervision. Representatives of the creditor nations were the decisive personalities on its board. To raise the amounts required for reparations the greatest possible strain was put upon the railwaymen and heavy sacrifices were demanded from them. Germany also lost her sovereignty as far as her currency bank was concerned. Mr. Parker Gilbert, an American business man, was appointed official " confidant " of the creditors. He became a kind of financial dictator, having for his offices a block of houses only a few minutes from Berlin's diplomatic and ministerial headquarters.

Methods such as these, long known to Western diplomatic and financial circles through experience in the Near and the Far East, were now applied to Germany. In reality, Germany became almost an annex to New York Big Business, completely dependent on fluctuations of American prosperity, a fact which was to prove disastrous when business in U.S.A. collapsed in the autumn of 1929. Her capacity to meet reparation obligations depended on these foreign loans. If Germany once failed to pay, her international credit would collapse and with it, perhaps, the political system so industriously built up by Stresemann.

These foreign loans gave to Germany such an impetus in the years 1924-1929 that she was able to raise the enormous taxes and also the reparation amounts. The whole plan was intended to be transitional until Germany could stand on her own feet again. The continuation of reparation payments depended, however, upon the uninterrupted inflow of foreign money and upon the avoidance of crises.

What did Germany really pay and how much did her individual creditors receive?

Up to the Hoover moratorium which began on June 30th, 1931, the payments on account of reparations[30] amounted, according to the German estimate, to 68,000 million marks. The Reparations Commission, however, credited the payments at about 21,000 million marks. The difference between the valuations of the payments on the part of Germany before the Dawes Plan came into operation are again striking. Germany estimated these amounts at about 42,000 million gold marks, whilst the Reparations Committee only credited them at 10,400 million gold marks.

The difference between the valuations appears mainly in the following items:

	GERMAN VALUATION	VALUATION OF REPARATIONS COMMISSION	
	In millions of marks	In millions of marks	As % of the German valuation
Confiscated German private property outside Germany	10,080	13.2	0.13
Imperial and Federal State property transferred	9,670	2,380.5	24.6
Residues not belonging to the army in non-German War zones	5,041	140.0	2.8
Shipping captured and transferred	4,486	711.5	15.9
Labour of German prisoners of War after the Peace Treaty in the zones of reconstruction	1,200	—	0.0

The estimates of the sums actually paid differ among the nations concerned. It has been said that the loans which Germany obtained in the U.S.A. and England were greater than the reparation payments. The Germans, however, argue as follows. According to the sums credited to Germany by the Reparations Committee, 8,100 million marks were paid up to the coming into force of the Dawes Plan. Then followed payments of 11,200 million marks until the Young Plan came to an end; that is, altogether 19,300 million marks. The Layton Report calculated Germany's obligations to the U.S.A. and England at 9,600 million marks (up to March 31st, 1931). In Germany, according to later estimates, this sum is alleged to exceed the true value by 2,000 to 3,000 million marks and the English and American loans were thus less than the reparation payments. Germany never recognised the statements of the Reparations Committee concerning the period before 1924 which differ greatly from those of the Washington Institute of Economics. This research institute estimates the total payments actually made to be 37,000 million marks, whilst Germany's foreign debts amounted at the most to 26,800 million marks in 1930. These foreign credits arose under the pressure of reparation payments which could not be met owing to the great lack of capital, and veiled the reparations problem for several years, but increased the actual foreign payments by the addition of an enormous interest. When the credit crisis came, it became evident that the repayment of debts which covered all the gold and foreign bill assets of the German Reichsbank was impossible. An increase of exports would have been necessary, which was impossible because of the protectionist policy of the creditor countries. With this arose the aggravated transfer problem of to-day, which is the same as the reparation problem of yesterday. The German reparations debt was fixed by the arbitary decision of the Reparations Commission (and without consideration of capacity to pay) in the ultimatum proclaimed in May, 1921, in London, at an amount of 132,000 million gold marks (plus 5,600 millions as balance of the Belgian War Debt to the Allies). These payments were to be paid in annuities of 2,000 million gold marks, plus 26 per cent. of Germany's export values. These payments, however, could neither be materialised in goods nor in foreign bills.

The Dawes Committee fixed the normal annuities at 2,500 million gold marks, but this figure was only to be reached by a rising annual amount in four years, beginning with September 1st, 1924. This amount could be increased if the cost of living index and the price of gold permitted higher payments. Eight hundred million of the first 1,000 million marks of the first annuity were lent to Germany through the Dawes Loan. Evidently it was not possible to raise the sums from her own exhausted trade and industry. The Dawes Plan was in operation for five years. The payments transferred in this time amounted to 7,970 million gold marks. Germany paid these sums out of loans from abroad. So in the following years she had also to borrow considerable sums to pay the annuities which in these five years were equally divided into cash transfer (in foreign currency) and payments in Reichsmarks ("*Sachlieferungen*"=in German goods, etc.). The proportion on account of these goods decreased according to the wishes of Germany's industrial competitors, whilst the proportion of cash transfer in foreign currencies increased from about one-third to one-half.

The offence against the established teachings of economics of compelling a country, forming a part of the world economy, to export foreign cash without corresponding goods, led to the plan of the Young Committee (June 7th, 1929). This included certain special agreements, such as those concerning payments to Belgium and to the U.S.A. (in repayment of the costs of occupation in Germany) and the claims of American property (mixed claims). The new plan brought about the end of the Rhineland occupation and the system of control established under the Dawes Scheme. The Bank for International Settlements took over the activities of reparations agent.

The annuities were fixed until 1966 between 1,642 and 2,353 million Reichsmarks, and from 1966 to 1988 at 900 to 1,700 million Reichsmarks. The scheme provided for the repayment of those sums by which the Allies were mutually indebted to each other. Again, the international loan burdened the German account. From September 1st, 1924, till 1931, June 30th, the payments had to be 10,172 million marks; altogether 11,128 million marks were paid.

On June 21st, 1931, the Hoover Moratorium ended the payments. This scheme was intended to enable Germany as well as other countries suffering from the world crisis to recover. France, however, insisted that Germany should repay the sums postponed.

The shrinkage of foreign bills had made it impossible to pay anew her annuities as provided by the Young Plan. The International Bank in Basle, through a committee of experts, declared Germany's inability to pay and asked for immediate measures against the world crisis.

On July 9th, 1932, a new plan came into existence at Lausanne, which provided for a change of method of payment of the German debts—35,500 million marks. If the plan had come into force, Germany would have had to pay first 180 million marks per annum, instead of the Young Plan sums, and additional sums amounting to roughly 90 million marks for special obligations towards Belgium and U.S.A.

Between 1924 and 1931 Germany, parallel with her policy of economic recovery, took the opportunity to set her currency up again. Thus the gold cover at the end of 1924 was 760 million Reichsmarks, whilst by May, 1931, it had increased to 2,390 million marks (see p. 285).

§3 *Boom and Crisis*

In the survey (Chapter II) of the system of combines in the pre-War period, their variety of forms was described rather as adaptations of opportunities than of distinct functions. To become a monopoly or part-monopoly (consciously or unconsciously aimed at) was the most important function. Whether these combines were loosely held by agreements or were more closely interlinked or even completely unified depended on the temporary fitness of these forms for the method of financing and for the legal cloak of the undertaking. Forms changed frequently according to the vagaries of the trade cycle, and of a multitude of economic and political factors. Sometimes these forms in their adaptations marked distinct stages of development in the enterprises in question. The power of an economic group, commanding the whole monopoly formation, was the more essential issue; while the question of such forms as " parent," " roof," " key," " control," " pool," and their dependent companies such as " daughter " companies, " organ " companies, etc., was, in principle, of minor importance. The early years of the boom, with their many flotations and issues, or the years of the slump, when the mistakes had to be salvaged, both show striking excesses in comparison with more tranquil periods.

The period of the Weimer Reich, politically and economically chaotic from beginning to end, naturally followed the development and adaptations of the combines of earlier periods of chaos. It was a golden time for promoters, as in the period of 1873 and at the beginning of the 20th century. Whereas in previous periods the banks had a decisive influence in industry, at the time of inflation the "*Flucht in die Sachwerte*" (flight from the mark to substantial values such as factories, houses, land, etc.) gave the great industrial trusts a predominance and a certain independence of their former financing institutions which belonged to the *Konsortium* for their flotations, issues and other banking activities. At a time when profits fell hourly, the man in the trust or the trust's banking expert who understood arbitrage and other means of adjustment to favourable transactions in various currencies became dominant. At this time the biggest trusts had relations (besides their *Konsortial* banks) with small banking houses and broker firms, and of these mushroom institutions some grew to a gigantic size. To these bankers and tradesmen there belonged, to give a few names only, men such as Herzfeld, who operated in potash and other commodities ; Michael, the leader of a promoting trust ; and Flick, a trust-monger of genius. This latter appeared like a meteor, and in spite of heavy setbacks, is still one of the greatest shareholders in Germany. Once he had an outstanding position in the great steel trust. Then he experienced its temporary downfall, and later he appeared as controller of the " Harpen " works which he developed into another mammoth formation. At this time big trusts again developed their own "*Konzern*" banks (examples have been mentioned on p. 91 ; others such as the Deutsche Länderbank were established by the I. G. Farben A.G.). Financing institutions were established abroad with the profits derived from export business. The possibilities of protecting the " *Konzern* " against failures due to the deficiency of the home currency and for the development of foreign business were as great as the possibility of veiling balance sheets.

One of the worst examples of " veiling " through pyramiding was the case of the " Nordwolle," the big wool trust which contributed so largely to the bad end of the Darmstädter und Nationalbank. Amongst other things the trust, in the time of inflation, had established in Amsterdam a daughter company, called Ultramare, in order to collect there foreign bills deriving from exports (a measure often applied at this time by German trusts). Shareholders of these trusts might, perhaps, find some figures in their balance sheet about " shares in other concerns " but did not know anything about special daughter companies and the secrets they hid. When the inflation ended, the Nordwolle did not greatly care about its daughter companies, but when a crisis arose on the wool market and the parent companies suffered heavy losses on its wool supplies these losses were simply veiled by the Ultramare. This undertaking bought raw wool on the world market and conveyed it to the Nordwolle in Germany below its actual price. Thus the daughter suffered heavy losses while the parent showed profits.

Daughter companies often served, on the other hand as " secret " reserves of supply stores with high values which were not indicated in the balance sheet of the mother company. Liefmann[31] mentions other dangerous procedures of *"Effekten Substitution."* One potash company owned another potash company which again possessed the majority of the first concern. (Such manoeuvres are now being excluded by the new Company Law of 1937.) The ephemeral " Sichelkonzern " of the inflation—and post-inflation—period, had in its main German " concern " company with a share capital of 100 million marks, a company which controlled companies of various trades and industries. A daughter company in Switzerland established *ad hoc* (with 12 million of francs) owned again the greater part of the German trust. Nobody, including the revenue offices, knew where, in fact, the actual control was, in Germany or in Switzerland.

It was not so much new forms of enterprise but rather matured ones that showed themselves since the beginning of the century, according to the increase of men and goods. Principally it was the expression of an accumulation of events which covered the fields of trade, transport and commerce. The details that are here relevant are well described in the books of Liefmann and H. Levy.[32] It can only be the task of this history to survey in very broad outlines some few examples of industrial organisation.

The penetration of trading interests into production and the great complexity of enterprise under this influence, which already showed itself during the War, advanced rapidly. In non-ferrous metals the Merton-Concern, the Beer, Sondheimer & Co. Concern, and the A. Hirsch Concern went ahead. But also in coal and iron, trading firms, such as Klöckner, Stinnes, Ravené, Friedländer, Arnhold, Otto Wolff, Julius Sichel, some of them well known before the War while others were newcomers, reached leading positions. Commercial textile firms such as Lahusen (Nordwolle), Simon, Blumenstein, showed similar phenomena in more extensive forms. This was, however, no new development in that industry. Trading companies bought up manufacturing companies. Wool, cotton and jute showed trusts of this kind. Departmental stores (Karstadt, Tietz) followed the same example. Beer, spirits, insurance and many other branches of industry and trade were linked up in certain big trusts. While horizontal concentrations were still going on, the vertical form was now the more prevalent. Events marched on so rapidly that, even in the short period of the Weimar Reich, trusts and amalgamations, but newly established, were in this short time also dissolved. The *Interessengemeinschaft* agreements sometimes established for 90 years, were not valid for even half-a-dozen. Even old-established houses were infected with the mania of greater trustification or amalgamation. So the Siemens electricity works merged into a " community of interest " with the Stinnes Concern. The Siemens-Rhein-Elbe, Schuckert Union G.m.b.H. comprised a curious mixture of works. The Deutsch-Luxemburgische Bergwerksgesellschaft which Hugo Stinnes, the coal trader and shipper, once invaded, was the starting point for his ambitious plans. Inside the coal and iron industry the new giant trust swallowed up the Gelsenkirchen Bergwerksgesellschaft, the foundation of Emil Kirdorf, for many years the economic and political leader of that industry. The Bochum Gussstahlverein of the old coal-owning family, Barre, and some other works joined the trust. There was scarcely any branch of trade and industry which did not finally come under Hugo Stinnes' power. He was interested in chemical and textile works, in works which began with forests, sawing mills, pulp, and paper mills and ended in the printing and publishing of newspapers, etc. Shipping lines, hotels, the food trade, ticket offices, musical instruments and big banks—all this medley passed through his hands. At first, his activities, like those of some of his fellow captains of industry, meant the salvage of profits in substantial values at the period of inflation, later it was mere gambling. And this man who in his time was showered with adulation could envisage, before his sudden death, the end of this embodiment of inconsistencies. In fact, with the exception of a large colliery firm and some shipping and cellulose interests, there was not much of this mammoth trust left by the liquidation to his family. But the year 1926 (the British coal strike) gave the firm a new start. The Siemens works regained their liberty.

The Klöckner-Concern, the Stumm-Concern, the Thyssen-Concern, the Haniel-Concern, the Krupp-Concern, the Hoesch-Concern, the Röchling-Concern, the Lothringen-Concern, the Otto Wolff Phoenix-Concern, also acquired many other companies but they were much more careful and the works acquired showed more organic connection with the key undertaking. These trusts merged concerns of old traditions, and one saw the penetration of the basic industries into every field of the finishing industries, locomotives, nuts and bolts, razors and other cutlery articles. But the reverse system, with the control springing from works of the finishing industry (formerly more exceptional as in the case of Krupp) became more common. But, before the Weimar Reich ended, new formations showed themselves especially with the big industries merging again in other mammoth formations of recent establishment. Among these the Vereinigte Stahlwerke A.G. and the I.G. Farben A.G. were the greatest concerns Germany ever saw. The interlocking of the supervisory boards of these two trusts was significant. On these boards there appeared the same names of banking and other industrial magnates.

The rapid changes in which the big iron concerns were involved is best illustrated by the history of certain works, including those which Hugo Stinnes once held in his hands. Deutsch-Luxemburg, Gelsenkirchen, Bochumer-Verein, Phoenix, Rheinische Stahlwerke, Thyssen Hüttenwerke, etc., merged in the Vereinigte Stahlwerke A.G. Such a merger of enormous trusts, whose representatives once shaped industrial history, was not a voluntary formation. Anyone who is familiar with the autocratic will of industrial leaders, will guess that such a subjugation would be submitted to only at the stern bidding of necessity. But with this foundation in 1926 the process of amalgamation was by no means ended; for a new chapter began which, from then to the present time, shows continuous alterations. The giant steel trust temporarily added such works as the Rombach Hütte and the Charlotten Hütte in Silesia, and parts of the Stumm-Concern. The ownership of the major part of one of the greatest Upper Silesian trusts brought the steel trust into connection with this second greatest German industrial area. The Vereinigte Stahlwerke became the greatest shareholder of the trust which, in Middle Germany, controlled by far the greatest number of steel works and rolling plant, a merger which has recently been dissolved. Participation in coal mining, in products derived from coal such as the Ruhr-Gas A.G., the Ruhr-Chemie A.G. and a company dealing with the utilisation of tar, and Austria's greatest industrial mining undertaking can only be mentioned in passing.

Emerging from the Thyssen engineering works, the Demag (Deutsche Maschinen Fabrik A.G.) arose as part of the trust which also comprised constructional work, bridge building, nuts and bolts, cutlery articles and so on. There were also works which were not organically related to the trust. I must, however, again refer to literature showing how the Vereinigte Stahlwerke, in swallowing up trusts of such great variety, showed an intensified verticalisation.

The real significance of this trust is shown in its great influence in the cartels, such as iron and steel, coal, etc., and finishing groups which was always outstanding ("from coal to pig-iron and from semi's to structural steel, hoop-iron, thick plates, bar-iron, tubes, and wire rods."[33]

The Great Depression was a disastrous time for these mammoth formations. In the worst period, when Stock Exchange markings were stopped and only bank to bank prices were fixed, the Vereinigte Stahlwerke shares sank to a merely nominal value. Without the support of the Government, which became a great shareholder, this trust was faced with alienation by the foreign buyers of its share and debenture capital.

The German Enquiry Committee points out that a mere statistical description of company concentration can easily overlook the fact that amalgamation is reinforced by the linking up of several independent undertakings through a close network of financial relations; such combination while leaving formal independence to the single enterprises brings them into the field of bigger groups of interest.[34]

With the merger of all these companies a process of rationalisation set in, which covered the technical as well as the commercial side of the concern. This meant a period of experimentation. The trust itself was clumsy inasmuch as its part-trusts which it merged were "inorganic." The history of this huge German merger (Vereinigte Stahlwerke) can only be written by one who is allowed to see the records. Nobody knows whether they still exist, and a history based on these records has never been written. Perhaps it was a great salvage operation amongst companies and works extremely unprofitable at the time of the slump. In addition, it may be that this salvage action was used by the industrialists and the bankers concerned, in order to get substantial promoters' profits. The period of experimentation after the merger and the reconstruction shows that the bringing together of such giant enterprises cannot be judged either as a necessity or a failure. The cheapening of a process by rationalisation, which was partly attained, or could be attained in time was, undoubtedly, necessary for certain sections of this industry. Retrospectively one can say that in the period from the inflation to to-day, great changes in the technical and commercial organisation of the trust took place every year or so, whereby many an alteration of the composition and holding of the shares was effected.

This giant process of trustification in the iron and steel industry gives me the opportunity to make some more general remarks following upon Chapter II. Figures in the note [35] show that Germany's iron and steel industry maintained its remarkable importance even after the War, in spite of the loss of the basic raw material, the loss of territory and the troubles caused by the political changes. The German gift of keeping house with scanty means was inspired anew by all these troubles which prevented the country from continuing her rapid industrial progress. Iron-ore now had to be imported, and in the first five years after the Great War, scrap was used in great quantities, thus necessitating systematic economy. There were many methods tried to achieve recovery. Already, in 1933, Germany ranked third in world iron and steel production, an astonishing achievement, and was not far behind France, which held the second place. But it was not only the quantity but also the quality of the various products which was raised to a high standard, and more economical methods of production were introduced, which formed a system in itself covering as many activities as the mind could explore.

This typical process of planning was achieved by the co-operation of many factors, to which not only the rationalisation of the technical and commercial apparatus of the enterprises belonged, but also the financing of these big trusts. In these trusts the amalgamated companies and works supplement each other in the process of production and distribution. At the time of the slump, in which the banks and industrial concerns of the whole world were shaken as never before, one could not judge the measures carried out in Germany by the standards of normal times. The process of economising found expression, among other things, in the cheapening of transport, in transferring works to the most economical shipping points (interesting in this connection is the migration of many industries to the Rhine from Westphalia and other districts) and here is a certain justification for the combination movement on a scale which was never so large before. Conditions improved when Germany in 1925 regained the right to conclude commercial treaties and could protect herself against the free import of her necessary raw materials and semi-finished goods. Her financial revival, due to the Dawes Loan and the large amount of foreign capital drawn to Germany in connection with it, has been described. Heavy compensation for lost works, now outside the German borders, was used by the trust for considerable investments in its works inside the Reich. So long as there is no higher Advisory Board to direct investments, there may be no other way to make use of these large amounts of capital which undoubtedly ultimately over-capitalised German industries and helped to bring about the slump. When the machinery of production has been built up far beyond immediate need, this immobilising of capital contributes to the slump. But from the point of view of the upswing of the "next" cycle, the available productive capacity of the German works, and their relation to cost worked out very favourably. So disadvantages of the former cycle became assets in the next—the period of German rearmament, which demanded this high productive capacity.

These brief remarks cannot in any way outline the complexity of the combine problem, but may give some motives for the movement. It would have appeared as merely nonsensical in this chaotic period of politics and economics for German industry to have followed the free play of competition. No doubt, at this time she would have been the only free trader in the world. Considerations of a co-operation of all industries and their finances under a general competitive scheme for the whole world seem very remote at a moment of self-defence. From this angle the problem ceased to be one of economic mechanics. Either way may be right according to which starting point we choose. The method of using combines which involve the human brain in a network of plans of such variety and numbers in consequence converts men into experimenters. Such experimenters were the men who formed this colossal block, the Vereinigte Stahlwerke, which taking all provinces of its activities controlled a very high percentage of German production. But trusts were not so powerful as to exclude competition, and so the cartels for regulating competition still persisted. The great exporting industry had to meet the competition of the world market.

The problem of combination can be judged only in the light of the tradition and peculiar conditions of German industry as part of a complex problem. From a system which connects a thousand parts like those of an organism, it is not possible to isolate the functioning of one part and to contrast it with its imaginary function under free competition. In contrast to the British coal, iron and steel trades, Germany's territorial distribution predestined the competitors located in a relatively small area to balance their interests. Figures show[36] how high was the percentage of persons employed in the heavy iron industry in Westphalia and the Rhineland, and how great was its share of the whole German iron production. Long before this period, horizontal and vertical combinations in this district cheapened the process of production, and here the " pure " works as compared with the " integrated " works are very few. " This applies to the making of pig-iron as well as to the steel-rolling mills. It has been estimated that 90 per cent. of the pig-iron produced in the territory comes from furnaces belonging to undertakings which possess steel-rolling mills of their own."[37] It is not within the scope of an historical description to go into further details so far as this combination movement is concerned. When this movement spread to the finishing industries also, the pure mining concerns which lost their best customers had to turn into vertical combinations by acquiring mixed undertakings, especially iron and steel works.

It is a peculiarity of German heavy industry, which started much later than the British industry, that it was from the beginning adjusted to work on a large scale. The efficiency of larger technical and commercial units made the larger size appropriate for technical reasons as well as for reasons of competition. The German Enquiry Committee gives on this point an interesting comparison[38] : "At the end of 1913 there were in the Reich 313 pig-iron furnaces in blast, the production of pig-iron being then 16.7 million tons ; in 1930 the production of pig-iron amounted to only 9.6 million tons, but there were not more than 107 furnaces working and the number of existing furnaces had been reduced from 330 in 1913 to 158. In England the pig-iron produced in 1927 amounted to $7\frac{1}{2}$ million tons, but the number of furnaces amounted to not less than 437 ! So, in 1925 the output of pig-iron per furnace in blast was on the average 138,000 tons a year in the U.S.A., 96,000 in Germany and not more than 41,354 in England." Throughout and prior to the period under review basic iron and steel manufacture differed widely from the British manufacture in the small number of German works and commercial units. The drive towards vertical integration early caused the great reduction in the number of commercial units. A cheaper production was better guaranteed by extending this integration (see p. 186) by the conservation of heat from furnace to the production of semi-finished products. Small works were bought up in order to get the supply of raw material or semi-finished products and so compete more easily with great finishing works. Cartel activities directly and indirectly supported this process. Before and during the War these units corresponded in size to the demand. At the time of the boom, 1924-1929, the increase of investments and the productive capacity did not correspond to the actual demand. At the time of big investment in basic industries, the extent to which the capacity may be increased and yet maintain profits is hardly measurable and belongs to considerations of expectations of the enterprise. The same holds good for the enlargement of a concern by other undertakings, which normally serve the same purpose of attaining a greater efficiency.

Levy[39] presents some interesting arguments on the problem of protection and cartels. " The duties on iron and steel would have been ineffective if competition among the producing companies within the Reich had brought prices down below the level of world market prices plus duty and freight." Cartels and syndicates by fixing prices had to achieve that. " . . . the desire to make the utmost out of the protection afforded by the State instead of losing its ' benefit ' by over-competition, became a very strong stimulus to the formation of industrial combinations. It will be understood that industrial associations have by no means been able to maintain permanently the highest possible level of prices, i.e., the world market price plus duty and freight. But this fact does not dispose of the argument that prices would certainly have developed at times in a very different way if the policy of effective syndicates had not prevented their ' free ' play."[40] Showing figures from 1924 to 1930 which compare German and Belgian iron prices, Levy concludes that " the German price, though subject to considerable fluctuations, has been oscillating around the level by tariff protection, sometimes easily advancing above the world market price plus German duty."[41] And this author continues : " that cartels and syndicates, however their price policy may be judged or criticised, have been the means of raising prices to the level conceded by the grant of tariff protection and that it has been one of the avowed objects of cartelisation to bring this about."[42]

The great iron and steel syndicates which were formed in the time of the Weimar Reich are further stages of a long development. One syndicate regulated pig-iron (*Roheisenverband*), another syndicate regulated the output of unmanufactured steel, (the *Rohstahlgemeinschaft*); both syndicates were annexed to the Stahlwerksverband A.G. in Düsseldorf, Germany's greatest and most effective cartel, and one of the greatest in the world. This was a framework, too, for other iron and steel cartels. It represented the commercial management of other part-syndicates such as bar-iron, thick plate, hoop-iron, etc.

Since 1904 the heavy branches of the iron and steel industry were united in the Stahlwerksverband which controlled output and prices of the simpler kinds of products. A strong tendency towards combination in either form, horizontal or vertical, ran parallel with the cartel activities. From early beginnings a heavy war was waged inside the cartel between the member firms of the cartels, which led in 1919 to its breakdown. During the succeeding years, in which steel and steel products were not regulated, the increase of productive capacity was as great as the tendency to vertical combination. The result was a lack of markets to absorb the increase of production beyond capacity, and a consequent price war. On November 1st, 1924, the *Rohstahlgemeinschaft* was established. It was a cartel which served as " frame " or " base " cartel. Levy mentions that in the group of wire and wire products alone there were, in 1930, 17 different syndicates.

In the establishment of cartels the *Stahlwerksverband* kept its roof organisation for the sale of the various products, the *Rohstahlgemeinschaft* regulating control and allocation of A and B products. The various cartels annexed to the *Stahlwerksverband* fix the prices of their products, but are subject to regulations of the *Stahlwerksverband* as far as production and distribution are concerned.

In the course of events this system of cartels became the partners of international establishments of similar national kinds. So far as experiences of various industries show, there was every transition possible from cartel to trust as well as a twofold system of either cartels or big vertical concerns. Cartels themselves gained much by the increase of rationalisation and economic and technical unifications. But the movement towards the formation of bigger concerns did not lead to the abandoning of the activities of the cartels.

The movement towards iron and steel combination was, from early times, that of integrating coal, iron and steel. This process was facilitated because there were only two big centres, the Rhenish-Westphalian and the Upper Silesian—which were of importance for coal-mining. When lignite became a competitor to coal, the development had already shaped itself. Before the War (1913) 190 million tons of coal were used as against 87 million tons of lignite. In the boom year 1929 lignite even reached 174 million tons, but in 1933 the figure was 122 million tons. Briquette-making production and that of raw lignite are found in Middle Germany and in the Rhineland.[43]

The territorial distribution led very early in the thirties of the last century to combined action by undertakings, but it rapidly grew in the seventies and eighties. The growth of larger technical and economic units, at first a consequence of heavy competition, was assisted by the favourable geographical conditions. There is a big contrast to British coal-mining in respect of output per colliery and per man. Technical progress very soon brought great differences between the three nations, the United States, Great Britain and Germany. As far as coal-cutting machinery is concerned, in U.S.A. at the beginning of the century 25 per cent. of bituminous coal was cut by machinery, and the proportion in 1924 was nearly 70 per cent.; whilst Great Britain in the years 1925 and 1928 had 20.8 per cent. and 26 per cent., Germany had 59.4 per cent. and 77.7 per cent. of her coal cut by machinery. The various coal commissions in Great Britain disclosed differences between the two countries. German collieries producing up to 500,000 tons a year in 1900 numbered 72.77 per cent. of all the collieries. After the War this figure diminished greatly to 23.75 per cent. But the percentage of collieries producing from 500,000 tons to 1,000,000 tons rose in the same period from 27.23 to 60.29. The closing down of collieries has largely been furthered by the process of cartelisation and trustification. It lay in the interest of the big collieries to acquire quotas of the competitors, to shut down their pits and add the quota to their own more economically working plant.[44]

Combination in the iron and steel industry had a close connection with the movement towards monopolisation of coal mining. Iron and steel undertakings integrated themselves with coal mines, forming great combined works. The Rhenish-Westphalian Coal Syndicate, in conjunction with some others, goes back for half-a-century. The Westphalian Coke Syndicate was already formed in 1890, and the Coal Syndicate in 1893, and this combined itself with the coke and briquettes selling associations. During its long life it was able to elaborate a thorough organisation, which regulated the quotas of the member firms, price fixing and pooling. A central selling agency to which activities such as exports belonged was included. Up to the outbreak of the War the production of coal of the member firms was immensely increased and sometimes could not satisfy the demand, which made imports from England necessary in certain years, although there was overproduction in other years. The fluctuations of the market can change in forms and extent for which no scheme might be provided. Shortly before the War the great Coal Cartel was faced with questions which threatened its very existence. Since blast furnaces and steel works were in the same big concerns with the coal-mining industry, new interests of these industries emerged which did not comply with the former aims of the coal cartel. The iron industry, which had an interest in getting as many coalfields as possible to supply their now integrated plants, felt disinclined to regulate the general conditions of coal outside their interests. The agreement of the coal syndicate expired in 1915. Long before, discussions hinted at the difficulty of coming to new arrangements. The position of the mixed works and the increasing number of outsiders were clearly realised in these negotiations. The Prussian State which had itself become, for some years past, a coal-owner in order to balance private interests for the sake of public welfare, now entered the syndicate (1912). But the Prussian Minister of Commercial Affairs was prepared in the same year to leave the syndicate again because of its price policy. In 1914 there was no possibility of reconciling the interests of the " pure " and the " integrated " collieries. The State decreed on July 12th compulsory cartelisation, if the syndicate was not reconstituted by September 15th. (One has to bear in mind that this was the very time of uniting all industries in such cartels under Government's control, the " War-Companies.") A transitional coal syndicate, in which the State with its mines again entered, was the result of the pressure. In October, 1916, the new cartel agreement was achieved and all Ruhr mines, including those of the Prussian Government, joined it. Of 93 mining enterprises of the coal industry, 19 were such as used their coal in their own iron and steel or other works. More has been said in another place about the insertion of the coal syndicates into the socialisation scheme drafted by the government in 1919, and only cursory mention will be made here of the main syndicate which combined the Upper Silesian coal interests and arranged also a selling office for their products.

A type of cartel brought together by governmental coercion was the compulsory syndicate which was established in 1910. Until certain *potash* industries were developed recently in other countries Germany possessed in Middle-Germany and Alsace-Lorraine a natural monopoly which freed her from every competitor. Although the War caused the abandonment of a large section of the potash mines to France, this has not greatly changed this monopoly character. The French agreed with the Germans to maintain it. The potash syndicate on its first appearance in 1879 contained only a few firms, of which the State owned two, but the number of these undertakings increased during the next two decades. Stock Exchanges and private people shared in a potash boom and the establishment of nearly 70 undertakings in 1910 led the State to combine the potash works compulsorily. The older and more efficient works at this time, which wanted to make good use of their productive capacity instead of seeing the output limited by the quota, were strongly opposed to combination. Some experts did not agree with the governmental step which they recognised would not greatly lessen over-competition. Levy[45] says: " that over-production in the potash industry would, in fact, have been abated with greater success by leaving competition alone, as this in the long run would have led to a survival of the fittest." In fact, the over-production resulted from the protection of the more inefficient competitors. In 1913 the number of the undertakings was already 167 and 207 in 1916. Liefmann says that about a hundred million marks of capital investment would have been sufficient for the whole demand, but even before the War 2,000 million marks were invested in this industry. During the time of the Weimar Reich, potash became one of the biggest objects of concentration. The " Wintershall " Concern became the owner of nearly half of the German production, whilst the shares of other groups were also very high. Thus the " Salzdethfurt " which owns the works of Aschersleben and Westeregeln have nearly a quarter of the whole production of the syndicate in their hands. Germany after the War paid much attention to the chemical side of the potash industry, in which great progress has been made. During the boom years, potash concerns, like others, became connected with other activities outside their province. No doubt, the history of the potash industry is a history of mistakes grown out of the cartel which had no regulating power.

In contrast to potash, which based its combination activities wholly on a natural monopoly, *cement* became one of the greatest objects of contrived monopolisation in Germany. Indeed, it is the size of the commercial and industrial unit which here has been of outstanding influence. The ubiquity of its appearance all over the world is characteristic, and it shows that no other monopolising influences need here be called to account. The increase of the cement supply in the main consumer countries led, already before the War, to severe competition as well as cartelisation. During the War the Government restricted newcomers and also regulated other activity through a governmental body. It was not possible to create a cartel comprising all German cement works, but a looser organisation was established. The concentration movement in the Portland Cement Industry in Germany was very strong. At the end of the period of the Weimar Reich two of the biggest concerns combined— not voluntarily—so that three concerns are now the dominant producers in Germany. Over-production and over-capitalisation have marked this sad chapter in German economic history.

The most important event in the field of *chemical* industry was the merger of the few giant undertakings which had been connected since the War period by a community of interest. From the " pooling cartel "—*Interessengemeinschaft*—the new " *Interessengemeinschaft Farbenindustrie Aktiengesellschaft* "—a complete merger —arose in 1925 ; this had at one time a capital, in ordinary and preference shares, amounting to roughly 1,000 million marks. The chemical industry, like the electrical industry, began as a large scale enterprise. It, too, demanded large amounts of fixed capital sunk in plants and processes, which had to turn upon the everchanging inventions and new needs. The existence of the monopoly formation made unnecessary or impossible either cartelisation or competition on a small scale. Cartels, however, of great significance dominate the main raw material of the chemical industry, tar, which is a by-product of coal.

The name of the great trust, directly referring to dyes, is misleading ; for the range of its activities and of those of its subsidiary concerns embraces many goods other than dyes, amongst them fertilisers, including artificial nitrogen (the Haber-Bosch patent), artificial silk, electro-chemical and metallurgical goods. The trust is a corner-stone in Germany's plan for self-sufficiency as well as for armament. Its economic significance is as interesting as its technical and commercial organisation, which is an example of German thoroughness.

In the *electricity* industry, as in the chemical industry, there is evident a dependence on certain progressive works which are better able to bring about technical development in order to meet changing needs and the growing financial obligations. The utilisation of patents in this industry made it subject to a continuous change caused by new inventions and new needs. (It is true that some works can develop on a small scale but that is rather the exception than the rule.) The strength of the pioneer companies depended mainly on the provision of their own consumption which linked up the two distinct groups of the electrical industry with each other : that is, the electrical engineering and manufacturing (generators, motors and transformers, electro-technical material, lamps, apparatus of all kinds) and power works and electricity supply. In sub-chapter 2 (*c*) (mixed public enterprise), the need for regulating the whole supply system will be shown and more details will be given. Here we have to show that there was no room for small private enterprises. There is hardly an industry for which, as a producer of cheap staple products for masses of consumers, it was more necessary to use every method of rationalising the process of production. Electricity is an example which shows that the usual conception of producer and consumer as separate entities is no longer applicable. The producer can only produce rationally if he finances a large amount of consumption. The consumption of a product which is one of the most important mass goods of a country involves public affairs ; so in one form or other, from the two points of view—exclusion of competition, because of collaboration with the consumer, and protection of the consumer of an essential mass good—compelled the construction of a large-scale organisation from the beginning, which is an inevitable product of the individual branch subject.

Levy approves the large unit when he writes : " As to the supply of electric power, about half the costs are due to the writing off and the interest on capital and the same feature of ' rigid ' costs applies to labour and staff, while the outlay necessary for the supplies of fuel and material are relatively secondary. This also explains the necessity of big units in this industry, as it is well known that the increase in the size of the industrial unit has in general been largely dependent on the increase of fixed capital as compared with other less rigid items in the cost of production scale."[46] Mention has been made of the Siemens Electrical Trust. The other great concern, Emil Rathenau's foundation, the *Allgemeine Electricitäts-gesellschaft* was a financial undertaking as well as an industrial one. As such it inserted itself into an outstanding process of verticalisation. The company, supported by many subsidiaries such as banks, power stations, electric railways, chemical and other companies, controlled basic as well as finished industries. Loans from abroad supported this giant trust, which like others had to be salvaged later from the ruinous effects of the slump.

With the increasing monopoly activity of the main basic industries and certain others on the finishing side I showed attempts at adaptations to altered relations caused by the artificially reduced economic Germany and the great economic changes of the post-War world. I do not wish to enlarge the picture by enumerating other trades and industries involved in the monopoly movement, of which some revealed a finance-capitalist basis, whilst in others already a certain co-operation with the State could be seen. This period marked the stage prior to the great metamorphosis of the German economic system. Conditions reflect a compromise between two clashing principles. The stronger note of a State policy of interference was due to a great extent to the effects of the Great Depression. I cannot do more now than outline the exuberant workings of a finance capitalism, revived in the form of promoter's capitalism. Another sub-chapter will show how these activities brought about a legislative intervention in the field of the combine system.

State interference in the economic sphere in varying degrees of intensity, which found strong expression in the Weimar Reich, will be described in a later chapter in a wider connection.

(2) SOME SPECIAL PROBLEMS

(a) INDUSTRY AND ITS FINANCING

The peculiarities of the German banks have been described in Chapter II. The reader will find many interesting further details on this subject in Mr. P. Barrett Whale's " Joint Stock Banking in Germany " (1930). The effect of the difference between German banks and those, for example, of France and Great Britain was revealed in the crisis of 1931.[47] The close relationship between German banks and industries made them feel this crisis like an earthquake whilst similar French banks did not receive such great shocks and the English banks had hardly any difficulties. Even in the years 1931 and 1932 the latter distributed big dividends and their liquidity was evidently not seriously affected. Cash, trade bills, treasury bills, and short loans maintained an almost constant ratio of 40 per cent. to their deposits. The traditional principle (which differs from that of Germany) of interposing risk bearers by the process of discounting bills, and by making short loans, no doubt vindicated itself during the banking crisis. Even the Acceptance and Discount Houses which bear the first risk did not meet with grave difficulties. The Bank of England may, perhaps, have assisted during the period of the German crisis in 1931. Even where loans of the deposit banks were used for speculation in securities, serious losses rarely occurred. It is unnecessary to go farther into details of the British activities in relation to State loans and loans to the trade and industry of the country. Where these were given directly by the deposit banks they adhered to their old traditions of giving short credits only and not entering the administration of industries. On the other hand, the world crisis did not prevent the freezing of credits and many losses consequent upon mistakes made in the immediate post-War boom. The principle of avoiding credits by way of long term investment was on the whole rigidly maintained. Some critics in England and many more in Germany hinted at the backwardness of British industries in comparison with the parallel German institutions as a consequence of this policy on the part of the banks.

Following Schulze-Gaevernitz and other experts, the German banking system was described as part of the whole national system, political as well as economic. Whether the rapid economic rise of Germany was sound or not, the banking system from 1850 to the Great War was successful at least in meeting the needs of Germany. The soundness of banking principles in Great Britain could not be followed, simply because the resources were not available and a more speculative procedure was unavoidable. The close relationship of German banks and industry brought insurmountable difficulties in the time of crisis. Out of four big branch banks, two, in July, 1931, were at the end of their liquid resources and the other two would not have been able to fulfil their obligations if the run had persisted much longer. This was at the time of the moratorium to which the short term foreign creditors agreed in connection with the collapse of the Darmstädter and National Bank. As a result of the moratorium and of the calm attitude of internal creditors, the liquidity of the bank improved to some degree. But balance sheets showed that there was not only a serious liquidity crisis evident in 1931, but also that the big branch banks had lost the greater part of their capital. At the eleventh hour the State salvaged the remains of the banks. The Darmstädter Bank was amalgamated with the Dresdner Bank which in turn was supported by the Reichsbank and its daughter institution, the Gold Discount Bank (which also took over the bulk of the capital of the Commerz und Privat Bank). Even Germany's greatest bank, the Deutsche Bank und Diskonto-Gesellschaft, in itself a not altogether voluntary combine of recent development, was also aided by the Gold Discount Bank, which took over a share of its new issue. In 1932 all the banks needed to put their houses in order; the Deutsche Bank and the Commerz Bank set about their tasks.

The breakdown of credit institutions is due to more than one cause. Before the War the German banks showed more and more caution in their use of sums deposited with them. At the end of 1908 the capital and reserves of the 169 German credit banks of which the capital exceeded one million marks, covered 45 per cent. of the total liabilities. At this time, relatively fixed investment (stocks and shares, mortgages of property, undisposed of blocks of new issues) amounted only to one-third of the capital and reserves. In 1913 also, the ratio between the capital and the deposits of the big branch banks was little more than one to four. Between the end of the War and 1931 a great change took place. The interesting figure of Mr. Jacob Goldschmidt (Darmstädter und National Bank) typifies this period, which is reminiscent of the early days of the then inexperienced German banks. To carry on the large scale financing activities of the bank while using only a very small capital was Goldschmidt's principle. He offered to one industrial concern alone an amount nearly equal to the capital of his own bank ! Goldschmidt's colleagues in big banking, however, had no better principle and less brain. The increase in the balance sheet totals of the Darmstädter und National Bank was enormous and stimulated other banks to a similar policy. When the Darmstädter (und National) Bank closed its doors, a chapter in banking history also drew to its close. The bank had been established in the early 1850's by Rhenish bankers for the purpose of developing the Ruhr industry by utilising Frankfort credit facilities. Frankfort was then the hub of the German credit market, but the bank itself was established at Darmstadt, a short distance away, because the Rothschilds and others who controlled the Frankfort Exchange, did not favour the establishment in Frankfort itself of the new speculative type of joint stock bank. Barely surviving the crisis of 1857, the new bank became the prototype of the German speculative banks and remained until its end as the characteristic speculative bank. During its whole life a series of great financiers, among them Dernburg, Dr. Schacht and Jacob Goldschmidt were in charge of its affairs.

The mutual competition of the big banks was one great stimulant of the boom. No doubt, there are extenuatory circumstances for the banking crisis. War and inflation resulted in the great diminution of capital, whilst the effective means of fresh accumulation were weak. Furthermore, the reparation payments frustrated the building up of capital. Germany, unable to shake off this burden, followed from 1924 to 1930 the economic policy of expanding production and foreign trade, thus hoping to increase public welfare. These processes were difficult because, both in the time of the War and afterwards, Germany's development suffered one setback after another. Technical progress, rationalisation, and no doubt the fascinating example of the U.S.A. inspired big business in this period. German financial resources, and in particular those of the banks, were inadequate for such tasks. It should be added that, during this period, private banks lost ground by reason of the enormous progress of public institutions. First there was a growth of the State banks, i.e., the banks of the federal States, and for many years a remarkable process of centralisation of municipal and provincial savings banks had been taking place. In the period under review, that process swept rapidly forward to a climax. Also, for many years, the State had been taking a greater and greater financial interest in the co-operative banks. That interest now grew until it reached the point of virtual control. What a change from the original ideas of co-operative brotherhood! The widely-drawn small deposits were now supplying the demands of the State, of industrialists and of the owners of large estates. From the middle of 1913 to the middle of 1930, according to the Enquiry Committee of 1930, the balance sheet totals of the State Banks rose from 958 to 2,117 million marks, and the deposits of the municipal savings banks showed an increase from 273 million to 3,000 million marks. Public institutions, such as the Gold Discount Bank, the Transport Credit Bank and the Reichs Kredit A.G. (a great Joint Stock Bank owned by the Reich) also had deposits of hundreds of millions. These last three banks invested mainly on the money market and not in trade and industry (as did savings and other municipal banks). Thus, the industrial crisis involved savings banks in the general slump, decisively an effect of the re-establishment of the gold standard by Great Britain in 1925 while, in addition, savings banks enhanced the already keen compeitition between the private banks.

The Joint Stock Banks were further handicapped by the fact that the encroachment of public and semi-public banking organisation into the field of investment forced them into more and more speculative activities. Furthermore, they were continuously and urgently being pressed to offer credits to the Reich and to other public institutions. But these Joint Stock Banks were operating chiefly with short term funds acquired abroad. There was no sort of equilibrium between the internal supply of capital and the demand for it. Consequently, the high rate of interest attracted foreign capital; in fact, in a few years, twenty to twenty-five thousand million marks came to Germany from abroad. The danger would not have been especially great if only long term capital had come to Germany, but large parts of this foreign capital came in the form of short term loans. The Joint Stock Banks took over the dangerous position of intermediaries acquiring short term foreign credits and changing them into long term internal ones. By the middle of 1930, short term credit from abroad, amounting to 5,500 million marks, represented 45 per cent. of the total Joint Stock bank deposits. The other 55 per cent. was more or less connected with foreign capital otherwise acquired. The Enquiry Committee of 1934 stated that this influx of short term capital was decisively an effect of the re-establishment of the gold standard by Great Britain in 1925, and in particular, of Poincaré's stabilisation of the franc in 1926. The consequent deflationary and other effects gave rise to the wandering of a large amount of capital in search of profitable investment. The amount of this wandering capital was greatly augmented from American sources. The high rate of interest offered in Germany led inevitably to the influx of large amounts of short term capital to German banks and industries, which were misled to over-expand business. Who ever reads

Dr. R. Kuszynski on "Wall Street and the German Loans,"[48] and especially the evidence of witnesses before the Official Investigation Committee of the U.S.A. Senate on Credit and Banking, will be aware that it was the importuning of American big business which largely inspired the borrowing of German businessmen and municipalities. Worse, the banks neglected their pre-War principle of retarding this expansion when they had no possibility of placing their own issues. So, in the big Berlin banks, the average ratio of their own resources (capital and reserves) to deposits changed from one to four in 1913, to one into fifteen by the middle of 1930. Irresponsibility showed itself in an increasing expansion. It was in this ill-omened period that municipalities, under the control of their political advisers, carried out an exaggerated social and educational policy. To the great buildings erected for these purposes were added town halls, opera houses, hotels, exhibition halls and so on. Dr. Schacht's[49] frequent warnings against borrowing with a "borrowed currency" (as he called it in one of his publications) proved right at a later time. Thus, the incredible lightheartedness of German banks, shared by trade and industry and by the municipal corporations, cramped Germany's foreign policy and became the main cause of the credit crisis of 1931. Uneasiness did not manifest itself among inland investors until a very short time before the collapse occurred. Even then, it was confined to distrust of individual banks and could probably have been overcome by a willing offer of credit on the part of the Reichsbank. The withdrawal of *foreign* credits, however, was a serious matter since it reduced to a minimum the reserves behind the currency. The enormous amounts of foreign credits placed Germany at the mercy of world fluctuations. Short term foreign loans were utilised not only for floating capital but also for fixed investment. In 1930 not less than 18,000 million marks of short term credit were used for long term purposes. Even at the time when the trade cycle declined, current account loans increased. Many of them were used by the borrowers for fixed purposes such as the building of factories. Even in 1929, the big banks in Berlin increased their debtors by 935 million marks, i.e., by nearly 20 per cent.—and in the first half of 1930, by a further 430 million. In the whole of the following year not even this last amount could be repaid. Later trials in the law courts revealed how imprudently credits had been offered by the big banks, which felt themselves impelled to throw good money after bad.

The scarcity of capital coupled with the urgent demands of industry, which at this time was carried away by the idea of rationalisation, was one of the influences accounting for this faulty policy of the banks. In consequence of the period of inflation, the relative power of industry and banks had greatly changed. Industries had their resources at least in tangible form; the resources of the banks were merely intangible rights which could easily disappear in the maw of inflation. An activity of concentration, the biggest that Germany ever saw, was in progress at this time, the banks themselves sharing in the forming of these giant trusts, of which only two need be quoted here, the Vereinigte Stahlwerke and the I.G. Farben. The capital of each of these concerns almost equalled the combined capital of all the large Joint Stock banks. This chemical concern, by reason of its foreign relationship, was nearly independent of the German big banks. It is said[50] that the great steel trust could even dictate terms to the banks by pitting one against another. It may be added that even smaller industrial undertakings could enjoy offers of credits from foreign banks. The business of private investors was insignificant in comparison with that of the great industrial trusts. The tyranny over the banks by the great industrial administrations was further strengthened by interlocking directorates, which at this time enabled industrialists to control bank policy, whereas under other conditions, the same device had enabled bankers to control industrial policy.

(b) CARTEL POLICY AND LEGISLATION

In Chapter II, I have touched upon the road to a " Cartel law " and a "*Marktordnung.*" The period of the Weimar Reich forms the transition to this stage.

If cartels were inevitable, then the fiction of the undisputed rule of free competition must fall, and price agreements would have to be inserted into a law of competition. If cartels were obnoxious, then their formation would have to be prohibited. The Weimar Reich, owing to its inherent weakness, living by bargaining with, and making promises to all parties, showed an ambiguous attitude towards cartels. The changing cabinets variously declared themselves as favourable or unfavourable to the cartels. Reactions changed according as cartels were regarded as institutions of big business or of socialist economic planning. This condition found expression in the decay of competition principles within the law courts. State policy till then was only sporadically engaged with cartels, whenever public excitement asked for interference. From pre-War periods, when personal competitive troubles were insurmountable, the Prussian Ministry of Trade had intervened to enforce systematic organisation of an industry as a unit. This it did in the coal, lignite, potash and alcohol industries. On the one hand, the legal code held to the fiction of free competition (not by conviction or consideration, but by old custom). Civil law and the Judiciary, however, allowed an extension of private power positions and of certain organisations to settle market situations. This stage, transitional and inconsistent in itself, has not yet come to an end. Great progress was made by a governmental decree in 1923. This was the so-called " cartel decree," or officially, the decree against " abuses of economic power." This law was a product of its time, that of the inflation period, before the genuine post-War combination movement began. It was by no means directed by its supporters against the anti-combine argument of orthodox theory, but against certain abuses of the inflation period. The preparation of the law coincided with that of the stabilisation of currency. If success of the stabilisation had been known at this time, the new act would, perhaps, never have been decreed, at least in its peculiar form. As shown in Chapter II, paragraph I, combinations could be considered as factors in the expansion of the home and export markets, as far as the maintenance of prices, restriction of output, and the role of export stimuli were concerned. As Miss D. Warriner says, these considerations changed; in contrast to Great Britain, where there was a general industrial interest, Germany showed other conditions. " Each cartel or trust is the outcome of a peculiar situation and must be judged on its efficiency in that situation only . . . "[51] " In a country with its heavy industries in a state of continuously threatening over-production, with new industries enjoying sustained prosperity, older finishing branches retaining a weak hold on the protected home market, numerous small branches relying almost entirely on export, a country which has financed the re-equipment and expansion of the whole, first by inflation, and then by foreign borrowing, the combine's functions are too various and complex to permit of summary out of the particular setting." The new decree intended to get rid of certain abuses brought about by cartels above all disturbing the consumers. Now a written form was prescribed. Following clause 8, a cogent reason gave the parties to certain contracts a right of rescission in certain circumstances.

Paragraph 4 gave the president of a law court established *ad hoc* the right to nullify a cartel, if the State moved its dissolution. Paragraph 9 turned out to be of no less importance; it took away the power of the cartel to prohibit delivery to outsiders, and gave it to the president of the cartel court. This decision practically had its end in the coercive provision of the special goods of the cartel even to a limited extent. That certainly contrasted with every legally recognised position of monopoly.

The numerous decrees following this cartel law did not change its essential character. The period of deflation stressed an anti-cartel tendency. The Emergency Act, of 26th July, 1930, empowered the Government to dissolve all linking up of prices. But this Act was only used to influence cartel prices; cartels themselves were not touched in their existence or their extent. A certain significance of this Act was expected for agreements between an entrepreneur and the single tradesman to whom he provided his goods—" linking up of prices through an intermediate party " as these agreements were called. But this extension of the conception of the cartel as aimed at by the legislator remained legally useless, because law courts ignored the Act completely, indicating that the presupposition in the character of combination which made the conception of cartel, was lacking.

The alternative of lowering import duties on articles whose prices were "tied up" (*gebunden*), instead of proclaiming the nullification of a cartel, was a great failure. More effective was the Emergency Act, of 30th August, 1930, which prohibited the linking up of the prices of goods and services of non-cartel origin, which had aimed at preventing traders not too dependent on cartels from buying and transmitting goods from outsiders. Some cartels, among them the "Benzine-convention," at this time collapsed. An Emergency Act of June, 1932, became the protection against "*Liefersperre*" (blocking of delivery), a measure which tried to guarantee against blockades (*Sperren*) by examining those already in force. The cold attitude to the outsider later, in the early days of the Third Reich, led to weakening of the clauses concerning the protection against blockades (cf. Chapter IV (3) (*a*) (§2)). This announced already the stronger attitude of the State which recognised cartels as main instruments in the Law to provide a *Marktordnung*. Taken all in all, the cartel decree of 1923 was successful in giving legal means to private enterprise to paralyse exaggerations of cartel organisations and of private coercion of organisations by the means of self-help. It was a progress as against the Civil Law, by which it was intended not to make impossible the formation of cartels.

(*c*) Mixed Public and Private Enterprise

There is nothing that would more clearly mark the transition between liberal and socialist philosophies than the idea of the mixed public and private enterprise. If we are forced to compromise between the two opposed philosophies, here is, perhaps, an ideal solution for at least the transitional period between the two epochs, of capitalism and a new one, which we cannot yet name. The idea of a "mixed enterprise" was not an artificial product; it arose out of practical needs. The public servant and the industrialist desired a scheme of joint action which they found empirically. Nearly thirty years of development, crowded with examples in countries all over the world, have shown that the idea of a "mixed enterprise" had potentialities of which no one could have had an adequate conception at its commencement.

It is typical that this development should start in State-socialist Germany. There is a mercantilist element in this form of undertaking. The mercantilist forms, however, at this period, were pure State and municipal undertakings, such as agricultural estates, forests, mines, iron and steel works, armament works, china factories, printing and publishing undertakings, and even health resorts, canals, docks, and harbours. In a later period the local utility services, such as water, gas, and electricity supply, municipal transport, and the national utilities such as railways and railway workshops, road transport, telegraphs and telephones became mere parts of the public administration.

At the beginning of the 20th century, the mixed enterprise arose. In its country of origin, there were differences about the definition of this form of undertaking. According to the German liking for definition in legal terms, some authors explain mixed enterprises as organisations under civil and company law, whereby the invested capital is jointly subscribed by individuals and by public corporations, and where the management is carried through by both factors.[52] Dr. Most expressly requires that the public authority should hold a financial share in mixed enterprises but Dr. Passow reserves the term " mixed enterprise " for concerns where the public authority has not only a financial interest but also voting rights. One cannot agree with these more formal definitions,[53] which do not deal with the motives of the joint action between individual and public corporations. C. J. Asriel[54] rightly says, that this joint action represents an economic principle and it is immaterial which particular form of expression is chosen. This principle of mixed enterprise will be better understood if we first survey its historical development.[55] Electricity supply furnishes the best examples of this new scheme. The Frankfort electricity exhibition of 1891, a turning point in the history of the German industry, made it quite clear that electrical energy would be the outstanding factor in the future development of industry. The initiative for this movement lay with the electricity companies. With the production of rotary current in power stations a new chapter started, which brought its own problems. In no way can rotary current be stored; production and consumption must coincide. Each power station must have the machinery to cope with the maximum demand. It is obvious that the most rational type of unit for this industry is a large scale producer in the centre of a district demanding current for a variety of purposes. These and other technical and business reasons motivated the change from the state of affairs where a large number of isolated producers were each supplying a small area. But there were many difficulties; local patriotism and rivalries between neighbouring towns everywhere hampered the development. It was also shown that the officials of a municipal supply department could not match the experience of the industrialists. The co-operation of public bodies could facilitate the activities of private companies which operated the electricity supply and the tramways; for the roads were controlled by public authorities, which also had a certain influence in encouraging new industries, and with whom rested the decision of establishing new suburbs. Before the Great War the co-operation of publicly owned credit organisations facilitated the financing of such " mixed enterprises." The rise of the German heavy electrical industry arose to a large extent out of its position as the supplier to power stations and other electrical undertakings. Basic industries such as coal, and iron and steel, benefited enormously from these activities. There were certain private power stations which within their limited range, no doubt, worked profitably by keeping high their prices for current, fares and so on, when already their product was no longer a luxury. It was a common good for everyone using tramways (and the use of electricity for transport completely altered ideas of town planning), electric light for industrial and domestic purposes, and electrical power, the greatly-needed motive force for the development of industries all over the country. Electricity supply was a question of outstanding public significance. Birthrates in consequence of employment, wages and spending power, were still high at this time, emigration decreased to a minimum, and the maintenance of this state of affairs was strongly desired. German industry, already a great exporter, could only work with a cheap and efficiently produced motive power. To leave a social and industrial need of this magnitude to be satisfied by laisser-faire methods would have been an enormous blunder. Furthermore, if the State were to interfere, was it only to give an impetus to the new industry or was it to become joint owners? The answer given by a State-socialist country such as Germany could not be difficult. An outstanding example was the *Rheinisch-Westfälisches Elektrizitätswerk*,[56] mainly planned by Hugo Stinnes. It was intended to provide electricity for the largest industrial area, the Rhineland and Westphalia. This gigantic plan could be carried through only with the co-operation of the corporations of towns and rural districts, since they controlled the roads and possessed local monopolies of electricity supply. The private management of the *Rheinisch-Westfälisches Elektrizitätswerk* started by giving shares and seats on its " *Aufsichtsrat* "* to municipal corporations. Even the greatest towns, such as Essen, Mühlheim, Gelsenkirchen, shared in this undertaking as early as 1905, this year being called the year of birth of the mixed public and private enterprise (*Gemischt-wirtschaftliche Unternehmung*). The name for the new form of undertaking was given by Dr. Wilhelm Freund, who later in his life was Permanent Secretary of the Prussian Home Office. The idea as well as the practical development met with great opposition, even new establishments being set up to counteract the movement. But the *Rheinisch-Westfälisches Elektrizitätswerk* became the greatest organisation in German electricity supply. The feature of the new formation was that a freely organised body of self-administration in legal form combined the main producers of electrical energy and their consumers throughout a large district containing a great variety of economic interests.

It may be mentioned in passing that, by 1914, 75 great German town corporations participated in 95 mixed enterprises (mostly electricity, gas, water and tramway undertakings) Dr. Leoni, deputy-mayor of Strassbourg, emphasising the efficiency of the new

* What in England is the Board of Directors is under German Law split up into two bodies, the *Vorstand* (committee of managers, managing directors) and *Aufsichtsrat* (supervisory committee), elected by a third body, the General Meeting. It will depend on the power of the economic factors and of the personalities of members of either bodies, whether the *Vorstand* or the *Aufsichtsrat* has the real lead.

scheme, mentioned in 1914 that if all municipal works had followed the example of working in co-operation with private enterprises, the German public economy would have saved 100 million marks in one year. In the period of the Weimar Reich roughly half of all power supply institutions existing in Germany were mixed enterprises.

The great Enquiry Committee of the Weimar Reich tried to throw light on the question whether the electricity supply undertakings should be public or private. In 1931 the quantity of electricity supplied by public works was 14.4 million kilowatt-hours, while that supplied by private works was 11.4 million. I should like to cite here some further differences noted by Levy.[57] The best utilisation of plant, calculated on the average time during which the plant supplying electricity is actually used, was shown in the private works affiliated to certain groups of industry, such as chemical or metal manufactures, mining or the iron and steel industries, as also the paper and printing trade. As the Enquiry Committee stated, the degree of efficiency of the public works lagged far behind the figures for the private ones, as these works handled only part of the electricity supply to the big industrial concerns and were mostly suppliers to small and domestic consumers of electricity. The tendency recently since 1926 has been towards a diminution of newly-created privately-owned industrial power plants (*Eigeninstallationen*) in favour of an increasing supply of electricity from plants not belonging to the industrial users of electricity (*Fremdstrombezug*). The industrial undertakings have been working their own power plant to its utmost capacity, but to obtain additional supplies they have not enlarged their electricity plant but have relied on an increasing supply by " outside power plant," especially by the large works in the branch. This has been partly effected by electricity supply contracts between manufacturing companies and large electricity concerns.

The principle of arranging the whole economic system according to general plans once again subjected the electricity supply to measures intended to produce greater efficiency during the period of the Third Reich.

The mixed enterprise marks for the first time a unit in which public and private interests were combined. The example of the electrical branch shows that political units with divergent interests (urban as well as rural areas, and most of them involved in inter-municipal rivalries) were working in part independently, in part in conjunction with private concerns in the interest of the general consumer. Among the private forms, too, were divergent interests. It was a tremendous task to balance all these divergencies in *one* organisation so as to ensure cheap and safe electricity supply. In the above-mentioned example the advantage of combining the particular abilities and legal powers which both partners possessed was clearly recognised. The increase in population of the great industrial towns was resulting in increased prosperity of the undertakings such as electricity, gas, and waterworks. The general feeling was that such profits were not to be used solely to enrich private persons but were also to be shared by the community.

Some remarks on the legal aspect. As mentioned above, the public authorities possessed in their control of roads the right to license electricity supply. Municipalities concluded agreements with certain companies to carry out the service. This system led to the opinion that agreements alone could not express the public will and that, therefore, public capital must share in the jointly run undertaking. A formal legal definition of the undertaking and a certain legal protection for public corporations when co-operating with private people, were demanded. Dr. Freund wished to give by law control and right of veto to the public part of such enterprise. All these tendencies derived from the German inclination towards codification in all spheres of activity. The rapid change of development, however, prevented the creation of rigid legal forms.

There are certain legal forms in which the mixed enterprise is formed, mostly the Joint Stock Co. and the G.m.b.H. (comparable to the English private limited company). It was thought by certain experts that the limited company was proved an appropriate form which enabled the influence of both partners, public and private, to be balanced. Freund's suggestion, therefore, did not require a new legal form. An interesting experiment took place when the Deutsche Gasgesellschaft applied a new form of co-operation.[58] A " twin-company." as Thierbach called it was established. One of these was a kind of holding company (through this legally established company), in which public interest had the majority, so that the direct inroads of red-tape measures and of changing political parliaments should be avoided. The second company carried out technical and business functions partially; in it private interest prevailed.

The mixed enterprise is flexible enough to permit a variety of forms. So the public part was linked up with individual companies, cartels, and co-operative societies.[59] During the War, as mentioned, mixed public and private enterprise became the " be all " and " end all " of the formations officially designed to rule German industry and trade. I once called these types of *Kriegsrohstoff—und Ernährungsgesellschaften* " mixed public and private cartels." The will of the public authority, as representing general interests, can, of course, be expressed in other ways. Great Britain is familiar with this instrument as instanced by the London Passenger Transport Board, Imperial Airways, the Central Electricity Board and the British Broadcasting Corporation. An example is furnished by the Third Reich in the period under review, and by Italy and Soviet Russia. The totalitarian State assumed the right of complete interference in private affairs including the economic sphere. In the last chapter of German Economic History we again find the State working in closest co-operation with cartels these (a kind of self-government in industry) proving an important instrument of Public Administration.

Whither the development leads nobody knows. It can well outstrip conditions in Soviet Russia where former private prerogatives and self-regulation of economic forces are excluded. But there may be a retrograde movement to conditions of economic equilibrium which our experience has shown to be more " normal." Then, the mixed enterprise will become of even more outstanding significance. No doubt it is the ideal economic scheme of our transitional time.

Chapter IV
THE THIRD REICH
(1) IDEOLOGICAL REMARKS

This investigation cannot do more than hint at some striking features of the ideology of the Third Reich, since, as this ideology is still in the making, it does not yet permit of a thorough analysis.

It is common knowledge that when once industrialisation had passed its first youth, the part played by economics within political systems became increasingly important. Even before the War various schools of political thought were mainly concerned with the place of Labour inside the political system. The consequences of the War offered the first real opportunity for putting these ideas into practice. New methods have been devised and are expressed in the written and unwritten constitutions of various countries, and although they have not yet achieved a perfection they at least show the trend of development. Both the Weimar Reich and the Third Reich had to face the same problem, that of determining the position of Labour within the system. But the great economic problem which imposed itself upon the social conditions still remained sectional subject to general political ideas.

The democracy of the 19th century was split up in the Weimar Reich into a political and economic pluralism (in Germany called " atomism ") of the citizen who voted for parliaments and was himself a party in the economic system. Naked and undisguised the representatives of economic powers, organised in large bodies, became the virtual mouthpiece of so-called public opinion in the parliaments, and the " atom citizen," as politician, lost his individual importance as did the " economic atom "—the individual competitor, who was once proclaimed as the unit of the laisser-faire system. In his stead the big monopoly organisations openly took control.

The constructive ideas of the State policy in the 18th century and their continuations into the 19th, in which they found material expression, lost much of their value under the changed conditions of political and economic life, and counter-movements advanced new ideas. The search for new creative factors and forces in the State machinery became, and continues to be, general throughout the world. All this took place at a time when there was a general increase in population in every country. These masses, to a great extent organised into strong bodies, demanded, and in part succeeded, in getting, a say in public affairs. Through this a new and decisive factor was revealed in post-War political systems. The masses both used and abused their power; the " atoms " fought for control, and there came into being " power atomism " which expressed itself in a struggle of all against all. Creative ideas could only be carried through in the State when there was power behind these ideas, and they had to contend with many and varying opponents. Even the idea of a social "democracy" was abused in the divergent views of socialists of different creeds who used their power to paralyse their socialist opponents more or less by violence as was evidenced in the Weimar Reich. As in time of War, the nation again took to uniform and the "atoms" assembled in army formations. "Uniformed ideologies" were identified by shirts or coats of various colours or other symbols of their faith during the last years of the Weimar Reich. Other great countries followed this example, arraying their political ideas in military-like forces. And where successful revolutions made new political systems possible, two movements made a concomitant appearance. There first came the idea of overcoming the "atomism" by more vital spiritual forces in the State and social organism. Secondly, there appeared the need for powerful defence against enemies abroad and opponents at home, which led to the formation of new power systems and power states. This second movement ran counter to many of the ideals of the first.

Germany in 1933 already possessed models for new forms which other nations, such as Russia and Italy, were just acquiring by degrees—a development accompanied by setbacks, failures and fresh starts. Undeniably, German National Socialism established a system modelled on that of the other revolutionary countries: a use which not only embraced the ideas prevalent at that time, but which also envisaged the "technique" of maintaining power. I have described two outstanding factors in the revolutionary States, first the political, in the role of the "one party system" which excludes other opinions and makes its measures more efficient by avoiding sectional interests without parliamentary control; secondly, economic planning, which in one form or other became the type of the economic system which was accepted in the dictator States and even, to a lesser degree, in the liberal countries. However, it is clear that the peculiar conditions and the traditions of different countries shaped their economic systems. Germany, as the example of cameralism and planning, gave a lead in the management of the economic system.

The Liberalism of the 19th century was established as a result of a doctrine promulgated in the 18th century and advanced as a consequence of both the French and American revolutions. In contrast the ideologies of the modern dictator State develop as "ideologies *post hoc*." When the old régime collapsed there was no political system ready to fill its place in any of the States concerned; this is true of the various socialist creeds whether national or international. Enough has been said in the chapter on socialism in the Weimar Reich of how the change in the capitalist system brought about alterations in economic and political ideas and forms. It was a socialist spirit and socialist views of material policy which took the lead in inserting themselves into the still existing but declining liberal economic system. But the socialist ideas of exercising the power of government which were expounded in the 19th century neither met the reality of present-time economic conditions nor proved possible of execution in Public Administration. Socialists themselves when in a position of great power after the breakdown of 1918 had, therefore, to modify their plans. Germany's contributions to these systems (which were suitable for application to the planned system of other countries) have been described in a previous chapter. It seems only fitting to touch upon the pattern furnished by other countries. In this section, therefore, I shall select some outstanding features and I shall show how this "ideology *post hoc*" is still in the making. For *natura non facit saltum:* The elements of this new ideology are continuations of former ideas, based, consciously or unconsciously—as far as the supporters of this new creed are concerned—on various existing elements in which I include Mercantilism, Romanticism, the German War-organisation system and certain Russian and Italian patterns.

The decline from the more or less democratic political forms to the "one party system" was not a superimposed issue but sprang from the flow of development. In this respect I mentioned the development from the democratic Soviets to the all-embracing and dominating Bolshevist Party (see pp. 152, 153).

In the same way, the Fascist State developed gradually with the "one party system" which has been so often described.[1] The dictator States are still consolidating their power: to this effort ideological issues belong, and so the shaping of an ideology and of the rôle of the Party is far from being at an end. The claim of the Bolshevist Party to be selected by the masses as the missionaries of World Revolution and World Liberation finds its parallel in the idea of "Eternal Rome," the motto of the Fascist Party, and in the German "Nordic Nation." These ideas then aim at developing a religion on the basis of the system.

The Italian movement started very modestly in March, 1919, with "a defence of the victory" programme in the foundation meeting of the Fasci di Combattimento in Milan. The Fascists were then composed of groups of different political views, each of which had their own programmes. This lasted two and a half years till Fascism gave up the anti-party idea. The fight for power became the main object of the Fascist policy as it was then. The attitude of Fascism to the form of State, its relation to the crown, and to the Pope developed slowly, in contrast to former more radical ideas. It was a completely "realistic" policy, which led, for instance, to the foundation of Fascist trade unions forming a group within the Corporate system. Finally the Partito Nationale Facista was created in the autumn of 1921 and with this the "one party system" in Italy came into being. But with the destruction of other Italian parties many of their ideas were transferred to the expanding ideology of the Fascist party. In particular, the newly established Roman Catholic Party, the Partito Popolare Italiano, which wished to unite the ecclesiastical hierarchy not as before with the crown and nobility but with the masses of the working class—this " Social Catholicism " provided many ideas which were ripe for adoption by the Fascist party. The principle of equal right for employer and employees in the framework of the Corporate State and the share of these corporate elements in the political constitution were doctrines of the then dissolved Popolari. It is interesting to note that revolutionary syndicalism also contributed to this new ideology. The atomism of democracy, as expressed in the parliament as the centre of political struggle, had now to give way to the trade unions as exponents of the corporative principle foremost directed against the centralist official socialism.[2] Other Italian groups provided further ideas and were precursors of Fascist anti-parliamentarianism. One group called "Nationalists," in reaction to the Tripolitan War, called for protectionist Imperialism. This is hardly the place to go into further details. But for our investigation of Germany it appears important in showing the comparison with another nation's development in the attempt to mould a new political system.

National-Socialism encountered ideas of both derivations—from the Italian opportunist and from the German romanticist. A bridge between these ideas can be seen in Othmar Spann whose system of Universalism is propped up by the idea of the Corporate State. In the active propaganda in Germany which led to the rise of the new régime both elements during the Weimar Reich were extensively used.

German National-Socialism had already a programme for economic policy which was formally adopted when it came into power in 1933, and the main propagandist, at this time, the engineer, Gottfried Feder, became one of the Secretaries of State for Economic Affairs. But these principles soon yielded to the exigencies of practice. Some clauses of the official economic " party " programme are here given:

" §11.—Abolition of unearned income : Overthrow of the slavery of interest."

" §13.—We claim the Socialisation (*Verstaatlichung*) of all trade organisations, hitherto established in the form of companies (*Vergesellschaftete Betriebe*)."

" §14.—We claim the share of the profits in large scale enterprise."

" §16.— . . . The immediate communalisation of big departmental stores."

" §17.—We claim a reform of the land adapted to our national needs, creation of a law for expropriation of the land for common purposes. Abolition of the interest on investments in land and prevention of any speculation in land."

" §18.—We claim the replacement of the Roman Law, which serves the materialist order of the World by German common law."

§24.—Points out : " Common weal before private interest."

These few paragraphs clearly show elements of different ideological origin and without an analysis of their derivation it would be difficult, if not impossible, to understand the economic programme.

The further stages of development since 1933 are marked first by the adaptation of the new system to the needs of a practical policy which had to be carried out when the consolidation of political power at home and abroad was the primary concern. The dissolution of the many political parties and economico-political organisations and the alteration of the federal States, as it were, into tribal districts of a national administration, are events belonging rather to general history. The ideological parts of the programme were greatly affected by those events which carried on emergency measures of the Weimar Reich, such as the foreign trade monopoly and the idea of self-sufficiency. Even now the emergency character of these and other measures which, in themselves, represent very definite economic systems, is only too clear. Thus it would be difficult to forecast whether they really belong to the ideology of the Third Reich.

The stages of development seen in the transition from cameralism through the War economic system and on to the later planned economy were clearly influenced by practical needs. Obviously this planned economy could not but have been influenced to some degree by other pre-War socialist doctrines, and there appeared a still further modification due to ideas belonging to another political field. This represents the trend of thought from Herder, Adam Müller, Gobineau, Nietzsche, Houston Stewart Chamberlain, Möller van den Bruck, to Alfred Rosenberg, Hitler's lieutenant and official spiritual leader of the movement, the author of " The German Race and the German Myth." The aspect of the political problem is destined to end in a religious system. Professor Carl Schmitt, a jurist and political philosopher, one who had great influence in the early days of the movement, once epitomized it as " *Staat, Bewegung, Volk* " (State, movement, people).[3] During the first four years of the Nazi régime he took an extremely active part in the preparation of a new system of German law and of a new German Constitution. He was the exponent of the tripartite structure of the new political system. New constructive forces were sought, which perforce were the embodiment of the second of the attributes first mentioned, viz., *movement*,* and these were inherently opposed to the earlier forces of the liberal and democratic State. The former conception of the State Schmitt dismisses as the outcome of atomism (also called pluralism) on the one hand and of Marxism, with the idea of class struggle, proclaimed by him as " *Staatsfeind* " (public enemy), on the other ; both elements having to be opposed with the utmost force by the Constitution, Administration, official law and the whole community. The " Party," according to various official proclamations, is an integral part of the State ; as such, it is the centre and embodiment of the " movement " and the organ through which to fight anti-Nazi State forces. According

* The new sense of the term " movement " is illustrated by the proclamation of Munich (where most of the headquarters of the party are still to be found) as the " capital of the movement."

to Schmitt, Adolf Hitler, when appointed Chancellor, first gave this political lead and with it gave to the German State the forces to destroy Marxism, the public enemy.[4] Again he says, "On January 30th the Hegelian '*Beamtenstaat*' (public official State) of the 19th century which made the *Beamtentum* (the officialdom), the *staatstragende Schicht* (the class upholding the State) a unity was replaced by another new conception of the State," and "One can say that on this day Hegel died."[5] The tripartite structure is based (1) on the politico-static (the State), (2) the politico-dynamic (the Party) and (3) the non-political element (the People).[6] As against the liberal conception of the State, which opposed the State and the private individual, the national-socialist State aims at uniting State and People.[7] The "movement," on this basis, derives from the people. Here is the link, the connecting idea, seen in the trend from Herder to Alfred Rosenberg, and which may be expressed in the statement, that the movement springs from "blood and soil." The movement is in every way in harmony with the Führer principle considered as Germanic in origin. The "*artgleiches Volk*" (equality of kindred people) of the Germanic people is the presupposition of the conception of the political leader principle. This presupposition is not concerned with those parts of the German nation which derive from Eastern races, Alpine Slav and Baltic, or from the Dinaric race. The system ends as a faith, the nation as represented by the Führer, the leader of the party. The role of the party as the dynamic force in the State is the same as in Russia, though Stalin is general secretary of the Party and not President of the Soviet Union, or in Italy where Mussolini is the leader of the Party whilst the king remains sovereign. Hitler, however, combines in himself the leadership and the sovereignty. The typically German habit of conceiving and realising things in a spirit of thoroughness and unification manifests itself conspicuously in the whole religious, political and economic system. Here is the idea of *one* Germanic State from blood and soil, *one* nation embracing all German people, throughout the world, *one* party represented by the leader, *one* system of public administration of this national State (including the economic system) and belief in the *nation* is the article of *faith*. So the idea leads to *one* religion.

The State is to be led by power only and so *one* national army and *one* public opinion support this system, under the control of the party, once again the centre of the movement. Legislation, law, and administration are no longer divided as with the French school of political thought of the 18th century. The "objectivity" of the law up to 1933 (recognised as of Roman origin) was overthrown; the new law—alleged to be of Germanic origin—has to assist in carrying out the idea and faith of national-socialism which direct the judgment instead of the former judicial "objectivity." It is not easy to reproduce this world of ideas into which the economic system is inserted. From its inception the party called itself the National-

Socialist *Workers'* Party. In this are involved nationalism and opposition to internationalism : the nation unites in the corporate system the two main poles, employers and employees. So it is anti-Marxist, anti-Communist. It will recognise only kinsmen and not two opposed and militant classes. There is, without doubt, an anti-capitalist current within the party and thus State interference, State supervision and control will, from this side, undermine the capitalist system by degrees. Opinions with regard to the precise character of the present conditions vary. There are some, who, because of the presence of the employers, tend to regard this transitional system as capitalistic. This, however, must be examined very carefully and conclusions must not be arrived at with superficial knowledge.

Summary.—A closer examination of the economic sections of Nazi ideology reveals that the continued War economic system has been adopted as a corporate system, influenced by similar Italian experiments. Control of social policy is now mainly exercised by the National Labour Front—which is not divided into employers and employees but into " the leader and his following." Here again outside critics fail to agree as to whether this means a strengthening of the capitalist and anti-socialist spirit or not. I believe rather that, despite some inconsistencies brought about by the emergency character of the economic system and the transitional state of economic affairs—so often described in this history—the strong note of a socialist planned economy is evident. The transformation of the capitalist entrepreneur into a pensionable civil servant of industry or even a public functionary still continues. The party, as it has consolidated its power, has elaborated many more details of ideology. And to produce this not a stone has been left unturned, old traditions faded away ; and at the same time they aim to build up upon the basis of the party a new " selection of leaders " and a new aristocracy of the State. It follows naturally that if this object were achieved it would also affect the whole economic system. The employer would make way for the leader of the enterprise, the trustee of the community. There are obvious unsolved problems (with which all anti-capitalist countries are concerned) underlying these ideas, as, for instance, that of finding the incentive for the individuals directing or initiating enterprises and the question as to who is to bear the risk during a period of slump, in an enterprise which is dependent upon profits. But I shall deal with these questions in another connection.

(2) ECONOMIC POLICY IN THE THIRD REICH
(General Survey)

As I have pointed out, the stages of development in the national economy since the new régime came into power, make it difficult to distinguish how far things belong to the ideology of the leading party and how far they are measures necessary to meet emergency conditions. There are still some differing tendencies among the forces concerned—including the party—as to the aims and the tempo of the movement. These are expressed by radical socialists, wholesale planners, and moderates, who may be opportunists or else former liberals managing businesses. No doubt, behind these tendencies lie the great problems of political science and economic theory of which, however, few are conscious. But I must stress the fact that within the last-mentioned group of business people there are no capitalists—except, perhaps, a few families—comparable either in fortune or in income, to those in Great Britain to-day. The change from capitalist-entrepreneur, or the representative of finance capitalism, to a civil servant of industry marks, as I have shown, no new event in German development. But finance capitalism changed into a capitalism in which interference by the State plays the decisive part in business management. The intensity of State interference is a revolutionary event. It is not only that public capital has a great share in production and distribution, which I have described as modern cameralism or a kind of nationalisation; but the system of the regimentation of the whole economic life has further stressed the long-existing socialist note, and there is no need to distrust the words which certain leaders of the movement or the organisation have often uttered : " economy has to serve the nation " (Dr. Schacht in Nürnberg, *Einsetzung des Reichsarbeits-und Wirtschaftsrat*, 1935). It is true that this principle was proclaimed a long time ago by socialists and writers of other creeds. Certainly the system does not show itself as thoroughgoing socialisation; it is a peculiar mixture between a market and private economy on the one side, and a public economy on the other. It is difficult to follow the Government's organs when they speak of the " still existing or necessary private initiative of the entrepreneur " or claim " that the national-socialist conception deviates from an economy planned by the State," or again, that " self-administration is the organisation to which the problems of economy are entrusted." The German Institute for Business Research (Weekly Report, March 11th, 1936) elaborates this : " Self-administration in its new form has for the most part public and not private functions. It is organised in complete accordance with the principle of leadership and is based on the principle of compulsory membership."

It is true, units of trade and industry still exist as companies of a private character. The contradiction which lies in the existence of private enterprise and its regimentation by the State, requires more detailed explanation. But this explanation will also show how the economic system changed its character as a capitalist one. In Soviet Russia there is a planning committee which adjusts all the needs of the population to the existing means, both those which come from the country itself and those which have to be imported from foreign countries in exchange for Russian goods. In Germany the strict combination of the centralised headquarters of the departments of economic affairs, including the currency bank of the country, is to be compared with this planning committee, which provides the general plan for the current needs of a given period, at present for four years. And even the changes in the leadership of national economy do not change the principle. It just shifted from Dr. Schacht to General Goering's staff. More details of the methods of planning are given on p. 217. The State of the 19th century regulated the official budget for State income and expenditure and left private enterprise outside its activities : the new State which, according to its ideology, wishes to combine the formerly separated tasks of the State with all the activities of private life (and especially economic activities) reveals itself as a new and different thing, which can only be paralleled in Russia.

It is a mere matter of method of execution whether public departments directly control economy, as in Russia, or whether the former private entrepreneurs (in direct contrast to their former prerogatives as exponents of private capitalism) are used as trustees of the whole economy of the country.

As to the policy of Dr. Schacht, the former leader of the Ministry of Economic Affairs and Governor of the Reichsbank, I can best give his own words, which may show the practical exigencies which made it necessary to co-operate in the fight to reduce the army of more than six million unemployed, the effort to build up a national economy on constructive ideas. He said in a speech characteristic of his whole approach : " The secret of financing Germany's political and economic tasks lies in a centralised and rigid concentration of the whole public and private activities of the German Reich, that is, public finance as well as private economy. This concentration is only possible within a State based on authoritative rules."[8] Dr. Schacht admits that this task was not to be accomplished under a democratic and parliamentary system. This confirms the fact which has so far always appeared in connection with all modern planned systems, that they are achieved at the price of liberty. Greater efficiency is, therefore, always accompanied by setbacks in social progress.

The stabilisation loan of 1923 and Papen's loan of 1932 (based on a system of payment of taxes by private enterprises for a year or more in advance) suggested the means of coping with unemployment (I give further details in the note[9]). At a time when there was a general lack of money, when money was hoarded and credit was frozen—all the outcome of the Great Depression—another loan had to be started to set in motion the economic machinery which was then at a standstill. The " employment creation loan " was to perform again the miracle of providing capital for trade and industry to carry out their normal private and now greatly extended public orders. In the above-mentioned speech, Dr. Schacht stressed the fact that the revenue income had improved with the progress of economic employment. " The liquidity of the money market enabled the Reich to issue treasury loans, some interest bearing and others not so to any considerable extent. The Reichsbank was capable of aiding these measures as far as it was possible without damaging the currency, and that because the private economy did not approach the bank owing to the existence of reduced activity." The German Currency Bank was always the rediscounting bank—the banker's bank—which supported the deposit banks (as the former main financiers of trade and industry). " The release of debtors of deposit banks enabled these to support employment by offering credit to the trades." Again, circulation of money (and corresponding circulation of goods and services) was restored.

Dr. Schacht recalled that the very small extension of the money circulation and " to a certain extent bigger increases of the *bargeldloser Zahlungsverkehr* (i.e., payments made without the use of cash) was a natural consequence of the increased turnover of the national economy." He went on to say that they thus anticipated the later permanent financial arrangements by debiting short term money. He admits that the consolidation of the latter will, of course, be an important and unavoidable task, and makes it clear that " the programme of the government to create work and especially the provision of all needs for warfare was the only means of getting rid of the big army of unemployed. Of course, the costs of these purposes, measured with a normal rod, are of unheard-of greatness and can only be settled by the services and savings of the people." . . . " For, an improvement of wages cannot take place at this moment, economising of means is everything." In fact, during the period of the Nazi régime, the Government stuck rigidly to this principle. The anxiety to keep prices stable contradicted all other wage policy. The direct connection between the work creation programme and the increase of the purchasing power of the people seems to be clear. Dr. Schacht, in his first-mentioned address, then appealed to the German people's inherent sense of thrift and warned them against hoping that any plans of devaluation could help.

In a more recent speech, about two years later, when surveying four years of activities of the national-socialist régime, Dr. Schacht repeated : " All the great achievements could only be carried through with Germany's restored sovereignty for military dispositions and freedom of action . . . So the financing of the expenditure by using her own resources alone succeeded because everything which concerned the money and capital market was subject to strictest control and compelled everybody to the strictest discipline. No expenditure was permitted in this financial apparatus, which could not serve the creation of work and the enabling of the nation to arm (*Wehrhaftmachung*)."[10]

I shall return to these plans advocated by the then helmsman of the Reich and will show in more detail how they might be carried out. Schacht's words left no room for doubt, and later events testified to their truth. So the Government felt obliged to introduce a thorough-going regimentation, with the two great departments of economic affairs (Currency Bank and Cabinet Ministry) at the head. The so-called "Leadership and Guidance of national economy" established a system of organising all political and economic forces, which had to serve both political and economic ends.

This construction of an economic organisation first found its legal basis in the law for the Preparation of the Organic Structure of German Economy of February 27th, 1934, followed by the first "*Durchführungsverordnung*" (decree to execute this order) of November 11th, 1934. The organisations embrace divisions such as "*Reichsgroups*": (1) industry, (2) trade, (3) handicraft, (4) banks, (5) insurance, (6) power producing industries; sub-divisions ("main groups" which are again divided into "economic groups" and "special groups"). The economic groups are the basis of German industrial organisation. Furthermore, German industry is divided into fourteen economic districts which correspond to the districts of the socio-political organisation (Trustees of Labour). A wide network of centralised and decentralised groups, committees and boards embraces all branches of economy. The head departments of industry, transport and food are the Advisory Boards, i.e., councils for the respective Reich Ministries. As nothing is overlooked, neither person nor undertaking, working in trade and transport, so the Reich Food Estate (*Reichsnährstand*) embraces all farmers, whether owners or employees, co-operative societies or agricultural associations, etc. The market or buying associations are of special importance, because of the complete *Marktordnung* which regulates all matters relating to food and agriculture, including price formation. To this organisation belong also handicrafts and industries concerned in any way with food (bakers, butchers, flour mills, packing companies) while trade in agricultural products is supervised by the Reichs Food Estate alone.

The organisation of industrial economy was based on previous associations which served the economico-political tasks of entrepreneurs (e.g., for commercial policy, cartel policy, taxation, etc.) and of employers' associations (*Arbeitgeberverbände*) which, as opponents of the labour unions (*Gewerkschaften*) supported the wage policies of the entrepreneurs. Most of the former organisations of producers (federations of industries and socio-political employers' associations) as well as the unions of workers and employees were dissolved by the new régime. The large resources of the latter, as well as the funds of the parties of the left were placed at the government's disposal. The present economic associations are forbidden to undertake any activity connected with social policy. This is the field of the German Labour Front. No doubt with the dissolution of the social political associations of entrepreneurs, an important chapter of German political history was closed. The associations combined in the new organisation of German industry were (as groups in the sense of a corporate system) at first not allowed to pursue their own market and price policies. These fell under the special problems of the " cartels." But such questions as general economic policy, money, banking and credit policy, foreign exchange control and questions of law belonged to the " special groups " of German industrial organisation. While cartels were allowed to continue their old activities (mainly market regulation) and certain new ones, both on a voluntary and compulsory basis, they were not allowed to pursue the " economico-political " aims of the groups. So, there was temporarily a two-fold organisation—cartels, side by side with special trade and industrial groups. By the law of November 12th, 1936, to these groups were given rights to supervise cartels in conjunction with governmental organs. A greatly extended chapter of the new policy is that of the *Marktordnung* which was settled by certain official decrees (see §2). Another group, the chambers of industry and commerce, which, in addition to certain internal administrative work which was legally described as their duty, fulfilled various other tasks of representation of industry, have been now inserted in the new system of " groups " (law of July 7th, 1936). In fact, these highly regimented groups and cartels act as part of the Public Administration.

The Weimar system, the consequence of a kind of workers' revolution, legalised all the rights of workers to combine and strike, but tried to establish peace in the labour market by an elaborate system of arbitration. No doubt it was really based on the creed of class struggle. One of the corner stones of the Nazi system was that it broke completely with this idea, and combined the two opponents of production in one " Labour Front " forbidding in principle both strikes and lockouts.

A central office is entrusted with the execution of a far-sighted scheme of land settlement which will cover the whole Reich and provide for the planned development of agricultural as well as industrial districts and the lay-out of houses and communications, especially roads.

The system of the totalitarian State, to which the economic system is subordinated, is still in the making and is, therefore, subject to changes. But more and more tasks are comprehended in the great scheme, which seems to aim at completeness. An innate inclination once awakened finds scope for expression in every exaggeration of planning. As early as 1934 the following typical utterance was made by Herr Ph. Kessler, whom Herr Kurt Schmitt (Dr. Schacht's predecessor in the Ministry of Economic Affairs) appointed " to the highest office as leader of the German National Economy " : " Every part group or branch of industry must know where its place is and may not wander from it."[11]

The four year plan continues this work of planning, making the retreat to any kind of liberal economy ever more difficult. The question arises, at which I previously hinted, whether self-sufficiency is a mere emergency measure or becomes an issue of the ideology.

Supporters have, for a long time, advocated these ideas: the soil of the homeland has to provide for the nation; if this soil does not suffice then the claim to a greater Germany is raised.

I might indicate some stages in the course of development which have revealed themselves since 1933 : (1) Whilst the pre-1933 ideological programme (see p. 207) with its radical socialist claims was still valid, the first outlines of the corporate system (during the Ministry of Kurt Schmitt) and the Labour Front were visible, as also were preliminary steps to combine the economic system in which currency and banking policy should play an outstanding part. (2) The leadership of the currency bank and the Ministry of Economic Affairs were united in the person of Dr. Schacht—and the whole national economy becomes subjected to a general plan. (3) The four years plan of 1936, which is backed by the Party through General Göring. This stage began only recently, so I cannot record its accomplishments. The activity of a price-commissioner, coming from the party hierarchy, appointed to regulate the whole price system, might, no doubt, be a most interesting subject for the economist. For instance the " price-stop decree " (1936) did not care at all whether the costs of production in a certain industry were greatly increased owing to the rise of the world market level and to other factors. The importance of certain goods for the community gives the State the right to enforce or reduce their production.

In his survey[12] of the first four years of the Hitler régime, Dr. Schacht pointed out that the whole money and currency problem had been to aim at a circulation of as small an amount as possible, so that " for the same money token the same amount of goods could be bought." In the last four years the increase of production corresponded to the increase of the money circulation. He then faced " the question whether it will be possible to increase further the production of goods or whether a state of stability may be achieved. The future money policy might depend on this fact; the relation of production to money circulation had to be in a balanced proportion . . . the stability of the German currency was due to the necessity to keep prices stable. Every increase of prices would necessarily spread to other districts. Therefore, the economy of a people as a whole had to be guided." In the words of Dr. Schacht, the " substance " (economic resources) of the German people is not yet big enough to justify the risk of leaving its economy unguided. Therefore, economising and aiming at efficiency had to be the watchwords of his economic policy, which he inaugurated in 1934. And these principles influenced Germany's foreign trade relations. Germany's indebtedness compelled the selection of those goods which could enter her borders without damaging her currency. However, 11,000 million marks of foreign debts still existed and compelled Germany to negotiate with foreign countries, but in the last four years 8,000 million marks were repaid.[13] The selection of what had to be imported and produced necessitated a *list of preferences*, in the foreground of which is placed "security and food" for Germany's vast population; these two main objectives involve, also to quote Dr. Schacht's words, the absorption of the unemployed. The guidance of the whole economy is subject to this scale of preferences which in the general plan is similar in all countries furnished with planning committees.

In order to fulfil the plan, industry, the greatest absorber of the army of unemployed, has been divided into two sections, the first of which provides "security,"—mostly "production goods industries"; and the second meets less urgent needs, which can be postponed—mainly "consumption goods industries" (to these belong the building trade, household goods, furniture, cloth, etc.) which can be economised for a certain number of years. To the initiators of such a policy it seemed clear that the stream of new investments " in such a State controlled economy has to be directed " to the production goods industries, which at the same time must receive foreign raw material in preference to the not so urgently needed consumption goods industries. This reasoning determines the control of foreign bills as well as all foreign economic policy.

Later chapters will make clearer how the State through various channels influences the carrying out its dictates, intended to privilege certain trades. Quite apart from its power as a great monopolist on either side, supply and demand, it operates a kind of "machinery of compensation" between all trades of the country; and does not scruple to enforce its wishes.

To give only a brief example[14] of the working of the system of the list of preferences, I might instance the building trade, and its economical use of iron and steel raw materials. In 1936 the production of the building trade was valued at about 9,000 million marks as compared with 7,500 million marks in 1935 and 2,300 million marks in 1932, the year of the crisis. The year 1936 marked a new record. Although the production of steel rose from 7,200,000 tons in 1932 to 19 million tons in 1936, this increase did not by any means fully correspond to the increase in the building trade, which in 1936 received 35 per cent. of the steel production. But the building of dwelling houses, despite the increase in value to 2,000 million marks, as compared with 800 million marks in 1932, was greatly overshadowed by public works, and so did not receive the share of raw materials which it needed in proportion to the lack of dwelling houses. Even the building of small houses up-country was less than in 1935.

The list of preferences from 1936 to 1937 regulated the use of iron and steel, and secured first of all the export needs of iron-works, then export quotas for iron products, and iron and steel for those works which were urgently needed in the State's interests. To these belong such State and municipal works as were within the framework of the Four Year Plan and were urgently needed for transport undertakings. A "Department for the distribution of raw materials" decided whether iron was to be delivered to branches of industry in which it is an essential material, such as machine-building, mining, furnaces, ships, boilers, etc.; and special orders for public buildings. As stated, for the remaining industries, among them the building trade, there was only a small quota left. The distribution of material for building lies within the province of the National Institute for Labour Exchange and Labour Insurance, and their local branches, because employment figures are here decisive. There were further regulations for the economical use of iron. The National Institute only gave permits if buildings planned for trade purposes were in the public interest or where the national food supply was concerned. Dwelling houses for workmen are preferred, especially those which pay a monthly rent or interest of 40 marks. Where the rent reaches 80 marks, special permission is required. Buildings for administrative purposes, larger detached houses and big blocks of flats are not allowed. That the iron is being used in the most economical manner must be proved in every case. The necessary iron and steel had then to be bought in the free market, but only up to the limit which building plans permit. The " planning " of iron and steel consumption has now been elaborated and refined, and this is not the end.

* * *

What were the results of the Government's policy of State regimentation which set to work the great army of employees after so long a period of idleness ?

Not only was agricultural and industrial production increased in quantity, but this policy was also reflected in an augmented purchasing power, and in the higher figures of saving deposits. There was, too, an increase in exports and in revenue income, together with a decrease of foreign debts. Such improvements in the economic condition of the nation have opened up new opportunities for future development. These figures foreshadow yet another important aspect of the great structural changes in which the world market of our days is involved.

As far as industrial production is concerned, according to Hitler's speech (Reichstag, February 20th, 1938), this increased from 37,800 million marks in 1932 to more than 75,000 million marks in 1937. Of this sum, 22,000 million is in respect of handicrafts, which in 1932 amounted to 9,500 million marks. The share of retail trade in 1937 was 31,000 million marks.

As to the growth of production between 1932 and 1937, coal increased from 104.7 million tons to 184.5 million tons—lignite from 122.65 million tons to 184.7 million tons, steel from 9.66 million tons (1933) to 19.207 million tons, German iron ore from 1.3 million tons to 9.6 million tons. The using of low grade iron ore deposits from German soil are officially expected to increase the German iron ore production by 21 million tons in 1940 (cp. p. 239). The total estimate of German iron ore production in 1941 has been mentioned by Hitler as being 41 to 45 million tons. Correspondingly high figures are shown for by-products of coal, including oils and fats. The German petroleum production rose from 238,000 tons in 1933, to 453,000 tons in 1937. The same applies to the various synthetic products. Amongst them, synthetic rubber, artificial silk and soap from coal and other synthetic oil and fat materials have to be mentioned.

All branches of transport show corresponding increases in their traffic. Canals and inland waterways have been greatly enlarged, their utilisation cheapening the cost of production and distribution. The building of new vehicles, steamers, etc., greatly improved their figures. The *"Reichsautobahnen"* (roads for motor cars), completed or in building, have reached 2,300 kilometers in length.

The increase of dwellings since 1933 has been mentioned as being 1·4 million.

The Government believes that its measures only succeeded because of its action in lowering interest. For short term credit, the reduction was from 6.23% in 1932 to 2.93% in 1937; for long term credit, from 8.8% in 1932 to 4.5% in 1937.

The latest figures of the trade balance do not allow prophecies; for unexpected events, such as wars or slumps cloud many future aspects. The enormous increase of production is due to be absorbed to a great extent on the world market. Under favourable conditions this might increase the export capacity of Germany. The following figures of the trade balance are not without interest in this connection. The import increased from 1933 to 1937 from 4,200 million marks to 5,500 million marks; the export during the same period increased from 4,900 million to 5,900 million marks.

(3) SPECIAL PROBLEMS

In this brief survey of the facts of topical history still in a state of flux, the author can do no more than hint at the great theoretical problems which lie behind them.

(a) MONOPOLIES AND MARKTORDNUNG

§1 *The motives for planning*

Frequent comment has been made on the increasing adoption by the State, during the last 60 to 70 years, of activities in production and distribution, either by control or by interference. These activities have been emphasised in the National-Socialist system, where the Power State regiments organisations by command, and enforces economic orders by the threat of retributive punishment. The above-mentioned activities influence the monopoly problem, the treatment of which has to undergo a revision, since the demand side is no longer occasionally in the hands of several combinations, but has become completely subject to the will and plans of one great demander. This great demander is the State, already a leading factor in production. It takes this position either by directly receiving supply (i.e., railways and other transport, public utilities, State owned industries, banks of various kinds, building, army and navy) or by using its power to " guide " (i.e., dictate to) the consumers (*Verbrauchslenkung*). This act marks the latest stage of development of a State which has been cameralist in its trade policy throughout its history. The Power State not only organises production (Schmoller in his historical survey speaks of a " *Markt-Ordnung,*" "the State allows as much free competition or as much monopoly as is appropriate for the community " (see quotation p. 222 *et seq.*) but now it also guides distribution and consumption. What under free competition results from the free action of forces, directed by self-interest, the State plans and carries out by conscious guidance of supply and demand.

MacGregor's argument that all combination movements, especially exaggerated ones, are signs of abnormal times and that there will be a reversion to some kind of competitive system of satisfaction of wants, is certainly not to be ignored. Emergency produces exaggerations of planning in order to make the best use of small resources. Moreover, the special circumstances in Germany have led to special measures. How is a growing population of 68 million inhabitants to keep alive? That means finding work and wages and thus purchasing power and setting and keeping the wheels of industry in motion. And a smooth working economic machine eases disturbed political conditions and makes government simpler. This requires nothing less than planning and all that goes with it in State policy (foreign and domestic), managed currency, managed labour policy, managed adjustment of production to distribution. This means an internal market of a certain buying capacity and a certain export market. Germany paid with her exports for her vital imports of raw materials and foodstuffs. These imports gave work and purchasing power. It was thus that the population could grow so immensely. It is not to be denied that the contraction of export markets and all its corollaries in political, economic and social affairs, enforced the planning of the government. True, the most disastrous effects, the outcome of the destruction of Germany's previous economic equilibrium through the Treaty of Versailles, are already overcome. The utter destruction of an organisation of production built up by the elaborate work of a century and operating under conditions which could attain a product cheap enough for the world market, has now to some degree been replaced by a new system. Yet, the system which the German Government uses, to finance her expenditure, hints at a currency system which, measured by pre-War standards is completely abnormal. The gold cover of the currency bank is so small that it cannot back in any way the enormous expenditure of the country. The normal access to foreign raw material and food resources which Germany urgently needs is thus prevented. The problems which emerge from such a precarious situation can hardly be overlooked in their vital importance for the whole world.

If the international market, now without exception protectionist, would again permit an appropriate quota of export from Germany, sufficient to keep industry and the population alive, it might be that the most advanced measures of State planning would have to be dropped. But this process of changing the conditions of the international market is a task of *international planning*, politically as well as economically. Thereby combines will not disappear but new ones will be formed.

International policy in recent years has not been encouraging. The only free traders left in the world, Great Britain, Holland, and some other countries, followed extensively the opposite policy. Is there any prospect of these policies changing? How can one expect the most broken industrial Great Power, dependent on export and yet so widely prevented from exporting, to begin with laisser-faire? Dr. Schacht himself has often proclaimed that he does not wish to undermine the competition principle as such. So an economic system excluding individual entrepreneurs, like that of Soviet Russia, was not envisaged at the time he was in office. This opinion, in contrast to that of more advanced economists and politicians, is still widespread in Germany, judging from public utterances. Dr. Schacht (in a pamphlet in the " *Zeitschrift der Akademie fuer deutches Recht*," January, 1938) made it quite clear that, to his mind, the necessary retreat to an automatic price mechanism could be achieved only on an international basis. The presupposition for such a step must be an international political understanding disposing of what he calls " the spirit of Versailles."

Again and again in this history the fact is stressed that the ideal schemes of the liberal economy as far as circumstances favour their application, and political conditions permit their execution, might be the ideals for planning and management of exchange between nations. But there are two questions to consider: first, that of who is to begin such favourable political conditions?; and second, how can national and international competition continue in a world of monopolies?

I have attempted to divide the history of trustification and cartelisation into three periods during which the whole face of the commercial policy of the last sixty years has changed (see p. 92 *et seq.*). The quantity of change ultimately produced a truly qualitative change. There is no doubt that the natural development of markets, the influencing of markets and the exclusion of the market economy made great strides. The two-sided monopoly became an economic organisation of its own. How can it return to recovering a free market? It seems, therefore, justifiable to conclude that (even if the most important difficulties which have led to the crescendo of State planning were to disappear) a very great part of governmental and private combined policy would be left.

Under these general outlines we must examine how *the demand side* fell subject to State invasions, so changing an essential assumption of deductive monopoly theory and forcing us to resort to inductive methods.

Before going into the details of the inroads of the State into the demand side, it should be noted that this interference can be pursued by many means. These are (1) all inroads by private combined forces which the State permits with or without its active support. (2) State regulation by law. (The extent to which the law will regularise State interference will depend upon some view of economics. It may vary from slight deviations from free competition to enforced combination or, conversely, enforced competition.) (3) State regimentation. (Here there are two possibilities : (*a*) private enterprise is still retained. This is the condition which alone interests us as regards the German economy. (*b*) Private enterprise is abolished, e.g., the Russian example.)

§2 *Cartels since* 1933 *and the Marktordnung*

The Third Reich continued to reconcile the idea of combines with that of a corporate system. Later the part which combines as instruments of another principle were to play became more evident. The reform of trusts at the beginning ran separately from that of cartels but later the line of both became more clear. The first decisive act was the law of July 15th, 1933, by which the Administration was empowered to submit all organisations and agreements which tied up prices to its regimentation. The Minister of Economic Affairs could arbitrarily decree the nullification of cartel agreements or cartel decisions, or he could forbid certain ways of carrying out the transactions of cartels. " Compulsory cartels " could be decreed by the Minister, in order to combine enterprises. Even the settlement of individual Cartel Agreements could be decreed by the Minister. The cartel decree of 1923 for these " compulsory " combines also remained in force ; although, without the aforementioned clause 8 which gave members the possibility of giving notice to the cartel. The decisive change evidently lies in the complete submission of the economic system to the State in all those cases which were not explicitly reserved to competition. Now the State is empowered to prevent the restriction of free competition as well as to create or enlarge it. Through this act the Government takes over the responsbility of seeing that the abolition or alteration of certain market situations does not injure public welfare. The State controls the entire formation of prices and " calculation " of cartels. In a special decree of May 16th, 1934, the Minister claimed the censorship of all tied prices. Without his permission a new tying up or raising of prices of existing agreements was not allowed. The establishment of a register of cartel agreements and measures was fulfilled. Automatically all reports are forwarded to the Minister, who backed this measure by proclaiming an obligation to communicate all changes concerned to the Commissioner of Prices. The hitherto valid principles of fixing cartel prices according to the costs of the marginal entrepreneur were now in many cases no longer pursued. A very important clause of this law is the power of the Minister to prohibit or direct investments. This might also serve to prevent over-production or lavish use of capital. Before continuing these general remarks on State and economy, I shall give some few examples, in chronological order, of how the new State, since its ascent, has interfered in trade and industry.

* * *

The first year of the new régime was referred to as a " *Cartel hausse.*" Under the influence of certain more or less vague corporative ideas, the State made far-reaching interference in the affairs of market policy. The State then made inroads into the system of combines, as I have just mentioned in touching upon the laws of 1933. The principle already shown in the Weimar Reich, that the cartel movement extended into the province of finished goods, advanced rapidly to include such goods as cigarettes, soap, glass and porcelain goods, playing cards, wireless sets, gas stoves, enamelled goods and slates.

In the next year, however, the cartels were deprived of the rôle of sole maker of " *Ordnung* " in the industrial market. For a year and a half no compulsory cartels were allowed and the formerly existing cartels became more independent and permits for new cartel arrangements were only given for a short time. Some of these, such as those of cement, potash, automobile tyres, and cigarettes were not continued. But in these years no dissolution of cartels took place; on the contrary, the cartels established in 1933-34 were consolidated and extended in the favourable conditions of trade cycle.

The year 1936 brought a strong wave of market agreements, activities which have a certain connection with stimuli offered by the developments in the corporative organisation, which simplified the technique of formation of cartels and created a good psychological situation favourable to their appearance. The branch groups (*Fachgruppen*) of the first organisation of 1933 sometimes exercised cartel functions. In the next period these compulsory organisations were forbidden to continue any such activities. Later again, a loosening of these rigid distinctions followed, and branch groups were able to act as observers, advisers, and trustees. The personal and official union between general economio-political policy and the associations which regulate the market, was not forbidden. The latter were strengthened by the support of the branch groups. The condition of the outsider became public knowledge through the statistical returns which he was compelled to make, and the pressure exerted upon the outsider was increased. Even where in some industries such cartels did not formerly exist, organisations for regulating market conditions were now established. The branch group made use in this way of their knowledge of all statistical material. Some industries such as packing-case manufacture or that of the cartel of domestic candelabra which are under the guidance of the branch group are worth noticing. Wholesale trade through these channels tried to secure for itself old claims such as certain rebates, fair prices, and quantitative limitation of recognised firms. The iron trade, coal trade, sheet glass wholesale trade, fixed agreements, and others can be seen in the making, as also parts of motor cars and the electrical industry. It is true that firms are not officially compelled to join these agreements, but the influence of branch groups to form cartels became stronger and stronger. Payment cartels have easily gained extension by these measures. In other industries again the obligatory fixation of prices of certain factories took place between producers and the trade, e.g., in wireless, linoleum, motor-cycles, cigarettes, automobiles, books, etc. The rebate system found a corresponding regulation. I need not enumerate more instances of special questions in which the co-operation of producers' and consumers' associations is instrumental.

There are, at this time, some new types of a *Marktordnung* through cartels which have to be mentioned. The former " calculation cartels " found new principles.

The " calculation cartel " of which experience is now being gained in the foundry industry (*Grauguss*), printing, radiator, and fishing industries, etc., plays an important part. The casting industry offers an interesting model of an industry whose members are compelled to join the cartel and to consider it the official organ for regulating the market under governmental control. Much research has been undertaken to arrive at principles of technique and of organisation for efficiency. Comparison of costs of the various works concerned furnishes guiding principles for an unification of cost accounting, etc. An elaborate system of recommendations and formulae is provided for the member firms by the examination office of the cartel in order to control costs and prices. The recent change in the allocation of tasks between the " group " and the cartel does not greatly change the principle: the State transferred functions of Public Administration to associations of entrepreneurs.

The prohibition of new investment in cement, which was reintroduced in March, 1936, was supported by a compulsory membership of firms concerned, and a compulsory quota system for outsiders on the basis of their last year's output. The steel wire association and razor blades organisation were submitted to the same regulations. The " calculation cartel " is above all one of those forms mentioned above which help to open up clearer vistas in important business transactions (see p. 94). No wonder that the idea of managed price was used to the utmost at a time when free price formation had to be abandoned within a world of trade restriction and protection.

In the three corporate sectors, food production and consumption (which became completely subject to *Marktordnung*), forestry (where associations to provide calculations for saw mills are organised), and inland shipping, progress has been made in widespread interference through old and newly-established authoritative agreements and organisations. First of all the general prohibition of investments presupposes that every firm concerned must get a permit for any new establishment and extension. Interference by the State-controlled bodies shows itself not only in old-established cartelised industries such as sugar, starch, yeast, but also in others such as the flour-mill bakeries, preserved goods, margarine and vinegar industries. An indirect and looser quota system, whereby raw material becomes specially distributed to the individual producer, exists in the chocolate and confectionery industry, prepared cereals, certain other foodstuffs and, to a limited degree, also for malt mills and breweries. Price control following the line of the calculation cartels holds sway in fruit and vegetable preserving industries, and in the fishing industry. The cartels which were formerly concerned with sugar and potato starch manufacture extended their activities by adding rice starch, foodstuffs consisting of sugar, certain waste products, like molasses, and the refining of sugar—all these are now rigidly organised in price agreements as well as in quota. Breweries had, through these new regulations, certain decisive means of financing restaurants, hotels, etc.

A compulsory association of all entrepreneurs of motor transport is obliged to settle with the National Railways all questions as far as tariffs are concerned. The creation of premises collecting railway and motor vans provides a centralised distribution of freight supply.

The cartel law received a further emphasis at this time of growing expansion of the principle of cartels. I do not wish to enumerate here all new regulations in various industries such as heavy industry, motor oil, super-phosphate, paper. It is not without interest that after the crisis, which revealed some very questionable price cartels and syndicates in the paper industry, a system of thirty cartels now regulates completely all questions involved. Wallpapers, glass, porcelain, have a fixed system of mutual understanding between producers and the trade.

Statements of the Business Research Institute and of other publications differ as to the percentage of cartelised products of trade and industry, but they agree as to the enormous and ever-increasing extent of this process.

A certain wider significance for this wave of cartels is gained by their growing international extension. England, Belgium and France show progress in this direction. The International Iron and Steel

Export Cartel has to be mentioned in this connection, the tinplate cartel, the iron wire export cartel, and the cartels for tubes, coke, potash, nitrogen, aluminium and some other articles.

Governmental decisions regarding control of the economic system are considerably assisted by the fact that in Germany one part of economic doctrine, that is, " business management," is very well developed. From secret wrappings, the " invisibility of capitalism," economic and connected financial transactions seem now largely unveiled. An army of academic accountants, well instructed in business management for a generation in the German Schools, of which Professor Schmalenbach's was outstanding, made possible the disclosure of almost every secret of costs[15] or of the setting up of a balance sheet and the unravelling of all financial and legal transactions leading to the promotion and working of trust companies. One may say that the orgies of promotion during the boom periods brought about the disappearance of the legendary financier and man of Big Business, nor has legislation since given any opportunity for restoring such figures.

* * *

The Police State found a new instrument in the institution of Public Accountants (established 1931), whom some people have called " detectives of business." The duty of the legal adviser of the undertaking to inform the appropriate Government department of any offence against the law extended equally to the Public Accountant when making his " compulsory " audit. Now, the Revenue Department is equipped with a personnel which already includes hundreds of experts on the previous secrets of private economy. The practice of scrutinising costs and prices and comparing the profits of the individual members of cartels in the cartel and syndicate office was, no doubt, itself a splendid school for investigations of the Revenue Department. For instance, the writing off of depreciation, which formerly was an instrument for veiling profits, is now regulated in such a way that the State can go back ten years in assessments and add to taxation the written off values which later turned into boom profits. Claims of this kind by the Revenue Office are in fact very frequent. The packed State budget in this way brought about the controversy between Schacht and the other leaders as to how far a system of taxation can proceed. The State income from taxation has been more than doubled during the five years since 1932, and refinement of taxation is still going on to provide for the ever-increasing needs of the State. It is said that, all in all, the various taxes constitute a burden of 60 to 70 per cent. of the net profits of industrial undertakings (*Frankfurter Zeitung*, 24th October, 1937). The business corporation tax alone absorbs almost a third of the surplus profits. This is a case of double taxation ; for the profits of the individual shareholders are again taxed. There should be added also the expenses which industries have to bear for extensions forced upon them by the four years plan (see p. 239). In mentioning this drastic reduction of the profits of private enterprise I have anticipated some facts which will complete the picture of German Public Finance (see p. 253). (For certain other burdens on private enterprise see what I have said regarding individual loans mentioned on p. 239.)

* * *

It is to be noted that at present great activity in the control of trusts and cartels exists, as the outcome of the enormous economic activity since the rapid increase of employment. The policy of the Government is caused and directed by the general plan mentioned elsewhere. The cartel policy is strongly influenced by these measures in which production for export and the cheapening of the process of production are outstanding factors. This development is older than the Third Reich. It began after the slump of 1931.

No doubt, the Government, when conditions were precarious, employed cartels for purposes of a general political and economico-political nature, which had nothing to do with market or cartel policy. The problem of maintaining political power, internal and external, has confronted the present Government as well as its predecessors, and political and economic exigencies have led to the continuous modification of far-reaching plans.

But the above-mentioned deviations from the peculiar cartel-purpose, are not the only troubles with which this new economic policy is faced. They are of a more fundamental and theoretical character. It is repeatedly being proclaimed that thorough legislation upon "*Marktordnung*" will, in time, be decreed. What an enormous task it is to formulate laws for general application on such a highly controversial subject! Evidently, it is intended that practice will first have to show how far special cases, now under experiment, justify possible generalisations. It is a stage of tentative experiment. So far as I can see, the monopoly problem in Germany as it finds actual expression in recent development, has been but little studied. The German Institute for Business Research is engaged in investigations on the demand and consumption problem. Miksch, in a book just published,[16] comes to certain conclusions—no doubt completely different from and foreign to the British economist's point of view—he says : " The progress of economic science furnishes to-day the equipment for the reorganisation of the policy of competition. The two essential facts are : (1) one is not allowed to put one's house in order by means of private economic forces, this is the work of the State ; (2) the actual form in which free competition or linked-up organisations show themselves should be the decisive criteria for the establishing of a working procedure." Miksch states five facts : " (1) Where complete free competition exists as the form of the market, this form has to be introduced and secured as the legal market constitution (*Marktverfassung*). (2) Where complete free competition can be brought about there it must be brought about. (3) Where this is achieved, the legal market constitution has to be applied and secured. (4) Where imperfect competition exists as the market form, the legal market constitution of tied-up competition has to be substituted for free competition. (5) Where imperfect competition exists and a private market regulation is introduced, a legal market constitution of ordered and tied-up competition has to be set up."

Nos. 1, 2 and 3 do not seem comprehensible at all as long as the "totalitarian" type of imperfect competition of the present system exists.

The policy here suggested reflects Miksch's recognition of combines as an inevitable phenomenon of the economic system. Furthermore, these combines are now conceived as institutions of Public Administration. Maybe a monopoly theory will have some future for application when both inductive and deductive methods and results are sufficiently mature.

In Party and Government circles there is, as with Dr. Miksch, an opinion that future legislation must involve the whole " Law of Competition," into which the law relating to combines has in some manner to be inserted. The former law of competition merely dealt with unfair competition and its punishment and so it dealt with only a side issue of the competition problem. Nobody can, at this moment, say how a law embracing the wider problem will eventually be shaped. The new Company Law of 1937, which embraces the highly controversial " concern " problem, is not so much concerned with competition as such and is new only in other aspects (see §4).

§3 *Growing demand-monopolies*

On both sides, supply and demand, monopolies are created, such as that of the Manuring Syndicate brought into being by the *Reichsnährstand* (Reich Food Estate), which was formerly not organised, as it is now, by monopolisation through syndicates and cartels. Examples, *inter alia*, of partial monopolies on the demand side are the National Railways and the Post Office, in so far as they have requirements, e.g., for various vehicles or apparatus. The Post Office, for instance, constitutes the dominant part of the demand in certain electrical industries.

Concentration of production very often provoked parallel measures on the consumer's side, and where production passed through a series of divided processes, there would arise monopolistic organisations at the various stages, each of which would represent demand for the preceding stage. Formerly these monopolistic positions would be met only at the early productive stages, but since the War finishing industries have been organised similarly. Conversely, monopolistic control on the demand side would provoke similar organisation on the side of supply. A significant example of this kind is found in the industries making locomotives, wagons, and nuts and bolts.

These are suppliers of the National Railways and are for the most part, or even wholly, dependent upon this gigantic undertaking. This monopoly of demand, arising from the State ownership of all tracks, was still more powerful when foreign orders to the supplying industries dwindled during the Weimar Reich. It is interesting that the cartel schemes which were evolved in the industries concerned (such as in the locomotive and wagon industries) were established by the will of the Transport Authority itself. Finally, at the time of the Third Reich, the State regimented the whole transport system when all means of transport were subjected to one great scheme. State ownership or control was partly carried through during the Weimar Reich and involved every sector of the economic sphere in its great range of influencing and guiding activities of production as well as consumption. State and municipal departments hereby created an instrument for managing an active trade cycle policy (see next page).

The demand monopoly throws light also on other theoretical problems. First, there is here a difference from the case of supply monopolies where the extent of supply is adapted to its curve of costs. This issue of price formation does not exist on the side of demand. The National Railway can vary its orders to a great extent, owing to its monopolist position in transport activities. Thus a demand monopoly can apply differentiated prices, according to the costs of suppliers. The possibility of enforcing low total prices upon suppliers corresponds exactly to the differentiation of prices by supply monopoly. The differentiation creates a greater demand and thus an increase of markets. Just because of this, suppliers through the existence of demand-monopoly will be induced to combine. If this is not possible as soon as desired, then price wars will bring about combination. The National Railway has made full use of its monopoly position as a public undertaking; therefore, it has induced cartelisation on the suppliers' side. If, however, monopoly of supply is opposed to a monopoly of demand, it is evident that what still existed of the free formation of prices, under the less complete restriction of competition, is now completely excluded.

As Dr. Miksch[17] puts it, an expedient should be sought to create a condition of quasi-competition, in order to make possible a certain formation of prices for the sake of the technical progress which he considers dependent on it. Since 1926 the wagon builders have been united in a common board of control, which investigates the costs of every individual factory, not only the costs for the " complete wagon " but for every single part. From these figures, average costs are calculated, which are communicated to the individual companies. The National Railway pays all works a price which corresponds to these average costs with a certain addition for profit. It was stated that this system was a foundation of regulation to which the suppliers agreed. It worked well. The costs of the worst entrepreneur would be greater than the average, so he was compelled at least to strive to reduce them. Companies are induced to reduce their costs in order to increase their profits. Continuous and meticulous calculation of cost can be an advantage to the concern. But this system has its weakness. When output decreases, cost per unit rises. Thus when the National Railway decreased its orders it was inevitably faced with the increased costs of the suppliers. In 1932, when such a situation occurred, the wagon companies were induced to forfeit the increase of their costs brought about by this restriction of output. Other examples of the State as purchaser restricting a free market can be found.[18] The public (State and municipal) demand for supplies was stimulated by the Government in order to reduce unemployment, and for special political and new cultural purposes. Some distressed branches of industry were kept above water by special orders of the Government, e.g., the small domestic industries in the mountains of Middle Germany. Some supply boards of Nazi party unions and the winter relief organisations gave orders which normally would not be needed. There are other cases where the Government secured for poorer classes certain standard goods. In these cases and others, the Government as main purchaser enforced a very low price based on the cost records of selected producers. These examples of deviations from free competition are sufficient to show that important consequences may result. In normal times undertakings will provide from their profits certain reserves, either secret or disclosed, against less prosperous times. With profit-making kept to a minimum by means of cost calculations, there are no longer large profits from which such reserves can be built up. When the monopoly position of the Government as purchaser becomes so strong and when this results in such a tight control of trade and industry, the Government itself is involved in responsibility for many frictions forced upon the economic system. The more the demand is concentrated with public boards, the more can it be employed for economico-political purposes. Yet, "the control of the trade cycle according to central plans" is one of the major tasks of the Government. The *Reichsausgleichsstelle für öffentliche Aufträge* (Compensating Board for Public Works) adjusted employment by the allocation of public orders to districts according to their need, as measured by the degree of unemployment existing. The orders were given to certain cartels and co-operative societies which are subject to publicly controlled and compulsory auditing. (The board also "examined," on behalf of the Government, calculation of prices.) But this office here referred to might rather serve as an important example to cope with the problem at issue. The longer the new four years plan overshadows the economic system the more the whole private and public economic machinery becomes subject to thoroughgoing planning and adjusting supply to demand and vice versa.

There are some other concentrations of demand. The so-called co-operative societies of consumers did not affect the free competition of their different and vast suppliers. Their purpose was always directed towards the wholesale provision of goods and the cheapening of costs of distribution. The co-operative associations of consumers, which suffered greatly during the slump, have meanwhile been placed on a sound basis. With the sequestration of the trade unions and relative institutions their properties went under the governmental scheme and so the Reich association of co-operative societies has been established, which since then has shown an increase in membership, as well as in turnover (510½ million marks in 1936) and output (8,833 offices of distribution existed).

Considerable consequences resulted from the concentration of consumers in the German Labour Front (see pp. 214, 269) (in which employers are included). This combination can easily influence certain markets. For example, the " Strength through Joy " union of the National-Socialist Party, aims at mass travelling for more than seven million people. It has been mentioned that a new style of travelling has been evoked by this movement, which influenced the whole hotel and restaurant trade, the building and managing of hotels, overseas steamers and so on. Classes of the population which formerly did not travel participate in these journeys. Strong organisations on the side of demand everywhere result in a fixation of prices. Only some instances showing organisations formed on the side of demand have been mentioned and they represent a small sector of the whole. First of all the German Government believed it was its task to interfere in those forms of market which are no longer "free."

When the Government attains a position of virtual monopoly on the demand side, thereby dominating vast sections of the economic life, quite new problems arise, among which is that expounded by German economists, which Dr. Wagemann calls the " manipulation of consumption."[19] Demand and consumption, according to writers such as Wagemann and Miksch, become new focussing points of practical economic problems. It is not only the direct share of the Government as shareholder; the State influence is marked by the power which the new system of State, as planner and regulator, has of interfering in the former private fields of the economic sphere; and this interference is often as strong as when the State is a large shareholder. Therefore, the Government partly sold the shares in banks and industrial undertakings which it bought during the slump. But, nevertheless, the active share of the State as Capitalist in trade and industry is still very strong, as the sub-chapter (*b*) on " Public Control " will show.

§4 *New Joint Stock Law*

Mention has been made in the previous chapter of the change in Joint Stock Company Law, introduced on October 1st, 1936. The remarks on the ideology and the practical policy of the new system in this chapter will make more comprehensible the idea of the leadership, with which the chief manager of the company is now entrusted.

Since the Government directs the investment of the deposits of saving banks, and of co-operative society banks, without asking either saver or member of the small co-operative whether or not they agree with the way in which the State makes use of their deposits for the State's purposes, it is quite clear that the shareholder of the Joint Stock Company will not be treated differently. The shareholder's choice is restricted, since decrees cut off investments abroad or inland securities even if they were to the investors' liking. There is for the investor no possibility of choosing *a la carte* (to use a comparison from H. Levy given in another connection); the shareholder has to take the menu offered by the quasi-planning committee of the Government, which thinks for him and takes his savings and deposits for whatever purposes the Government believes to be enlightened.

Already during the Weimar Reich, old ideas of shifting the boundary between private and public interest gained favour. No wonder that this movement flung itself against the heart of the capitalist system, the private enterprise. The whole German Company Law was based on the fundamental principle that the holder of responsible capital who, therefore, bore the risk, was to be respected as the owner of the enterprise. The whole body of owners had the formal right to decide the undertaking's affairs, even to liquidate or to destroy it. Only the interests of the creditors were protected by the law. Labour was protected only through some preferential rights as creditors in case of liquidation. The law had no cognisance of the claim of the worker to his job. Shortly after the War, in connection with the establishment of a special Ministry for Demobilisation, certain State kommissars obtained the right to collaborate with the owner in so far as closing down of plants and mass release of labour were concerned.

Germany's development in the most recent period of this dominant trustification shows a totally different picture from that seen before the War or at the beginning of this century. In those days, millions of small and middling businesses characterised her economy, so that the consequences were not so grave if some capitalists closed down their works. When enormous trusts came to dominate entire industries and trades, involving the destiny of hundreds of thousands of families of workmen, suppliers and customers, and even the budget of the State, the unlimited rights of private ownership were challenged. Bankruptcies, collapses of entire groups of industries with enormous effects of temporary, and in many cases of permanent unemployment, impelled a new law to protect the community and especially labour, the major sufferer. The behaviour of certain businesses accelerated the process of averting these unwholesome conditions. In referring to special events I have to add, in fairness, that critics have to distinguish between failures originating in the system itself, such, as in this case, of trustification and cartelisation in German trades, and those due to fraudulent manoeuvres, the conditions for which were highly favourable in a time of unprecedented crisis. The law of September 19th, 1931, sought to do justice in this respect. Whether it was too weak to be effective is not clear. The crisis, with its very unfavourable conditions for capital issues, and the short duration of the law, make it difficult to judge. The 1931 law aimed at an increased accessibility to public inspection and almost completely prohibited the acquiring of shares in one's own company. It contained rigorous provisions for balance sheets and compulsory auditing. In addition, capital increase was to be facilitated in prescribed ways.

I may mention here that the German Commercial Law of 1869 provides the Joint Stock Company with three organs. First there is the *Vorstand*, that is, a board of the higher servants of the company (committee of managers), but similar to the Board of Directors of British Law, in so far as they do much initiatory work. Rarely are they capitalists but rather highly-paid civil servants of industry. Departmental heads of works were frequently among these personalities. Henceforward I shall call this *Vorstand* the Administration. In Germany the decisive power of the undertaking ultimately rested in many cases in this Administration, in other cases in the second statutory body, the " *Aufsichtsrat* " (Supervisory Board). This was generally the seat of representatives of the main capital and also some important experts of the special branch of industry, often long connected with the enterprise. It is not without interest that some trusts found their real leader in the chairman of the *Aufsichtsrat*. In contrast to this principle, e.g., Emil Rathenau and Deutsch, the decisive leaders of Germany's gigantic Electricity Trust, were chief managing directors without votes in the *Aufsichtsrat*.

The German Joint Stock Company profited extraordinarily from its two-chamber system. The main difference between the statutory bodies in this country was that the German Supervisory Board was not so intimately engaged in current work as the British Board of Directors, and that the management of the Administration undertook much initiative work and not only executive work.

The third body was the general meeting representing all shareholders. In a nutshell, the new law wishes to bring the Administration to the fore, and to condemn the *Aufsichtsrat* and the general meeting to a life of shadows. The general meeting, as Dr. Schlegelberger (the chief official of the Ministry who prepared the reforms) once said, will be " a deposed King." It will no longer be allowed to protect certain votes. There is no doubt that, since the Great Depression, the plural-vote share—a type very foreign to German companies prior to that time—created for Germany's whole trade and industry great new problems, prompting the ideas for reforming the whole system. In future, the Administration, according to the " Law for the order of National Labour " will also be the legal leader of the company. The Administration, from which a chief manager with a decisive vote can be appointed, is independent of ownership of shares. The original plan to authorise the Administration to exercise a voice equal to one-fifth of the votes carried by all the shares has been abandoned. In August, 1935, at the meeting of the National-Socialist Union of Lawyers in Hamburg, Dr. Schlegelberger, pointed out that this authority (the Administration) would be able to fight effectively against the selfishness and ignorance of the shareholders. The wording of the new law gives to the Administration so prominent a position that it is believed it could exercise its power without the support of a certain percentage of shareholders' votes. Commentators say[20]: "The former company law understood the Joint Stock Company as a company of shareholders, formed in order to make joint profits." " In future the share will be merely a method of financing, offered to the Administration as an *Unternehmer auf Aktien* (entrepreneur supported by shares)." The wording of the official interpretation of the law says: "The Administration has to lead the company according to its own responsibility in order to serve the welfare of the company and its following and the common weal of people and Reich." The increased power of the Administration is alleged to be expressed by the taking away of the rights of the general meeting, and by its greater independence of the supervisory board, which, however, still retains the right to appoint or retire the Administration. According to the law, this Administration decides the "annual report" and the balance sheet of the company, without the approval of the general meeting, which formerly exercised this prerogative. With this privilege the Administration is intended to carry corresponding responsibilities. With these new decisions, these members of a junta inside the private undertaking, still the representatives of private interests and not the officers of the Government or a Council for Joint Stock Companies, have become the "champions of public interests." Officially the law is announced as socialism of the proper national-socialist colour but it still preserves important rights of private groups. Who guarantees that this privileged Administration would, in a conflict between block and small holders, vote against the former? It is not easy to decide whether an action is for or against the community or the enterprise, especially when interests conflict.

A peculiar condition of the law has authorised the general meeting to elect, actually by majority vote, the Supervisory Board which, in turn, appoints the Administration. According to this, it still remains an employee of the Supervisory Board, but once chosen, it may, according to its special right, influence the election of the Supervisory Board. This still receives the right of a merely formal veto on the exercise of voting by the Administration. This limitation again has created the possibility of a dependence of the Administration on the Supervisory Board and may unite them to act against the interests of the small shareholder. No guarantee against this is available. On the surface, it is true, the idea of leadership is given, but who on earth can guarantee independence against the blockholder of shares? The preponderance of power now rests with the individual leader. According to the new regulations, in the case when several members form the Administration, its chairman has to be the leader. It is true that most influential captains of industry in preceding decades have been compelled to provide themselves with sufficient blocks of shares to keep a leading position, but this fact of acquiring majorities often led to great evils. The Supervisory Board is, in certain respects, not unlike the British Board of Directors; it has outstanding economic functions. These comprise all potential authority for providing new capital issues, special orders in undertakings which, perhaps, have been connected with the company, providing markets, etc. In discussing trusts, we considered this problem more closely. How far is the influence of these groups important or even vital for undertakings, when the Supervisory Board is to be excluded from real power without damaging production and distribution as an entity? Where is the power of the almighty leader of the company, when he is compelled to provide new sources of capital, e.g., in times like those of the recent past, when in a crisis the stock and share market is unwilling to accept new shares? On such occasions the natural dependence of the power of the leader finds its limits. With regard to these important problems, left untouched by the authors of the new decree, it is no great thing that, as Dr. Schlegelberger said, in order to provide capital, the conditional enlargement of capital is to be introduced. It might be so constituted that it could be carried out only when third persons made use of its right of issue. Beside the conditional increase of capital, the " authorised " capital is to be added, that means that the Administration is empowered for a given time, say five years, to issue new shares over and above the nominal capital.

As regards the privileged position of the leader, I ought to mention, that many objections to these leading " captains of industry " were made, especially in the time of the slump; e.g., that the Supervisory Board did not supervise enough and that thus many collapses were not averted!

One point more—the position of the shareholder. So long as the private economy exists, his sharing in the capital is voluntary. According to the new law, the shareholder is no longer allowed to ratify the annual report, balance sheet and declaration of dividend, his former most important prerogatives. His organ, the general meeting, as Dr. Schlegelberger said, will only have to vote in cases where it is expressly authorised by law or company rules, as, e.g., in formal confirmations (which right it probably has for lack of anybody else). Hereby it had only to accept as foundation the balance sheet; it was not allowed to test it, or approve the appointing or dismissing of the Supervisory Board, or the alteration of the company rules. It is very significant that the general meeting is said to be the instrument of its leader, and has to be prepared merely to listen to proclamations about management, if he so wills it.

Without doubt, the small shareholder, after changing his functions as the most important financier, has become a factor of minor significance. The speculative character of buying shares with certain chances for profit, which stimulated the shareholder, will still exist to a certain degree, though limited by the law which cuts his dividends. The law is formed according to the peculiar conditions of an artificially provoked boom period. Will it prove satisfactory in other phases of the cycle? There is now practically no difference between the holder of shares and the holder of debentures, the one is a creditor for the interest, and the other is a creditor for the dividend, which may not exceed six per cent. But the new law permits him little more than to buy the shares and to obey the leader of the company.

The Government is deeply concerned to subject also other legal forms of undertakings to far-reaching reforms. Thus the G.m.b.H. (see p. 78) is now under consideration by the official Enquiry Committee. This form of company served, among other things, undertakings of smaller size and enabled the enterprising partners to limit their liability. Much the same as in England, the private limited company is not obliged to publish the facts leading to its formation, or its balance sheets, as is the case under the stricter provisions relating to public limited companies. So the G.m.b.H. was sometimes called a "financial camera obscura." The years of crisis revealed this character of them; it became especially obvious during the last crisis. This saw the collapse of a good many newly-established undertakings, and other private limited companies which, as part of great trust undertakings, had been engaged in manoeuvres which could not be carried out under the legal scheme of the public limited company. At the end of 1933 nearly 65,000 G.m.b.H's existed which decreased to 38,000 in 1936.

In recent times, probably as a consequence of the new Company Law, undertakings of a very great size were transformed into private companies. Sometimes, as the *Frankfurter Zeitung* (25/7/37) says, "to escape the intended social will of the legislator which was expressed in the new law."

The new Companies Act and other statutes caused various changes in the legal form of trading associations. For example, public limited companies were transformed into limited partnerships (*Kommanditgesellschaft*) which form, e.g., the "roof organisation" of the Flick Trust or the great Julius Pintsch Concern and the Brassert Concern. It has been stressed that the private limited company in changing its original purpose might become a transitional stage between the public limited company and such *Kommanditgesellschaften* or partnerships limited by shares (*Kommanditgesellschaft auf Aktien*). As far as can be seen at this moment, the economic principle of finance capitalism is not much touched by the changes of legal forms, from one to another, effected from within or by legislation. The tentative character of transitional economic and legal forms of undertakings is evident.

What has been changed is the State influence, oft-quoted in this history, which subjects the whole policy of the quasi-private undertaking to its will. The preservation of some quasi-entrepreneurs in this system without whom, according to one part of the Government advisers, a sound production for the present Government purposes cannot go on, marks the compromise character. There is no possibility of prophesying whether the tendency to undermine these remainders of the capitalist system, containing certain quasi-entrepreneurs, will continue or whether economy might fall back to a certain degree, to a more capitalist system with entrepreneurs.

§5 *A few remarks on Trusts*

One word more on trusts: This problem remains largely untouched, in spite of an enormous literature, in newspapers and periodicals, which blustered about trusts and called them antinational socialist, alien bodies and pernicious influences. In the law to promote the conversion of certain capital companies into personal companies, i.e., partnerships (5.VI.34), a prior stage of this process was attempted. The minimum capital of Joint Stock Companies is now fixed at 500,000 marks as against 50,000 marks previously. The minimum value of a share is now 1,000 marks.[21] The often-repeated heading " from anonymity to the personal leader of the enterprise," has made clear the aim of the legislation, which, however, has hardly succeeded in changing materially the nature of the trust. Many changes took place within and between big trusts such as separation or absorptions of auxiliary companies. Blockholdings of shares have changed hands, and in certain cases, such as the Vereinigte Stahlwerke, a new stage in reconstruction has again been reached. In fact, the new law did not greatly change the structure of the trust in principle (nor did the trusts themselves); rather, it contains further provision against abuses or criminal offences. The law maintains in a definition of the subsidiary enterprises of the concern (trust), (which remain legally independent companies), the state reached previously. So, the trust is a combine, holding directly or indirectly in one hand the majorities of numerous enterprises, thus actually controlling many undertakings from one place. It therefore remains true that the Administration of a trust subsidiary, in spite of its legal independence as a Joint Stock Company, is nothing other than an employee.

National-Socialist legislation did not prevent the continuation of trusts. It is true, they did not occur with the frequency and extent of the preceding period of trustification, but its extent is still considerable. Some reasons for this phenomenon have been mentioned. The policy of the Government of creating work led to an increase of liquidity in the economic system. Public orders directly and indirectly animated industry, trade and banking. Partly the increased turnover resulted in more effective use of the productive capacities, partly new investments were needed, as in the motor car industry. But those works which, owing to import restrictions, were not in a position to reproduce their stocks of raw materials and could not sell as much as in former normal years, had, in fact, liquid resources. The same is true where certain branches of industry was deliberately restricted, as the margarine industry. These resources have been partly absorbed by State loans which were issued for the consolidation of short term debts resulting from the creation of work. But other resources have been used for new investments and for the reconstruction of concerns whose structure appeared to be partly " organic " and partly " inorganic." This latter term was a reproach frequently levelled against certain combinations during the inflation and boom periods. Several transactions were brought about by the necessity or desire of holders of blocks of shares partly or wholly to get rid of them. Great private shareholders, banks and industrial concerns, participated in these transactions. All big industries were affected by these measures. The State, which in times of emergency had become a shareholder, again sold its shares (Vereinigte Stahlwerke, Deschimag, Atlaswerke). The Middle German iron and steel works had to be dissociated from the Vereinigte Stahlwerke as well as its majority in the big mining trust, Essener Steinkohle. Mr. Flick, the former blockholder of shares of the Vereinigte Stahlwerke, again played a leading part in these transactions, now taking over majorities of shares in the Harpen mining trust dominated by this financier. That these changes in trust shares or their majorities really serve in the reconstruction of trusts to make their composition more rational surely holds good for certain concerns, but not for all transactions which have taken place since 1933, of which I give here only a glimpse. The heavy industry, which acquired new tasks in the self-sufficiency programme, for instance, for gaining oil by liquifaction of coal, or obtaining synthetic rubber and similar processes, developed new subsidiary enterprises or changes in trust structure. The same holds good for cement and all forms of transport.

There may not be a single big trust in which such transfers of companies, of blocks of shares or reconstruction of their economic or legal forms, have not taken place during the Third Reich. Nevertheless, no essential alteration has been made in the economic power of the leading *Konzern*-firm in regard to its dependent companies.

A little hint at one of the latest events may be permitted. Apart from other far-reaching changes of General Goering's four years plan, the decision of the German Government to develop as a national enterprise the hitherto unworked low-grade iron in three great German ore-fields (in North Germany, especially in Brunswick, in Baden and Franconia) marks a new epoch in the history of the iron industry. The loss of Lorraine, with its great resources of iron-ore, early drew the attention of Germany to the problem of making use of the extensive deposits of " lean " iron-ore in the homeland. The Corby works are using the English " lean " ores with great success, an experience which gradually influenced the creators of the four years plan. Already three processes have been worked out in Germany. It has been said that one process has cheapened the cost of a ton of Thomas iron produced from that ore by 33 per cent. It is true, up to now, none of the processes developed has been completely satisfactory economically, and the German iron and steel industry cannot afford to let its production costs rise above those of its foreign competitors. The industry has had to invest hundreds of millions of marks in the production of oil from coal (and other processes), and was accordingly the more reluctant to undertake the enormous capital expenditure required to develop the ore-fields. Already, before the four years plan, the industry was influenced by the Government to take over many new tasks which made it necessary to economise on the capital of the works or to apply to the capital market, supported by the Government, which " guides " investment. Private enterprise was much restricted, besides the many official and " voluntary " obligations (see p. 253), in accumulating reserves for lean years or making use of boom profits for capitalist enrichment. I mention in passing that compulsory loans have been obtained not only from the banks and the insurance companies (4½ per cent. of 2,000 million marks for long periods, and several of the short term loans have been converted into medium term issues) but also from a levy on industry which aimed at 1,000 million marks for the purpose of subsidising export.

The four years plan regulated in exact manner the distinct tasks of every enterprise. To give only one example, the Kloeckner works stated at their last general meeting (29/10/37) that the four years plan made necessary an increase of their coal production to about six million tons per annum (in the year of the report production reached only 4.41 million tons), and an increase in the production of coke to two million tons (1.49 million tons in the year of the report). The increase demanded in raw iron production, from 1 million to 1.25 million tons per annum, together with the increase in their rolling mill products made necessary the reconstruction of a certain iron-ore mine. As Herr Peter Kloeckner pointed out, these extensions of the factories alone would need three to four years and would require unheard of sums of money. At the same time, he continued, costs were increasing through the increase in prices of iron-ore on the world market and the rise in overseas freights. And he then mentioned the increasing costs for his trust of the hitherto unworked low-grade iron-ore deposits.

These figures give only a slight idea of the great change in which German industry is involved by new buildings and new machinery.

Experience already gained convinced the German authorities that the German ore could be developed without involving economic disaster. The risks of action probably appeared less than those of a shortage of iron and steel due to inaction. The hesitations of the industrialists, among other things, seem to have decided General Goering and his advisers that the undertaking could be carried through more speedily and efficiently by the State than by private enterprise. The iron and steel required to erect the works will have to be taken away from other branches of industry and official agencies, which are already complaining of the inadequacy of their quotas under the rationing scheme. Without State interference there could be no smooth running of the process of rationing. State interference is also necessary to find labour at the expense of other branches of the industry, there being no skilled men unemployed in Germany. Regulations have been made to prevent employers from enticing away each other's skilled workers. The new iron and steel works has been founded as a company controlled by the State, which appointed the chairman and board. This company will acquire undeveloped mining property and claims in exchange for shares, and generally act as a holding company, while the firm of H. Brassert & Co. will erect the works and put them into operation. It is already hinted at from various sides that this scheme is the forerunner of a new and rather socialist mining law. The ideas of former programmes of the national-socialist party foreshadow the strong socialist note as far as the ownership is concerned. The prospector whose claim to ore is taken over will receive compensation like the holder of a patent.

Apart from the interesting legal form of the new giant company, the recovery of the national ore resources, if possible at reasonable costs, will mean an enormous increase in the wealth of Germany. The country will certainly not be self-sufficient in iron-ore, although it may be able to produce, as mentioned, as much as 50 per cent. of its requirements. But the basis of the whole economic system will have been substantially strengthened. Towns will grow up round the coke ovens, blast furnaces and rolling mills, where only villages existed before, and a substantial part of German iron and steel requirements will be produced in regions less vulnerable to air attack than the congested Rhineland and Westphalia. Again, a change in the factors determining location of industry will take place; previously coal-mining decided the location of industry, now a migration to the iron-ore field might happen.

The State always had a grip on the ironworks of the country, but now the intensity of its holds has become stronger. The share which the Prussian Treasury took at the beginning of the century, with the buying of the Hibernia works, permitted to the State membership of the great cartel. This assured it of influence in the formation of prices. The former participation in the Vereinigte Stahlwerke surely strengthened the influence of the State, but did not have more than temporary significance. The new scheme, in addition to securing partial independence of foreign iron-ore, will increase the whole capacity of rolling mills.

(b) PUBLIC CONTROL AND PUBLIC FINANCE

(§1) Before dealing in detail with Public Finance, I wish to summarise the advanced stage of Public Control now reached in economic and in other affairs.

During the period of the Weimar Reich, public enterprise developed rapidly. Where formerly undertakings such as railways, tramways, public utilities and banking institutions, were in the hands of public authorities, these activities were enormously enlarged and other fields were taken under public control. The form through which these authorities showed their interests changed from a policy of sustaining certain undertakings or whole groups of trade, into legal support offered by certain laws, by subventions or by sharing in the capital. This could be done by complete control or partial ownership or by retaining certain sovereign rights.

As for the transport system, the German Reich has recently regained all its sovereign rights lost in the Treaty of Versailles. The State has co-ordinated all parts of the national transport system under its command. The *Kleinbahn* system (light auxiliary lines)—a remainder of private enterprise—is now completely subject to State regulation. Certain laws and decrees regulate entirely transport by rail, road and waterways under a co-ordinating scheme. Whilst railways and waterways had been State-owned and State-managed for a long time, motor transport has only recently been subjected to special rules. It belongs partly to the national railway and postal departments, partly to other State and municipal authorities. For such motor transport as remains in private hands there are certain schemes which regulate competition between the transport vehicles in respect to passengers and goods. All forms of transport, since they are institutions fulfilling important functions in the community, are now provided with a long series of public duties, which they must perform regardless of considerations of private profit. The principle mentioned on p. 98 of a " public profitableness " applies to the transport system and its profitability as a whole, leaving open the question of how compensation for public uses will be introduced when once the private undertakings have to meet losses. Where transport is in public hands, there is no longer any difference, as regards problems of personnel, between the State and municipal servants.

As I have outlined in Chapter II, German savings and other deposits went mainly into three channels : deposit banks, municipal banks, and co-operative banks. To this system, however, some other types of credit institutions have been added, among them some of an outstanding public character (see pp. 194, 283.).

It might be shown from the following context that National-Socialists inherited from their predecessors actually all that they required to have complete cont~~! over the banks. The totalitarian State became the greatest borrower in the market. As will be shown later, the municipal savings bank system was bound to buy the short term treasury notes. The Currency Bank with its auxiliary institutions, such as the Gold Diskont Bank, offered assistance either directly or through various channels and methods, among which a great part was played by the establishment of companies for public works, which issued bills eligible for re-discount. And these re-discounting facilities were offered abundantly to the deposit banks by the governmental banks, if they had bought enough of these bills. So bills for armaments, roads, ships, party and other edifices were easily discounted in increasing quantities.

The *deposit banks* had experienced—as mentioned elsewhere—disastrous shocks during the great crisis. It was not the principle of German deposit banks which brought about the collapse, but rather the misguided post-War political and economic development throughout the world. The Banking Enquiry Committee (1933-34) still recognised the German banking organisation as a main factor in Germany's rise during the reign of the two Williams, and the " law concerning credit " of December 5th, 1934, which was designed to be fundamental for future banking activities, aimed at preserving the union of deposit and industrial finance business, though, no doubt, with alterations as to the goal of private banking. In accordance with these aims, up to 1937 current account advances (*Debitoren*) decreased by many hundred millions of mark and were replaced by short term bills for the financing of intermediate industrial credit. The collapse (in 1931) was prevented by governmental support which made the public banks wholly or partly owners of the big private deposit banks and some of their greatest industrial foundations. Without such support they would have faded out of existence, as did the Darmstadt and National Bank which had to close its doors for ever after a hundred years' activity, finally merging with another of the big German banks, which in turn had to be prevented from definite failure by the salvage action of the Government. There has certainly been some return to private ownership of deposit banks and concerns hitherto owned by the State, but Government influence has changed only in the manner of execution ; from owning blocks of shares to ruling these credit institutions by commanding their main business activities. This complete control having been achieved, State ownership is no longer necessary. An economic system which excludes the main activities of the self-regulation of private forces must, no doubt, affect most the main exponents of the previous liberal economy. These former initiating activities are now being transferred to State organs and to the publicly controlled associations of private enterprise. These direct the stream of all existing capital into the channels which serve the present State's purposes as provided by the " general plan." And where the State itself—for its own purposes—is the creator of money, it does not allow competition with its own loans on the money market by private stocks, shares or debentures, unless these serve the Government's purposes for employment, or work in the interest of its "list of preferences." Many functions of banks and Stock Exchanges (such as private issues, arbitrage business and the financing of exports and imports) are so reduced or extinguished that these have become to a great extent mere executive organs.

Once, when the Banking Enquiry Committee (1934) was holding its sessions, more far-reaching plans were considered. It was intended to transfer the German " Giro "-Business of the credit account customers of these big private banks to the Reichsbank, which would have secured for itself the great profits, in order to help the State. This revolutionary measure would generally have transferred this enormous apparatus, both personal and material, to the State Bank, or else, this apparatus would have had to act merely as a State bank department. As an authentic report said, it was proposed to create a single form for all credit account transactions for the customer, to be carried out by the Reichsbank and no longer by private banks. Thus to take over one of the most lucrative tasks of the private banks would have been to alter the whole system. This measure has never been carried out, but the power of the great private banks has been broken by the State, not through ownership but through regimentation of the whole deposit bank system. This, as it exists at present, stands and falls with the credit of the National-Socialist Government.

The important law concerning credit policy, of December 5th, 1934, led the long line of laws regulating the interplay of credit and economy. Supervision by the State had existed before, as far as mortgage banks, savings banks and certain other special institutions were concerned. The banking crisis of 1931 had already established a general control of credit banks by an emergency law, which was subsequently replaced by that of 1934. All credit institutions, amounting to about 30,000, are subjected to the official organs established by the new law. Not only Joint Stock Banks, but also private bankers, all public and semi-public banks fulfilling deposit and financing functions, municipal savings banks and their " centralisations," the system of co-operative societies, insurance banks, transport banks, institutions of the building trade including such as promote housing and settlement, associations for certain guarantees to back certain special investments, and others are now subjected to the supervision of the control office of credit policy (" *Aufsichtsamt für das Kreditwesen* "). This latter body shows its close connection with the currency bank by the appointment of the governor of this bank as its chairman. It has no great offices, but has rather a kind of liaison office between public and private organs concerned, giving general directions for control. This committee, containing seven members, also gives directions to the " *Reichskommissar* " and is a kind of appeal court against his decisions. This " *Reichskommissar für das Kreditwesen*" is the chief liaison officer between the currency bank, the Ministry of Economic Affairs, and private economy. He is an all-powerful person, to whom every institution has to give all data of its articles of association, of its organisation, of its books and transactions. But this control does not exclude that of the currency bank. The "*Reichskommissar*" is not the chief of a big staff, but he uses the staff of local Reichsbank branches for his purposes. By the furnishing of interim balance sheets, which have to be produced periodically, the Reichsbank has to be constantly informed of the condition of credit institutions. This affects the German " Big Five," which now comprises the Deutsche Bank, the Dresdener Bank, the Commerz-Privat Bank, the Reichs-Kreditgesellschaft, and the Berliner Handelsgesellschaft. But 70 special credit banks, 22 banks of former federal States or provinces and 20 "*Giro*"-*Zentralen* (regional "centralisations" of municipal credit are subject to the same rules. The other credit institutions also have a distinct form of State supervision, so that on the credit side an elaborate network enables the State to control the German economy and to examine thoroughly all the transactions of finance. The whole credit organisation is now practically a privileged system, admission to which has to be sought as a concession, by every credit institution or its branches. Security, ability and need have to be examined because the banking trade is considered to be overcrowded. The "*Reichskommissar*" has to provide security for deposits and so he can close existing institutions. Deposits of savings banks are subjected to the same principle. There is a certain paragraph which contains provisions for the investment of these for the satisfaction of the demands of the Reich. All control of deposits lies in the discretion of the *Kommissar*. Every month, credit organisations have to announce the names of borrowers whose debts exceed one million marks, a provision which prevents them from obtaining credits at the same time with other creditors who are ignorant of the amount of credit offered by their competitors. Credit institutions are now informed by the *Kommissar* of how things stand with individual firms. Former abuses influenced a paragraph which deals with the percentage of their own capital which credit institutions can use for any individual purpose. Such credits have to be agreed to unanimously by all managers of the banks and the *Kommissar* has to be informed about these transactions, if the regulations are disregarded. The personal union of the Governor of the Currency Bank and the Economic Department of Public Administration expresses itself in the offerings of big credits which are given according to the general lines of the governmental policy. Post-War abuses in the clearing of payments where no cash payments were provided for are prevented by certain rules of the new law. Through these means, banks came to possess a power of creating credit which proved to be unhealthy. I can only deal briefly with what has been called " credit creation "—the measures of private banks which have been applied by post-War

Germany and many other States in an attempt to expand credit beyond the deposits of their customers. These measures, at the time of the bank control, now became instruments for the State and the currency bank which could use these activities of private institutions within the framework of a " managed currency policy." Severe prescriptions of the liquidity of the banks were provided. The *Kommissar* has plenary powers over all credit affairs such as rates of interest, conditions of loan, broker's fees, etc.

It may be mentioned that a clearing system such as exists in England was not far developed in Germany, where bigger cash resources have always been kept. Now, however, numerous regulations to prevent these " mistakes " and to promote easier clearing have resulted in an old item of the programme—the " *Verrechnungsverkehr* " (clearing)—of private and public banking institutions becoming more and more widespread.

State interference is marked by a number of other measures, of which we may mention that the conduct of a bank has been made conditional on the approval of the Board of Supervision. This approval may be withheld because of the unsuitability of the head of the bank, or of economic conditions, or deficiency of the necessary funds. Changes in ownership or capital fusions, and other alterations must be notified. A part of the profit of the directors is to be earmarked for guarantee fund purposes. Liquidity is to be ensured by the gradual formation of a cash reserve of ten per cent., and a further reserve in short term trading bills or discountable securities is to be formed up to 30 per cent. A further bill " anent the distribution of dividends by joint stock companies " amends an earlier bill which referred to companies having paid a dividend of less than six per cent. on their capital in the current year. The ruling idea was that the improvement in trade to be expected from the lavish use of public funds in stimulating industry should not benefit the shareholder alone but should help to alleviate the financial burdens of the State. The bill, however, had practically no effect. It was extended by the Dividend Limitation Law of December 4th, 1934, to all companies. The maximum cash dividend, in future, is to be six per cent. on paid-up capital, or eight per cent. in the case of companies having paid more than six per cent. during the last year. The number of companies which have previously paid more than eight per cent. is comparatively small. Any surplus must be transferred to the Gold Discount Bank, for investment in State securities. The sums transferred no longer remain the property of the company, but are administered by the Gold Discount Bank as trustee for the shareholders, who, however, are to receive interest payments only after four years. A decree of the 9th December, 1937, requires the distribution of the accumulated loan stock to be carried out by a Government issue of Advance Tax Certificates. The measure should first lead to the creation of another source of income for further financing of emergency schemes. The implications of the Bill cannot yet be fully seen. Companies have in the last few years taken the opportunity of rebuilding their factories and machinery on a very large scale. (In regard to the distribution of boom profits not used for dividends, see pp. 239, 253.)

Dr. Schacht made it clear that a time of shrunken markets is no time for speculation; for the need to economise the national resources must determine everything. State control likewise includes the prevention of competition with the great loans of the State and of those trusts which undertook big tasks for the " general plan " (e.g., production of oil from coal or development of natural sources of oil and development of low grade iron-ore deposits). In accordance with these intentions we see the number of German Stock Exchanges reduced by closure or fusion from 21 to 9. What a change in the sociological picture when such old mercantile cities as Bremen, Cologne and Dresden lose their economic centres of gravity!

The enormous development which characterised the local government both of the provinces and the town corporations during the Weimar Reich showed itself in the increased power of these authorities over the system of provincial and municipal banks, which increased the state of national dissolution greatly. These banks were mainly the central offices of all the many branches of municipal savings banks scattered over vast areas. Provincial institutions such as those of Westphalia and the Rhineland, Germany's greatest industrial provinces, made the "*Landeshauptmann*" (the communal governor of a province) a mighty territorial prince and so also some chief burgomasters of the big towns (in Germany paid and pensionable officials) showed a mania for spending money with the help of either municipal banks or credit loans from abroad or State support, secured by the influence of certain parties. The collapse of some of these banks—provincial and municipal—was not astonishing.

It is now the same both for the municipal savings banks or the co-operative banks (banks of the great system of urban and agricultural societies) : at the bottom private people give their savings or deposits, at the top the State decides how these enormous amounts are to be used. The "list of preferences" again serves as an indicator. All the great loans for providing employment used these instruments. The municipal authorities under the employment scheme were instrumental in providing work and paying for it on behalf of the Government.*

* Up to 1937 deposits of savings banks increased to more than 17 thousand millions of marks. The increase first served to liquidate the influences of the Great Depression. The dependence of these institutions on the general policy of the Reich will be clearer when we read in an article of the German Institute for Business Research (Weekly Report, April 8th, 1936, p. 29) : " The savings banks were in a position during 1935 to share to a great extent in the refunding of the Reich debt. Savings banks and Giro Centrals were able to take over up to February, 1936, about 1,000 million RM of the refunding block of 2,350 million RM (including the refunding loan of the German Railway). This was done through 1,000 million RM worth of the so-called " savings bank loan " as well as through the purchase of small amounts of ten-year treasury certificates offered to the public. In addition, the Giro Centrals took a decisive part in selling these certificates to the public" (cf. note 22).

The extent of public banks formed for special purposes showed an enormous increase during the period after the War. The former Prussian State institution for co-operative credit (established in 1895) became a national institution in 1932, having at its disposal the great deposits of the whole co-operative system (now a further resource for Government purposes). The German currency bank affiliated itself with the Gold Discount bank (1924), and the "*Deutsche Rentenbankkreditanstalt*" (1925), both serving various purposes. The latter served the financing of export, the *Osthilfe* (subsidy for estate owners in East Prussia), purchase of blocks of shares in banks and industries, etc. The bank originated in the redemption of industrial debts for reparation purposes. As mentioned, the Rentenbank became an important institution for agricultural credit. The " Bank for industrial debentures " offered long term credits to industry. The National Railways owned a bank for their purposes. The services for building houses and establishing urban and agricultural settlements had various public institutions at their disposal, either institutions offering mortgages and financing of intermediate and current credit or serving the Administration. These activities reflected the public control of the greatest part of the building trade. During the period of the crisis (1931), the " Acceptbank A.G.," the " Diskontkompagnie A.G." (1932), the " Deutsches Finanzierungsinstitut A.G. (Finag) " in 1932, and the " Tilgungskasse für gewerblichs Kredite (Tilka) " in 1932, were established to provide credit for suffering trade.

The numerous public companies for various purposes of insurance greatly widened the activities of State financial policy.

The *Deutsche Gesellschaft für öffentliche Arbeiten* ("*Öffa*") has to be mentioned as a public credit institution which was inserted in the employment creation scheme. The undertaking, which in collaboration with other public credit institutions served the great schemes providing public work, has concluded its task in 1937, after an existence of more than six years.

Some kinds of State monopolies, heirs of the mercantilist age, have to be mentioned. Such schemes were first of all applied to agrarian products. I mention also in this connection certain schemes for price regulation and prevention of foreign exports. Foodstuffs such as maize and potatoes were related to these institutions. The German spirit monopoly was a State monopoly which was the same as a kind of tax on consumption. It was established in 1918. The monopoly administration received the exclusive right to import and to take over and manufacture the product of the German distilleries. Existing distilleries produced according to a certain quota which fixed the output, and which was agreed upon by the administration in collaboration with the producing firms. In order to develop the cultivation of potatoes on the light soil in Eastern Germany, prices which the monopoly paid were fixed very high, whilst the sale was made mostly at a loss and big stores were accumulated. The Treasury in this way subsidised the cultivation of potatoes, a subvention which benefited only the existing distilleries because new ones were not allowed to be established. Other provisions of a decisive nature followed; amongst them in 1931 a compulsory addition of a percentage of this spirit to motor petrols was introduced which by degrees was increased to ten per cent.

Figures as to the extent of the public banking activities in relation to those executed by " private banks " will be given in the note.[22]

How " the State is playing an ever greater part in the mechanism of the security markets " and in the capital market policy has been drawn to our attention.[23] But even during the Weimar Reich the saving and investment habits had already altered. The activities of security markets in industrial financing decreased, " when the concentration of industrial enterprises increased the importance of self-financing and favoured stock turnover outside the markets." Saving in co-operative banks became preferred to securities for savings and investments. As pointed out in the article mentioned, social insurance had also caused fundamental shiftings in investment habits, because it undertook the provision for old age, which was formerly made by purchase of bonds. The Research Institute holds that half of the present funding block of five billion RM has been taken over directly by the banks and insurance companies, thereby avoiding use of the exchanges.

I need not do more than refer again to what I said about the Government's security market policy since the time when, with the decree of May 31st, 1933, a Cabinet committee under the leadership of Dr. Schacht was established in order to control all matters relating to the money and security markets. To these measures, which were consequently carried out, belong the easing of the capital market, especially reduction of interest rates. Then follow: use of savings in accordance with Dr. Schacht's " national economic policy "—and prevention of a speculative boom, and especially prevention of speculative utilisation of the economic revival. I do not wish to enter here into Dr. Schacht's policy in respect of open market policy and interest reduction, measures which were laid down in special decrees. I propose to give, rather, some interesting figures of Dr. Wagemann's institute on the direction of saving of capital. " The tremendous importance of public investments makes it necessary for regular savings to be used first of all for the financing of such investments. This means an absolute precedence for public demands on the capital market and a retirement of private demands for capital, for which a certain scale of precedence can be introduced. In order to assure precedence for public means, measures were taken which meant the practical exclusion of private concerns from use of the capital market. This *exclusion* included all securities, excepting Reich loans." The issue was permitted only of those industrial bonds and stocks which served " almost solely for conversion purposes or financing the four year plans.

While the issues of *public* securities *amounted to over ten billion RM* in the years from 1933 to 1936, the amount of stock and industrial bonds issued amounted to just about one billion RM."[24]

I hinted at what Dr. Wagemann's Report calls the ever-increasing power of the Government in the administration of the stock exchanges. What has become especially decisive is the *Emissions-Sperre*, the power of the State to allow or veto issues and quotations at will. The Government, by permitting only its own issues to be made, or only such others as served the purposes of its general plan, made every effort to keep district businesses from the exchanges. Some clauses of the law regarding Securities Trading (December, 1934) are obviously introduced for this reason.

Thus the Minister of Economic Affairs is empowered to withdraw securities with a nominal value of three million RM or less from the Berlin Exchange, if a large majority of the issue is held by one or by a few people. Since the reopening of the stock exchanges in April, 1932, credit business on the exchange has been forbidden, and exchange credits are rarely demanded, and buyers have to use their own capital. Further price-restricting measures were contained in certain laws which I mentioned in another connection (Capital Investment Law, of March 29th, 1934, and the Dividend Limitations Law, of December 4th, 1934). According to the former law, companies themselves had to invest surplus dividends in a loan stock; but later, if investment exceeded 100,000 RM, capital stocks were regulated by the latter law. Mention may be made in passing that the trade in foreign securities is completely restricted. Investment became, through the variety of measures described, more and more what has been called "totalitarian investment."

In a more liberal State, measures such as the Ottawa preferences (1932), together with the British capital embargo during the last few years—which to a great extent prohibited the provision of capital to non-Empire countries—correspond to the "guidance of investment." Also with these measures the free-trade principle has been very largely abandoned.

The achievements of public control in the province of internal banking affairs, although much simplified and improved, are as nothing in comparison with the degree of regulation of international payments. Since the time of the War, currencies have been disturbed and shaken by the ever-increasing degree of State interference in the currency system in most countries, and followed by counter-activities on the part of the foreign countries concerned. Germany very early initiated a control of foreign bills (*Devisenbewirtschaftung*), a principle now followed in many other countries. The technique of international payments in this way became changed in principle. This system is in closer relation to a foreign trade monopoly than to a self-regulating economy. So the description of this system as a mere emergency measure seems doubtful. Abnormal conditions once transferred to normal ones may certainly change the spirit of wholesale planning. Formerly the German term "*Devisen*" meant foreign bills which had to be bought in the homeland: with the extension of communications all over the world, other means of payments, credits with certain foreign banks, widened the former narrower term. The rates of these foreign bills were calculated according to the so-called international rates of exchange which reflected the fluctuations of the currencies of individual countries. The *Devisen* " arbitrage " (the balance between these fluctuations) is now hardly possible in Germany or in other countries with a foreign bill control.

The foreign bill control was much further elaborated by the governments and the currency banks concerned. It changed the conditions of payment completely. Instead of the possibility of buying voluntarily, the acquisition of foreign bills was controlled and permitted only for certain purposes. A central office regulated the whole system of quotation of foreign bills. Currency banks took over these transactions where they existed. There may be certain general principles which govern the running of the foreign bill office. Important reasons for the introduction of these measures were chiefly heavy losses of gold or foreign bills, which resulted from the withdrawal of foreign capital or from the flight of capital of inhabitants of individual countries. Later, a codification of all the processes involved took place in Germany. Not only the export of capital from the homeland but also the whole interplay of capital became controlled. The new system arose in which all import and export transactions were subjected to control. The control office distributes to the importers only a part of the imports desired by him which is calculated from his former turnover. The ratio of this proportion is determined by the plan of the control office, which depends on the general market and the situation of the home currency. Political influences based on preferences to certain countries also play a part. A presupposition is that foreign bills will be distributed only at an official rate, fixed in the homeland; the exporter of German goods is compelled to deliver his proceeds to the control office. Experience in certain countries shows that foreign bill control was sometimes temporary, but in Germany the institutions not only became ingrained but *proceeded under their own momentum*. It is not a new invention of the Nazi system—the emergency decrees go back to July, 1931, when a heavy drain of foreign money took place in connection with the collapse of the Austrian Kreditanstalt. Step by step, the Reichsbank, in conjunction with the provincial revenue offices of the Treasury, evolved a thoroughgoing system to create a planning office as well as one to carry out these plans. Up to September, 1934, when the "New Plan" of Dr. Schacht came into operation, the importer was more free; now permission has to be granted by the office before any bargain takes place. An elaborate network has been invented to fix the amount of the distributions which the importer receives.

Here the personal union between currency bank and Cabinet Ministry of Economic Affairs again becomes clear. The distribution takes place only in accordance with general plans, which contain a certain list of preferences—those which are urgently needed for Germany's economy. In regard to Dr. Schacht's levy on industry for the purpose of subsidising exports, see p. 239. I need not dwell upon all the measures by which in individual cases imports come to Germany. There is, of course, a throwback in economic history to be noted, certainly promoted by emergency. Barter of individual goods to be imported or exported is its basis, and not a general exchange of goods following supply and demand of the world market. Figures of German foreign trade in the last twenty to thirty years cannot easily be compared; one can state roughly that in both imports and exports a decrease took place which lies between 50 and 30 per cent., as compared with more normal years before and after the War.

(§2) The system of *Public Finance* has undergone a complete change since the War. This has been mainly due to the same circumstances which caused the growth of the share of Public Control in the whole of the economic and social life. The tutelage of the German cameralistic State and its financial policy were restricted in the age of the liberal economy to the institutions which were directly subject to Public Administration; yet, the State there, in contrast to other countries, followed a strong economic policy, mainly through legislation, in order to help private enterprise to develop Germany as a Great Power and as an Industrial State. It is true, that taxes and duties always influenced economic development, but the policy of the latest system of public finance has gone much further in most great countries. Activities, hitherto largely left to the private economy, now became an essential part of State financial policy. The obvious influences of the phases of the trade cycle on the labour market of overcrowded industrial peoples compelled the State—especially in countries with high social standards—to adopt an active trade cycle policy. Therewith, State finance and general economic policy were fused into a complete whole. States, which are to-day the greatest direct and indirect givers of orders—through promotion or restriction of public contracts—made use of their power of influencing the fluctuations arising from the irregularities of the private investment market. But this restriction of public expenditure during a boom, together with other measures, was merely the first step in the new financial policy by which the accumulation of liquid resources not only permitted a reserve of deferred orders and employment, but could also be used to prevent too violent an upswing, since a diminished velocity of circulation of money would result from the accumulation of almost immobile credit at the banks. The State might mitigate the effects of a crisis with its accumulated resources and deferred orders; but in a time of great alarm the German State "substituted" for accumulated resources, which it lacked, new ones created through an inventive process.

Public creation of employment thus directed economic policy as a whole, as well as State financial policy. Loans on a huge scale have to be the medium for creating work if the machinery which makes the wheels go round is greatly disturbed by extraordinary circumstances such as have been characteristic of the post-War period. There is certainly a difference between the policy of creating work through these loans and the afore-mentioned policy of flattening out the cycle. When, e.g., in 1932 the work created by Reichskanzler v. Papen's advance taxes loan began, no accumulated reserves of the preceding boom period were available. The future was mortgaged by the creation of an enormous debt through credit acceptances. Certainly the attempt made during the crisis of 1930-31 to rationalise Public Administration was a great support for this action. No doubt, the adjustment of expenditure to income in the Reich budget showed itself in unusual forms; a special supplementary budget had to be introduced to explain the expenditure for employment creation and the mortgaging of the future. The creation of employment, which was initiated in 1933-34, was made possible mainly through the medium of " employment creation bills," mentioned elsewhere, which in a similar form also served other great departments of the Administration, such as the imperial railways, motor lines and the postal department. I do not wish to repeat here in detail what I have already said of the way in which, by the help of municipal authorities, certain public corporations and banking organisations, the process of creating work and its payment restored the corresponding circulation of goods and money. I should mention in passing that the German economic dictator made good use of " the psychological moment to fleece the short term money market." Capitalists at home and abroad showed little confidence in German economy, and they were, in consequence, loath to invest on long term. But they were willing to employ their capital somehow, and Dr. Schacht exploited this situation by issuing those " work creation bills " by which a large percentage of the Government's expenditure was met (see notes 9 and 22). Industry and trade, receiving these bills in part payment, kept them as short term investments, whilst sending a relatively small percentage to their banks, which in their turn also kept them as short term investments. Statistics indicate that between April, 1934, and April, 1935, the circulation of commercial bills increased by 2,500 million marks; the whole of this increase was surely caused by these work creation bills.

I give these other following figures, completely topical in significance, with due reserve, knowing that all criticism and judgment may be premature. At the time the main budgetary sources of income were the floating debt in its official sense (i.e., excluding work creation bills), the funded internal debt, and thirdly, tax receipts. An income from the dissolution of certain official funds, and the contributions for winter relief, etc., which amounted to 400 million marks, have to be added.

Altogether these sources brought in 2,500 to 3,000 million marks. "A dense veil hides German taxation." Mr. Alwin Parker, one of the directors of Lloyds Bank (in the Monthly Review of his bank, July, 1937) says: "The Reich revenue in a budgetary sense is not known." The numerous items of the revenue besides tax yields make the picture no clearer. Mr. Parker adds ". . . the domination of the National-Socialist Party and the creation of numerous public bodies have introduced new payment liabilities, which do not appear in the tax revenue returns, but virtually are taxes. Some are legally compulsory, some virtually compulsory, and only a small part really voluntary" (p. 385). Besides some afore-mentioned contributions and other subscriptions to the Party, charitable funds, fees to corporative organisations, fees for import and raw material supervision boards and export subsidies have been mentioned. Mr. Parker adds an interesting remark: "No official report has been published for many years as to the amount or incidence of taxation; but the final estimates of three experts, working independently outside Germany, go to show that between 42 per cent. and 47 per cent. of the national income is now swallowed up in various forms of taxation and contributions, as against 20 per cent. or at most 25 per cent. before 1933. The sum which may be *legally* deducted from wages for income tax and social benefits is from 12 per cent. to 14 per cent., but other deductions are also made" (p. 386) (cf. also my p. 239).

The immense increase of taxation revenues (see also p. 226) hints at the great share which the Government felt justified in claiming from the boom profits. It argued that there would not have been such boom profits, without the government policy.

Hitler (Reichstag speech, 20th February, 1938), gives the following figures of the Reich revenue :—

1932	..	6,600 million marks.
1933	..	6,800 ,, ,,
1934	..	8,200 ,, ,,
1935	..	9,600 ,, ,,
1936	..	11,500 ,, ,,
1937	..	14,000 ,, ,,

and adds that they would increase to 17,000 million marks in 1938.

I shall give later some figures concerning the budgets during the period 1933-36.

It has been mentioned that the Government did everything to exclude the competition of other securities (private investments not serving directly or indirectly the Government's purposes) in order to keep funds at its disposal, whether they came from public or private deposits and savings. I touched lightly upon the new municipal reserve policy inaugurated through the Reich decree of May 5th, 1936, regarding reserve funds of the municipalities. Again, through these great distributors of public works, the principle of flattening out fluctuations by building up reserve funds during the upswing of the cycle and using these funds in times of crisis was laid down here. But these ideas were first applied for other purposes, as the German Institute for Business Research (June 4th, 1936, No. 21, 22, p. 46) points out : " Hence the most important prerequisites for such a financial policy are on hand . . . in the case of the Reich the entire financial power must still be used for the financing of employment creation and rearmament."

If financial policy is subject to general economic policy, then the State is compelled to tackle the main problem from various sides. The State as a great debtor is interested in the level of interest which, if it decreases, allows the State to convert long term obligations, either because the State enjoys the best credit in well-regulated communities, or because it assumes this prerogative of lowering the general level of interest. Most countries afflicted in the crisis made use of great conversions, following the liquidation of the capital goods markets since 1932. Germany also made abundant use of this interest reduction policy. The German Institute for Business Research[25] distinguishes here three stages : (1) the law for the conversion of agricultural debts (June 1st, 1933) and the law for the conversion of municipal debts (September 21st, 1933) which converted the block debts of municipalities, etc., and reduced the interest charges. In Prussia the average rate of interest was in this way reduced from a little more than 6 per cent. to 4 per cent.—the 4 per cent. Reichsloan of 1934 was used for the redemption of the tax free 6(7) per cent. Reich Loan of 1929 (called Hilferding Loan). (2) The law of January 30th, 1934, started the reduction of excessive interest rates on private credits and loans. The Land Credit Institutes were to reduce the interest of 6 per cent. and over on their mortgage and municipal bonds to $4\frac{1}{2}$ per cent., if the actual holder agreed to this reduction. Owing to this, it was possible for these institutions to grant their mortgagors a similar reduction in interest. On February 27th, 1935, the interest reduction was extended to public loans, and on March 1st, 1935, bank interest rates were reduced. Savings banks and insurance companies had paved the way for these measures by an early reduction of their interest rate for long term credit. (3) An expansion of the agreement of the main banking associations in regard to interest on debts, brought about by the "highest cost" regulations of the Reich Banking Commissioner for small credits. With this action control over the credit and loan business on the free money market was introduced for the first time.

Owing to the improvement of employment, and especially the measures which reduced interest, the total savings of public and private business increased immensely.[26]

The financial policy of the Government in connection with its programme for employment creation was also bound up with certain obligations in the form of guarantees. The various large amounts of short term obligations of the Reich early brought about certain conversions which I have mentioned before. The savings banks loan was the first step on this road, and enabled the Government to change over to this loan about 500 millions of employment creation bills. The savings banks loan was redeemable in 28 years, a period which corresponds with the obligation to repay the municipal corporations which gave the work under the employment creation scheme, as agents of the Government. The goal was the consolidation of the floating debt. The funded debt of the Reich was, in consequence of the inflation, not as big as might have been expected, a circumstance which alleviated the burden on the future created by the employment creation loan. It has been indicated that this funded loan, March 3rd, 1935, was at about 10,000 million marks, of which 1,730 millions were held abroad. As far as the funded debt is denominated in Reichsmarks, it is composed partly of Treasury bills with interest which have to run for some years, partly by redeemable loans. To these loans has to be added a debt which arose from the revaluation of pre-War loans. The textbook distinction between a floating debt intended to balance the differences between ordinary and extraordinary income and expenditure—arising in one budget period—and the funded debt, which has to cover the loans established for extraordinary expenses, is at present without value. Debts from former budget periods had to be transferred into following years and the financing of the extraordinary expenses of an employment creation policy had to be financed on short term. There is one word more to say about the close relationship between financial policy and the currency policy of the bank. As in other States, open market policy of the currency institute now plays a great part as a means of regulating the money market, and the Reichsbank has made use of it since 1933 and, later on, as has been mentioned, in its capacity as the bankers' bank, it rediscounted employment creation bills. As the German Government has not published a budget since 1934, there is no clarity about the amount of its expenditure, which is, therefore, subject to much speculation and discussion. A series of articles in " The Banker "[27] (February, 1937) gave a very critical review of probable budget items. This survey seemed to be written to prevent the City of London from offering credit to Germany (such as had been done not long before) because Germany's foreign as well as financial politics seem to " The Banker " to be untrustworthy and such as must lead to intolerable conditions which at some time will bring about a change for the worse. But this is only one aspect of the article of " The Banker "; for the period which must elapse between now and the probable occurrence of the disaster of which " The Banker " warns City people is a long one and the journal admits that a collapse, which its figures suggest as likely, is by no means inevitable. " The present financial situation," as " The Banker "[28] goes on, " is unsound, but it is not dangerous in the sense that Germany . . . is heading for a financial collapse. It is true that in normal conditions the existence of a floating debt—that is, inclusive of creation of work bills of as much as 16,000 million marks would constitute a most dangerous potential inflation . . . In Germany to-day this danger can be ruled out." " The means of control of the totalitarian State are so complete and powerful that it is well within the power of the Government to nip such a danger in the bud. The Government could, in fact, quite easily refuse to grant rediscounting facilities, and thus transform the bills into a kind of perpetual loan. For precisely the same reason it would be mistaken to believe that Germany will shortly be forced by financial considerations to reduce her expenditure on armaments. Just as the Reichsbank, with its dictatorial powers over the money and capital market can prevent a sudden currency inflation, so can it assure the continued issue of bills by which to finance the deficit of the Reich." It is remarkable that Mr. A. Parker, despite all the deficiencies of the economic system (which he clearly surveys) has no objections to recommending a collaboration between Great Britain and Germany : it is for this his interesting article pleads.

Who can foresee what may happen in the future ? Who can say what might happen in world politics and world economics ? To prophesy about, or believe in the German economic system and State financial policy as seen through the eyes of " The Banker " or Dr. Schacht might both prove wrong.

The figures of " The Banker " might agree with the more or less authentic ones available from Germany. These figures for the German Reich budgetary expenditure show the following increase : 1932-33, RM. 6.7 ; 1933-34, 9.7 ; 1934-35, 12.2 ; 1935-36, 16.7 ; 1936-37, 18.8 (approximately) in thousands of millions of marks ; and from these figures have been estimated, in the mentioned report, Germany's armament expenditure as follows : 1933-34, RM. 3.0 ; 1934-35, 5.5 ; 1935-36, 10.0 ; 1936-37, 12.6 ; total for four years=31.1 in thousands of millions of marks.

As to the figures of the total debts, " The Banker " considers for instance, that of 1935-36 " for a modern State, quite moderate. But debt of which 50 per cent. is not funded, and of which the floating part is rapidly increasing is a constant source of danger."[29]

(c) AGRICULTURAL POLICY
For some General Remarks on the Agricultural Problem,
see footnote p. 264.

In dealing with the new policy which aims at organising all farmers for economic, cultural and political purposes into a single unified organisation under National-Socialist leadership in the corporative style, I can best make it easy to understand by quoting some significant words of the leader of the movement, Herr Walter Darré, who says : " To understand fully the importance of the land law for our modern German State, we shall have to go beyond the value of a stable, permanent, agrarian Constitution, asking the question what the farmer means for the German people. It is at this point where National-Socialist agrarian policy differs from the agrarian policies of other countries. It is our duty to create economic conditions required not only for preserving national agriculture but for attaining the greatest possible perfection of efficiency. It is the peculiar character of our procedure that we co-ordinate the economic aims with the necessities of human betterment and cultural policy in the sense of the one, central and dominating idea of National-Socialism. The agrarian policy of National Socialism is not only concerned with the business of nutrition, but at the same time with the preservation of our farming population as the source of life of our people."[30]

" . . . The farmer is no entrepreneur in the ordinary sense of the term. The food producer cannot and should not take part in the game of price-making; he must not be thrown upon dangers connected with this game, because his function for the nation is extremely important . . . "[31] The agricultural leader is, in addition to his capacity as Cabinet Minister for food and agriculture, the " *Reichsbauernführer*." Mr. J. B. Holt[32] assumes that the best translation may be " Reichs yeoman Leader " (" *Bauerntum*," following Charles Beard=" Yeomanry " which may be taken as " the totality of independent, diligent farmers of small holding "). This title is undoubtedly intended to express the significance of the yeomen in the whole National-Socialist State and to contrast the difference between the peasant and the great landowner, the outstanding figure in the Prussian-German monarchical Power State. The Cabinet Ministry in 1936 edited a book,[33] " The Yeoman in the revolution of time," which vigorously attacked the big estate owners. This book, written by outstanding agricultural politicians of the National-Socialist party, was designed as a reply to a book of Dr. von Rohr : " The great estates in the revolution of time." Rohr, advancing the case of the great estate owners, wanted to attribute to them special political tasks and special positions in the Third Reich. The great estate owners had, as the National-Socialist agrarian politicians say, not so much an economic aim as a merely political one, i.e., the aim of power extension, from which has resulted the changing of most of the great holdings into organisations for profit making. The disappearance of sixty thousand small holdings (in direct violation of the Stein-Hardenberg Act, called " the liberation of peasants ") at the beginning of the 19th century and the capitalistic organisation of agriculture in the 20th century have been the work of the landed nobility, and not of those with big and medium-sized peasants holdings. Some contributors to this book characterise the yeomanry as the bearers of the Nordic element in culture and race as opposed to alien influences, and they acclaim the yeomanry as the backbone of the national army. As to the efficiency of great estates in supplying the country's needs, which claim was always advanced against peasant holdings, there always was and still is a marked difference of opinion. One argument (advanced in Dr. Clauss' book) was: The percentage of the whole product of the country furnished by great estates was 28 per cent. in respect of corn food, and about 32 per cent. of food potatoes, but even an improvement of the great estates could not change greatly the percentage of the corn and potato crops which they furnished. Their percentage of the quantitatively most important supply of live stock, dairy produce and meat was 15 per cent. Here, according to national-socialist supporters, the small farmer holdings alone could be of practical use. The significance of plant products as against animal products is clearly shown by the following figures[34] These are estimated gross cash income from farm production (in 1,000 millions of R.M.).

	1925-26.	1927-28	1928-29	1930-31	1931-32	1932-33	1933-34
Plant products ..	3.0	3.6	3.7	3.2	3.0	2.6	2.9
Animal products ..	5.1	5.7	6.5	5.4	4.4	3.8	4.6

I shall deal with the problem of the size of holding later.

A new land constitution has been attempted in the corporative style. The former order of landlords (at least as it existed in the East) has to be changed into an order in which the community forms the whole "food estate" (*Reichsnährstand*) embracing all groups of producers (pp. 214, 228,). The nucleus of this form is the mass of 700,000 hereditary free-holders. Even the agricultural worker—for whom training is provided—is enrolled in the agricultural order by means of a kind of tenant system. In Darré's words: "By being able to take fast root in his inherited soil, the yeoman should be enabled once more to become the instrument of the racial regeneration of the German People."[35] The titles of some pamphlets of Darré, such as, "In the struggle for the German yeoman soul," or "The yeomanry as source of life of the Nordic race" (1933) reflect the spirit of the ideal at which I have hinted. The principle of having pure stock goes so far in Herr Darré's eyes as to demand the exclusion of all live-stock not of German origin from taking prizes at agricultural shows, with the exception of certain breeds of horses.[36] The State demands, as Darré says, that the rural population tolerate only such marriages as will ensure a healthy posterity. And there are many biological and other qualifications which must be satisfied by the yeoman holder of an "inherited freehold." The "Inherited Freehold" Act, of September 29th, 1933, is the main law dealing with this type of farmer, whose "inherited freehold" must be large enough at least to provide a family living, and may not be larger than 125 hectares (about 310 acres). The number of farms eligible as "inherited freehold" is anticipated to be about one million; of the remaining four million holdings, about 20,000 are too large (over 125 hectares), and some three million are below two hectares and can scarcely be called independent farms. This leaves almost another million small farms, which are not eligible for the " inherited freehold " register. I can select only a few clauses from this law. The freehold cannot be sold : it must be bequeathed undivided according to the rules of primogeniture, and provision is made for the " next of kin " and compensation for other heirs. The decision to enter a freehold as an " inherited freehold " lies with the Government. A moratorium against foreclosures in connection with real estate debts already incurred is automatically declared upon the entrance of the "inherited freehold" into the "Register."[37] Claims against the farm produce can be made only by public institutions in the public interest. The taxes are also regulated in order to preserve here a distinct class. " Inherited Freehold Courts " both local and national, were created.

The provision of land for settlers continues the ideas of the Land Settlement Acts of 1919—Max Sering's plan—by which the acquisition of land could be made possible through " land delivery " associations built up out of the big estates of certain provinces. Portions around the big estates could be separated for settling rural workers or others, and increasing their holdings to the size of a subsistence farm.

National-Socialist ideology, in its anti-capitalist attitude, is especially directed against regarding price mechanism as the most important goal. The financial independence of the yeoman had to be guaranteed. The time was favourable for finding supporters of this theory ; for many a farm in 1933 was threatened with foreclosure, owing to the impossibility of paying interest charges from the reduced income.[38] From 1927 to 1932, 23,551 forced sales of farms (area=608,922 hectares, 1 hectare=2½ acres) were carried through in Germany. The low prices of agricultural products no longer covered costs. The Nazi Government held that agriculture is something entirely different from trade and industry because apart from considerations of natural phenomena, " security " required a sufficient supply of foodstuffs—in other words, making the country as independent as possible of imports—and agriculture should also be a main source of the growth and health of the nation. So the whole National-Socialist literature stresses the importance of the separation of agriculture from the ups-and-downs of capitalist economy. Therefore, in contrast to industry, the whole agricultural policy comes entirely under *Marktordnung*.

Roman Law, a stumbling block for the Nazi philosophy in many respects, is alleged to be the cause of the subjection of " the farm soil as individual private property to the same conditions as any commercial commodity."[39] The soil has to be withdrawn from the real estate market, thus making impossible the incurring of debts secured by it. The German pre-Roman Law, according to Nazi philosophy, regarded the soil " either (1) as common property of the community, to be tilled partly in common and partly individually by the community members, but remaining under the co-operative jurisdiction of the community in either case, or (2) as the property of an overlord whose relations with his peasant subjects were as full of obligations as they were of rights."

The attempts to remove the economy of agriculture and food from any kind of capitalist economy meant eliminating supply and demand as price determining factors. A price level was intended to be one which could claim to be a " just " price according to given conditions of production, and it was desired to stabilise this level, in order to serve as a basis which allowed the farmer to make plans of production for a long time to come. At the same time, the food supply of the population should be guaranteed by this State-managed economy. The mere regimentation of prices was impossible, so a compromise arose between central guidance and the existing organisation of production and distribution. But as time went on, the weight of State guidance biassed the new principle. Since scarce harvests occurred (from 1934 onwards), the *Marktordnung* has changed into a complete organisation of all processes, beginning with production or import and the last stages of distribution. A division of functions has been aimed at in carrying through the plan, which varies according to the peculiar conditions to which the individual commodities are subject. There is one function performed by corporative bodies of producers and distributors, whilst the other is performed by State organs. The regulation of the *Marktordnung* is in the hands of a central corporative body, which is authorised by the Government. This board the *Reichsnährstand* (Reich food Estate), or its regional or local branches, embraces all producers and tradespeople down to the last shopkeeper or, if necessary, the last manufacturer of the product. The State, which has only to approve the decisions of the corporative boards, established as its organ certain Government offices which control the production and marketing of the individual products to an extent which varies from a certain supervision up to a complete monopoly. The detailed regulation shows itself in an elaborate network of board offices, officials, prescriptions of prices, minimum delivery quotas for producers and for the various stages of the manufacture of all agricultural products. Grain, potatoes, milk, cattle, fruit, vegetables, are included in these groups and sub-groups, as well as beer, malt, yeast, chocolate, sweets, honey-cake, icecream, alcoholic spirits, pudding powder, mayonnaise, soda water, vinegar, bread, etc. Importation and control of imports are regulated in co-operation with various Government offices which manage the foreign bill control and the barter and compensation business.

The co-operation between the various governmental departments and private persons represented by their corporative boards, which is necessary for an undertaking of such vast dimensions, is attained through a complete military-like regimentation, accompanied by threat of punishment if offences are committed.

The co-operation between all offices regulating the labour market is specially close. I may mention in passing, for instance, the prohibition of migration to cities, in order to combat simultaneously the high unemployment in the industrial regions and the shortage of workers in agriculture.

The self-sufficiency problem arose out of various conditions which have been described repeatedly in previous chapters. It is probable that measures which were originally purely of an emergency nature may turn out in the end to be permanent phenomena. No doubt, since the machine age has overcome difficulties of distance and has made possible the world-wide exchange of goods and services, self-sufficiency is a setback. The troubles which prevent a frictionless exchange have their roots in political motives. Self-sufficiency must reveal obvious calamities when hypertrophic production, either by using a natural monopoly or by using synthetic substitutes, reaches the point where (through over-production and under-consumption) it is no longer profitable to continue these methods. The results may be equally injurious to the original producer and to the new competitor. Nations are still bound to live by mutual exchange, and the customer-nation will lose its purchasing power—take, e.g., the case of artificial fibres or synthetic rubber—if the prosperity of this nation depends on the production of cotton or natural rubber. But history has also revealed the inevitable process whereby products have sometimes been successfully substituted by others—thus bringing about to some extent an economic revolution.

Modern self-sufficiency is assumed to make a country independent of those goods, imports of which are too costly or disadvantageous to the currency. It is an entirely political problem, when nations wish to decide whether they will break away from the exchange of certain goods against certain others, which they lack. Independence in time of war plays a great part in the decision. But even in this case, a 100 per cent. self-sufficiency could hardly be achieved, but only independence in respect of certain foodstuffs or industrial raw materials. This, in a nutshell, was the problem which Germany had to face during the War, the Weimar Reich and again in the Third Reich. Its climax was reached in the Four Year Plan. It is not for the historian to prophesy whether an action is likely to be especially harmful when it is only in the experimental stage. Therefore, it is doubtful whether the bitter criticism of the present agricultural and food system, which calls this policy a failure, is justified. The more Government expenditure with a view to achieving self-sufficiency and ideological aims grows—and it is alleged to be 5,000 million marks in direct payments—the more truth is claimed for this criticism. When account is taken of higher prices, reduced retail margins for foodstuffs, the cancellation of agricultural debts and the provision of unpaid labour to the farmer, the German people has indirectly paid much more. But we are more interested in the statistical and scientific analysis as given by the critics.[40] It has been assumed that the inability to increase the output of staple foodstuffs like cereals, potatoes, and sugar beet, the production of which is entirely domestic and not dependent upon any foreign imports, is undeniable. Before 1933, 45 per cent. of German food requirements, measured in nutrition units, was met by these home-grown staple crops, which was supplemented by 30 per cent. imported high quality foodstuffs, whilst the remaining 25 per cent. was supplied by high quality foodstuffs raised entirely on the basis of German products. The critics indicate, therefore, that in the interest of the self-sufficiency plan, all or most of the 30 per cent. high quality foodstuffs hitherto imported have to be replaced by a corresponding increase in the production of home-grown staple foodstuffs. An increase of at least 60 per cent. in the production of grain and potatoes and of 40 per cent. in that of sugar beet is needed. But in 1935, despite a favourable harvest, official figures show themselves below the 1928-1934 average, and in 1936 the harvest, which could not be considered bad, fell by 15 to 20 per cent. The second failure has been described as the great deterioration of the productive capacity of German agriculture through its inability to replace fodder imports by home-grown fodder supply (Banker, loc. cit.—page 140). Formerly, less than half the fodder requirements, measured in food value, was produced at home; since 1933 the production of home-grown fodder has only been increased by about 8 to 10 per cent. In these circumstances, the compulsory reduction of fodder imports by almost 75 per cent. must have serious consequences. Still, the large reserves of former years to some extent prevented a deficiency in fodder and a fall in the numbers and quality of livestock. The figures of the critics show that the numbers of first-class milch-cows and laying-hens have already declined by 12 per cent., and unless substantial fodder imports are available, the decrease in 1937 will be nearer 25 per cent., thus bringing the numbers of first-class livestock and poultry to what they were at the end of the War year, 1916. The critics conclude that 30 per cent. of the total peace time requirements must be imported. Moreover, productive capacity has diminished, and Germany is to a great degree dependent on the supply of staple foodstuffs from abroad. The " inability to buy foodstuffs in concurrence with a bad potato harvest might bring about a most serious situation." The incorporation of Austria might, perhaps, change the prospects of the critics to a certain degree.

As pointed out by these critics, plans to increase the staple crops could be carried through only on the basis of large-scale collective farms, not on that of small independent " land-conscious " owner-farmers. The small farmer is dependent on those products which give him the highest profit, combined with the greatest labour intensity, and these products are the highest quality foodstuffs, not the staple crops.[41] In this connection the critics call the new agricultural policy an almost complete destruction of the liberty of the independent farmer. The famous "hereditary" farm law which forbids the sale, splitting up or mortgaging of peasant property, and lays down that the eldest son alone has the right to inherit the farm (which he is not allowed to leave) while the other children have to be paid off, according to the critics has proved an acknowledged failure. Its only effects have been an enormous increase in the number of landless younger sons, the breakdown of the highly organised agricultural credit system, and the promotion of a slackness, since the farm cannot "come under the hammer." The regulation of production and distribution had destroyed the agricultural co-operatives which now continue to exist only as controlling and auditing agents of the central totalitarian authorities (Banker, p. 141). Compulsory delivery of fixed quotas of various crops at fixed prices, under penalty of long term imprisonment or death, which has been introduced in 1936, has been described as a further destruction of the liberty of the farmer. The critics, in summing up, come to the conclusion that Germany will very shortly be faced with the problem of deciding whether the present system with its multitude of independent farmers is to be maintained; and then either all hope of self-sufficiency must be abandoned, or agriculture must be remodelled to achieve self-sufficiency through the replacement of the independent farmer by the "grain factory" on the Russian model. The attitude of the governing party towards large estates, as has been shown on p. 257, seems to be quite clear. Holt[42] expresses the opinion that "the very active '*Anliegersiedlung*'" (i.e., delivery of land at the expense of large estate owners to settlers) "and the tone of the National-Socialist speeches in respect to these estates may indicate their coming dissolution."..But he adds, "the food problem may become acute enough to delay such subdivision." The large estate owners in Central and Eastern Prussia who "before Hitler, were on the verge of collapse because of the inability to compete with world markets, have prospered from the monopoly of cereal and potato production which they enjoy."[43]

It would not be out of place to add to the more political survey, given in previous chapters, a few general remarks on agricultural problems, of which that of agricultural protection is one of the most prominent. The development of Germany into a more industrialised country became clearer in the period under review. The German Institute of Business Research, 1935 (No. 28/29, p. 60), in a comparison between the "net production of Agriculture and Industry" (in 1,000 million RM), gives the following estimates :

	1928	1931	1932	1933	1934
Agriculture	11.9	9.6	8.3	8.2	9.2
Industry	33.4	23.4	17.6	18.5	23.3

Germany, like certain other countries, has made great strides during the last hundred years towards making her agriculture very efficient. The figures given by Rybark, who attempted to estimate Germany's agricultural achievements, can hardly be questioned. Bringing all the figures of the various agricultural products raised at home to a common denominator—the basis of meat substance—he calculated that the total agricultural production increased between 1800 and 1900 by about 212 per cent. (quoted from August Müller, "*Die Deutsche Volkswirtschaft*," Berlin, 1931, p. 157). In giving these figures

I do not wish to enter into more details, e.g., of the outstanding per acre increase of corn and potatoes, or that of the amount of milk per cow, etc. It is only fair to add that the progress was achieved by enlightened farmers of every size of holding. Scientific breeding of plants and cattle, progress in agricultural chemistry, the use of machinery, improvement of legal, technical, and educational organisations and the very extended system of co-operative societies, all contributed to the remarkable results achieved. In 1930 77 per cent. of the more than 50,000 co-operative societies in Germany belonged to agriculture. During the period 1929 to 1934 the yearly average of savings deposits of these agricultural associations was between 1,500 and 1,600 million marks. Co-operative societies and savings banks were the main institutions for providing personal credit to the majority of farmers, whilst the big estate owners were more dependent on deposit and other banks. I have already mentioned that the urban and agricultural co-operative societies finally combined in a common national institution which became of the greatest importance as one of Germany's credit resources. The whole system of personal credit was severely shaken by the world crisis. To avoid the coming into force of the mutual liability on which the co-operative system was based, the Government completely safeguarded this system by itself meeting the obligations of the societies. But with this action only one part of the debts of the farmer was met, other personal and funded credit had to be safeguarded by the Government. For a long time various credit institutions served the funded credit, among which I may mention the banks of provinces and of minor federal States, so-called *Landesbanken*, and Joint Stock Mortgage Banks (*Hypothekenbanken*). These lent money on mortgages on real property while they raised money by issuing a special class of obligations or debentures (*Pfandbriefe*), which were covered by the mortgages. In addition, I may mention again the *Landschaften*, agricultural banks of land owners. Mortgages on their lands were raised, which were secured by their collective credit. Whilst the *Landschaften* held the mortgage, they did not give the landowner money but *Pfandbriefe* in the name of those banks. By selling these *Pfandbriefe* the landowners received the money required. A general guarantee by the entire resources of all the members secured the payment of interest upon these obligations and their redemption. All these institutions for funded credit were suffering severely from the crisis.

After 1925 the *Rentenbank-Kreditanstalt* provided every kind of credit for the farmer. During the period of the inflation the agricultural debt of Germany was almost completely discharged, but already one decade later new debts had arisen which, owing to the high rates of interest, oppressed the farmers more than those before 1913. This was partly due to the vain endeavours to meet by technical rationalisation the pressure on prices, which were dictated by the world market. I do not wish to enumerate the numerous emergency measures of the Government to support agriculture by special subsidies, reduction of interest, etc. Holt (loc. cit., p. 137) gives some figures about the German agricultural indebtedness (quoted from *Deutsche Agrarpolitik, Friedrich List Gesellschaft*, I, p. 399) : 1925, 7,300 ; 1927, 8,728 ; 1929, 10,831 ; 1930, 11,392 ; 1932, 11,765 million marks. For some figures showing how the world crisis caused compulsory sale of estates, see page 259.

In previous chapters the political role played by the big landowners has been mentioned. These held one-fifth of the total agricultural surface. The German East, "East-Elbia"—the former Germanised Slavonic land—was the very centre of these large estates. In parts of Pomerania, Mecklenburg and East Prussia even more than 50 per cent. of the agricultural area belonged to great estate owners. Their estates in contrast to West Germany, in which the big estates amounted to less than one-tenth of the agricultural surface, were administered directly by the owners. In the German West, the tenant system prevailed on the big estates. In the class of peasant farmers who possessed twenty to fifty hectares of agricultural land, 93 per cent. were run entirely by the owners ; of the class holding between 50 to 100 hectares, 86.8 per cent. (1 hectare = 2½ acres) ; of the class, 100 to 200 hectares, 77.9 per cent. ;

and of the big estates, 200 hectares and over 75.1 per cent. of their land was run under their own administration. The former *Sachsengänger*—seasonal agricultural workers on the great estates from the former Western Russian provinces—numbered in 1914 still 372,000 people. The post-War policy prevented this influx of workmen which had been in force for about two generations. Recently arrangements have been made to satisfy the demand for agricultural labourers from foreign sources (1937).

Of the German agricultural soil, roughly 63 per cent. was devoted to cereals and leguminous products, whilst potatoes and beets (including sugar beets) occupied more than 20 per cent. of the surface. The arguments for and against peasant farmers, who held 40 per cent. of the surface and 75 per cent. of the holdings, as against the bigger estates, have been mentioned. This problem, like that of how far Germany can be self-sufficient, is a vast field of different opinions. During the Weimar Reich great activity in land-settlement took place, and in the years 1919 to 1931 alone, 50,000 new settlers were placed on a surface of 550,000 hectares. Settlement, however, serves not only for self-sufficiency purposes but also for the transfer of unemployed. It has to be mentioned that in pre-War times the expropriation and purchase of land in the East for Germanising Prussia's Polish provinces by agricultural settlement has to be considered more or less as a failure.

(d) Social Policy before and during the Third Reich.

The conception of the employer as the master in his own house, and of the essential neutrality of the State with regard to capital and labour, has been abandoned for ever : the changes in the position of labour, both in public and private life came into being as aftermath of the War, as did the kind of social revolution such as I have described in the previous chapter.

No new social order, however, resulted in Germany : neither the sole ownership of the means of production by the community as the centre of all affairs, nor the rule of labour over individual units of economy in the anarcho-syndicalist manner. This latter has never been applied to any real degree ; the former, in Soviet Russia alone. Both the Socialists of the Weimar Reich and those of the National-Socialist Workers' Party compromise with the mainstay of capitalism ; both show an evolutionary socialism, doubtless with different objectives. But in each case the policy is a mixture of self-regulation by economic forces and economic planning. In the two régimes private ownership and the employer are still preserved, and with that about 90 per cent. of the income earners of a 68 million population remains far removed from having an income of £150 per annum. While preserving the capitalist system, even though this is dictated by opportunism, the National-Socialists have attempted to mitigate class contrast through the new methods of forbidding class struggle and dissolving the former organisations of the two parties concerned. Two main points show themselves clearly : first, the labour market is almost completely controlled ; secondly, practical policy is dominated by the dependence of the labour market on general problems of the world market. The two governments, those of the Weimar Reich and of the Third Reich, arrive at their social policy by making an employment policy the basis of their objectives. In principle, the execution of these was evolved by the government of the Weimar Reich, even if it was unfortunate in application. The schemes for creating work by loans and through the activity of the *Reichsanstalt für Arbeitsvermittlung und Arbeitslosenversicherung* (National Institute for Labour Exchange and unemployment insurance) have been taken over by the Third Reich. For the first time the Weimar Reich connected general economic and social policy as an organic whole, thereby far outstripping the activities of pre-War social " reform." Among the measures which continued this policy were those which were made for workers' protection during 1918 and 1923, and which culminated in the laws in respect of an eight-hour day.

The individual wage-agreement between employer and employed of the individual plant was transferred to the organisations representing both parties, and a collective wage agreement (*Kollektiver Tarifvertrag*) emerged, which was compulsory for both parties, unless appeal courts consented to its modification. The governmental system of arbitration was an attempt to preserve the peace of industrial society. The principle of collaboration between the two parties in the individual plant itself, later called a " cell," found expression in certain works councils (*Betriebsräte*).[44] This constituted the democratic method of seeking industrial peace. With it the class struggle was not abandoned, but transferred from individual shop agreements to collective ones. An old claim of the German Socialist Party was thus carried out, but the cleavage among socialists themselves made many advantages illusory. The influence of Communists in certain trade unions became stronger and their anti-democratic tendencies undermined much of this legislation. For the first time, then, the democratic State supervised the peace of the workshops. The " *Betriebsrätegesetz* " (law for shop councils) from 1920 endeavoured to regulate conditions from the bottom. In spite of all good intentions the monopolist organisations of the labour market proceeded in an unintended way. The rigid standardisation of conditions of labour led to a levelling of wages among different categories of workers without sufficient regard to grades of skilled labour. The whole wage level lost its elasticity, a fact which had very bad consequences in times of decreasing trade cycle, and led to increased unemployment.

Already in connection with the general economic policy the housing and land settlement problem appeared outstanding as a corner-stone in the Weimar Reich. In the Imperial Government and the governments of the former member-States, special Ministries for Social Policy, charged with the planned transfer of workers from distressed areas, were unknown. Settlement of unemployed workers now became a feature which served social as well as general economic policy. Following this, the juvenile inhabitants of big industrial centres joined labour camps and the unemployed went to settlements which were mainly localised in the agricultural East. The unemployed living in the heart of the town settled in the agricultural outskirts. This is an example of how a whole system—beginning with *Randsiedlung* (marginal settlement)—served the needs of transplanting labour in connection with schemes for the productive creation of work, among them, that of home colonisation. Many schemes now being carried out had been planned long before the present régime. Already during Dr. Brüning's chancellorship the labour camps, largely supported by the Government, included about 300,000 young people. The labour service was introduced by an Emergency Decree of June 5th, 1931, and supported by the Reich Institute for Employment Exchange and Insurance and the various political associations which were the mainstay of the movement. As soon as the National-Socialist Government came into power, the labour service became a party instrument, all other associations being dissolved. For the labour service an appropriate State office with a Permanent Secretary at the head was established, and the Treasury undertook all expenses. A law regulates the labour service of every German before entering the Army, both being obligatory duties. It must be added that the survivors of the " old régime," including the great owner class, were violent opponents of land settlement. What formerly was governmental support, not far removed from poor law legislation came in the Weimar Reich to be demanded by the men who had not only to be protected against the fluctuation of the market, but to be provided with healthy homes, and support during old age and sickness. The housing policy gradually led to a building trade financed and supported by the State, causing the private market to tend to recede into the background. Objections have been raised that some tens of thousand million marks were wasted on housing and settlement by public authorities during the Weimar Reich, but in comparison with money wasted on warfare, miscalculation of cyclical fluctuations and promoters' profit in the period under review, such objections seem to lose much force. In this connection it must be mentioned that slums hardly exist in Germany.

In this history I can touch only on some of the more striking activities of social policy during the Weimar Reich. So I wish to draw attention to the organic school system, which divided tuition in elementary and continuation schools on technical or commercial lines. The system was adapted to the typical German apprenticeship, which extended over all branches of commerce and craft. Employers were now compelled by law to send their apprentices to these schools, which during this period were opulently established in imposing buildings.

The National-Socialist Government also attempted to unify its economic, social, and political system. For this purpose, certain distinct organisations have been created.

The "*Gesetz zur Ordnung der nationalen Arbeit*" (law for the order of national labour) of January 20th, 1934, has been the first and main instrument to deal with labour problems. Organisations of employers and employees having been dissolved, a new order attempted to combine the parties, which had to agree to wage and salary scales. The combination, which will be dealt with later, starts its work in the individual plant. Mutual obligation of faith between the former employer and the former employee, now called leader and following, has been established as a principle. The leader of the plant, according to the leader principle, regulates conditions of labour for the plant, according to certain rules laid down. Co-operation between him and the workman is guaranteed through the Confidential Advisory Board. To prevent excessive rigidity in orders which are applied to vast regions or great groups of branches of industries, allowance was made for peculiar conditions in localities and district branches. As the government declared, however, it did not wish to suffer social setbacks from this return to the principle of efficient work for private profit and to the liberty-principle of the individual entrepreneur. In order to prevent abuses troubling an elastic order of labour conditions, certain institutions have been set up. First, the *Trustees of labour* have been instituted, which preside over a big district—14 of these exist, corresponding to the divisions of the Party. They are civil servants and belong to the Reich Ministry of Labour, whose advice they follow. Their discretionary powers are indeed great. They not only have the right to interfere in the internal organisation of the plant, but they may also decree of their own will certain individual scales of wages or tariff orders for certain districts or subjects. And these decisions are compulsory. Through these trustees of labour, the State has an instrument to supervise also the determination of wages, in which capacity it is omnipotent. In recognition of the fact that the State cannot bear the full responsibility for the entire determination of wages there still exists a certain possibility of collective wage-agreements. As already mentioned, the Government emphasised its unwillingness to permit any organisations which would return to the idea of the class struggle. It has been stated[45] that up to the end of 1935 more than 1,300 wage regulations were declared, so that the greatest part of the wages and salaries has actually been determined by the Trustees. There are several institutions through which the State wishes to regulate labour conditions by co-operation of employer and employee; the trustee of labour is assisted by a council of experts which can be heard before a decree of wage regulation is made. Co-operation between the National Labour Front and organisations of economic branch groups had been decided upon in 1935; certain committees consisting at the most of twelve members, including leader and following and members of the expert council of the trustees, collaborate in this. Chambers of Labour and Economy have to co-operate with these bodies in local districts. A centralisation of these chambers is affected by the Reich Chamber of Labour and Commerce.

Social Courts of Honour, with a second appeal court, as the name suggests, have to judge offences of social honour and determine whether the obligation of faith between leader and following is being fulfilled. These courts have been known to dismiss leaders from time to time.

The National Labour Front is one of the most important constituents of the National-Socialist system, and was established to embrace all relations between employer and employee. All working Germans, from the labourer to the entrepreneur are members of the Labour Front. It is alleged to be based on the principle of voluntary membership. The activities of this organisation are directed towards political ends, and to those of social welfare. The functions are partly laid down in the above-mentioned Law of National Labour. The National Labour Front has to carry out educational functions "on the basis of the National Socialist philosophy." The Labour Front is a public law corporation, which unites employer and employee, and took over the whole property of the former organisations of employers and trade unions. The organisation and task of the Labour Front were settled by a party decree of October 24th, 1934, which decree has the same legal force as government legislation. In the ideological sense, the Labour Front is an organ of the governing party, intended to overcome the class struggle and to pursue the aim of forming an actual community of interests among all members of the German population. This organ deals with nearly all problems of social welfare, and has an enormous apparatus of offices and officials at its disposal. The office for Economy of the Labour Front is identical with the central office of the Reichs Chamber of Commerce. A certain significance lies in the organisation "Strength through Joy" (*see* p. 231) which is distributed in various departments throughout the whole Reich.

Certain centralising offices exist. As the successor of former trade unions and their properties, the Labour Front has at its disposal membership fees, besides returns of economic undertakings. One bank actually belongs to it, the *Bank der Deutschen Arbeit A.G.* (the successor of the "Workman's Bank," established in 1924). The total income of the Labour Front from fees in 1935 was 300 million marks, obtained from 16 million members. The cost of administration, including offices to advise members in legal affairs, was in that year 82 million marks. The head of this organisation, Dr. Ley, is leader and originator of many new schemes of this organisation.

Germany during the Weimar period followed the example of certain other countries in building up a system of unemployment insurance. Before the War, unemployment even in times of slump did not exceed some hundreds of thousands. Labour, which in good times had entered industry, in times of crisis returned to agriculture to a considerable extent. The world crisis, however, revealed some millions of workmen unemployed, though the phenomenon became outstanding as a sign of continued industrialisation. It became recognised not as a temporary and seasonal problem but as one which changed the whole structure of the economic system. The policy of the Weimar Reich expressed the feeling that the State as social trustee had here to interfere to an extraordinary degree with the free play of forces in the labour market.

Compulsory unemployment insurance, first introduced in England in 1911, was decreed by law in Germany in 1927, a measure which followed some regulations of minor importance. Labour exchange and Labour insurance are dependent on the investigation and announcement of openings. The discovery of vacancies and the allocation of labour to them was once a weapon in the struggle between Capital and Labour for wages. First trade unions created offices of their own, announcing the openings, and also associations for social welfare, and municipal authorities established similar offices. In 1912, more than 2,200 labour exchanges of these categories existed in addition to numerous private ones. It was typical of pre-War Germany that the work of the employment exchange was felt to be no more than a private need of a local character. The idea of building up public exchanges for larger areas first emerged during the War. The short-lived union of employers and workers' associations which was formed in November, 1918, attempted to regulate the employment exchange on the basis of equal right and denounced the use of the employment exchange as an instrument of social struggle. In 1922, the Labour Exchange Law created a system of public Labour offices of a more municipal nature. These were embraced under the Reich employment exchange office. Experience of their working brought about the law of 1927 which created a central national office and official services of central, regional and local character, The insurance was linked up with the State Labour exchange, and the Government established the Institute for Labour Exchange and Labour Insurance. Federal States or bigger provinces received a system of regional branches, which were again divided into local ones. The obligation to be insured against unemployment was joined with the obligation of the worker to be insured against disease. Contributions were shared by employer and employees, and were graded according to classes of wages and salary. Originally, the assistance was limited to 26 weeks, which under certain conditions could be extended—whilst in times of crisis the so-called " crisis assistance " could be given. In principle these regulations are still valid, but they operate under other conditions than those existing at the time of the Weimar Reich.

During the Weimar Reich the unemployed for the first time had a legal claim to assistance. That was adapted to the scale of income.

The amount of the premium did not depend upon political influences. The first budget was based on an annual average of unemployment of 800,000, an estimate calculated on the basis of conditions prevailing during the boom period of 1927. The slump, however, destroyed these—at one time unemployment outstripped six millions—and made the accumulation of a reserve for the insurance impossible. The consequence naturally was a heavy increase of contributions, whilst on the other side the benefits paid had to be repeatedly reduced. The crisis subsidy ("*Krisenunterstützung*") was provided in the proportion of four-fifths by the Reich and one-fifth by the municipal authorities. The unemployed insurance fund was also forced to seek assistance from treasury loans. The emergency decree of the 14th June, 1932, introduced a scale of contributions according to income, which went to the Reich Institute to be used for supporting the unemployed; the contributions were obtained from all receivers of wages and salary. These measures were ultimately bound to lead to the abandonment of the principle of insurance. This became clearer when a means test (after six weeks " crisis support " for the unemployed) was introduced; its effect was to reduce the legal claim of the unemployed. But it was not the Reich Institute itself which was faced with the main difficulties; for the other authorities, such as municipalities, had to take over those unemployed who had exhausted the permitted period of unemployment payments or crisis support. Thus the liability for unemployment support was transferred to the municipal welfare department. So three types of unemployed emerged: (1) those entitled to assistance from the Reich Insurance Fund; (2) those receiving Crisis Support, and (3) those assisted by the municipal welfare (*Wohlfahrt*) departments. The effect on the finances of big towns with a working class population was disastrous. In 1932, the Reich first established support for the approved "*Wohlfahrts*" unemployed, who, altough they had exhausted their 26 weeks' benefit otherwise satisfied the conditions of " Reich unemployed." The great employment creation activity of the National-Socialist Government through its various loans so changed conditions that no transfer of Reich unemployed to *Wohlfahrt* unemployed took place. The government stressed the principle that it gave work and with it profit so that business enterprises had to take care of many unemployed, whether they wished to or not. The Reich Institute now has various obligations, which include training in new jobs, the training of cripples and so on. The identity book of the worker, which indicates his unemployment is another instrument for keeping down the numbers of unemployed.

Some few words are here necessary about the financing of the German Social Insurance policy since the War. All the reserves previously collected faded away during the period of inflation. Still, claims had to be satisfied, especially from the old age and disablement insurance (*Invalidenversicherung*) which was established in Bismarck's time. The more recent salaried workers' insurance was less burdened with claims. There was no other way out than to meet commitments out of the current income of State and Municipal authorities and the parties concerned. There never was a return to actuarial principles during the Weimar Reich. So higher outgoings and lower incomings during the crisis led to enormous deficits. Emergency decrees attempted to mitigate the troubles in the financing of the Reich Insurance, but the actuarial deficit was still 17,000 million Marks in the old age and health insurance, and 17,000 million marks in the salaried workers' insurance. A law of December, 1933, which first tried to simplify the organisation of insurance, stopped the drain on current budgetary expenditure, but set up the Public Insurance bodies with separate accounts. The improved condition of the labour market meanwhile alleviated the financial situation of the insurance-bodies. The new law of December 21st, 1937, which is too complicated to be described in detail, combines for joint action the former independent authorities for public insurance and the treasury—creating with this the principle of a general Public Insurance, of which the parts must balance their expenditure under each other. At the same time, every German is now allowed to insure himself by the old age and the salaried workers' insurance—a further evolutionary step of the policy towards nationalisation. The insurance for miners has also been subject to a reform similar to that mentioned above.

Social policy is now an instrument of State guidance influencing the whole economic policy, of which it became a marked constituent. The study of the trade cycle and unemployment status furnishes the foundation of governmental interference, creating as it does at the same time a new financial and banking policy, both private and public.

NOTES TO CHAPTER I.

1. WIESER (Friedrich) v. *Theorie der gesellschaftlichen Wirtschaft. Grundr. d. Sozialökonomik.* I. Abt. 1914. p. 141.
2. In this analysis of the application of the theory of cognition by the various economic schools I follow LEDERER (Emil), *Aufriss der Oekonomischen Theorie.* 3rd Ed., 1931., Chap. 1. (Lederer is here influenced by H. Rickert whose philosophical explanations of the *Methodenstreit* were of great value.)
3. LEDERER, loc. cit. pp. 17-18.
4. Ibid.
5. SPIETHOFF (Arthur), *Allgemeine Volkswirtschaftslehre als geschichtliche Theorie. Die Wirtschaftsstile. Festgabe für Werner Sombart* München, 1933, pp. 51 seq.
6. LEDERER, loc. cit. pp. 8-9.
7. LÖWE (Adolf): Economics and Sociology, London, 1935, pp. 81-82.—" Middle principles " is a term used by J. S. Mill and revived by M. Ginsberg, to describe such " sociological elements which constitute ' uniformities of co-existence between the states of the various social phenomena ' because ' not every variety of combination of these general social facts is possible, but only certain combinations.' " (Löwe, p. 54).
8. LÖWE, loc. cit. p. 82.
9. BRUCK, W. F., *Die wandelnde Rolle von Unternehmerbild— und Funktion in verschiedenen Epochen der Wirtschaftsgeschichte und die Theorie von Unternehmer und Unternehmung. (Festgabe für Werner Sombart,* 1933, p. 95).
10. TROELTSCH, E., *Der Historismus u. seine Probleme,* Vol. I, 1922, and MANNHEIM (Karl), *Historismus (Archiv. f. Sozialwiss,* Vol. 52, 1924), pp. 29-31.
11. London, 1935.
12. HEIMANN (Eduard), " Sociological Pre-conception of Economic Theory " (Social Research, Vol. I, No. 1, pp. 22-44).
    NEISSER, H., *Archiv. für Sozialwissenschaften,* Vol. 65, pp. 225-250).
13. ROBBINS (Lionel), An Essay on the Nature and Significance of Economic Science, 1933. His footnote p. 20.
14. LÖWE, loc. cit. p. 20.
15. LÖWE, loc. cit. p. 103.
16. LÖWE, loc. cit. p. 77.
17. LÖWE, loc. cit. p. 78.
18. LÖWE, loc. cit. p. 88.
19. LÖWE, loc. cit. p. 92.
20. LÖWE, loc. cit. p. 86.
21. LÖWE, loc. cit. p. 78.

22. Translated as literally as possible.
23. I use a phrase of BONAR (J.), "Philosophy and Political Economy," 1893.
24. See the first chapters of ONCKEN (August), "Adam Smith and Immanuel Kant," 1877.
25. The Acquisitive Society, London, 1922, p. 96. See also COLE (G. D. H.) and COLE (Margaret), A Guide to Modern Politics, 1934, pp. 370-414.
26. *Nationale Selbstgenügsamkeit (Schmollers Jahrbuch)*, Vol. 57, pp. 565-66.
27. *Handwörterbuch der Staatswissenschaften*, Ed. 4, Vol. VII, 1926, p. 581.
28. Observer, Dec. 2nd, 1934.
29. Quoted from a review " A scientific Civilisation " (The Webbs on Soviet Communism) by F. A. v. HAYEK, " Sunday Times," Jan. 5th, 1936.
30. BERDYAEV (Nicolas), The origin of Russian Communism (London, 1937).—He, an anti-Bolshevist, says, Communism is essentially Russian; the passion for "wholeness" governs it too. But wholeness thus conceived must be set over against any form of individualism : it results in " the love of the man far off, not the love of one's neighbour."
MEYER (Karl), *Die geistige Haltung Russlands und die Sovietpresse.* (*Zeitungsseminar*, Vol. III, *Münster in Westfalen*, 1931, p. 11).
31. MEYER, loc. cit. p. 12.
32. Official German Statistics quoted from DAWSON (W.H.), Evolution of modern Germany, 1919.
33. MOST (O.), *Bevölkerungspolitik*, Leipzig, Philipp Reclam, 1934, p. 26.
34. MOST (O.), loc. cit. p. 28.
35. HÄPKE-WISKEMANN, *Wirtschaftsgeschichte*, II, Leipzig, 1936, p.16.
36. WARRINER (D), Combines and Rationalisation in Germany, 1924-1928, London, p. 148.
37. PALGRAVE'S Dictionary of Political Economy, p. 313-314, 1923 " Historical School of Economists."
38. Here I refer only to the world of German officialdom.
39. SPEKTATOR-BRIEFE, *Tübingen*, 1924, p. 5 seq.
40. LÜTGERT (Wilhelm), *Die Religion des deutschen Idealismus und ihr Ende*, 4 Volumes Gütersloh, 1923-1930.
41. *Nationalwirtschaft*, Vol. 2, 1928, p. 11 seq.
42. English Edition, London.
43. KEYNES (J. M.), loc. cit. p. 40.
44. The Theory of Social Economy, London, 1923.
45. CASSEL, loc. cit. p. 116.

46. CASSEL, loc. cit. p. 117.
47. CASSEL, loc. cit. p. 119.
48. CASSEL, loc. cit. p. 119.
49. KEYNES, loc. cit. p. 31.
50. cf. I (2) (*b*), §4.
51. " Observer," Jan. 5th, 1936.
52. *Weltbürgertum und Nationalstaat*, Ed. VI, 1922.
53. VORLÄNDER (Karl), *Von Machiavelli bis Lenin*, Leipzig, 1926, p. 158 seq.
54. Quoted from DAWSON (W. H.), Evolution, etc., p. 37.
55. VORLÄNDER, loc. cit, p. 145.
56. VORLÄNDER, loc. cit. p. 106.
57. VORLÄNDER, loc. cit. p. 205.
58. MEINECKE, pp. 98-129.
59. WEBER (Adolf), in *Conrads-Jahrbücher*, etc., 1935.
60. KLUCKHOHN (Paul), *Persönlichkeit und Gemeinschaft, Studien zur Staatsauffassung der deutschen Romantik*, 1925.
61. KELSEN (Hans), *Sozialismus und Staat*, Ed. II, 1923, p. 128.
62. 1929.
63. pp. 17 and 27.
64. London, 1935, p. 14.
65. See loc. cit.
66. In " History of Christianity, in the Light of Modern Knowledge," ed. Hugh Martin, London, 1929, Chap. V.
67. I recommend to the English reader GOOCH (G.P.), Germany, 1925, p. 372.
68. loc. cit.
69. *Weltgeschichtliche Betrachtungen " Kröners Sammlung,"* Leipzig, 1935, p. 50.
70. *Reichstags-Debatte*, 26/11/1884.
71. " *Die Bauernbefreiung und der Ursprung des Landarbeiters in den östlichen Teilen Preussens.*" Leipzig, 1893-1894.
72. *Deutsche Wirtschaftskunde, Statistisches Reichsamt*, Ed. II, 1933, p. 8.
73. *Statistisches Handbuch des Deutschen Reichs*, 1904.
74. *Deutsche Wirtschaftskunde*, loc. cit. p. 28.

NOTES TO CHAPTER II

1. The new industrial system, London, 1936, p. 270.
2. loc. cit. pp. 125-126.
3. "*Die Betriebswirtschaftslehre an der Schwelle der neuen Wirtschaftsverfassung*" (*Zeitschrift für handelswissenschaftliche Forschung*), 22. Jahrg., 1928.
4. Quoted from DAWSON (W. H.), Evolution, etc., 1919, pp. 91-92.
5. *Vom Aktienwesen*, Berlin, 1917, p. 25 et seq.
6. *Die deutsche Kreditbank* (*Grundriss der Sozialökonomik*), V. Abt., 1918, p. 12.—I have followed closely Schulze-Gaevernitz's conceptions in this history. His book is not a mere survey of banking, but covers the whole field of political and economic activity in which banking is included. BONN (M. J.) gives an interesting analysis in "*Das Schicksal des deutschen Kapitalismus*" (1926 and 1930).
7. *Bankpolitik*, Tübingen, 1915, p. 272.
8. p. 274.
9. p. 36.
10. p. 145.
11. p. 38.
12. *Finanzielle Organisation der Industrie und Monopole* (*Grundriss der Sozialökonomik*), VI. Abt. 1914, p. 199.
13. SOMARY (Felix), p. 201.
14. Quoted from SCHULZE-GAEVERNITZ, p. 147.
15. p. 101.
16. p. 100.
17. p. 99.
18. RIESSER (J.), *Deutsche Oekonomist*, 1905, p. 697.
19. LIEFMANN (R.), *Kartelle und Truste*, 6th Ed., 1924, p. 112.
20. SCHMOLLER (Gustav), *Grundriss der allg. Volkswirtschaftslehre*, 1908, Vol. I, p. 462.
21. loc. cit. p. 147.
22. I quoted here from the description and some detailed facts on cartel policy, given by Dr. L. MIKSCH (*Handelsteil e. Tageszeitung*, Frankfurt, 1936, p. 364). For the more recent facts on the cartel and monopoly problem (and the interference by the State) I used in addition to official publications, the various writings of the economic editors of the *Frankfurter Zeitung*, among them Dr. E. WELTER and Herr L. MIKSCH and others (see pp. 280, 284), the *Kartellrundschau*, the *Deutscher Volkswirt*, the publication of the German Trade Cycle Institute. The books of Professor D. H. MACGREGOR (Industrial Combination, 1906) and Mr. H. W. MACROSTY (Trust movement in British Industry, 1907) are still a mine of information for students of the combination movement. Professor H. A. MARQUAND in his book "The Dynamics of Industrial Combination," 1931, gives a thorough analysis of the problem which I can trace here only in brief outlines.

23. Enterprise, Purpose and Profit, 1934, Chapter I.
24. *Verein für Sozialpolitik*, Vol. 180, pars. II, pp. 152 and 154.
25. loc. cit. pp. 8-9.
26. loc. cit. pp. 119-126.
27. *Planwirtschaft und Verkehrswirtschaft*, München, Leipzig, 1931, pp. 21-27.
28. WARRINER, loc. cit. pp. 148-150.
29. WARRINER, loc. cit. pp. 148-150.
30. Professor WAGEMANN said recently that two-thirds of all prices in Germany are cartelised prices (Weekly Bulletin, Business Research Institute, December, 1936).
31. loc. cit. p. 126.
32. loc. cit. p. 241 et seq.
33. loc. cit. p. 21.—I have taken here the views of LANDAUER (p. 18 et seq.) and condensed them.
34. loc. cit. p. 26.
35. loc. cit. p. 26.
36. LIEFMANN (Robert), *Kartelle und Truste*, VI Ed., Stuttgart, 1924, p. 107 et seq.
37. *Marktform und Gleichgewicht*, Berlin, 1934.
38. "*Fragen der Verbrauchskonzentration*" (*Wirtschaftskurve*), 14 Jahrg., pp. 213-218.—See also my quotation of Dr. MIKSCH'S work in Chapter IV.
39. Economics of Imperfect Competition, 1933.
40. *Sozialistische Monatshefte*, Nov., 1905, quoted from DAWSON (W. H.), Evolution, etc., 1919, p. 342.
41. I follow here ADOLF WEBER'S *Volkswirtschaftslehre*, Vol. IV, Chapter III, Section IV, München, Leipzig, 1933.
42. ibid, Vol. IV, pp. 544-545.
43. ibid. Vol. IV, p. 544.
44. ibid. Vol. IV, p. 546.
45. In my description I follow A. SARTORIUS VON WALTERSHAUSEN'S representation (*Deutsche Wirtschaftsgeschichte*, 1815-1914, Jena, 1920 (see his Chapter VI, Section III)).
46. See footnote 45.
47. ibid. p. 399.
48. Again I use SARTORIUS' history as regards German trade policy with the Great Powers.
49. ibid. p. 400.
50. ibid. pp. 410-411.
51. ibid.
52. RIESSER (Jacob), *Grossbanken*, 3rd Ed., Jena, 1910, p. 135.
53. PAISH (George), Statist, Dec., 1910 (quoted from SCHULZE-GAEVERNITZ, loc. cit. p. 160).
54. HELFFERICH (K.), *Bankarchiv*, 15th April, 1911 (quoted from SCHULZE-GAEVERNITZ, p. 158).

55. SCHULZE-GAEVERNITZ, *Deutscher Oekonomist. Die Entwicklung der deutschen Aktienbanken*, 1903, p. 19 et sq.
56. WARRINER, loc. cit. p. 1.
57. SOMBART (Werner), *Die Deutsche Volkswirtschaft im* 19th *Jahrh.*, 4th Ed., Berlin, 1919, p. 431.
58. loc. cit. 1931, p. 11-13.—There was little change by 1928 when the official statistics (quoted from the *Frankfurter Zeitung*, January 8th, 1937) record that approximately 90 per cent. of the German population had an income of less than 3,000 Marks per annum and 57 per cent. less than 1,200 Marks, of the 32 million in employment. Ten million lived with their families and so their income was merely additional to that of other members of the household. Corresponding figures for the year 1934 are not directly comparable with former statistics because a different method of assessment came into force which does not relate so much to the net income as before (see Vol. 499, Statistics of German Statistical Office; results of the income assessment, 1934).
59. cf. Professor PIGOU'S and COLIN CLARK'S estimate of English incomes (the London & Cambridge Service, Spec. Mem. No. 43, April, 1936) and earlier work by Professor BOWLEY and Sir JOSIAH STAMP (1924).
60. Statistics taken from DAWSON, Evolution, etc., p. 159.
61. HEYDE (Ludwig) in his "*Abriss der Sozialpolitik*, Leipzig, several editions, surveyed briefly facts and statistics of the socio-political events of this period. I followed here his description.
62. HEYDE, loc. cit. p. 34.
63. Figures taken from DAWSON, Evolution, etc., p. 116.
64. DAWSON, loc. cit. p. 154.
65. *Psychologie der antikapitalistischen Massenbewegung* (*Grundriss der Sozialökonomik*, Vol. IX, I, 1926, p. 277).
66. BRUCK, "*Die Kriegsunternehmung*," etc. *Archiv für Sozialwissenschaft*, 1920-21.—A short survey of the War Economy was written by BRIEFS (Goetz) in *Handwörterbuch der Staatswissenschaft*, 4th Ed., Bol. 5, p. 984 et seq.
67. Out of the various pamphlets on the subject dealt with in this chapter I mention here from RATHENAU (WALTHER): *Deutschlands Rohstoffversorgung*, Berlin, 1915—*Vom Aktienwesen*, Berlin, 1917—*Autonome Wirtschaft*, Jena, 1919—*Probleme der Friedenswirtschaft*, Berlin, 1916—*Von kommenden Dingen*, Berlin, 1917; MOELLENDORFF v. (Wichard), *Konservativer Sozialismus*, Hamburg, 1932 (in this book Moellendorff's publications and official reports are reprinted).
68. *Von kommenden Dingen*, p. 130.
69. *Vom Aktienwesen*, p. 61.
70. ibid p. 62.
71. cp. note 66.

NOTES TO CHAPTER III

1. HÖVEL (P.), *Grundfragen deutscher Wirtschaftspolitik*, Berlin, 1935, p. 5.
2. I use here C. E. M. JOAD's description and quotations from authors such as LENIN (quoted from Introduction to Modern Political Theory, London, 1924-1935, Chapter 5). See also my quotation from KELSEN, p. 60.
3. JOAD, ibid.
4. JOAD, ibid.
5. ROSENBERG (Arthur), loc. cit. p. 21.
6. ibid.
7. *Archiv für Sozialwissenschaften*, Vol. 45, 1918-1919, p. 527 et seq.
8. ibid p. 533.
9. ibid p. 529.
10. ibid. p. 536.
11. BRADY (Robert A.), The Rationalisation movement in German industry, 1933, p. 68.
12. Reprinted in MOELLENDORFF von (Wichard), *Konservativer Sozialismus*, Hamburg, 1932.
13. ibid, pp. 235-36.
14. ibid.
15. ibid. p. 234.
16. ibid. p. 227.
17. Quoted note 12.
18. ROSENBERG (Arthur), loc. cit. p. 178.
19. ibid. p. 181.
20. ibid.
21. ROSENBERG (Arthur), pp. 181-82.
22. ROSENBERG (Arthur), p. 183.
23. Quoted from ROSENBERG (Arthur), p. 184.
24. loc. cit. p. 185.
25. SCHACHT (Hjalmar), *Die Stabilisierung der Mark*, Berlin, 1927, p. 61.
26. HALM (G.), *Geld-Kredit-Banken*, München-Leipzig, 1935, p. 79.
27. SCHACHT, loc. cit., p. 98.
28. EISELE (Julia), *Die Reichsbankpolitik seit der Stabilisierung*, Berlin, 1933, p. 22.
29. *Deutsche Wirtschaftskunde, Statistisches Reichsamt*, 1933, p. 348 et seq.
30. ibid.

31. LIEFMANN, loc. cit. p. 115.
32. LIEFMANN'S book has been translated into English. LEVY (Hermann) published "Industrial Germany," 1935, and "The New Industrial System," 1936. The German literature on post-War industrial development is voluminous. Besides the works already quoted, I may refer here to von BECKERATH (Herbert), "*Kräfte, Ziele und Gestaltungen in der deutschen Industriewirtschaft*," Jena, 1924, and "*Der moderne Industrialismus*," Jena, 1930.—As regards the effects of the crisis, Professor L. ROBBINS' book, "The Great Depression" (1934) widely contributes to the explanation of underlying events.
33. LEVY, The New Industrial System, p. 184.
34. LEVY, Industrial Germany, p. 56. See reports of the German Enquiry Committee. The volumes are published as *Ausschuss zur Untersuchung der Erzeugungs-und Absatzbedingungen der deutschen Wirtschaft* (published Berlin, Siegfried Mittler, from 1928 onwards).
35. LEVY, Industrial Germany, p. 47, published an interesting comparison of the output of iron and steel in Germany with that of other countries:

In millions of tons.

	Pig-iron.			Steel.		
	1913	1929	1933	1913	1929	1933
United Kingdom	10.26	7.59	4.12	7.66	9.64	7.00
Germany without Saar	10.73	13.19	5.18	11.99	15.99	7.44
France	8.93	10.20	6.21	6.86	9.55	6.40
U.S.A.	30.97	42.61	31.75	31.30	56.43	23.57

36. LEVY, Industrial Germany, p. 49.
37. ibid.
38. ibid. p. 57.
39. ibid. p. 58.
40. ibid. p. 58.
41. ibid. p. 59.
42. ibid. p. 59.
43. ibid. p. 25.
44. ibid. p. 26.
45. ibid. p. 35.
46. ibid. p. 75.
47. The Banking Enquiry Committee under Dr. Schacht's leadership offers a good source for this Chapter of the History of German Banking. The economic editors of the "*Frankfurter Zeitung*" (at the same time of "*Die Wirtschaftskurve*") published comments to the Reports of the Committee ("*Bankensystem im Umbau*," 1933). I have made use of these reports and comments for several of the causes and effects of the crisis here outlined. M. J. Bonn and P. Einzig (London) have written numerous pamphlets on the German Post-War situation.

48. *Wall Street und die deutschen Anleihen*, Leipzig, 1933.
49. *Eigene oder geborgte Währung*, Heft 16, Weltwirtschaftliche Gesellschaft zu Münster in Westfalen, Leipzig, 1928.
50. loc. cit. p. 21.
51. loc. cit. p. 125.
52. MARX und MOST. *Gemischte wirtschaftliche Betriebe, Handwörterbuch der Kommunalwissenschaften*, Jena, 1922 ; MOST (O.), *in Ergänzungsband, Handwörterbuch*, etc., Jena, 1927, p. 646 et seq. SCHMELCHER (E.), *Gemischtwirtschaftliche Unternehmung, Handwörterbuch der Staatswissenschaften*, 4th edition, 1927 ; PASSOW (R.), *Die gemischt privaten und öffentlichen Unternehmungen*, 2nd edition, Jena, 1923.
53. BRUCK (W. F.), " *Die Kriegsunternehmung,*" *Archiv für Sozialwissenschaften*, Vol. 48, 1920, p. 547 et seq., and " *Zur Systematik der Unternehmungsformen,*" *Archiv für Sozialwissenschaften*, Vol. 52, 1924, p. 623 et seq.
54. ASRIEL (C. J.), *Das R.W.E. Rheinisches-Westfälisches Elektrizitätswerk A.G.*, *Zürcher Volkswirtschaftliche Forschungen*, Vol. 16, 1930, pp. 196 and 197.
55. SCHMELCHER, loc. cit. p. 847 et seq., on Electricity Supply and Mixed Enterprise.
56. ASRIEL, loc. cit., pp. 75-168, pp. 205-244.
57. LEVY, Industrial Germany, p. 82.
58. *Die Fortbildung der gemischtwirtschaftlichen Unternehmungen und die Vergesellschaftung der Betriebe* (*Technik und Wirtschaft*, 1919, Heft 5).
59. Professor LAVERGNE (Bernard) illustrates (*L'orde co-operatif*, Paris, 1926, and the extract, " *Regies co-operatives,*" Paris, 1927) from the Belgian experiment some of these interesting forms of mixed public and private institutions, of which the latter are co-operative societies.—Also in Germany co-operative societies are tied up with public authorities. See SCHMELCHER, loc. cit. p. 846.

NOTES TO CHAPTER IV

1. MARSCHAK (J.), *Archiv für Sozialwissenschaften*, Vol. 52, 1924, p. 695. See also the corresponding chapters in FINER (Herman), " Mussolini's Italy," 1935. See also COLE, loc. cit. p. 160 et seq., p. 323 et seq., pp. 370-414.
2. MARSCHAK (J.), loc. cit., pp. 708 and 709.
3. In " *Der Deutsche Staat der Gegenwart*," *Heft I*, Hamburg, 1933.
4. SCHMITT, loc. cit. p. 11 seq.
5. SCHMITT, loc. cit., p. 32.
6. SCHMITT, loc. cit. p. 12.
7. SCHMITT, loc. cit. p. 24.
8. *Königsberg, Deutsche Ostmesse*, August 18th, 1935, quoted from KRAUSE (A. B.), *Organisation von Arbeit und Wirtschaft*, 5th Ed., 1935, p. 77.
9. Professor WAGEMANN, the financial expert and head of the German trade cycle institute, in describing the procedure and effect of the loans (" The Secret of Employment Creation Financing in Germany," Supplement to the Weekly Report of the German Institute of Business Research, August 22nd, 1935), assumes the same political and economic foundations for the loans of 1932 and 1933 as for the Rentenmark of 1923. The new loan had to overcome the liquidity crisis due to the frozen resources of industries, banks, and farms. The lack of money was disastrous for all business men, though the mass of consumers, who were now supplied with cash which was secure in value, suffered less than they did during the inflation of 1923. As in the latter year a Public Loan had to revive economic activities by refilling the consumers' coffers, so at this period State loans set industry, banking and agriculture in motion again. The employment creation loan of 1933 was, together with treasury bills and certificates, and intermediate term loans, instrumental in bringing about this activity, and offered, as Wagemann says, an excellent and " secure " investment. By 1935 the circulation was as follows :

Bills*	12,500	million RM.
Reich Treasury Certificates†	3,500	,, RM.
Advance Tax Certificates‡	900	,, RM.
Total	16,900	,, RM.

* Commercial bills, employment creation bills and bills to pre-finance special Reich expenditures. † Interest-bearing and non-interest-bearing Treasury certificates, without security, and 4 per cent. work Treasury certificates (*Arbeitsschatzanweisungen*), Reich bills and operating credit at the Reichsbank.
‡ Not including advance tax certificates deposited at the Reichsbank.

These 16,900 million RM. of bills and certificates are distributed as follows :

	Bills.	Treasury Bills.
Note-issuing Banks*	3,800	400 million RM.
Public Banks†	1,200	1,500 ,, RM.
Gold Discount Bank (*Golddiskontbank*)	200	100 ,, RM.
Private Banks	2,100	800 ,, RM.
Railway Bank (*Verkehrskreditbank*)	400	—
Co-operatives	400	—
	8,100	2,800 million RM.

* Including holdings of covering securities, largely advance tax certificates. † Prussian State Bank, Giro Centrals, Savings Banks and Communal Banks.

Together this makes 10,900 million RM. The remainder is held by insurance institutions and especially by industrial enterprises. The amounts held by the banks, of course, represent at the same time liquid reserves, if not savings capital, of the whole economic system.

In its turn industry used these bills to repay its credits to the banks, which passed them on to the Reichsbank, or bought employment creation bills for themselves. The recovery increased the deposits of industry and tempted the hoarded money to return to the banks. The recovery, too, helped the savings banks to reduce their debts to the currency bank, which in its turn was able to decrease the issue of these bills by 500 million marks. The deposit of savings increased enormously :

Deposit of Public Savings Banks, Giro Centrals and State Banks. (Million Reichs-Mark)

	Public Savings Banks		Giro Centrals	State Banks (*Staats and Landesbanken*)
	Savings Deposits	Demand Deposits	Total‡ Deposits	Total Deposits
1932—June	9,800	1,625	859	1,344
1933—June	10,467	1,484	864	1,357
1934—June	11,668	1,702	828	1,532
1935—June	13,158	1,874	812	1,612

‡ Excluding deposits due to other banks and savings banks.

It is unnecessary to elaborate the whole process by which this system set in motion the whole machinery of public and private economy.

The forerunner of the employment creation loan, Papen's advance tax certificates reduced the debts of the entrepreneur to the bank and of the bank to the Reichsbank (in its capacity of the "banker's bank"). The Government sold Creation Loan and treasury certificates which were acceptable by the Reichsbank as collateral, and returned the proceeds to industry which carried out its orders.

10. Official German News Agency, January 24th, 1935, referring to the Festival Meeting of the Central Chamber of Trade and Industry of the Reich.
11. Quoted from FRITZSCHE (Rolf), Press Attaché of the Ministry for Economic Affairs : *Aufbau der Wirtschaft im Dritten Reich.* Berlin-Charlottenburg, 1934, p. 82.
12. Official German News Agency, quoted from *Frankfurter Zeitung* January 24th, 1937.
13. German News Agency, ibid.
14. *Deutscher Volkswirt*, April 9th, 1937, No. 28, p. 1350.
15. SCHMALENBACH (E.), " *Selbstkostenrechnung und Preispolitik,*" 6th Ed., 1934 ; " *Dynamische Bilanz,*" 6th Ed., 1933 ; " *Finanzierungen,*" 5th Ed., 1932.
16. MIKSCH (L.), *Wettbewerb als Aufgabe. Die Grundsätze der Wettbewerbung*, Stuttgart, 1937.
17. *Fragen der Verbrauchskonzentration (Wettbewerbsbeschränkungen auf der Konsumseite) Die Wirtschaftskurve*, Frankfurt/Main, 14th Jahrg., 1935-36, p. 215—cp. also " *Wo herrscht noch freier Wettbewerb* ? " and " *Marktordnung und Marktregelung* " in *Die Wirtschaftskurve*, 15th Jahrg., p. 339, resp. 412, and the same author's articles on Competition and *Marktordnung* in " *Wie liest man den Wirtschaftsteil einer Tageszeitung* ? " Dr. Miksch's various articles on the actual changes in market and cartel policy have been a reliable source for this history.
18. Quoted from Dr. MIKSCH.
19. WAGEMANN (E.), The Manipulation of Consumption. *Vierteljahrshefte für Konjunkturforschung*, 1935, Heft 3, Teil A, p. 249, in English in Weekly Report of the German Institute for Business Research, February 12th, 1936, p. 14.
20. *Frankfurter Zeitung*, January 31st, 1937.
21. By 1940 all existing joint stock companies with a share capital below 100 thousand marks have to be dissolved. These are not more than one-fifth of the 7,204 joint stock companies, existing on December 31st, 1936. These companies represent

a capital of 18,780 million marks in ordinary and 444 million marks in preference shares. The average share capital of all these companies increased constantly during the last few years and amounted at this date to 2.67 million marks. This increase was due partly to the effects of the concentration movement and partly to the compulsory dissolution of smaller joint stock companies (figures quoted from *Vierteljahrshefte für Statistik des Deutschen Reiches*, 1937, Heft 1).

22. The *Debits in the different banking groups* show the enormous influence of governmental financial policy. The following figures (quoted from Weekly Report of the German Institute of Business Research, 1936, p. 53) are the more striking as the " eight large banks " contain deposit banks which are wholly or partly State owned.

Millions RM.

	Eight Large Banks		State and Provincial Banks		Giro Centrals		Special Banks	
	Total	Customers' deposits	Total	Customers' deposits	Total	Customers' deposits	Total	Customers' deposits
1935								
June	6,447	4,804	1,859	1,351	3,712	630	2,204	1,595
Sept.	6,213	4,669	1,842	1,355	3,820	654	2,306	1,667
1936								
Jan.	6,208	4,660	1,853	1,322	3,744	704	2,491	1,794
May	6,334	4,874	1,883	1,335	4,149	773	2,286	1,598

The *bill holdings of certain German banking groups* (quoted from ibid p. 54) show exactly the interdependence of the German Public Financial Policy and the German banking system (see second part of this sub-chapter).

In connection with the work creation bills, through which the currency bank's note circulation received a substitution for gold as a backing, I quote here the Status of the Reichsbank, comparing January 31st, 1933, with June 23rd, 1937 :

	Jan. 31st, 1933	June 23rd, 1937	
Gold	822	69	—753
Bills	2,459	4,468	+2,009
Note circulation	3,338	4,429	+1,091

(PARKER, loc. cit. p. 387.)

Millions RM.

Period	Reichsbank Bills and Checks	Reichsbank Reich Treasury Bills	Gold Discount Bank Bills	Gold Discount Bank Treasury bills and non-interest bearing Treasury certificates of the Reich and the States	Konversionskasse Investments	Eight Large Banks Bills	Eight Large Banks Treasury bills and non-interest bearing Treasury certificates of the Reich and the States	State and Provincial Banks Bills	State and Provincial Banks Treasury bills and non-interest bearing Treasury certificates of the Reich and the States	Giro Centrals Bills	Giro Centrals Treasury bills and non-interest bearing Treasury certificates of the Reich and the States	Special Banks Bills	Special Banks Treasury bills and non-interest bearing Treasury certificates of the Reich and the States
1935 June	3,878.7	389.6	714.1	91.7	172.0	1,746.0	615.2	595.6	477.6	376.7	754.1	827.7	176.4
Sept.	4,143.6	385.7	1,043.0	139.7	191.4	1,473.9	651.5	666.5	434.4	437.9	744.4	928.8	160.7
1936 Feb.	4,025.7	391.8	1,282.8	147.2	223.0	1,734.1	666.5	562.1	443.4	645.4	785.4	776.3	202.0
May	4,606.4	256.8	1,197.4	137.0	194.0	1,863.1	682.7	553.8	413.8	676.1	938.2	916.4	190.9

23. Weekly Report of the German Institute for Business Research, April, 1937.
24. ibid, p. 3.
25. ibid, July 15th, 1936, pp. 57-59.
26. Figures as regards savings for the time the employment action came into force, can be taken from German Institute for Business Research, Supplement, August 2nd, 1935, which I quoted note 9, p. 282). Cf. also 246, 252-255.
27. " The Banker," February, 1937, p. 118.
28. ibid, pp. 115-116.
29. According to figures issued by the Reichs Ministry of Finance, the German funded debt stood at 13,750,100,000 marks (about £1,146 millions at current rates) on March 31st, 1937, an increase of 870 million marks (about £73 millions) since the end of 1936. This is, of course, apart from the floating debt, which decreased in the same period by only 60,000 marks.
30. " Times," August 12th, 1935.
31. HOLT (John B.), German Agricultural Policy, University of North Carolina Press, 1918-1934, p. 200.
32. HOLT, loc. cit. p. 189.
33. Editor, Dr. Wolfgang CLAUSS (Press Attaché to the Ministry of Agriculture).
34. Supplement to the Weekly Report of the German Institute for Business Research, June 8th, 1935, p. 47.
35. DARRÉ (R. W.), *Im Kampf um die Seele des deutschen Bauern* Berlin, 1934, p. 42, quoted from HOLT, loc. cit. p. 206.
36. *Reichsbauerntagung*, Goslar, Autumn, 1935, quoted from Official German News Agency.
37. HOLT, loc. cit. pp. 206-207.
38. HOLT, loc. cit. p. 139 (quoted from *Deutsche Allgemeine Zeitung*, May 3rd, 1933).
39. HOLT, loc. cit. p. 205.
40. Articles of " The Banker," loc. cit. p. 139.
41. " The Banker," loc. cit. p. 141.
42. HOLT, loc. cit. p. 211.
43. " The Banker," loc. cit. p. 142.
44. Mr. C. W. GUILLEBAUD gave an excellent study on this subject: Works Council: German Industrial Democracy, Cambridge, 1929.
45. Supplement to Weekly Report of the German Institute for Business Research, March 11th, 1936.

INDEX

Administration, *see also* Public Administration; A. and Economics in German teaching, 35-37, 101, 102.
Agriculture: Banks, 69; Big estates and their owners, 30, 31, 147, 257, 259, 264, 265; competition, 113 *seq.*, 257; Co-operatives, 69, 264; indebtedness, 259, 261, 264; Inherited freehold, 258, 259; A. and industry, 263; A. in National Socialist corporate organisation, 214, 260; A. and National Socialist ideology, 256-259; A. and self-sufficiency, 261 *seq.*
Ashley (Sir William), 36.
Associations, employers', 92 *seq.*, 214.
Austria, 113, 117.
Banks, 80, 92; agriculture, *see* Rentenbank, 264; control, 241-251; *see* co-operative movement; crisis, 191-196, 232, 242 *seq.*, 250; deposit banks, *see* joint stock banks; Enquiry Committee, 242; history, 80 *seq.*; public b., 194, 243-248, 283-286; *see* Reichsbank; Rentenbank, *see* currency; savings b., 69, 82, 194, 243, 246, 283; B. and building trade, 247; B. and industrial cartels, 80, 86; B. and loans, *see* loans.

Barker (Ernest), 31, 47, 48.
Batocki (A. v.), 141.
Beckerath, von (H.), 280.
Berlepsch, 128.
Berliner Handelsgesellschaft, 88, 244.
Bernstein (Eduard), 59, 130, 149.
Beveridge (Sir W. H.), 6.
Bismarck, 31, 40, 66-72, 73, 113, 114, 128, 143, 158.
Boehm-Bawerk, xv, 2, 3.
Boetticher, 128, 129.
Bonn (M. J.), 276, 280.
Bowley, 278.
Brentano (L.), xiv, 101.
Briefs (G.), 278.
British and German conditions compared: banking, 80-92; individualist view, 26, 42 *seq.*, 103, 104; subject matter of economics, xii-xv, 103, 124.

Bruck (W. F.), 273, 278, 281.
Brüning, 147, 267.
Buecher (Karl), xv, 36, 101.
Bülow tariff, 116 *seq.*
Building trade, 217-219.
Business management (as instrument of *Marktordnung*), 226.

Cameralism, 24, 36, 37, 205; *see also* mercantilism.
Capitalism, 21, 24; finance c., 80-92, 211.
Caprivi, policy of tariff, 115 *seq.*, 121.
Cartels, 92 *seq.*, 100 *seq.*; calculation c., 94, 224; coal c., *see* coal industry; compulsory c., 188, 197, 222, 223, 225, 230; decree of 1923, 196 *seq.*, 222 *seq.*; export policy, *see* c. and protection; history of c., 92 *seq.*, international c., 11, 97; iron and steel c., 95, 137, 181, 185, 186; war c., 135-139, 188, 202; C. and banks, 80, 86; C. and *Marktordnung*, 222-228; C. and protection, 93, 95, 185; C. (as organs of) public administration, 215; C. and transport, 95, 96.
Cassel (Gustaf), 45 *seq.*, 76, 100, 103.
Cement, 96, 189.
Chemical industry, 77, *see also* I. G. Farben.
Christian Socialism, 60 *seq.*
Clapham (J. H.), xv.
Clark (J. B.), xv, 4.
Coal industry, 86, 96, 147, 158, 159, 186, 187, 218.
Cole (G. D. H.) and (M.), 20, 22, 274, 282.
Collective bargaining (wage agreement), 266.
Colonial policy, 120 *seq.*
Communists, 57, 150, 163, 266.
Commercial policy, 110-119, 221; *see also* export; import.
Company law, 231 *seq.*
Constitution of the Weimar Reich (economic system), 158.
Consumer's associations, 224, 230, 231.
Consumer's guidance, 220.
Co-operative movement, 69, 82, 88, 230, 231, 243, 264, 283.

Corporate system, 207, 216, 223.
Crisis, 31, 233, 243, 264.
Cuno, 162 seq.
Currency: foreign bill control, 148; Gold cover, 177, 285; Gold discount bank, 192, 194, 242, 245, 247, 286; see also loans; Reichsbank, 82, 88, 162-177, 213, 242 seq., 256, 283-286; Rentenbank and Rentenmark, 167-171, 180, 247, 264, 286; stabilisation, 162-177.

Darmstadt (National) Bank, 86, 88, 121, 178, 242.
Darré (R. W.), 256, 264.
Dawes (C. G.), General, 145, 167, 171-177, 183.
Dawson (W. H.), xv, 275, 276, 277, 278.
Debts: National D., 218, 254, 255, 264; War D., 173 seq.
Demand-Monopoly, 228 seq.
Deposit banks, see Joint Stock banks.
Depression (Great), 181, 191, 212, 280.
Deutsche Bank, 88, 92, 121, 122, 244.
Devisen-Control, 249, 250.
Dialectical process of history, 5, 6, 23, 49.
Diehl (Karl), 27.
Diskonto-Gesellschaft, 86, 88, 92, 121, 122.
Dividend limitation (law), 245, 249.
Dresdner Bank, 88, 122, 244.

Economic schools of thought and their observational approach, 1 seq., 6; dynamic theory, 3; mercantilists, 2; physiocrats, 2; Ricardo, 3; static liberal theory, 3, 15.
Einzig (P.), 280.
Eisele (J.), 279.
Electrical industry, 8, 78, 190, 199-201, 228.
Employer's associations, see associations.
Employment creation, 212, 213, 230, 251-255, 283-286.
Employment exchange, 270 seq., 267.
Enquiry Committees: banking, 194 seq., 242 seq; cartels, 101, 102; German economic conditions, 182, 184; socialisation, 155 seq.
Ethics (in relation to the political and economic systems), 23 seq.
Ethnology, 27 seq.
Evangelisch Sozialer Kongress, 129.
Exchange (bourse, Börse), 87, 246, 248.

Export, 110, 116, 219.
Export industrialism, 73 seq.
Fascism, 53, 206, 207.
Feder (Gottfried), 207.

Fichte, 49, 51, 52.
Finance capitalism (Joint Stock capitalism), 80-92.
Finance, see Public Finance.
Finer (H.), 282.
Flick, 178, 236, 238.
Food problem, 141, 214, 228, 256-265.
Foreign bill control, 148; see also Devisen control.
Four years plan, see Goering.
France, 117.
Frankfurter Zeitung, 276, 278, 280.
Frederick the Great, 32, 37: as mercantilist and planner, 38.
Functional society (functionalism), 19, 22.

Gas industry, 78, 202.
Gelsenkirchen Bergwerks A. G., 86, 180, 181.
Gemischtwirtschaftliche Unternehmung, see Mixed enterprise.
Ginsberg (M.), 273.
Gilbert (Parker), 174.
Giro centrals, 244, 246, 285.
Gold, see stabilisation; see also currency.
Gold discount bank, see currency.
Goering's four years plan, 212, 216, 217, 238, 240.
Goldschmidt (Jacob), 193.
Gooch (G. P.), 275.
Great Britain, trade relation with Germany, 119.
Guilds, 93.
Guillebaud (W. C.), 287.

Haber (Fritz), 136, 189.
Halm (A.), 170, 279.
Hamilton (Alexander), 11.
Handicrafts, 214, 218.
Hegel, xiii, 3, 5, 19, 22, 36, 49, 51, 53, 56, 209.
Heimann (E.), 12, 155, 156, 273.
Helfferich (K.), 124, 142, 166, 168, 277.
Herder, 52 seq.; see also National Socialist ideology.
Heyde, (L.), 128 seq., 132, 278.
Hilferding (R.), 89, 155, 169, 254.
Hövel (P.), 279.
Höchstleistungsbetriebe, 138.
Holt (J. B.), 257, 263, 287.
Housing and Settlement (see building trade and settlements, agricultural).
Hoover moratorium, 145.

Idealistic school, 43, 51-65.
Ideology, National Socialist, 204 *seq.*, 256, *seq.*
I. G. Farbenindustrie A.G., 107, 178, 180, 189, 196.
Import, 110, 116, 219.
Income distribution, 126, 127.
Individualism (and socialism), 19 *seq.*
Industries, statistics, 218.
Inflation, 162-177, 178.
Insurance (social), 127 *seq.*, 270 *seq.*
Integration in industry, 77, 89, 182, 184.
Interessengemeinschaft, 107, 180.
International cartel, *see* cartels.
Investment, British embargo since 1931, 249 ; totalitarian I, 232, 239, 249.
Iron and steel industry, 110, 147, 159, 182, 184, 217, 218, 280.
Italy, corporative system, 207 ; *see also* Fascism.

Joint Stock banks (deposit banks), 81-83, 87, 88, 121 *seq.*, 191-194, 196, 242.
Joint Stock Companies, 78, 233-237.
Joint Stock Law, 231-237.
Joint supply and demand enterprise, 8, 78, 79, 190, 221.

Kalkulation, 94, 138.
Kant, 19, 20, 27, 51, 62.
Katheder Sozialisten, 3, 131, 132.
Keith (Sir Arthur), 29, 30.
Kelsen (H.), 54, 60.
Keynes (J. M.), 25, 45, 47, 103, 274.
Kirdorf (A.), 77.
Kirdorf (E.), 86, 131, 180.
Knapp (G. F.), 37, 68, 166, 167.
Kohlensyndikat, *see* coal industry.
Klöckner, 179, 180, 239.
Konzernbanken, 91, 92, 178.
Krupp, 180.
Kuscynski (R.), 195.

Labour : camps, 267, 268 ; difference in English and German literature, 124 ; l. exchange problem, 218, 230, 266, 270 ; l. front, national, 214, 215, 269 ; law for the order of national labour, 268 ; l. service, 267 ; *see* social policy and also employment.
Landauer (C.), 101, 104, 105, 106, 126, 127, 277.
Large scale organisation, 4, 8, 16, 75-79, 92-100.
Lassalle, 49, 50, 56 *seq.*
Lavergne (B.), 281.
Lederer (E.), *see* Motto, 1-3, 155, 273.

Levy (H.), xv, 73, 179, 185-187, 188, 190, 280, 281.
Ley (R.), 269.
Liberalism, 13, 19 *seq.*, 26, 41 *seq.*, 74.
Liberal State and Authoritarian State (difference in dealing with the economic system), 215, 251.
Liefmann (R.), xv, 89, 101, 104, 107, 179, 277, 280.
Lignite, 186, 218.
List (Friedrich), 11, 38, 115.
Loans, *see* Dawes l, 167 *seq.*, *see* employment creation, 212, 252, 282-286 ; foreign l. 121, 195 ; Papens advanced taxes l, 212, 245, 252 ; *see* stabilisation and *see also* debts.
Locomotives, 180.
Löwe, (A.), 4, 12, 14, 15, 16, 17, 18, 273.
Losses through Peace Treaty, 145 *seq.*
Lütgert (W.), 64.
Luther (H.), 169, 195.
Luther (Martin), 48, 64, 65.

Macgregor, (D. H.), 99, 220, 276.
Macrosty (H. W.), 276.
Management, *see* business.
Mannheim (K.), 273.
Marktordnung, 93, 109, 220-228, 259, 260.
Marquand (H. A.), 276.
Marschak (J.), 206, 207, 282.
Marx (Karl), 2-6, 16, 20, 22, 27, 49, 50, 56-58, 60, 76, 90.
Marxism, stages of, 5, 60.
Meinecke (F.), 51 *seq.*
Mercantilism, 37 ; Prussian m., 26, 49 *seq.* ; theoretical approach of, 35 *seq.*
Meyer (K.), 32, 274.
Michels (Robert), 133, 134.
Miksch (L.), 108, 227-229, 231, 267.
Mixed public and private enterprise, 98, 139, 198-203.
Moellendorff, von (W.), 22, 136, 141, 142, 155, 157-162 ; planning, 159 ; *Reichswirtschaftsrat*, 22, 158 ; socialisation, 158 *seq.*
Monetary problem, *see* currency.
Monopoly problem, 8, 105, 107, *seq.* ; demand monopolies, 228-231 ; influence of fixed costs to destroy free competition and develop monopolies such as cartels (Brentano in 1888, 101), (Cassel, 47, 76), (Schmalenbach, 76) ; imperfect competition, 109.
Montesquieu, 37.
Most (O.), 199, 281.
Müller (Adam), 53 *seq.*

Müller (August), 155, 157, 263.
National Economic Council, *see* Reichswirtschaftsrat.
Nationalism, 10 ; nation as incentive, 10-12, 38.
Naumann (Friedrich), 64, 65, 129.
Neisser (H.), 12, 273.
Nietzsche, 55, 208.
Nitrogen (synthetic), *see* I. G. Farben and chemical industry.
Nordwolle, 176-179.

Oncken (A.), 274.
One Party and One Class system, 152, 153, 206-210.
Oppenheimer (Franz), 4, 38, 58.
Oxford movements, 65.

Parker (Alwin), 253, 256.
Party as movement, 208.
Party system, the " one," *see* One party, etc.
Payments (War), *see* reparations.
Peace Treaty (Versailles), *see* Treaty of V, and losses, etc.
Pigou (A. C.), 109, 278.
Planned systems and liberty, 34, 212.
Planning, 6, 7, 22, 31, 75, 76, 99, 135, 137, 159, 211, 221, 245 ; *see* P. and cartels ; *see also* Frederick the Great ; and *also* P. and Public Administration.
Planning Committee and central Pl., 211, 242.
Planning, limits of, 25, 135, 142.
Population problems, 72.
Posadowsky, 131 *seq.*
Potash industry, 96, 147, 159, 188, 189.
Preferences, list of, 214-217.
Price mechanism, exclusion of, Ch. II, A (1), (c.), Ch. III, (2), (b), Ch. IV, (2) (3), (a)-(c).
Price regulation, 140, 197, 216, 260, 263.
Profitableness, public, 97, 98, 241.
Protection, 70, 93, 113 *seq.* 185.
Public Administration, 35-39, 203 ; cartels as organs of P.A., 7, 22, 103, 135, 215.
Public control, 234, 242 *seq.*
Public finance, 71, 241-256.
Puttkamer, 128.
Pyramiding, 91 ; *see also* Nordwolle.

Raiffeisen, 69.
Railways, 108, 122, 174, 229, 241, 246, 247, 283.
Rathenau (Emil), 190, 232.
Rathenau (Walter), 22, 77, 135-142, 156, 157.

Rationalisation (industrial), 182, 183, 195.
Reich Economic Council (*Reichswirtschaftsrat*), 22, 158.
Reichsbank, *see* currency.
Reichskredit A. G., 194, 244.
Religious movements and liberal spirit, 60 *seq.*
Rentenbank, *see* currency.
Reparation Committee and payments, 173-176.
Report business (as instrument of German power policy), 81, 83, 87.
Revisionism (socialist), 59, 60.
Rhenish-Westphalian Coal Syndicate, *see* coal industry.
Riesser (J.), 88.
Ricardo, 2, 3,
Robbins (Lionel), 13, 273, 280.
Robinson (Joan), 109.
Roman Catholics, 63, 128-130, 141, 144, 151, 152, 154.
Romanticism, 51-56, 206.
Rosenberg (Alfred), 35, 208.
Rosenberg (Arthur), 59, 145, 163-165, 167, 279.
Russia, 98, 145 ; German trade relations with, 118 ; Soviet Russia as model for Dictator States, 21, 22, 31, 149, 150, 152, 153, 206, 211.

Sartorius von Waltershausen (A.), 115, 116, 117, 118, 119, 277.
Savings banks, *see* banks, and *see also* employment creation loans ; deposits of, 246.
Schacht (Hj.), 168, 171, 193, 195, 211-213, 216, 217, 221, 246-252, 279.
Schmalenbach (H.), 76, 103, 226.
Schmitt (Carl), 208, 209.
Schmitz (Hermann), 136.
Schmoller (G.), 37, 41, 49, 93.
Schulze-Delitzsch, 69, 88.
Schulze-Gâvernitz, v. (G.), 80, 81, 82, 87, 277, 278.
Schumpeter (J.), xv, 2, 4, 18, 75, 93, 102.
Self regulation of economic forces, 6, 9, 25.
Self-sufficiency, 11, 134, 135, 261 ; *see also* agriculture.
Sering (M.), 259.
Settlements (agricultural), 147, 215, 259, 263-267.
Shop councils, 276.
Siemen's works, 92, 180, 190.
Slavs in Germany, 28 *seq.*, 33 *seq.*
Smith (Adam), 2, 19.

Social democrats, 58 *seq.*, 61, 68, 69, 128, 130, 133, 144, 149, 162, 163, 266.
Socialism, 19 *seq.*, 149-162.
Social policy, 124-134, 265-275; hours of work, 129; insurance, 127, 269 *seq.*; wages, 129.
Social psychology, 12 *seq.*
Socialisation, 97, 125, 154-158.
Sociology, 3, 4, 12 *seq.*
Sombart (W.), 126, 273, 278.
Somary (F.), 75 *seq.*
Soviet Russia, *see* Russia.
Spann (O.), xv, 54, 207.
Spiethoff (A.), 3, 273.
Spengler (O.), 38, 159.
Stabilisation 1923, 14, 162-177, 212.
Stahl (F. J.), 53, 54.
Stamp (Sir Josiah), 278.
State, S. banks, *see also* public banks; S. monopolies, 247 *seq.*; S. socialism, 26, 48 *seq.*
Stinnes (Hugo), 89, 179, 180, 192, 200.
Stock Exchange, *see* Exchange.
Stoecker) Pastor), 129.
Strength through joy, 231, 269.
Stresemann, 165, 166, 172-173.
Syndicate, 94, 98.

Tariffs, *see* protection.
Tawney (R.), 19, 20.
Taxation, 221, 226, 253.
Temple (W.), 61-65.
Textile industry, 94, 137, 178, 179, 261.
Thyssen, 180, 181.
Trade unions, 128, 130, 131, 214.
Transport, 95, 96, 108, 219, 228, 229, 241.
Treaty of Versailles, 10, 145 *seq.*, 148, 172, 220, 221.
Treitschke, 49, 56.

Troeltsch (E.), 17, 39-41, 63.
Trusts, 90, 92 *seq.*, 104 *seq.*, 177-182, 233-241, 251.
Trustees of labour, 268.

Unemployment, *see* employment, etc.
Unternehmer auf Aktien (entrepreneur supported by shares), 234, 235.
U.S.A., 110, 113, 115, 118.

Verein für Sozialpolitik, 14, 101, 129, 131.
Vereinigte Stahlwerke A. G., 89, 181, 182, 183, 196, 238, 240, 241.
Versailles, *see* Treaty of
Vierkandt (A.), 44 *seq.*
Vogelstein (Th.), 84, 155.
Vorländer (K.), 51 *seq.*

Wagemann (E.), 231, 248, 249, 277, 282.
War economics, 134-142.
War cartels (companies), 137 *seq.*, 157, 188, 202.
Warriner (D.), 36, 94-95, 101, 102, 124, 197, 274, 277, 278.
Weber (Adolf), 54, 81, 113, 114, 115, 275, 277.
Weber (Max), xv, 36, 37.
Welter (E.), 276.
Whale (P. B.), 191.
Wiedenfeld (K.), 104.
Wieser, v. (F.), 1, 5, 10.
Wilson programme, 144-145.
Wissell-Moellendorff, 22, 162.
Wolfers (A.), 101.
Working class, 134.
Workmen's bank, 269.

Young committee and plan, 176, 177.
Youth movement, 63.

DATE DUE

NOV 19 1970	
DEC 9 '71	